Geneva 3 April 199[?]
To Corinne ;

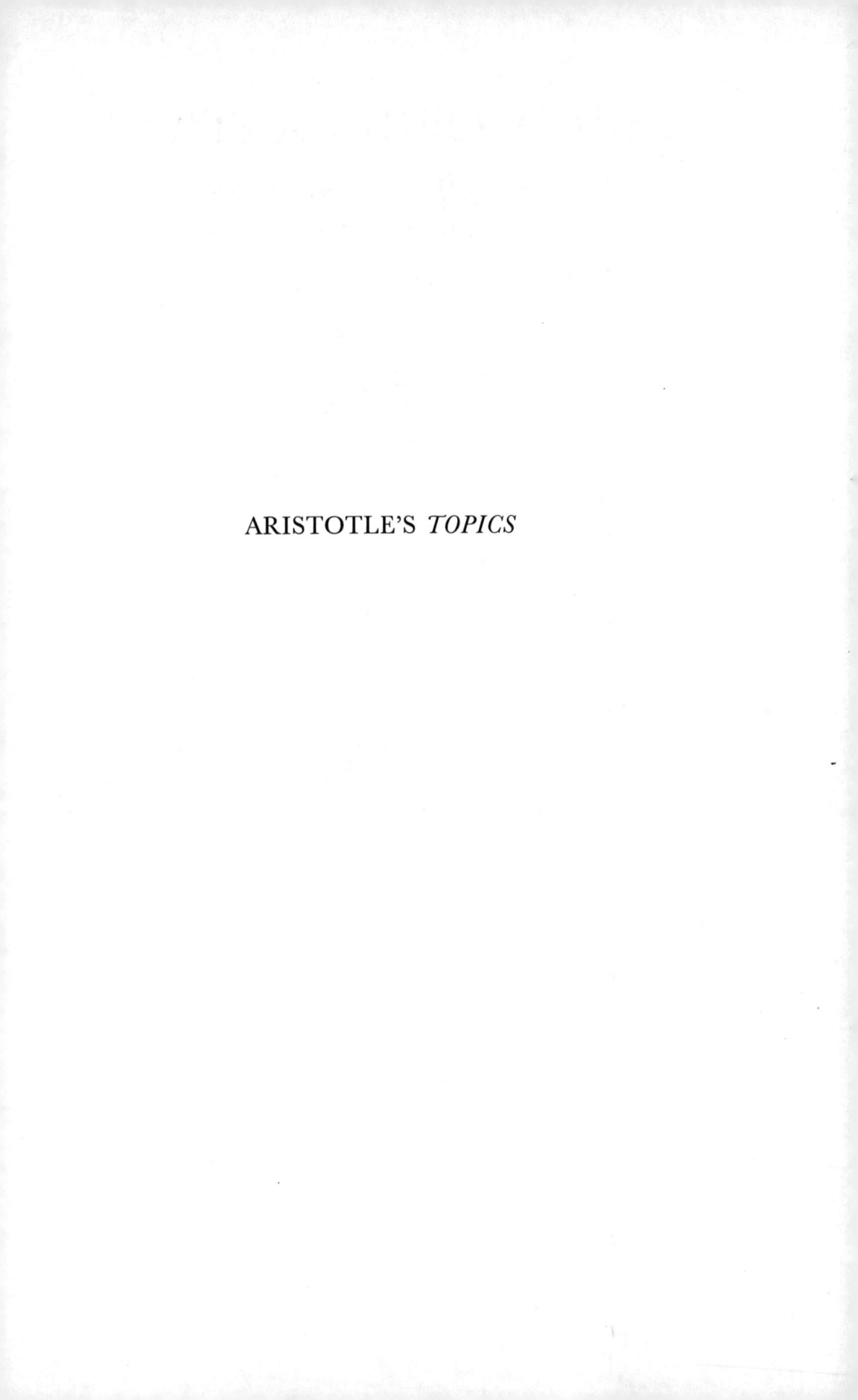

ARISTOTLE'S *TOPICS*

PHILOSOPHIA ANTIQUA

A SERIES OF STUDIES
ON ANCIENT PHILOSOPHY

FOUNDED BY J.H. WASZINK AND W.J. VERDENIUS

EDITED BY

J. MANSFELD, D.T. RUNIA
J.C.M. VAN WINDEN

VOLUME LXXIV

PAUL SLOMKOWSKI

ARISTOTLE'S *TOPICS*

ARISTOTLE'S *TOPICS*

BY

PAUL SLOMKOWSKI

BRILL
LEIDEN · NEW YORK · KÖLN
1997

The paper in this book meets the guidelines for permanence and durability of the Committee on Production Guidelines for Book Longevity of the Council on Library Resources.

Library of Congress Cataloging-in-Publication Data

Slomkowski, Paul.
　　Aristotle's Topics　/　by Paul Slomkowski.
　　　　p.　cm. — (Philosophia antiqua, ISSN 0079-1687 ; v. 74)
　　Revision of the author's thesis (doctoral)—Oxford, 1994.
　　Includes bibliographical references and indexes.
　　ISBN 9004107576 (cloth　:　alk. paper)
　　1. Aristotle.　Topics.　2. Logic, Ancient.　I. Title.
II. Series.
B442.S56　　1997
160—dc21
　　　　　　　　　　　　　　　　　　　　　　　　　　　　　96-49113
　　　　　　　　　　　　　　　　　　　　　　　　　　　　　CIP

Die Deutsche Bibliothek - CIP-Einheitsaufnahme

Slomkowski, Paul:
Aristotle's topics / by Paul Slomkowski. – Leiden ; New York
; Köln : Brill, 1997
　(Philosophia antiqua ; Vol. 74)
　Zugl.: Oxford, Univ., Diss., 1994
　ISBN 90–04–10757–6
NE: GT

ISSN　0079-1687
ISBN　90 04 10757 6

© *Copyright 1997 by Koninklijke Brill, Leiden, The Netherlands*

All rights reserved. No part of this publication may be reproduced, translated, stored in a retrieval system, or transmitted in any form or by any means, electronic, mechanical, photocopying, recording or otherwise, without prior written permission from the publisher.

*Authorization to photocopy items for internal or personal use is granted by E.J. Brill provided that the appropriate fees are paid directly to The Copyright Clearance Center, 222 Rosewood Drive, Suite 910 Danvers MA 01923, USA.
Fees are subject to change.*

PRINTED IN THE NETHERLANDS

CONTENTS

Preface	IX
INTRODUCTION	1
I. DIALECTICAL DEBATES	9
A. Training in disputation	11
B. Form of dialectical disputations	14
1. The part of the questioner	15
1.1. Problema	15
1.1.1. Form	15
1.1.2. Content	17
1.1.3. Construction and destruction	18
1.2. Protasis	19
1.2.1. Form	19
1.2.2. Content	19
1.2.3. Universal and particular protaseis	23
1.2.4. Syllogistic protasis and syllogism	24
1.2.5. Necessary protaseis	27
1.2.6. Auxiliary protaseis	32
2. The part of the answerer	36
2.1. Solutions (λύσεις)	38
2.2. Objections (ἐνστάσεις)	39
II. WHAT IS A TOPOS ?	43
A. Definition of the topos	43
B. Topos as a principle and a protasis	45
1. The passage in *Top.* Θ 14, 163b22-33	46
2. The passage in *Rhet.* A 2, 1358a10-20 & 29-33	47
3. The passage in *Rhet.* B 26, 1402a32-34	49
4. The synonymous use of "element" and "topos"	49
C. Other interpretations of topoi and how they square with the interpretation of topoi as protaseis and principles	50
1. Topoi as rules of inference	50
2. Topoi as laws	54
3. Topoi as investigation-instructions	54
3.1. Organa	54
3.2. Structure of the organa (and topoi)	57
3.3. Conclusion	58

D. Objection and induction in book Θ and in the central books	58
E. The evidence of Theophrastus	61
1. Tradition of the interpretation of the topos as a protasis	61
2. Theophrastus' distinction between parangelma and topos and his definition of topos	62
2.1. Dinstinction between parangelma and topos	62
2.2. Theophrastus' definition of topos	64

III. PREDICABLES AND THE SPECIAL STATUS OF SUMBEBEKOS — 69

A. Definition of the predicables	69
1. The passages in *Top.* A 5 and 8	69
2. The clash between the definition of the predicables and the explanation of their use in *Top.* H 5, Z 1 and A 6	71
B. Brunschwig's interpretation	73
1. Critique of Brunschwig's interpretation	74
1.1. Genus	74
1.2. Proprium	76
C. Sainati's interpretation	78
D. My interpretation	79
1. The passage in *Top.* H 5, 155a3-36	79
2. The form of problemata/theses in *Top.* Δ-Z	85
2.1. The form of problemata in Δ	85
2.2. The form of problemata in E	87
2.3. The form of problemata in Z	87
2.4. The form of problemata in B	88
2.4.1. To belong (ὑπάρχειν)	88
2.4.2. Sumbebekos in B	89
2.4.3. The meaning of sumbebekos	92
2.4.4. Accident	93

IV. HYPOTHETICAL SYLLOGISMS—THE MAIN FORM OF ARGUMENTS IN THE *TOPICS*: — 95

A. Hypothetical syllogisms in the *Prior Analytics* A 23, 29, and 44	95
B. Theophrastus' list of hypothetical syllogisms	96
C. The topoi for the construction of the corresponding hypothetical syllogisms found in the *Topics*	97

1. Hypothetical syllogisms proceeding by way of a continuous proposition together with the additional assumption ... 98
2. Hypothetical syllogisms proceeding by way of a diairetic proposition ... 103
3. Hypothetical syllogisms procceding by way of a negated conjunction ... 104
4. Hypothetical syllogisms on the basis of analogy ... 105
5. Qualitative hypothetical syllogisms ... 106
6. Other varieties of hypothetical syllogisms ... 106
D. Confirmation by Galen's *Institutio Logica* ... 107
E. Origins of Galen's and Alexander's terminology ... 108
F. Alexander's explanation of the working of the metaleptic and diairetic hypothetical syllogisms ((Hm) and (Hd)) ... 108
G. Further arguments for topical arguments working as hypothetical syllogisms ... 110
H. Reductionism ... 111
I. How does a hypothetical syllogism work ? ... 113
  1. Locus classicus on the hypothetical syllogism: *APr.* A 44, 50a16-28 ... 113
  2. The hypothesis has to be endoxical ... 116
  3. Concluding on the basis of a hypothesis ... 117
  4. Argument per impossibile ... 118
J. Hypothetical syllogisms in the *Topics* ... 120
  1. The mode of expression: aorist-future perfect ... 121
    1.1. The case of the Law of Subalternation ... 121
  2. Hypothesis ... 125
    2.1. Is it a protasis ? ... 125
    2.2. What kind of protaseis are the hypotheses? ... 126
  3. Consequence in the metaleptic hypothetical syllogism (Hm) ... 129
    3.1. In the constructive case of (Hm) ... 129
    3.2. In the destructive case of (Hm) ... 130
  4. Consequence in the diairetic hypothetical syllogism (Hd) ... 130
K. Hypothetical syllogisms in *APr.* A 46 ... 131

V. SELECTIVE INVESTIGATION OF CONCRETE TOPOI ... 133

A. Introductory chapter to B: B 1 ... 134
1. Universal versus particular problemata: 108b34-109a10 ... 134
2. "To belong" versus "to be": 109a10-26 ... 135

3. Definition of two errors: 109a27-34	138
3.1. The first error: false statement	138
3.2. The second error: violation of the established terminology	139
B. The most opportune topoi	140
1. Topoi from the contradictories, contraries and relatives	141
1.1. Topos from the contradictories	141
1.2. Topos from the contraries	142
1.3. Topos from the relatives	145
2. Topoi from the greater, lesser and the like degree	146
2.1. The first topos from the greater and lesser degree	146
2.2. The three remaining topoi from the greater and lesser degree	147
2.3. The three topoi from the like degree	150
C. Selection of topoi from book B	150
1. The first topos in B: 2, 109a34-b12	150
2. The second topos in B: 2, 109b13-29	153
3. The fourth topos in B: 2, 110a10-13	154
4. The third topos in B: 2, 109b30-110a9	155
D. Topoi of "what is more worthy of choice" and of "what is the same"	156
1. Topoi of "what is more worthy of choice"	156
2. Topoi of "what is the same"	157
E. Origins of categorical syllogisms in the *Topics*	160
1. The topos in B 4, 111a14-32	160
2. The topos in B 2, 110a14-22	164
2.1. The topical argument interpreted as a hypothetical syllogism	165
2.2. The topical argument interpreted as a categorical syllogism	166
3. Categorical syllogisms in dialectical debates	166
Summary	169
Bibliography	175
Classified Bibliography	195
Greek-English Glossary	199
Index of Passages	203
General Index	215

PREFACE

This book is a revised version of my D. Phil. thesis undertaken in Oxford and conferred as such in May 1994. Firstly, I would like to thank Prof. Wolfgang Wieland through whom my interest in the *Topics* was first aroused in one of his colloquiums at the University of Heidelberg and who was my first teacher in the study of Aristotle and Plato. The comments made by my two D.Phil. examiners, Mr Christopher Kirwan and Prof. Mario Mignucci were of great help. In addition, the suggestions of the publisher's anonymous reader helped make the thesis more readable. I am grateful to the British Academy for enabling me to study for a D. Phil. at Oxford; to the Studienstiftung des deutschen Volkes which supported me throughout studentship; and to the editors of Philosophia antiqua for accepting my thesis for publication.

I came to Oxford first as a Visiting Student in 1990 and I feel that my stay here was of great advantage to my studies and in particular to this book, and there are many teachers to whom I am indebted. I should like to thank Dr. Katherine Morris and Dr. Stephen Blamey, from whom I learned much about formal logic, and Dr. David Charles, with whom I studied Aristotle's syllogistic. Then, as a D.Phil. Student, I had the chance to learn a great deal about Hellenistic philosophy, esp. in Prof. Jonathan Barnes' classes on Sextus Empiricus and Prof. Michael Frede's classes on Stoic Logic. A paper based on Chapter Two was read in a doctoral seminar held by Prof. Bernard A. O. Williams who made useful comments. I am also grateful for the comments of the participants of my lecture series held in Trinity Term 1996 at the University of Oxford which coincided with the revision of the book.

I am of course especially indebted to the supervisors I had whilst writing my thesis. I would like to thank the late Mr. Michael Woods who supervised my work for one term in my second year. Sadly, he died prematurely; he was a very gentle man, and I am personally very indebted to him. I also have to thank Prof. Michael Frede who supervised my work in the two remaining terms of the second year; through his initially heavy critique of my interpretation of hypothetical syllogisms I had to find more and more arguments in favour of it which was certainly beneficial to my thesis. I also thank my wife Claire for all sorts of editorial help in turning my thesis into a book.

Most and above all, I would like to thank Prof. Jonathan Barnes, who supervised my work in my first and third year. I have learned a great deal from him about how to treat philosophical texts. As will become clear from the references in my thesis I also learned very much from his articles, especially those on hypothetical syllogisms; they were of great help to me in developing my own thesis. Having tutorials with him was always very helpful and stimulating. I suspect that I am more indebted to him than he is even aware.

PAUL SLOMKOWSKI

Brasenose College, Oxford
July 1996

INTRODUCTION

Brief summary of modern research
Aristotle's *Topics* is a handbook on how to argue successfully in a debate that is structured in a certain way. It consists of eight books which fall into two main parts: the six middle books (B-Z) deliver a list of the so-called topoi[1] which are designed to help a disputant win a debate; the outer books (A and Θ) describe what could be called the context of the debate as well as certain notions that are important for the understanding of the topoi. The *Topics* is also, so to speak, the official version of Aristotle's dialectic that originates in the argument between two persons who learn through debate how to find arguments pro and contra a thesis as displayed in the *Topics*.

For a very long time the Aristotelian *Topics* was a fairly neglected work. One important reason for this seems to have been the wide-spread opinion that its contents were just a muddled theory of argumentation out of which the *Prior Analytics* finally crystallized: Aristotle proceeded from Platonic dialectic to his syllogistic.[2] Hence, it appeared to be better to work on the latter straightaway.[3] Another reason seems to have been the generally agreed opinion that Aristotle had a low regard for dialectic.[4]

Of course, these opinions are not entirely incorrect. Clearly, the *Topics* was strongly influenced by Plato, especially the late dialogues, and it is also true that many concepts are found in the *Topics* which only crystallized later in the *Analytics* or various other writings. Even so, scarcely any scholar seemed concerned to demonstrate this: the *Topics* was simply ignored. Thus in the period between 1900 and 1950 we do not have many pertinent texts; however the texts we do have are very useful, even though they usually only deal with certain aspects of the *Topics*. Thus Hambruch (1908) shows many similarities between Plato's dialogues and Aristotle's *Topics*. Von Arnim (1927) investigates the ethical content of book Γ of the *Topics*. Solmsen (1929) deals mainly with the *Rhetoric*, but also deals much with the *Topics* and clearly recognizes that the notion of syllogism in the *Topics* is not that of a categorical syllogism, but of something different. Le Blond (1939) stresses that despite the fact that dialectic has merely to do with reputable opinions and Aristotle sometimes speaks derogatively of it, dialectic and reputable opinions actually have a great importance in Aristotle's method of work in his writings.

---

[1] Topos (pl. topoi) is the transliteration of the Greek τόπος (pl. τόποι) which I shall be using throughout this book rather than any of the possible English translations such as 'topic' or 'commonplace' which can be misleading.

[2] Cf. e.g. Maier (1896-1900), II, 2, p.77, Chroust (1963), pp. 27-57, Kneale (1989[10]), p. 33.

[3] Cf. e.g. Ross (1995[6], 1923[1]), p. 57: "We have neither the space nor the wish to follow Aristotle in his laborious exploration of the τόποι, the pigeon-holes from which dialectical reasoning is to draw its arguments. The discussion belongs to a by-gone mode of thought [...]; it is his [Aristotle's] own *Analytics* that have made his *Topics* out of date."

[4] Cf. Maier (1896-1900), II 1, p. 29; Hamelin (1920), p. 230.

The fifties saw an important publication in an article by Bocheński (1951a) who was the first scholar in this century to deal with topoi in the *Topics* and define the question which later occupied many scholars, namely whether a topos is a rule or a law; as the title of his article shows—"Non-analytical Laws and Rules in Aristotle"—Bocheński does not commit himself to either. Colli (1955) writes a commentary on the Organon, which includes the *Topics*. Braun (1959) represents the first book which is entirely dedicated to the *Topics*; the author tries to show the unity of all eight books of the *Topics* and points out their similarities.

From the sixties onwards scholars began to take more and more interest in the *Topics*. The erudite and exact work of de Pater (1965) is certainly the best monograph on the *Topics* to date. Not much later, probably the most important book on the *Topics* appeared, namely the edition of the first four books of the *Topics* with a long introduction and notes by Brunschwig (1967).[5] The Third Symposium Aristotelicum was devoted to the *Topics* and there are many interesting articles in its published proceedings edited by Owen (1968a). Sainati (1968) offers illuminating theories about the predicables and the topoi. The works by de Pater and especially those by Brunschwig and Sainati are certainly the best on the *Topics* and most pertinent to the subject of this book and their views will be scrutinized accordingly.

A few more books have been published since then, such as Zadro (1974) who provides a full-scale commentary on the Topics and, more recently, Pelletier (1991), but none of them as impressive as those mentioned above.[6] Interestingly, excellent books have been published on the tradition and influence of the *Topics* in Late Antiquity and the Middle Ages, especially by N. J. Green-Pedersen and E. Stump.[7]

However, substantial research has been published in the form of articles on various dialectical notions such as predication, predicables and dialectical syllogism and especially on dialectical method in other Aristotelian writings; to cite some of these authors—J. Barnes, E. Berti, T. Ebert, D. Hadgopoulos and, more recently, especially R. Bolton and R. Smith.[8]

One important result seems to have been achieved as a result of most of these works, namely the insight that the *Topics* is not just a predecessor of the *Analytics*, but that it represents something quite different, which is of great importance with respect to Aristotle's philosophy as a whole.

There are also a number of articles on the topoi and how they work. However, the authors do not seem to have gone further than de Pater, Brunschwig or Sainati: either the views of the above-mentioned three scholars are adopted or the authors try to find something out about topoi without taking the larger context into consideration and using all sorts of modern theories of logic or argumentation. However, if one does not take the larger

---

[5] Regrettably, the edition of the four remaining books has still not appeared.

[6] Most recently, a monograph by Oliver Primavesi, *Die Aristotelische Topik*, Zetemata 94, München 1996 has been published which unfortunately could not be taken into account in time for this publication.

[7] Cf. section U in the classified bibliography.

[8] Cf sections Q, especially Q 5, P, M and N in the classified bibliography.

context into consideration and tries to find out what topoi are by looking merely at individual passages in which they are stated, one is inevitably confronted with many possible interpretations of how they work and cannot possibly tell what Aristotle had in mind exactly. The situation here is the same as Bocheński[9] formulated nearly forty years ago: "So far no-one has succeeded in saying briefly and clearly what they [topoi] are."

The aim and argument of this book
Thus, the aim of this book is to answer the question of what a topos is. In addition, this book also aims to answer a closely related question, namely: How do arguments constructed with the help of the topoi work?

I shall argue that a topos is a universal proposition and functions as a hypothetical premiss in hypothetical syllogisms[10] which in turn are constructed with the help of the topoi. As we shall see, the interpretation of the topos as a proposition and premiss is not new but has a long ancestry. I shall provide evidence from Aristotle's text that there are clear signs that he himself considered topoi to be a particular type of proposition according to which hypothetical syllogisms were constructed. Thus, the later tradition of the *Topics* was not an invention which had nothing to do with Aristotle's *Topics*, but clearly originates in it.[11] The topical arguments are thus not predecessors of categorical syllogisms which finally crystallized in the *Prior Analytics*, as many scholars have thought. Nor is it the case that the *Topics* teaches how to *discover* categorical syllogisms displayed in the *Prior Analytics*.[12] The topoi tell us how to discover arguments which Aristotle mentions only sporadically in the *Prior* and *Posterior Analytics*—hypothetical syllogisms. Now, of course the categorical just as the hypothetical syllogisms originate in dialectical debates—the entire dialectical terminology and the assumed context in the *Prior Analytics* clearly demonstrate this.[13] And we do find a few topoi which tell us how to construct predecessors of categorical syllogisms. However, such topoi, which I shall deal with at the very end of this book, seem to be exceptions. The vast majority of topoi tell us how to construct hypothetical syllogisms. In the *Prior Analytics* A 27-29 Aristotle explains how to discover categorical syllogisms of a given conclusion which has to be proved, which coincides with the discovery of the middle term. Interestingly, the term topos is not mentioned here—it seems to have been reserved for the discovery of hypothetical syllogisms. In books Γ and H of the *Topics* we find topoi which tell us how to construct arguments which are

---

[9] Bocheński (1970²), p. 51 (English translation of the German edition first published in 1956).

[10] By syllogism I simply mean 'deductive argument' (with at least two premisses); cf. p. 15n.31.

[11] I would stress that I derived my interpretation from Aristotle's text alone, learning only of the ancient interpretation at a later stage. I found it reassuring that the Ancients interpreted the topos along the same lines.

[12] This is the thesis of van der Weel (1969) who assigned what he calls *pars inventiva* to the *Topics* and *pars iudicativa*—judgement of arguments—to the *Posterior Analytics*.

[13] With respect to syllogistic (i.e. the system of categorical syllogisms) this has been very clearly shown by Kapp (1931).

neither hypothetical nor categorical and which have been classified later as relational syllogisms.

Bocheński and de Pater hinted that some arguments in the *Topics* might have something to do with hypothetical syllogisms; but neither expanded upon this. Brunschwig was the first scholar who suggested that the arguments in the *Topics* work according to the rules of Modus ponens and tollens. Now, this interpretation of the working of the topoi sounds slightly anachronistic—Brunschwig does not explain why it is that we suddenly find these rules in Aristotle which are usually attributed to the Stoics and of which we do not seem to find much in the *Analytics*. In essence, however, Brunschwig is indeed right: a large number of topical arguments seem to work similarly to what we would now call Modus ponens and tollens. I shall show that there are some other forms of arguments according to which the arguments in the *Topics* function: arguments which rest on exclusive disjunction, negated conjunction, relational arguments, and some others. I shall show that these arguments are hypothetical syllogisms which Aristotle already indicates by names in the *Prior Analytics* and promises to deal with later—he never fulfils this promise. However, Theophrastus seems to have developed the plan of the master and the hypothetical syllogisms which we find in his writings seem to correspond to those named in the *Analytics* as well as to those arguments which are found in the *Topics*. Solmsen (1929) recognized the possibility that for nearly every topos one can construct a corresponding hypothetical syllogism. However, he regarded this as a completely un-Aristotelian interpretation and further development of the *Topics* by Theophrastus and later Peripatetics, and he argued that what we find in the *Topics* is a completely different sort of syllogism. I shall show that there are many places in the *Topics* which very clearly indicate that the arguments therein function as hypothetical syllogisms, in places that Solmsen apparently failed to note; the entire book shows signs of development in this direction. I do not maintain that, when writing the *Topics*, Aristotle was fully aware that the arguments he was writing down were hypothetical syllogisms; I do believe, however, that when he was writing them he had arguments in mind which he later classified as hypothetical syllogisms. Further, I do not want to maintain that for every single topos we can construct a hypothetical syllogism. I do however think that we can do this with the vast majority of topoi.

Initially, I intended to write a work which would be to a considerable extent an analysis of the topoi found in the inner books. However, so many difficulties emerged which had to be solved first before one could embark on an adequate interpretation of the topoi that only in the last chapter have I included an analysis of a selection of concrete topoi.

In the first chapter I investigate the dialectical debates as they are described in the last book of the *Topics* which is book Θ; these dialectical debates provide the context in which the topoi in the central books have to be understood: Aristotle expresses himself very concisely and obviously presupposes that his hearers and readers know the context. In a dialectical debate, there is a questioner and an answerer, and the questioner tries to refute the answerer's thesis by deducing the opposite of his thesis from the questions answered positively or negatively by the answerer. Some notions concerning the dialectical debates are only explained in book A or have to be deduced from their usage in the central books B-H, so that at times I shall refer to those books as well. However, there are some notions in the central books which are not even mentioned in Θ. These are in the main the predicables—I shall deal with them in the third chapter—and, more importantly, the notion of the topos, with which I shall deal in the second chapter. The function of the topoi in the central books seems to be fulfilled in Θ by a certain kind of universal propositions, which are established by the questioner usually by induction and can be objected to by the answerer using a counter-example. We merely find some predecessors of the topoi in book Θ of which the core has obviously been written earlier than the rest of the *Topics*.

In Chapter Two I turn to the central question of this book: *What is a topos*? I concentrate firstly on what Aristotle says *about* the topoi. Aristotle does not give a definition of the topos anywhere in the *Topics*, but he does give a quasi-definition of it in the *Rhetoric*, the only other Aristotelian work in which a list of topoi, albeit a brief one, is given (*Rhet.* B 23-24) and in which Aristotle says something about the topos. I investigate this passage along with a few others in the *Rhetoric* and in the *Topics*. Aristotle explicitly says that a topos is a proposition and a premiss (πρότασις) and this is also confirmed by the fact that many topoi are found in the central books of which Aristotle explicitly says that these should be established by induction and can be objected to by objections, just as the universal proposition in Θ. I show that these complex topoi-propositions obviously function as hypotheses in a hypothetical syllogism. My results are confirmed by Theophrastus.

In Chapter Three I deal with the notion of the predicable. Predicables play a very important rôle in the *Topics* because all the topoi are divided according to them. Each topos contains a predicable and with the help of every topos one of the predicables is supposed to be established or destroyed. In order to understand the topoi in the central books and the dialectical procedure generally, it is essential to understand the predicables and how they are expressed. I shall deal in particular detail with the notion of what is usually called the accident, since Aristotle's definition of this term in book A on the one hand and its use in the central books on the other, differs—this has been observed by both Brunschwig and Sainati. I shall show that the Greek term συμβεβηκός of which "accident" is the usual translation is best understood in the central books as meaning "attribute"; the topoi of this predicable establish the predication of an attribute, not an accident.

In Chapter Four I discuss various kinds of hypothetical syllogism found in the *Topics* and the workings of hypothetical syllogisms in general. In looking at a considerable number of topoi it becomes clear that many arguments which are constructed according to them function in a similar way to what we now call Modus ponens and tollens. However, some clearly also function according to different rules. By knowing the hypothetical syllogisms which are ascribed by some scholars to Theophrastus one discovers that the arguments constructed according to topoi function in exactly the same way.

There are passages in the *Topics* and in the *Analytics* which suggest that Aristotle had a fairly clear notion of the hypothetical syllogisms which occur in the *Topics*. Aristotle describes the workings of a hypothetical syllogism in only one passage in the *Prior Analytics* (*APr.* A 44). Many articles have been written on the way in which Aristotle thought of hypothetical syllogisms, but the interpretations do not fit the hypothetical arguments found in the *Topics*. Thus, I had to answer anew the question of what a hypothetical syllogism is and how it works. The answer to this question occupies the larger part of Chapter Four.

Only having made all these investigations can I at last proceed to the investigation of the concrete topoi in the *Topics* in Chapter Five. Given the vast number of topoi, the number of those examined is necessarily small. I have chosen topoi which I consider to be the most important and through these, demonstrate that my interpretation given in the earlier chapters is correct. I also discuss some topoi according to which arguments can be constructed which were later classified as relational syllogisms. At the very end I present one of a few exceptional topoi from which a categorical syllogism can be derived.

I am not concerned directly with questions of *chronology* and at the start of this research I had intended to avoid them altogether. Questions of chronology are a precarious matter and things can very easily go wrong. The issue is complicated by the fact that Aristotle seems to have been revising the text, making additions, adding references etc. How wrong chronological investigations can go can be especially well observed in the investigations which have been carried out on the *Topics*. Gohlke, for example, had to change his mind three times.[14] On the whole I agree with Evans (1977), p. 4, who "believe[s] that before these [chronological] questions can be embarked upon, it is necessary to obtain an accurate assessment of the absolute character of Aristotle's doctrines, and that in the case of dialectic this has not yet been done".

However, despite these deterrent examples I have found that with regard to clear differences of content it has not been possible to avoid the questions of chronology altogether. I have restricted myself to just a few important points with regard to this work; I do not prove them properly,[15] but simply state them relying on a number of points which seem to be obvious enough to confirm my view. The most important point is about book Θ. Most scholars assume that it is later than the rest of the *Topics*. Some scholars point out that the reasons given for this are fairly poor and that there is no need to assume this. It seems to me to be fairly obvious that the core of Θ is earlier than the rest of the *Topics*. If Θ really postdated the rest of the *Topics* one would have to assume that topoi, which do not occur in this book, have been substituted by a certain kind of universal propositions.[16] However, the

---

[14] For a nice summary of his different views cf. Braun (1959), p. 51f.

[15] In order to do this one would be best advised to satisfy all the aspects which Owen (1959) used in determining the chronological place of *Timaeus* among Plato's dialogues.

[16] This has indeed been argued by Sainati (1993), 48-56.

universal propositions in Θ are much less sophisticated than the topoi in the central books; besides, in the transitional passage at the very beginng of book Θ Aristotle mentions topoi and explains in what way they fit in with what he describes in Θ. Theophrastus, Aristotle's immediate disciple, and other Peripatetics worked on topoi and always considered the *Topics* to be the book on dialectic—obviously they did not think that topoi were out of date in any way. I shall give some further points of evidence in Chapter One.

Apart from that I am in harmony with the common opinion. Thus, I believe that the *Topics* (with a few possibly very late additions) lies within the earliest works of Aristotle. I also think, together with Brunschwig and Sainati, probably the most prominent experts on the *Topics*, that the notion of the accident obviously went through a certain development in the *Topics* which I shall describe in Chapter Three.

I am not concerned with the notion of *dialectic*. The reason why the *Topics* is regarded as the "official version" of it becomes clear from Chapter One in which the dialectical situation which is presupposed in the *Topics* is described. In order to deal adequately with the notion of dialectic one would not only have to rely on the *Topics* but also take into consideration the *Rhetoric* and some parts of the *Metaphysics*. There are some very good works on dialectic, especially by Le Blond (1939), Evans (1977) and Irwin (1988). As far as the origin of it is concerned we find a very good account in Wilpert (1956/7) who shows that the influence by Plato and Zeno and Aristotle's own contribution do not exclude each other.

Most scholars agree nowadays that Aristotle's method in his writings is to a large extent dialectical and much research has been published on this.[17] On the whole, this research is praiseworthy and has shown how Aristotle uses various dialectical devices, such as division, analogy, reputable opinions and others in the context of other writings. However, it is striking that no adequate reaserch has been done on the use of the central notion of dialectic—the topos—in other writings; perhaps this is due to the fact that scarcely any scholar was absolutely sure as to what a topos was. Unfortunately, an investigation of the use of topical arguments in other writings could not be included in this work and would in fact go beyond its scope; however, I intend to write on this elsewhere.

As for the use of secondary literature, I am aware that the bibliographical references in this book are fairly scarce. The results of this work are fairly new and I did not deem it reasonable to point out on every page with whom I disagree; I usually confined my criticism to the most important works on the *Topics*. However, in order to give the reader a guide to current research I have provided an extensive bibliography at the end of the book and a classified bibliography which is subdivided into different sections on all possible areas of research connected in some way or another with the *Topics*.

---

[17] Cf. section Q 5 in the classified bibliography.

CHAPTER ONE

DIALECTICAL DEBATES

Arsitotle's *Topics* is a handbook on how to win a debate organised in a certain way. At the very beginning of the *Topics* Aristotle stipulates the primary purpose of the *Topics* (100a18-21):

> The purpose of the present treatise is to find a method by which we shall be able to reason syllogistically (συλλογίζεσθαι) from generally accepted opinions about any problema brought forward, and also shall ourselves, when defending a proposition (λόγον ὑπέχοντες), avoid saying anything contrary to it.

The passage presupposes the knowledge of the structure of dialectical debates as they are described only in the very last book of the *Topics*—book Θ. There are two disputants—a questioner and an answerer—who hold two contradictory theses. The task of the questioner is to refute the answerer's thesis which he does by proving his own thesis: he asks the answerer questions which the answerer may either accept or not and he tries to deduce from the answers a conclusion which is identical with his original thesis and the contradiction of the answerer's thesis. The answerer tries to avoid his thesis being refuted.[1]

In the six middle books (B-H) Aristotle provides us with around 300 topoi which are, roughly, lines of argument designed to help the questioner to win the debate. However, in order to understand the function of the topoi it is essential first to understand the dialectical situation in which they are employed and which is taken for granted in the middle books. These dialectical debates are described in book Θ and some important notions which are used in Θ in turn are only defined in book A—the notions of the syllogism, proposition or premiss and problema. Thus, this chapter will concentrate on these two outer books, especially Θ; in very few instances will the middle books be consulted as well.

It is of course slightly peculiar that the book in which the very context of the topoi is explained comes at the very end. For a modern reader it is on the whole reasonable to begin the *Topics* with the eighth book. And in general, from a methodological point of view it is perhaps questionable as to whether the editor who was responsible for the order of the books as we now know it, be it Aristotle himself or someone else, did the right thing in putting book Θ at the end and not together with book A at the very beginning. There is something even more striking about book Θ: we do not find the notion of the topos here except in the transitional part at the very beginning of Θ in 155b4-17. There are actually two transitional parts. The first one is 155b3-16, starting with the first sentence of the book:

---

[1] For this "defending" of the thesis Aristotle often uses the Greek ὑπέχειν which usually takes θέσις or ὑπόθεσις as its object (Θ 3, 158a31f.; 9, 160b14f.), less seldom λόγος as in the passage cited above or in Θ 5, 159a38; instead of ὑπέχειν sometimes also the word φυλάττειν ("to defend") is used, cf. Θ 4, 159a23; 5, 159a36.

Next we must speak about arrangement and the way to ask questions.[2]

The other is in b17f.:

> The sources from which the topoi should be taken have been stated. We must now speak about arrangement and formation of questions and first to distinguish the propositions [...].[3]

Only between these strikingly similar lines do we find the word topos. It seems to me to be very likely that this passage was inserted later to connect the central books with the earlier book Θ. In 155b4-7 we find a quasi-explanation of why Θ comes at the end:

> He who is about to ask questions must, first of all select the topos[4] from which he must make his attack; secondly he must formulate and arrange them one by one to himself; thirdly and lastly, he must go on to address them to the other party.

Firstly, one first has to find the topos, which is dealt with in books B-H, and *secondly* formulate and arrange questions, which is dealt with in Θ. In b17 the last mention of topoi being made Aristotle starts speaking about propositions (προτάσεις) and does so until the end of the book. Some sort of especially general (καθόλου) and reputable propositions have a central rôle in the debates. It will become clear in Chapter Two that these propositions have an analogous function to the topoi in the central books. Book Θ has obviously been originally written independently of the rest of the *Topics* and subsequently attached to it.

Topos is not the only notion which is missing in Θ. In A 4-5 Aristotle develops his well-known theory of the predicables: every problema and proposition expresses either an accident or a genus or a proprium or a definition. All the topoi in the central books are ordered according to these predicables—I shall discuss this briefly in this chapter and in full detail in Chapter Three. Not only are no predicables (except definitions) found in Θ, there are not even any verbs denoting the predication of a subject by a predicate such as "to belong" (ὑπάρχειν[5]) or "to be predicated of" (κατηγορεῖσθαι) which are frequent in books A-H of the *Topics* and later in the *Analytics*[6]—the theses and propositions are simply expressed with the help of the verb "to be" or some other non-technical verb.

Curiously, since Maier (1896-1900)[7] most scholars are agreed, albeit with eminent exceptions,[8] that book Θ was written later than books B-H 2. The

---

[2] μετὰ δὲ ταῦτα περὶ τάξεως καὶ πῶς δεῖ ἐρωτᾶν λεκτέον

[3] τοὺς μὲν οὖν τόπους ὅθεν δεῖ λαμβάνειν, εἴρηται πρότερον. περὶ τάξεως δὲ καὶ τοῦ ἐρωτηματίσαι λεκτέον διελόμενον τὰς προτάσεις (...).

[4] The translation by Forster (1960) and Pickard-Cambridge (1984) of τὸν τόπον εὑρεῖν as "to choose ground" and "to select ground" respectively is misleading—clearly τόπος in its specific meaning is meant here.

[5] This verb actually occurs in 161b36, 162a26, and 163b13, but has a different meaning here.

[6] Let alone words denoting a predication of a specific predicable such as "being convertibly predicated of" (ἀντικατηγορεῖσθαι) or "belong as an accident" (συμβεβηκέναι).

[7] Vol. II 2, p.78 n. 3; followed by Gohlke (1928), Huby (1962) and others.

[8] Solmsen (1929), pp.151-153 very clearly shows the weaknesses of Maier's argument.

main argument is that in Θ, as well as in A and H 3-5, there are many occurrences of the notion of the syllogism (συλλογισμός) or conclude by a prosyllogism (προσυλλογίζεσθαι), but only four occurrences are found in the inner books B-H 2.[9] These occurrences are interpreted as later additions.[10] It is generally assumed that the arguments in the central books are some sort of topical arguments which are not syllogisms.[11] As we shall see this assumption is wrong: the arguments produced by the topoi are syllogisms, namely hypothetical syllogisms. There is no need to assume that the occurrences of "to conclude syllogistically" (συλλογίζεσθαι) are later additions: they fit perfectly well into their context.[12] The fact that the term "syllogism" does not occur very often in the central books is simply due to the fact that topoi deal with structures within the syllogism. Aristotle usually prefers to use "to construct" and "to destroy" (κατα- and ἀνασκευάζειν) a thesis; of course, in both cases the thesis of the opponent becomes destroyed, but the two terms make a fine distinction as to the form of the thesis the questioner establishes by destroying the answerer's thesis—I shall discuss the exact meaning of these two terms shortly. It is in any case characteristic of Θ that Aristotle merely uses the word "to destroy" (ἀναιρεῖν), without making any fine distinctions.

All these seem to me to be good reasons for believing that the main body of Θ predates the central books.[13] I shall show in this chapter some predecessors of the topoi and in Chapter Two I shall analyse a passage in Θ 14 where the very origin of the notion of the topos is obviously found.

A. *Training in disputation*

In A 2, 101a26-30 Aristotle gives three purposes for which the treatise of the *Topics* is useful and names the venue in which one argues about any subject

---

[9] E 2, 130a7; Z 2, 139b30; Z 10, 148b8 and Z 12, 149a37, and incidentally no occurrences at all in B, Γ or Δ.

[10] The same goes for the occurrence of some other words in the central books as e.g. objection (ἔνστασις).

[11] Cf e.g. Solmsen (1929), p. 34. Solmsen in fact does not interpret the occurrences of συλλογισμός in the central books as later additions, but assumes that they designate a particular type of 'topical' arguments.

[12] And after all the word συλλογίζεσθαι occurs already in the meaning of "to deduce" in Plato: *Phileb.* 41c9, *Gorg.* 479c6, 498e10 (in the two latter cases together with συμβαίνειν ἐκ τοῦ λόγου or ἐκ τῶν ὡμολογημένων; συλλογίζεσθαι here is usually understood as "sum up", "reckon up"), *Resp.* 365a8 (ἐξ), 516b9, 517c1, 531d2; cf. also *Theaet.* 165c9f. (ἐξ οὖν τούτων λογίζου τί σοι συμβαίνει).

In any case, Maier's contention that the syllogism in *Top.* H 3 appears as a new invention is clearly wrong. He argues that Aristotle having discussed the establishing of definition with the help of topoi in book Z discusses in H 3 their establishing with the help of the syllogism, thus applying a new method for the same purpose. Maier has obviously overlooked the fact that in Z Aristotle only deals with the *destruction* of definitions; thus in H 3 Aristotle deals with something new. Aristotle obviously takes it for granted here what a syllogism is—the problematic question for him here is whether definition can be proved syllogistically.

[13] Of course, there are later insertions; the most obvious ones are the two references to *APr.*: at 11, 162a11 to *APr.* B 2, 53b26ff. and at 13, 162b31ff. to *APr.* B 16, 64b28ff.—book Θ is certainly not later than the *Analytics*.

presented mentioned at the very beginning of the *Topics* as its first purpose: training in disputation (γυμνασία):

> They [i.e. the purposes] are three: training in disputation (γυμνασία), casual conversations and philosophical sciences.
> That it is useful for the training in disputation is obvious on the face of it: for if we have a method, we shall be able more easily to argue about the subject proposed (περὶ τοῦ προτεθέντος ἐπιχειρεῖν).

Thus, it would appear that what Aristotle offers us in the *Topics*—primarily the list of topoi in the middle books—is just a method for such disputations which will make arguing about any subject proposed *easier* (A 2, 101a 28-30). The purpose of the training in turn is of course to acquire the ability in disputation (τὸ δὲ γυμνάζεσθαι δυνάμεως χάριν).[14]

Now, what are these "trainings in disputation" which Aristotle describes in Θ? These are meetings for discussion (διαλεκτικαὶ σύνοδοι or διατριβαί) where the disputants argue "not in competition" (μὴ ἀγῶνος χάριν) but for the sake of "examination" (πεῖρα), "inquiry" (σκέψις) and "training" (γυμνασία)[15] on any subject proposed. Although Aristotle seems to denounce the competitive character of the debates here, there are other passages in which he seems to take the agonistic nature of them for granted and even advises how to win the argument at all costs.[16]

When reading book Θ it is quite clear that Aristotle is not the inventor of these dialectical debates or even the first author to write on them. For example, at the beginning of Θ 5 Aristotle justifies his work by pointing out that there are no definite guidelines (ἀδιόριστα) laid down for those who argue in dialectical meetings for the sake of training and examination,[17] obviously assuming the existence of such debates. He often uses some obviously standard terminology which he does not always explain but takes for granted that his hearers know what is meant. In A 11, having made exact distinctions between a problem and a thesis, Aristotle states that "practically all dialectical problemata are now called theses",[18] which obviously presupposes that these terms were widely used. The very beginning of the *Topics* cited above in which Aristotle offers a new method clearly show that he took for granted what the dialectical debates were about.

To a certain extent the debates seem to resemble sports games: the questioner "attacks" (ἐπιχειρεῖ), the answerer "defends" (φυλάττει) a thesis, they are arguing for the sake of "training" (γυμνασία) and there is an audience present whose presence appears to exert pressure on the disputants to

---

[14] Θ 14, 164b1f. Aristotle advises us here to learn from each discussion a reasoning or a solution or, above all, a proposition or an objection (164a16-b7)—these are the sources of the ability in disputation (164b1)—and to make records of arguments (ἀπομνημονεύσεις τῶν λόγων) in a universal form (καθόλου), even though they might be concerned with a particular case (ἐπὶ μέρους). It is striking that no mention of topoi is made.

[15] Cf. Θ 5, 159a25; 32-34; 11, 161a24f.; 14, 163a29.

[16] Cf e.g. Θ 4, 159a18-24 vs. 5, 159a30-34. In Θ 2 Aristotle recommends many cover-up tactics which I shall describe in this chapter.

[17] Θ 5, 159a25f. Or at any rate there are no definite guidelines for the answerer, as 159a31-36 seems to imply; the text is slightly obscure here.

[18] A 11, 104b34-36.

respect certain rules of fair play.[19] The performance of the disputants can be judged, taking into consideration the fairness of the opponent and the difficulty of the thesis to defend or to attack.[20] It is quite possible that such dialectical meetings were even institutionalized in the Academy as has often been suggested.[21] In the Platonic dialogue *Parmenides* there is a passage, 135c8-136c5, which shows that the idea of a training in disputation was familiar to Plato and which throws light upon the origin of such training. Parmenides, teacher of Zeno, who is considered to be the inventor of dialectic,[22] and Socrates' main interlocutor in the dialogue, advises Socrates to train himself first (γύμνασαι) before proceeding to philosophical enquiries. The form of the exercise (τρόπος τῆς γυμνασίας) is that which Zeno used in the treatise Socrates was listening to: one has to consider the consequences both of a hypothesis (σκοπεῖν τὰ συμβαίνοντα ἐκ τῆς ὑποθέσεως)[23] and of its opposite.[24] What follows in the second part of *Parmenides* is thus an exercise in which Parmenides discusses with his interlocutor named Aristotle[25] the consequences of the hypotheses, that there is, or is not, a one (137b 2-4).[26]

In order to be successful in disputations it is not enough to read Aristotle's treatise. In *Soph. El.* 16, 175a17-30 Aristotle says, with respect to paralogisms:

> It is not the same thing to take an argument in one's hand and then to see and solve its faults, as it is to be able to meet it quickly (ἐρωτώμενον ἀπαντᾶν δύνασθαι ταχέως); for what we know, we often do not know in a different context. Moreover, just as in other things speed or slowness is enhanced by training (ἐκ τοῦ γεγυμνάσθαι), so it is with arguments too, so that supposing we are unpractised (ἀμελέτητοι), even though a point is clear to us, we are often too late for the right moment (τῶν καιρῶν).

The *Topics* have also two other purposes mentioned above, which are of course at the same time purposes of the training in disputation: casual conversations (ἐντεύξεις) and philosophical sciences. The casual conversations might include dialogues as we know them from Plato's early dialogues but also more casual ones. For the last purpose Aristotle gives two reasons:

---

[19] Cf. e.g. Θ 8, 160b3, 6; also *Soph. El.* 8, 169b31; 15, 174a37.
[20] Θ 11, 161a16-b10; 161b19-33; 161b34-162a11.
[21] Cf. especially Ryle (1966).
[22] According to a fragment of Aristotle's largely lost dialogue *Sophistes*, fr.1 in Ross (1955), p.15.
[23] *Parm.* 135e9-136a1.
[24] Cf especially *Parm.* 128d4-6.
[25] It is tempting to think that the author of the *Topics* is meant and some scholars have maintained this (e.g. Ryle (1968), p.77f.). In *Parm.* 127d2f. however the interlocutor is introduced as "the man who was afterwards one of the Thirty" which obviously precludes Aristotle, the philosopher.
[26] On the relation between Aristotle's dialectical method and Plato's *Parmenides* cf. Berti (1980).

If we are able to raise difficulties on both sides (διαπορῆσαι), we shall more easily discern truth and falsehood on every point.
Further, it is useful in connection with the primary elements (πρῶτα) [i.e. first principles] of each science; for it is impossible to discuss them at all on the basis of the principles peculiar to the science in question, since the first principles are prior to everything else, and it is necessary to deal with them through the reputable opinions (ἐνδόξων) on each point. This task belongs properly, or most appropriately, to dialectic; for dialectic, being of the nature of an investigation, has a road towards the first principles of all disciplines.[27]

This last purpose shows the importance of the *Topics* for Aristotle's philosophy. The first point clearly says that dialectical method can be helpful in philosophy and it is now agreed among scholars that Aristotle's method in his writings is largely dialectical. As for the second point, Aristotle seems to say not only that with the help of dialectic the principles of each science can be discussed,[28] but also that they can be found—if this is what is meant by dialectic's "having the road to the principle".[29] Given the eminent importance of principles in Aristotle's philosophy, this claim gives dialectic a very important place in Aristotle's methodology.

I have now outlined the sort of discussions Aristotle had primarily in mind when writing the *Topics*—exercises in disputation—and their purpose. These exercises have a special form which I shall go on to describe in detail.[30]

B. *Form of dialectical disputations*

In a dialectical discussion there is a questioner (ὁ ἐρωτῶν) and an answerer (ὁ ἀποκρινόμενος). Aristotle describes the rôle of the questioner in Θ 1-3 and that of the answerer in Θ 4-10, as well as making various points about dialectical arguments in Θ 11-14. In book A he explains primarily the notions of a problema, a protasis[31] and of predicables (A 4, 5, 10 and 11).

---

[27] A 2, 101a34-b4. I have dealt with the reference to first principles as falling under the heading of the third purpose, the philosophical sciences, as Irwin (1988), p. 37 does. One could also argue with Brunschwig (1967), p. 116f. that the reference to the principles actually represents an independent fourth purpose. The issue is debatable and one could argue both ways, as in fact Alex. *in Top.* 29, 18-30, 12 does.

[28] The most prominent example of this is the discussion of the Principle of Contradiction given in *Met.* Γ 4.

[29] Smith (1993) disputes this.

[30] I agree with Kapp's description (1931). However, Kapp gives only a very rough structure, as he himself remarks ("grob") and no pieces of evidence. The dialectical situation is described in some detail by Moraux (1968) whose interpretation is at times slightly speculative; cf. also Weil (1956) and Robinson (1930).

[31] *Protasis* (pl. *protaseis*) is the transliteration of the Greek πρότασις and means literally "that which has been put forward", here the *question* asked. However, Aristotle uses protasis as referring to a question answered in the affirmative or in the negative, i. e. a *proposition*, as early as in the *Topics* and then of course later in the *Prior Analytics* (cf. the definition at *APr.* 24a16). However, it is important to bear in mind that a protasis is normally used in the context of a reasoning, i.e. a syllogism or induction, and thus means a *premiss*, as it is in fact most often translated (for an exception cf. *Met.* N 2, 1089a24f.). I shall be using the transliteration *protasis* to allow for the two nuances in meaning mentioned.

The questioner asks the answerer a question in the form of a problema, e.g. "Is pedestrian biped animal a definition of man, or not?" (A 4, 101b32f.). Depending on which alternative the answerer decides to take the questioner has to take the other one. The task of the questioner is to refute the answerer's thesis which he does by proving his own thesis. In order to achieve this he asks the answerer questions in the form of protaseis, e.g. "Is animal the genus of man?" which the answerer may either accept or not by saying "yes" or "no".[32] The questioner tries to deduce from the admitted protaseis a conclusion which is identical with his original thesis and the contradiction of the answerer's thesis. I shall deal with the part of the questioner in section 1.[33]

The answerer tries to avoid being refuted, respecting however certain rules of 'fair play'. Thus, if he does not accept a protasis which the questioner has proved by induction, he is supposed to give a counterexample (ἔνστασις). If he does not accept a conclusion which has been deduced by a syllogism, he is supposed to give a solution (λύσις). I shall deal with the part of the answerer in section 2.[34]

This is a rough sketch of the structure of dialectical gymnastics and I shall now comment on it, name some difficulties, refer to Aristotle's terminology, etc.

1. *The part of the questioner*

1.1. *Problema*

1.1.1. *Form*

It is quite clear that the problema comes at the beginning of the discussion. In A 4, 101b15f Aristotle says:

> Arguments (λόγοι) arise from protaseis (ἐκ τῶν προτάσεων), while the subjects of syllogisms (περὶ ὧν δὲ οἱ συλλογισμοί) are *problemata*.

And in the passage cited at the very beginning of this chapter Aristotle says that "the purpose of the present treatise is to find a method by which we shall

---

I am also using the transliteration problema (pl. problemata) for the Greek πρόβλημα discussed above, since the word 'problem' would to a large extent be misleading.

I am using the word syllogism in the same sense as συλλογισμός is defined by Aristotle, i.e."an argument (λόγος) in which certain things being laid down, something other than these necessarily comes about through them" (*Top.* A 1, 100a25-27; very similarly in *APr.* A 1, 24b18-20) and simply seems to mean 'deductive argument'. The word 'syllogism' in English usually refers specifically to a categorical syllogism (and Aristotle sometimes uses it in this way), and thus in order to designate just the definition scholars use the transliteration 'sullogismos' or the term 'deduction'. However, the word in English is clearly used in its broader meaning in 'hypothetical syllogism' and since this is a standard expression and a notion of eminent importance in this book, I have decided to keep to 'syllogism' rather than a transliteration, stressing that it is meant in its broader sense.

Similarly, "induction" just translates Aristotle's ἐπαγωγή as defined in *Top.* A 12, 105a13f.; cf. pp. 29-31 below.

[32] Θ 2, 158a16f.
[33] On pp. 15-36 below.
[34] On pp. 36-42 below.

be able to reason syllogistically from generally accepted opinions about any *problema* brought forward."[35]

The problema has the form 'Is P the case, or not?' (πότερον ... ἢ οὐ;), P standing for a proposition, in contrast to a protasis which has the form 'Is P the case?' (ἆρα ...;).[36] A problema could be "Is pleasure a good, or not?"[37] or one of the examples cited on the previous page.[38]

However, Aristotle only seldom uses the term problema in its primary meaning of a question in the form described above.[39] Usually he uses it to designate the thesis of the answerer[40] or the thesis of the questioner[41] (which is equal to the conclusion intended by the questioner) or the thesis generally (whether held by the questioner or the answerer),[42] i.e. he calls both opposite parts of the problema-question 'Is P the case, or not?' expressed in the affirmative a problema: 'P' or 'not P'. Even more often Aristotle uses the very word θέσις, from which the English word thesis derives, to designate the thesis of the answerer[43] or, less often, of the questioner.[44] He sometimes also uses the expression "that which has been laid down in the beginning" (τὸ ἐν ἀρχῇ or ἐξ ἀρχῆς (κείμενον)).[45]

One might wonder why the problema should have a different form from a protasis, since the answerer could have made his position just as clear by asserting or denying a protasis. Obviously the idea was to distinctly mark the

---

[35] ἡ μὲν πρόθεσις τῆς πραγματείας μέθοδον εὑρεῖν ἀφ' ἧς δυνησόμεθα συλλογίζεσθαι περὶ παντὸς τοῦ προτεθέντος προβλήματος ἐξ ἐνδόξων (A 1, 100a18-20).
Even if we omit προβλήματος with Brunschwig, (1967), p.1n.4, it is clear from 101b16 and 101a30 that προβλήματος is meant. But Brunschwig's reason for omitting προβλήματος is actually not particularly sound: he justifies it by Alexander's omission of it in his citation. Now, it is true that Alexander omits it in his citation in *in Top.* 5, 20f., not, however, in 7, 1. Brunschwig gives as further reason that Aristotle would not introduce a term which he has not previously defined. Unfortunately, this is common practice with Aristotle—in *Rhetoric* for example he first mentions the notion of enthymema in A 1, 1354a14f. without any explanation, which he gives only later (1355a6ff.), and in the *Topics* he uses the notion of the topos without ever defining it.
[36] A 4, 101b29-36.
[37] Cf. e.g. B 10, 114b39.
[38] Many other examples will be cited in Chapter Three.
[39] Examples of problemata in the full form are found in A 10, 104b7, 8, 16.
[40] B 2, 109b24, 110a10, H 5, 155a37f. (προβλημάτων ἐπιχειρεῖν); Θ 3, 158b16 (πρό-βλημα (...) δισεπιχείρητον).
It is actually not always easy to determine whether the thesis of the answerer or the questioner is meant. The reason for this is that the word ἐπιχειρεῖν (πρός), meaning literally "to put one's hand to", which Aristotle often uses in conjunction with "problema" can have two different meanings: it either means "to attack" or "to prove (dialectically)", "to argue". In the former case the object is of course the thesis of the answerer (155a7, 11, 17, 37, 158a31, b5, 13, 161a22), in the latter case it can be either way (156b20, 158b1, 16, 36, 163b1). The context usually makes the exact meaning clear.
[41] Θ 11, 161b32f. 34f., 162a6, 163a8f. The thesis of the questioner of course equals the conclusion that the questioner purports to reach. All the occurrences of problema in the *Prior Analytics* have this meaning: a conclusion which is to be concluded (περαίνειν) or proved (δεικνύναι) (26b31, 42b29, 43a18, b34, 45a36, b21 and in many other places).
[42] B 1, 108b34, 109a2, 28, E 1, 128b23, 24, 29, 129a19, 20, 30.
[43] B, 110a11, 111a11, b12, 36; Γ, 120a21, 27; Δ, 123a4, al.; Θ, 159a20., 36, 160b14, al.; the same goes for ὑπόθεσις which in Θ usually has the same meaning as θέσις.
[44] Θ 1, 156a13 and 156b5.
[45] Θ 1, 155b13, 156a8.13; 3, 159a8; 6, 160a11, al.

problema as the proposition which had to be refuted or proved from protaseis as the propositions which serve as premisses of the reasoning which was to refute or prove the problema. Problema itself, being the conclusion of the reasoning or its negation, could under no circumstances be a premiss of this reasoning—otherwise one would commit the error of begging the question.

1.1.2. Content

In A 10 and 11 Aristotle specifies a problema and a thesis with respect to content. We should not be concerned with every problema, he tells us, but only with a dialectical one. In A 11, 104b1-5 he gives a full definition of a dialectical problema:

> A dialectical problema is an investigation (θεώρημα) leading either to choice and avoidance or to truth and knowledge.
> Its subject is something about which either men have no opinion either way, or most people hold an opinion contrary to that of the wise, or the wise contrary to that of most people, or about which members of each of these classes disagree among themselves.

The main characteristic of a problema seems to be that it has to have a problematic or aporetic content, on which people disagree or even have no opinion at all.[46] The aporia (or puzzlement) should be of the sort about which doubt might be felt (ἀπορήσειεν) by the kind of person who requires to be argued with.[47]

The demonstration (ἀπόδειξις) of the problema or thesis should neither be too ready to hand—otherwise the problema would not really be aporetic, nor should it be too remote—this could involve difficulties which go beyond the scope of dialectical training (πλείω ἢ κατὰ γυμναστικήν).[48]

Aristotle also makes a distinction between a problema and a thesis. In 104b18-28 he gives the following definition of a thesis:

> A thesis is a belief contrary to general opinion (ὑπόληψις παράδοξος) but propounded by someone famous as a philosopher; for example, "Contradiction is impossible", as Antisthenes said (...); for to pay any attention when an ordinary person sets forth views which are contrary to received opinion is foolish.
> Or a thesis may concern matters about which we hold a reasoned view contrary to received opinions (περὶ ὧν λόγον ἔχομεν ἐναντίον ταῖς δόξαις); for example, the view of the Sophists that "What is need not in every case either have come to be or be eternal" (...). This view, even if it is unacceptable to some people, might be accepted by someone on the ground that it has an argument in its favour (διὰ τό λόγον ἔχειν).

Every thesis is also a problema, since in a thesis the wise disagree with the many or one or the other class disagree among themselves; but not every problema is a thesis, since some problemata are such that we hold no opinion

---

[46] Cf. also A 10, 104a4-8.
[47] Rather than the kind of person who needs to be castigated, as those who feel doubt whether or not the gods ought to be honoured and parents loved, or those who lack perception, as those do who wonder whether snow is white or not (A 11, 105a3-7).
[48] A 11, 105a7-9.

about them either way, which is not true of a thesis (104b29-34). Aristotle remarks that "all dialectical problemata are now called theses" and that, once having defined them, he will take the liberty to use the two expressions interchangeably (104b34-105a2), as he in fact does in the *Topics*.

1.1.3. Construction and destruction (κατασκευάζειν and ἀνασκευάζειν)

Depending on whether the answerer says "yes" or "no" to the proposed problema, i.e. depending on whether the answerer takes on the affirmative or the negative thesis (assuming P to be in the affirmative), the questioner endeavours to *destroy* or *construct* the thesis, i.e. to deduce a negative or affirmative conclusion. In the topoi in the central books destruction is clearly predominant. The reason being that "people more usually introduce theses asserting a predicate than denying it, while those who argue with them destroy it" (B 1, 109a8-10). Thus, the answer to the proposed problema is more often "yes" than "no", but both are possible.[49]

There are certain irregularities in the usage of "to destroy" (ἀνασκευάζειν/ἀναιρεῖν) and "to construct" (κατασκευάζειν) a thesis. The passage in B 1, 108b34-109a10 seems to suggest that "to destroy" a thesis means to prove a *negative* statement containing the verb "not to belong" (οὐχ ὑπάρχειν) or "not to be" and thus to refute a positive thesis while "to construct" means to prove a *positive* statement containing the verb "to belong" (ὑπάρχειν) or "to be" and thus to refute a negative statement. This understanding of the two terms is clearly assumed in many topoi in B[50] in which the theses contain no quantifiers "all" or "no", but which contain general terms so that their extension is best understood as universal positive and negative theses. In books Δ-Z as well, "to construct" a thesis obviously means to establish that A is a predicable of B, and "to destroy" a thesis means that A is not a predicable of B, A and B standing for terms.

However, we also find a different usage of the two terms in B, in those topoi in which Aristotle explicitly distinguishes positive and negative universal theses and where the quantification is of importance. Here, "to construct" a thesis means proving a *universal positive or negative* thesis, i.e. that the thesis does or does not belong universally, and thus refuting a particular negative or affirmative thesis; "to destroy" a thesis means proving a *particular negative or affirmative thesis*, and thus refuting a universal positive or negative thesis. We find this usage for example in B 2, 109b13-29, B 3, 110a23-b7, and in some other places.

To express the difference once again in slightly different terms, in the first case the thesis P in the problema 'Is P the case, or not?' always seems to be

---

[49] Thus, Moraux (1968), p.280, is wrong in maintaining that «le questionneur devra tendre à faire admettre au répondant des propositions d'où découlera nécessairement une conclusion identique à la réponse oui au problème posé». There is no set order of answers, and in fact, the answer of the answerer is more often "yes" than "no". If the answer was always "yes" or always "no" then the difference between ἀνασκευάζειν and κατασκευάζειν would become incomprehensible.

[50] B 4, 111a14-32, a33-b16, b17-23; 5, 112a16-23; 8, 113b15-26; 10, 114b37-115a14, and many others.

an affirmative proposition. In the second case, where we have explicit quantification and which certainly is a later development, P in 'Is P the case, or not?' is a universal affirmative or negative proposition. In both cases it is true that if the answerer says "no", thus picking out 'not P' the questioner "constructs", i.e. proves P, whereas if the answerer say "yes", picking out 'P', the answerer "destroys", i.e. proves 'not P'.

In Γ 6 Aristotle also admits problemata containing quantified predication other than universal. Here, P can also be an affirmative or negative particular proposition (120a6-20) or any of the other specified belonging (120a20-31; cf. p. 122n.98 below. But those other than universal quantifications do not seem to occur anywhere in the *Topics* except here.

In Θ Aristotle does not make this subtle distinction. He does not here use the terms "to construct" (κατασκευάζειν) or "to destroy" (ἀνασκευάζειν) at all. He uses the more generic term "to refute" (ἀναιρεῖν), which embraces both "to construct" and "to destroy". The understanding of the two terms is essential in order to understand the procedure in the central books.

1.2. *Protasis*

1.2.1. *Form*

The form of a dialectical protasis is 'Is it the case that P?' (ἆρα ... ;). That is, in contrast to problema, of which the form is 'Is it the case that P, or not?' (πότερον ... ἢ οὔ;), the 'or not'-bit is left out.[51] My English rendering of the protasis as 'Is it the case that P?', rather than as 'P?' which would be nearer to the original Greek, points to another requirement which protaseis (and problemata) must fulfil: the answerer must be able to answer them simply by "yes" or "no".[52] Thus, questions of the kind "What is man?" or "In what various senses can the good be used?" are not dialectical and hence not permitted. The questioner must give his own definitions and distinctions and then ask the answerer to accept or not.[53]

1.2.2. *Content*

In A 10 Aristotle specifies the dialectical protasis with respect to content. In 104a8-15 the following definition is given:

> A dialectical protasis is a question (ἐρώτησις) which is endoxical (ἔνδοξον) to everyone or the majority or the wise—either all of the wise or the majority or the most famous of them—and which is not paradoxical;[54] for one would assent to the view of the wise, if it is not contrary to the

---

[51] In Greek the interrogative pronouns are different as well: ἆρα in the case of protasis and πότερον (indicating the choice of two theses) in the case of problema.

[52] Aristotle says this only of protaseis, but of course the same is true of problemata. In English we would have to answer a problema by "yes, it is" or "no, it is not", but in Greek a "yes" or "no" is enough; cf. *Soph. El.* 10, 171a19-21 and Plato's *Euthydemus* 276a3f., 295b2f.

[53] Θ 2, 158a14-22; cf. 160a34. However, if the answerer refuses to accept a distinction it is fair to ask him to make his own suggestion (158a22-24).

[54] This word means literally "against common sense", thus could perhaps be translated as "implausible", "incredible". Aristotle stresses that the protasis reputable to the wise should not be paradoxical—if it was it would be a thesis, which is defined as a paradoxical belief of a philosopher, e.g. Heraclitus's thesis that all things are in motion (A 11, 104b19-22). Παράδοξος seems to have a similar meaning to ἄδοξος and the opposite meaning of ἔνδοξος.

opinions of majority. Views which are similar to received opinions (ἐνδόξοις) are also dialectical protaseis, and so are also protaseis which contradict the contraries of received opinions, and also views that accord with the arts that have been discovered.

In this passage the important notion of "endoxical" occurs. The passage which best explains this notion seems to me to be the one found in the very first book of the *Topics*, namely A 1, 100b21-23:

> Those opinions are endoxical which appear to be correct (δοκεῖ) to everyone or the majority or the wise—that is to say, to all of the wise or to the majority or to the most famous and distinguished of them.

Thus, endoxical protaseis express reputable or plausible views.[55] Accordingly, the content of protaseis is quite the opposite of that of problema and thesis: the latter are supposed to be puzzling, the former to be generally accepted—either by all or the majority, the wise or the scientists. The reason for this is of course that the questioner is dependent on the answerer's accepting the protasis and "no one would accept" a protasis which is no one's opinion (A 10, 104a5-8).

In Θ 2, 157b32f. yet another characterization of the dialectical protasis is found:

> A dialectical protasis is one which holds in several instances and to which no objection (ἔνστασις) is forthcoming.

In 158a3-6 Aristotle expresses himself slightly more exactly with respect to the objections saying:

> Either no objection should be forthcoming at all, or at any rate none on the surface (μὴ ἐπιπολῆς); for if men can see no instances in which the protasis does not hold good, they admit it as true.

This characterization of the dialectical protasis is of course in line with its endoxical character and may in fact be understood as an explication of its being endoxical.

Aristotle divides all protaseis and problemata into three classes:

> There are, roughly speaking, three classes of protaseis and problemata; for some are ethical, some physical and some logical protaseis. Ethical protaseis are such as "Ought one rather to obey one's parents or the laws, if they disagree?" Logical protaseis are such as "Is the knowledge of contraries the same or not?" Physical protaseis are such as "Is the universal eternal or not?" Likewise also with problemata.[56]

---

[55] For an exact explanation of the notion of ἔνδοξος cf. Le Blond (1939), pp. 9-19 and especially Barnes (1980), pp. 498ff. I shall usually render the word by "endoxical" sometimes by "reputable" or "plausible". It should at any rate be borne in mind that "opinion" or "belief" (δόξα) stands in high regard in Aristotle and is not necessarily opposed to truth. In *Met.* Γ 6, 1011b13 he even calls the principle of contradiction "the most indisputable of all beliefs" (βεβαιοτάτη δόξα).

[56] A 14, 105b19-29.

This is a famous passage in which we find the first textual evidence for the widespread division of philosophy into ethics, physics and logic in Antiquity which is usually attributed to Xenocrates, a member of Plato's Academy and a contemporary of Aristotle. Aristotle here does not actually subdivide philosophy but problemata and protaseis into three types: ethical, physical and logical. In a parallel passage[57] Aristotle specifies the purpose of the three different kinds of problemata and protaseis; he actually refers here to problemata only:

> (1) The knowledge of some of these problemata is useful for the purpose of choice or avoidance; for example whether pleasure is worthy of choice (αἱρετὸν) or not.[58] (2) The knowledge of some of these is useful purely for the sake of knowledge, for example, whether the universe is eternal or not. (3) Others, again, are not useful in themselves for either of these purposes but as an aid to the solution of some similar problema; for there are many things which we do not wish to know for themselves but for other purposes, in order that through them we may obtain knowledge of something else.[59]

The first passage is taken by Hadgopoulos (1976), p. 286 as evidence for his contention[60] that Aristotle does not adhere to the formal distinction between protaseis and problemata made in *Top.* A 4 and described above:

> [T]his formal distinction [between protasis and problema] is not adhered to by Aristotle. Later on (..) [Aristotle] forgets the formal distinction, and he distinguishes between them in other ways. We find examples of dialectical *protaseis* expressed in the form that had been earlier appropriated for the expression of *problemata*.

By "later" Hadgopoulos means as early as *Top.* A 14, 105b19-29 where the above passage is found. Now, it is true that in this passage Aristotle calls questions protaseis which have the form of problemata. However, this is the only passage where Aristotle does this (even though Hadgopoulos gives it only as one example) and I think this passage should not be pressed.

---

[57] A 11, 104b5-12.

[58] One might be tempted to think that the first mentioned sort of problemata, point to book Γ where we find topoi which tell us what is more worthy of choice (αἱρετώτερον). But the problemata Aristotle deals with in Γ are of a different sort as he explains at the very beginning of Γ (1, 116a4-9). There, both things are worthy of choice and the question is: which one is more so. We very seldom find problemata in the *Topics* which contain the word αἱρετός or φευκτός (cf. e.g. B 7, 113a1-19). The problema Aristotle gives as an example occurs very often in the form "Is pleasure a good, or not?" and I assume that it is this sort of ethical problemata Aristotle refers to, which are found in all the central books along with physical and logical ones; Aristotle in fact often uses "good" and "worthy of choice" interchangeably (cf. e.g. *Rhet.* B 23, 1397a21vs. 22).

[59] It is interesting to note that Aristotle here sees logic both as a part and as an instrument of philosophy. Later in antiquity it became an issue whether philosophy is one or the other, cf. Alex. *in APr.* 1, 7-2, 33, Mueller (1969), p. 184 and especially Lee (1984), pp. 44-54. Aristotle himself later divided all knowledge in a way which did not leave space for logic (*Met.* E 1, 1025b25ff.; K 7, 1064b1-3; and in fact already in *Top.* Z 6, 145a15f. and Θ 1, 157a10f.); logic seemed to have for him a merely propaedeutic character (cf. e.g. *Met.* Γ 3, 1005b2-5 and 4, 1006a5-8).

[60] Hadgopoulos' main contention is a correct critique of a surprisingly misguided interpretation of the function of problema and protasis given in Kneale and Kneale (1962), p. 34.

Aristotle was clearly inattentive here. Only the example of the logical sentence is, also with regard to content, a protasis, i.e. is endoxical.[61] The example of a physical sentence is, with regard to content, clearly a problema since Aristotle cites it twice as a typical example of a problema.[62] We do not find the example of an ethical question given here anywhere else in the *Topics*, but it is quite clear anyway that with regard to content it is a problema. It refers to the famous Nature-Law-antithesis which Aristotle mentions in *Soph. El.* 12, 173a7-18 and of which he says that "in the view of the ancients [sc. philosophers, mainly the sophists] what accorded with nature was the truth, while what accorded with law was the general opinion of the polloi." This is according to the definition in A 11, among others, the characteristic of a problema.[63] So one wonders which distinction Aristotle had in mind when naming protasis and problema as distinct entities in A 14 and saying that the division is "likewise also with problemata."

Also what Aristotle does in this passage is to make a new division of questions, namely into physical, ethical and logical. It is often the case that when Aristotle introduces a new distinction, he pays little attention to the distinctions he made previously. Thus in A 4, where he introduces the formal distinction between problemata and protaseis, he does not pay attention to the distinction with respect to their content, which he makes in A 10, using the same statement in different forms to illustrate the difference.[64]

Besides, it should not be assumed that Aristotle himself introduced the formal distinction. Rather, he was describing what was common practice in the gymnastical disputations to begin a dispute by posing a question in this form. Problemata presumably originated from geometry and already Plato has used them for investigations other than geometry. Thus for example in *Theaet.* 180c5ff. the mathematician Theodorus suggests trying to solve a question "like a problema" and Socrates specifies the problema by giving two opposed dogmas, those by Heraclitus and Pythagoras. And in *Resp.* 530b6 Plato lets Socrates say that the study of geometry is pursued "by means of problemata."[65]

---

[61] Cf. A 10, 104a16.

[62] In the passage cited on the previous page (A 11, 104b8) and again in 104b16.

[63] "The subject-matter of a problema is something about which (...) the polloi hold an opinion contrary to that of the wise, or the wise contrary to that of the polloi" (A 11, 104b4f.).

[64] Hadgopoulos gives another passage to support his contention, namely *De Int.* 20b23-30. The relevant lines b22-24 run: "So if a dialectical question consists in requesting an answer— *either* a protasis *or* one side of a contradiction, the protasis being one side of the contradiction ... ." This text seems to me rather to suggest that the distinction between two sorts of questions, namely protasis and problema, is still at work here, even though "problema" is not explicitly mentioned and protasis designates an answered question here. The first answer answers a protasis, the second a problema which offers a choice of two contradictory propositions.

[65] Cf. also *Resp.* 531c2-5: "They do not ascend to *problemata* and the consideration which numbers are inherently concordant and which not" and *Soph.* 261a6f.: "Evidently he [the Sophist] possesses a whole armory of *problemata*, and every time that he puts one forward (προβάλη) to shield him, we have to fight our way through it before we can get at him." On the notion of the problema see most recently Lennox (1994).

1.2.3. *Universal and particular protaseis*

Aristotle distinguishes between universal (καθόλου) and particular (τὰ καθ' ἕκαστα) protaseis,[66] most explicitly in Θ 8, 160a39-b1. He explains here how the answerer should treat these two different kinds of protaseis: the answerer should accept the particular protaseis if they are true and endoxical, but he should always try to find an objection (ἔνστασις), i. e. a counter-example, against the universal protasis. Aristotle does not specify the distinction any further and thus we have to look at examples to see what is meant exactly. Four examples will be sufficient; the first three examples of particular protaseis constitute objections to the corresponding universal protaseis:

Universal protasis (1)
    The angry man desires vengeance on account of an apparent slight.[67]
Particular protasis:
    We become angry with our parents, but we do not desire vengeance on them.[68]

Universal protasis (2)
    The man who has lost the knowledge of something has forgotten it.[69]
Particular protasis:
    If the thing changes, he has lost knowledge of it but has not forgotten it[70]

Universal protasis (3)
    A greater evil is the opposite of a greater good.[71]
Particular protasis.
    Health, which is a lesser good than sound bodily condition, has a greater evil as its opposite, since disease is a greater evil than unsound bodily condition.[72]

Universal protasis (4)
    He who sits writes.[73]
Particular protaseis:
    Socrates is sitting.
    Socrates is writing[74]

---

[66] Aristotle does not usually mention protasis explicitly but uses merely the expressions "universal" and "particular"; it is obvious from the context that protaseis are meant. As far as I can see there are only two places where Aristotle expresses himself explicitly: Θ 1, 156a28 (καθόλου πρότασιν) and 14, 163b32 (πρότασίν τε κοινὴν).
[67] Θ 1, 156a31f.; explicitly specified as a universal protasis in a28 and 30.
[68] Θ 1, 156a37f.
[69] Θ 2, 157b12f.
[70] Θ 2, 157b13f.
[71] Θ 2, 157b17.
[72] Θ 2, 157b18-20.
[73] Θ 10, 160b26f. For other examples of universal protaseis: cf. e.g. 1, 156b11-13 (explicitly specified as universal in b11 and b15); 2, 157b15f.
[74] Θ 10, 160b27 and b28. For other examples of singular protaseis: cf. e.g. 2, 157b5f. (two examples).

It can be seen that universal protaseis in Θ are obviously quite different from those defined in *APr.* A 1, 24a16-19 or *Top.* B 1, 108b34-109a1: there is no universal quantifier ('all' or 'no') explicitly stated. The protaseis are universal or general by virtue of their containing *general terms*.[75]

As for the particular protaseis (τὰ καθ' ἕκαστα), these are obviously protaseis which are less specific than the universal ones usually by virtue of their containing particular terms.[76] The particular (καθ' ἕκαστον) here is ambiguous and can either mean "specific" or "individual". Specific terms are specific *relative to* generic terms: "disease" in the third example is specific with respect to "evil", but can be generic with respect to, say, 'rheumatism', i. e. a specific disease. An individual is a border line case of a specific term, insofar as that there can be nothing more specific than it, e.g. "Socrates" in the fourth example.[77]

The distinction between universal and particular protaseis is very important with respect to induction, objection and syllogism, with which I shall deal later in this chapter.

1.2.4. *Syllogistic protasis and syllogism*
In Θ 8, 160a35f. introduces the notion of a syllogistic protasis (πρότασις συλλογιστική):

> Every syllogistic protasis either is one of the constituent parts of the syllogism [i.e. a premiss] or else goes to establish one of these.[78]

Aristotle makes here two important distinctions with respect to protaseis and with respect to syllogism.

There are protaseis which are the premisses of the syllogism with the help of which the questioner endeavours to prove his own thesis—these are the so-called *necessary protaseis* (ἀναγκαῖαι προτάσεις). Aristotle simply

---

[75] The universal quantifiers are of course implicitly contained in these protaseis and if we wanted to formalize them in modern predicate calculus, we would have to use the quantifiers: 'the man' becomes then 'every man', 'the evil' 'every evil', etc.

[76] I say 'usually' because in the second example the particular protasis contains the same terms as the universal one; the objection here is specified by pointing out that the thing ("something") changes.

[77] This ambiguity is found in other Aristotelian writings as well, cf. Barnes (1994²), p. 83. 'Particular' is ambiguous in English. Apart from the two meanings which it has in common with the Greek καθ' ἕκαστον ('specific' and 'individual') it also has a third one, referring to propositions affirming or denying something about only some members of a class of objects and which contains the quantifier 'some'. The corresponding word in Greek is ἐπὶ μέρου as it is found e.g. in *Top.* B 1, 108b34ff.; the example Aristotle gives there is "some pleasure is good". This third meaning is not meant here, although there is of course some connection between it and the 'specific' and 'individual'. The first example of a singular protasis, "we become angry with our parents, but we do not desire vengeance on them" is directed against the universal protasis stated above and can be seen as an instance of the protasis "some angry men do not desire vengeance".
Instead of καθ' ἕκαστον Aristotle in Θ also uses κατὰ μέρος (1, 155b35; 13, 163a1, 5f.;14, 164a9) or ἐν μέρει (14, 164a8).

[78] πᾶσα πρότασις συλλογιστικὴ ἢ τούτων τίς ἐστιν ἐξ ὧν ὁ συλλογισμὸς ἢ τινος τούτων ἕνεκα.

defines them as protaseis "through which the syllogism proceeds".[79] I shall call this syllogism the *main syllogism*.

There are also protaseis which are used for establishing the necessary protaseis of the main syllogism—Aristotle simply characterizes them as protaseis "other than those which are necessary".[80] I shall call them *auxiliary protaseis*. The necessary protaseis can be established with the help of auxiliary protaseis through induction or, again, through syllogism. The deducing of the necessary protaseis is sometimes described by Aristotle as "to conclude by a prosyllogism" (προσυλλογίζεσθαι).[81] I shall call this syllogism the *prosyllogism*. Of course, auxiliary protaseis in turn can be established by a syllogism as well, so that one gets auxiliary protaseis and prosyllogisms of the second (or more) degree.[82] Thus, we can distinguish different kinds of syllogism—main, auxiliary of the first, second, etc. degree—depending on the function of their conclusion

Now, what does Aristotle actually understand by a syllogism in the *Topics* exactly? He gives a definition at the very beginning of the *Topics* (A 1, 100a25-27):

> A syllogism is an argument in which certain things being laid down, something other than these necessarily comes about through them.[83]

Almost exactly the same definition is given at the beginning of the *Prior Analytics*, A 1, 24b18-20. The only slight difference is that in the *Topics* Aristotle says that something necessarily comes about "through" the protaseis, whereas in the *Analytics* he says "through their being so" (τῷ ταῦτα εἶναι). In the next sentence Aristotle explains that he means the two expressions in the same way and that he wants to say through these expressions that in order to make the consequence necessary nothing more is needed than the terms in the protaseis alone (24b20-22).[84]

The definition of the syllogism is a very broad one: all it says is that from some premisses something else, namely the conclusion necessarily follows

---

[79] ἀναγκαῖαι δὲ λέγονται δι' ὧν ὁ συλλογισμός γίνεται (155b20; cf b 29). Sometimes the syllogism is called more specifically συλλογιμὸς τοῦ ἐξ ἀρχῆς, i.e. syllogism of the original thesis (cf. e.g. 1, 156a8).

[80] προτάσεις (...) παρὰ τὰς ἀναγκαίας (1, 155b19; cf. 1, 156a3). Sometimes they are circumscribed differently still as e.g. "protaseis which are required to establish the necessary ones" (πρὸς ταύτας [sc. ἀναγκαίας] χρήσιμ[α]) (156a10) or arguably the expression ἐκεῖνα (sc. λήμματα) ὑφ' ὧν ὁ συλλογισμός (156a21f.) which I translate as "those protaseis from which we syllogize the necessary protaseis" and which is interpreted in this way also by Alex. *in Top.* 527, 18-22, Pacius (1597), 755, 10, Waitz (1844-46), ad 156a20, and Zadro (1974), 522, 5 (3); the term λήμματα, which only occurs in the whole Organon in two other places, namely *Top.* A, 101a14 and Soph. El. 183a15, as well as ἀξιώματα are used synonymously with protaseis in *Top.* Θ.

[81] Θ 1, 156a8. The only other occurrence in the *Topics* is found in Z 10, 148b8.

[82] Cf. Θ 1, 156a7-11 where Aristotle says that the final conclusion is better concealed when not only the necessary protaseis, but also some of the protaseis with which the necessary ones are established, i.e. auxiliary protaseis are established syllogistically.

[83] ἔστι δὲ συλλογισμὸς λόγος ἐν ᾧ τεθέντων τινῶν ἕτερόν τι τῶν κειμένων ἐξ ἀνάγκης συμβαίνει διὰ τῶν κειμένων.

[84] λέγω δὲ τῷ ταῦτα εἶναι τὸ διὰ ταῦτα συμβαίνειν, τὸ δὲ διὰ ταῦτα συμβαίνειν τὸ μηδενὸς ἔξωθεν ὅρου προσδεῖν πρὸς τὸ γενέσθαι τὸ ἀναγκαῖον.

and it follows due to the premises alone. The definition is of course broader than the categorical syllogism with which the *Prior Analytics* mainly deals and to which the word "syllogism" in English most frequently refers. An example of a categorical syllogism is:

> Every man is an animal;
> every animal is mortal;
> hence, every man is mortal.

Apart from categorical syllogism Aristotle in the *Analytics* also deals very briefly with another sort of deduction, namely with hypothetical syllogisms (συλλογισμὸς ἐξ ὑποθέσεως). An example of a hypothetical syllogism is:

> If man is an animal, then man is mortal;
> man is an animal;
> hence, man is mortal.

In *APr.* A 44 where Aristotle deals with the hypothetical syllogism he explains that the conclusion is not reached by a syllogism but through the hypothesis. This statement has often been misunderstood to the effect that the hypothetical syllogism was supposed not to be a syllogism at all. Now, Aristotle of course used the word syllogism here in the narrow sense of categorical syllogism; obviously, hypothetical syllogism is still a syllogism in the broad sense, i.e. a deductive argument—otherwise it would not be called a syllogism; cf. p. 128f. I shall deal more extensively with hypothetical syllogism in Chapter Four.

Aristotle uses the notion of the syllogism quite extensively in Θ and it is fairly clear that he has the same definition in mind as given in *Top.* A 1.[85] Aristotle does not distinguish here between categorical and hypothetical syllogisms nor does he make any attempt to explain why the conclusion follows from the premises. There are at least two clear examples of syllogisms to be found in Θ:

> Knowledge of opposites is the same.
> Contraries are opposites.
> Hence, knowledge of contraries is the same.[86]

and

---

[85] Cf. e.g. Θ 11, 161b29f. where Aristotle criticises that "sometimes people secure more premises than are necessary, so that it is not through them (τῷ ταῦτ' εἶναι) that the syllogism comes about."

[86] Θ 1, 155b32-34. Aristotle does not present here the syllogisms in the neat form I use above, but it can be easily extracted from what he says here: "If one desires to secure the premiss that the knowledge of contraries is the same, one should claim it not of contraries, but of opposites; for, if he grants it (τεθέντος γὰρ τούτου), one will then deduce by a syllogism (συλλογιεῖται) that the knowledge of contraries is also the same, because contraries are opposites." Similarly, one could express the paradigma of the categorical syllogism given above: From 'animals are mortal' 'men are mortal' can be deduced, *because* men are animals.

He who sits, writes.
Socrates is sitting.
Hence, Socrates is writing.[87]

These examples of syllogisms seem to correspond to categorical rather than hypothetical syllogisms, although the second one could also be interpreted as a hypothetical syllogism, i.e. "he who sits, writes" as "if someone sits, then he writes". However, there are certainly universal protaseis which when used in a syllogism would certainly create a hypothetical rather than a categorical syllogism, e.g. "if a person has lost knowledge of a thing while it still remains, then he has forgotten it."[88] Thus, it would appear that in Θ syllogisms are found which later would be classified as categorical or hypothetical syllogisms. From the two examples given above it is clear that the syllogisms have much in common with syllogisms as we know them from the *Analytics*, but there are also some striking differences. As already mentioned above, the premisses are not explicitly quantified by quantifiers 'every', 'no', or 'some'.[89] Further, there are also premisses containing individual terms such as "Socrates" which are not allowed in the syllogistic as expounded in the *Prior Analytics*[90] and which we also find in other books of the *Topics*.[91]

1.2.5. *Necessary protaseis: Θ 1, 155b29-156a3*

Having dealt with the notion of the syllogism and the function of necessary and auxiliary protaseis, we can now proceed to deal with the latter two in more detail. As already said, necessary protaseis are protaseis "by means of which the main syllogism proceeds." Aristotle enumerates four ways in which they can be established:[92]

(1) by prosyllogism[93]
(2) by induction[94]

---

[87] Θ 10, 160b26-28. Here, the syllogism is presented in a straightforward way: "For example, if someone secures (from the answerer) (λάβῃ) that 'he who sits, writes' and that 'Socrates is sitting'; for from these it follows that (συμβαίνει γὰρ ἐκ τούτων) 'Socrates is writing.'"

[88] Θ 2, 157b15f.

[89] Although the general sentences have an implicit quantification of which Aristotle is well aware and which he makes explicit if necessary. Thus in Θ 10, 160b32f. he points out that what is false in the second example is the first premiss because "not *everyone* who sits, writes".

[90] However, there are exceptions: A 33, 47b15ff. and B 27, 70a16ff. Cf. Patzig (1968), pp. 4-8.

[91] Cf. e.g. A 5, 102b7; 7, 103a30f.; 9, 103b29-35; Γ 2, 117b13-25; E 1, 128b20; 129a5; 3, 131b12, et al. They are also found in the *Sophistici Elenchi*: 5, 166b32, 33f., 14, 173b30, et al. On the whole however they are actually comparatively seldom. On the problems which singular terms create in book E cf. Barnes (1970), p. 148.

[92] Θ 1, 155b35-38.

[93] Aristotle does not actually use the word "prosyllogism", but the more generic "syllogism" (b35). Since the syllogism here does not establish the final conclusion but only the necessary protasis of the main syllogism, obviously a prosyllogism is meant.

[94] Aristotle deals with likeness (or analogy) in several passages and says explicitly that it is often used to establish the universal (Θ 8, 160a37-39). However, it is not included in the list here. In contrast to induction we do not proceed from particular protaseis, but from one or more universal protaseis to the universal (Θ 1, 156b10-17) e.g. "as knowledge and ignorance of contraries is the same thing, so is the perception of contraries the same thing." Obviously

(3) some by prosyllogism and some by induction
(4) by being advanced in their original form, if "absolutely clear" (λίαν προ-φανεῖς)

There is something very striking about the purpose of the four ways to establish the necessary protaseis. The main function of the first three is the *concealment of the conclusion* (κρύψις τοῦ συμπεράσματος) and the fourth one is only used when the first three cannot be used. The expression "concealment of the conclusion" is actually misleading. There is of course no way of concealing the intended conclusion since this is clear from the very beginning of the disputation—the intended conclusion is the questioner's thesis and the contradictory to the answerer's thesis. What is supposed to be concealed is of course that the protaseis the questioner wants to secure bring him nearer to deducing the intended conclusion. Aristotle sometimes describes this tactic as "keeping away (as far as possible) from the intended conclusion."[95] An explanation for the expression "concealment of the conclusion" can be extracted from a passage in which Aristotle says:

> To put the matter generally, he who wishes to conceal his purpose while eliciting answers (τὸν κρυπτικῶς πυνθανόμενον) should so put his questions that when he has put his whole argument and has stated his conclusion, people still ask "Well, but why is that?"[96]

Why should the questioner try to conceal his conclusion? The dialectical disputes clearly have a competitive character (ἀγῶνος χάριν) and are always directed against another party (πρὸς ἕτερον),[97] the aim being to win and not necessarily to reach the truth. If the opponent realizes that a protasis clearly leads to the conclusion which is the opposite of his thesis, he will promptly refuse to grant it—there are of course limitations to this, which I shall discuss later. It is in fact acceptable for the answerer to refuse to grant a protasis on the grounds of its being too close to the conclusion.[98]

The fact that the dialectician has an opponent and has to argue accordingly, including the hiding of the conclusion,[99] is in fact the main difference between the philosopher and the dialectician as described by Aristotle in the transitional part joining book Θ with the central books.[100] The philosopher,

---

Aristotle did not consider it to be at the same level as induction and syllogism—but he does not say why.

[95] Cf. Θ 1, 156a12f.: οὕτω γὰρ πορρωτάτω ἀποστήσειε τῆς ἐξ ἀρχῆς θέσεως. See also 1, 155b30, 38f. and 14, 163b35f.

[96] Θ 1, 156a13-15. Aristotle also often speaks of the "universal" being concealed, cf. 156b11 (λανθάνει μᾶλλον τὸ καθόλου); also a28f.

[97] Θ 1, 155b26-28. Πρός in the *Topics* is often ambiguous between "in relation to" and the more specific "against"; here, the latter is certainly meant.

[98] Θ 6, 160a3-6. The answerer can use the closeness to the conclusion as an argument for not granting a protasis only in cases where the closeness is very striking, i.e. where the conclusion necessarily follows from the protasis so that the answerer can argue, the questioner is begging the question (*Soph. El.* 17, 176a27-33). On begging the question cf. Θ 13, 162b34-163a13.

[99] "For all this [i.e. arrangement and framing of questions] is in relation to/against another party" (πρὸς ἕτερον γὰρ πᾶν τὸ τοιοῦτον, Θ 1, 155b10).

[100] Θ 1, 155b10-16.

seeking for himself, need not care whether or not the answerer will grant a protasis which is too near to the original thesis of the questioner. On the contrary, he tries to make his axioms (ἀξιώματα)[101] as familiar and near to the question in hand (γνώριμα καὶ σύνεγγυς) as possible.

However, the concealment of the conclusion has for the dialectician not only the agonistic purpose described above. As Aristotle remarks casually in one passage, "if it is unclear what is useful to the argument, people are more likely to state what they themselves really think."[102]

In 155b30-34 where the establishing of the necessary protasis by the prosyllogism is described, the concealment of the conclusion is given as the purpose: one should keep as far away as possible from the necessary protasis one wants to establish (ἀποστατέον ὅτι ἀνωτάτω). What is meant in the case of a syllogism is that one should find a more universal protasis from which one can deduce the protasis needed by a syllogism.[103] Aristotle illustrates this by an example of a syllogism already cited above. If one wants to establish that "the knowledge of contraries is the same" one should not ask this protasis directly but ask the more general protasis "the knowledge of opposites is the same", hoping that the answerer would not realize that from this the needed protasis follows. Together with the protasis "contraries are opposites", which is so obvious that the answerer can scarcely deny it, "the knowledge of contraries" can be deduced. Once the answerer has accepted the protaseis he will have to accept the conclusion which follows necessarily.[104]

There is also another way of keeping as far away as possible (πορρω-τάτω ἀποστήσειε) from the final conclusion: one should state all the relevant conclusions at the same time at the end.[105]

Let us now discuss induction (2). It is described as one of two dialectical arguments, the other being the syllogism (A 12, 105a10-12). Induction is

---

[101] "Axioms" in Θ usually have the same meaning as "protaseis".

[102] Θ 1, 156b6-9.

[103] Aristotle actually says here more specifically that "one should keep as far *topmost* as possible" (ἀποστατέον ὅτι ἀνωτάτω) (Θ 1, 155b30), referring to a more universal protasis, whereas "as far away as possible" leaves it open as to whether a more or less universal protasis is meant. Aristotle often uses the local adverbs "above" (ἐπάνω) and "below" (ὑποκάτω) to designate more or less general terms or protaseis (cf. Δ 2, 122a4, 9; also Θ 1, 156b17).

Forster (1960) reads ἀπωτάτω for ἀνωτάτω, meaning "farthest from" so that the sentence in b30 could be taken to refer to both syllogism and induction; in the latter case the protaseis are of course less general. This would perhaps make Aristotle more consistent, but ἀπωτάτω is not found in any codex and I suspect that he was mainly thinking of syllogism here which immediately follows.

[104] Although even then the questioner has to be careful. Thus, Aristotle advises, "one ought not put the conclusion in the form of a question; otherwise if the answerer rejects it, it looks as if the syllogism has failed. For often, even if one does not put it in the form of question but advances it as a consequence (ὡς συμβαῖνον ἐπιφέροντος), people deny it, and then those who do not see what follows from the previous admissions do not realize that those who deny it have been refuted. Whenever, therefore, one puts the conclusion in the form of a question, without even saying that it follows, and the other party denies it, it looks altogether as if the syllogism has failed." (Θ 2, 158a7-13).

[105] Θ 1, 156a11-14.

dealt with throughout the *Topics* only as a subsidiary means of attaining necessary universal protaseis, not as a direct way of attacking the original problema. As with the syllogism, no explicit definition is found in Θ,[106] but there is one in A 12:

> Induction is a passage (ἔφοδος) from the particulars (ἀπὸ τῶν καθ' ἕκαστα) to the universal (ἐπὶ τὸ καθόλου [107]); e.g. the argument that supposing the skilled pilot is the best pilot, and the skilled charioteer is the best charioteer, then in general the skilled man is the best at his particular sphere.[108]

By particulars and the universal, clearly particular and universal protaseis are meant. The particular protaseis establish the universal protasis by expressing something "similar",[109] which is expressed in the universal protasis.[110] In the case of induction the conclusion of the induction is hidden away as well,[111] but one keeps away from the conclusion from the other side so to speak, i.e. the protaseis are not more but less universal than the conclusion. Aristotle makes the following distinction between induction and syllogism:

> Induction is more convincing (πιθανώτερον) and clear and more easily grasped by sense-perception and is applicable to the mass of people; but deduction is more cogent (βιαστικώτερον) and more effective against argumentative opponents.[112]

Syllogism is more cogent because the conclusion follows necessarily: once the opponent has admitted the premisses he is compelled to accept the deduced conclusion. In the case of induction the conclusion normally does not follow necessarily. It is more convincing and clear because it argues from less universal protaseis than the conclusion and the answerer is more ready to accept an endoxical particular protasis than a universal one.[113]

Once the protaseis have been admitted the syllogism is more cogent than induction. However, it can happen that the universal protasis from which the questioner wants to deduce the necessary protasis needed for the main argument is not admitted by the answerer, and if the questioner has not

---

[106] But the definition of induction is obviously assumed in Θ and Aristotle deals with it explicitly in several passages, cf. esp. 2, 157a18-33.

[107] Reading with Ross (1958) and Kapp (1942), p. 76n.1 τὸ καθόλου, not τὰ καθόλου, as Brunschwig (1967) does.

[108] A 12, 105a13-16.

[109] τὰ ὅμοια (Θ 8, 160a36-39; 2, 157a27ff.; 1, 156b16f.; A 18, 108b9-12).

[110] Sometimes it is difficult to find a universal protasis which describes the καθόλου, since no such term exists; one has to say then: "So in all cases of this kind" (οὕτως ἐπὶ πάντων τῶν τοιούτων) (Θ 2, 157a21-24).

[111] Θ 1, 155b38-156a1.

[112] A 12, 105a16-19. This corresponds to the advice given in Θ 14, 164a12f.: "You should apply your training in inductive reasoning against a young man, in deductive (τῶν συλλογιστικῶν) against an expert" and in 2, 157a18-21: "In dialectical argument, syllogism should be used in reasoning against dialecticians (διαλεκτικοὺς) rather than against the multitude; induction, on the other hand, is most useful against the multitude. This point has been made previously as well."

[113] Θ 8, 160a39-b2. In 1, 156a5-7 Aristotle says that in induction one proceeds "from the known (γνώριμα) to the unknown (ἄγνωστα); and the objects of perception are more known, either without qualification or to most people."

adduced any instance in support the answerer does not even have to justify his rejection with a counter-example.[114] If the answerer plainly rejects a protasis the questioner can still resort to induction. If, as in the example given above, the answerer does not accept the protasis that "the knowledge of opposites is the same", from which the questioner wants to establish that "the knowledge of contraries is the same", he has to establish the latter by induction.[115] That is, he has to give particular instances of the universal protasis to be established, here cases of some particular pairs of contraries of which the predicate "the knowledge is the same" is predicable: e.g. "the knowledge of good and evil is the same", "the knowledge of black and white is the same", "the knowledge of cold and hot is the same", etc.[116] The answerer is expected to grant the protaseis if they are endoxical and true (ἀληθῆ καὶ ἔνδοξα)[117]—even if he sees that the questioner wants to establish a protasis which brings him nearer to victory. Once the answerer has accepted several particular protaseis he has to accept the universal protasis as well, except if he can find a counter-example (ἔνστασις). If he does not accept the universal without giving a counter-example, he behaves peevishly (δυσκολαίνειν).[118] Both induction and syllogism contain at least two premisses.[119]

The third way of establishing necessary protaseis (3) is trivial; of course, it is not necessary to establish *all* the necessary protaseis either by syllogism or by induction: some of them can be established by syllogism and some by induction.

Aristotle introduces the fourth way of establishing necessary protaseis (4) by saying:

> If the protaseis are absolutely clear, you can also advance them in their original form.[120]

Reading this sentence one might interpret it in the sense that protaseis which are clear beyond all doubt can be advanced directly, whereas protaseis which are not so evident must be established by syllogism or induction. However, the next few lines (155b38-156a3), which are explanatory to the enumerated four kinds of necessary protaseis, make clear that this understanding is not quite correct:

---

[114] Θ 2, 157a35f.
[115] Θ 1, 155b34f.
[116] The examples are all Aristotelian, cf. A 14, 105b36f.
[117] Θ 8, 160a39f.
[118] Θ 8, 160b3-5; 2, 157a34f.
[119] The definition of the syllogism (as well as that of the induction) merely expresses that protaseis (plural) have to number at least two. He never says in the *Topics* that they have to be exactly two (as he does with respect to categorical syllogisms in *APr*. A 25, 42a33ff.), even though his examples of syllogisms usually consist of two only. Syllogisms with too many premisses are criticised, e.g. in Θ 11, 162a24ff., and Aristotle says explicitly that syllogism is always based on a few protaseis only (Θ 2, 158a28f.). As for induction, cf p. 40n.169.
[120] Θ 1, 155b37f.: ὅσαι δὲ λίαν προφανεῖς εἰσι, καὶ αὐτὰς προτείνοντα.

> For the coming conclusion (τὸ συμβησόμενον) is always less obvious when it is still far off (ἐν τῇ ἀποστάσει) and in the process of induction, and at the same time, if you cannot establish the required protaseis in this way, it is still feasible to advance them in their original form.

Thus, what is obviously meant is that it is always best to establish protaseis by syllogism or induction, since in this way the final conclusion is best hidden. However, if the questioner is not able to establish a protasis in this way, because, say, he cannot find a more universal protasis from which to syllogize the required protasis or he cannot find particular protaseis which would inductively establish the required protasis, he can still advance it directly, but only if the protasis is absolutely clear—otherwise the answerer is unlikely to accept it.

1.2.6. *Auxiliary protaseis: 155b18-28; 156a3-157a17*

The necessary protaseis, if not advanced in their original form, are established with the help of auxiliary protaseis—normally through syllogism or induction. Aristotle devotes nearly the entire first chapter to this kind of protaseis. In 155b20-24 he classifies them according to their use into four different kinds, which are supposed to be complete (b24f.). They are used :

(1) either for the sake of induction <and> in general for the sake of the universal being granted
(2) or to add weight to the argument
(3) or to conceal the conclusion
(4) or to render the argument more clear.[121]

The auxiliary protaseis for establishing the universal (1) seem to refer to the universal necessary protaseis described in 155b29-156a7 and discussed above. It is striking that in the first-mentioned kind of auxiliary protaseis (1) Aristotle only mentions induction and not syllogism with the help of which universal protaseis can be established as well, as shown in the previous section.[122] Aristotle appears to have been slightly careless here.

It is also possible to insert with Ross the conjunction "<and>" (καὶ) in b22, not testified by any codex, and interpret it not as a so-called καὶ-explicativum which would simply clarify the rôle of induction, but as introducing a more general point, i.e.: "for the sake of induction and in general for the sake of the universal being granted." This would leave room for syllogism and any other means of establishing the universal protasis.[123] Thus, the auxiliary protaseis for establishing the universal (1) could be taken as referring to the

---

[121] αἱ δὲ παρὰ ταύτας λαμβανόμεναι τέτταρες εἰσιν· ἢ γὰρ ἐπαγωγῆς χάριν <καὶ> τοῦ δοθῆναι τὸ καθόλου, ἢ εἰς ὄγκον τοῦ λόγου, ἢ πρὸς κρύψιν τοῦ συμπεράσματος, ἢ πρὸς τὸ σαφέστερον εἶναι τὸν λόγον. παρὰ δὲ ταύτας οὐδεμίαν ληπτέον πρότασιν.
[122] Induction always establishes universal protaseis whereas with syllogisms one can also establish individual protaseis, e.g. "Socrates writes."
[123] A universal protasis can be established by likeness or analogy (ὁμοιότης) as well. In Θ 8, 160a37-39 Aristotle explicitly says that "people usually secure the universal by induction or by analogy." The word "usually" obviously leaves room for syllogism as well. For the workings of likeness cf. Θ 1, 156b10-17 (see p .35 below); cf. also p. 27n.94.

entire section in 155b29-156a7 which deals with the necessary protaseis discussed above.[124]

Aristotle deals next with the protaseis used for concealing the final conclusion (3). The entire passage in 156a7-157a5—more than half of Θ 1—is devoted to these protaseis. The passage clearly ends in 157a5, since in the next line (157a6) Aristotle explicitly says that "for concealment, then, the rules which should be followed are the above." The beginning is harder to determine, because the protaseis used for granting the universal (1) and those for concealment (3) cannot be neatly separated, since protaseis used for granting the universal are used for concealment as well.[125] I have already dealt with the concealment of protaseis in the section on necessary protaseis: the auxiliary protaseis used in prosyllogisms or induction for establishing necessary protaseis also fall under the subheading of protaseis used for concealment of the final conclusion. However, in the present section we find many other such protaseis.

I have already remarked that the expression "auxiliary protaseis for the concealment of the conclusion" is misleading in that there is no way of concealing the conclusion which is clear from the start. The expression is misleading in another respect as well, since not all that we find in this section can be expressed in protaseis. The term 'tactics' or 'covering up' would describe the contents of the section more accurately. Take for example the following advice:

> It is also a useful practice not to establish the admitted protaseis (ἀξιώματα) on which the syllogisms are based in their proper order, but to alternate one which leads to one conclusion with another which leads to another conclusion; for, if those which are closely related are set side by side, the conclusion which will result from them is more clearly foreseen.[126]

The advice here is obviously to intermingle protaseis of prosyllogims and syllogisms so that the respective conclusions are better concealed. This advice refers to the order of stating protaseis, not to some additional auxiliary protaseis which would conceal the conclusion.

There are many more pieces of advice of this sort. Thus, in other passages the questioner is advised to state all the conclusions, i.e. not only the conclusion of the main syllogism but also those of the prosyllogisms, at the very end;[127] not to insist too much, even though he really requires the point, for insistence always arouses the more opposition;[128] when to ask the most important questions, depending on the temperament and experience of the

---

[124] One can divide section 155b29-156a7 (with Forster (1960)) into two sections: 155b29-156a3 which strictly deals with necessary protaseis only, and 156a3-7 where Aristotle explicitly starts dealing with auxiliary protaseis, dealing first with induction.

[125] The very fact that these auxiliary protaseis are listed as two different kinds seems to show that the main purpose of establishing necessary protaseis is to compel the opponent to accept the contradictory of his original thesis, and only secondarily is it for concealment.

[126] Θ 1, 156a23-26.

[127] Θ 1, 156a11-13.

[128] Θ 1, 156b23-25.

opponent.[129] More instructions of this sort can be found, referring to the sequence and way of asking protaseis rather than establishing of auxiliary protaseis.

There are other pieces of advice where an auxiliary protasis is produced, but it does not contain another protasis or conclusion implicitly, but rather has the purpose of deluding the opponent about the status of a protasis or to put the answerer off his guard. Thus the questioner is advised to sometimes make an objection against himself, for answerers are unsuspicious when dealing with those who appear to be arguing fairly[130] or to add the phrase "so and so is generally held or commonly said" (σύνηθες καὶ λεγόμενον τὸ τοιοῦτον), since people are shy of upsetting the received opinion without good reason.[131]

The expression "auxiliary protaseis for the concealment of the final conclusion" seems to fit best the auxiliary protaseis with the help of which syllogism and induction are carried out, since in these protaseis the conclusion is to some extent contained implicitly. I have dealt with them in the section on necessary protaseis. Interestingly, Aristotle also lists some other types of reasonings in this section which are neither syllogisms nor induction. These types of reasonings are of special importance for this book, because they seem to be predecessors of a few topoi with which the central topoi deal. These reasonings here are arguments with usually just one premiss and one conclusion, which is itself a premiss of another. One of them runs:

> Moreover, do not put forward (προτείνειν) the very proposition which has to be established (ληφθῆναι), but rather something from which it necessarily follows (ᾧ τοῦτο ἕπεται ἐξ ἀνάγκης); for people are more likely to admit the latter, because what will follow from it (τὸ συμβησόμενον) is less obvious, and if the one has been established, the other has been established as well (ληφθέντος τούτου εἴληπται κἀκεῖνο).[132]

Another example is:

> You should also, whenever possible, establish the universal protasis (καθόλου πρότασιν) in the form of a definition relating not to the actual terms in question but to co-ordinates of them (ἐπὶ τῶν συστοίχων); for people let themselves be deceived when a definition is established dealing with co-ordinates, imagining that they are not making the admission universally. This would happen, for example, if one had to establish that the angry man is desirous of revenge for a fancied slight and were to establish that anger is desire for revenge for a fancied slight; for obviously, if this

---

[129] Normally the questioner is advised to ask the most important questions at the end, because most people are eager to secure them first, and their opponents, being aware of this, are especially inclined to deny them. However, with ill-tempered people and those who think themselves clever one should ask the most important questions at the beginning. The former readily admit what comes first and show their ill-temper at the end; the latter are confident in their skill and imagine that they cannot suffer any defeat (Θ 1, 156b30-157a1).

[130] Θ 1, 156b18-20.

[131] Θ 1, 156b20-23.

[132] Θ 1, 156b27-30; cf. B 4, 111B17-23 and 5, 112a16-23, with which I shall deal in Chapter Four, pp. 98-103.

were established (τούτου ληφθέντος), we should have the universal admission which we require.
On the other hand it often happens, when people make propositions dealing with the actual term, that the answerer refuses his assent, because he objects more rapidly when the actual term is used, saying for example, that the angry man is not desirous of revenge, for though we become angry with our parents, yet we are not desirous of revenge. [...] But as regards the definition of anger it is not easy to find an objection as in some other cases.[133]

Another example is likeness (ὁμοιότης):

> Further, you should carry out your questioning by means of likeness; for this is a plausible method and the universal is less obvious. For example you should argue that as, as knowledge and ignorance of contraries is the same thing, so is the perception of contraries the same, or conversely, since the perception of them is the same, so also is the knowledge. This method resembles induction but is not the same thing; for, induction, the universal is established from particulars, whereas, in arguments from likeness, what is established is not the universal under which all the like cases fall.[134]

There are other examples of predecessors.[135] To state the difference very briefly. In Θ the predecessors of topoi work as immediate inferences of the form 'P, hence Q', establishing a *protasis*. In the central books the topoi have the form of a hypothesis in a hypothetical syllogism: 'If P, then Q.' Having established P, Q can be deduced. With the help of them the *conclusion* of an argument is established.

Aristotle deals with protaseis used "to add weight to the argument" (2) and those "to render the argument more clear" (4) very briefly at the very end of Θ 1, in 157a6-13 and 157a14-17 respectively.

The expression "to add weight" (εἰς ὄγκον) itself does not actually occur again. In 157a6-13 however Aristotle discusses protaseis used "for ornament" (εἰς τὸν κόσμον), which are obviously meant to be the same and which are not in any way necessary for the final conclusion.[136] Two means of achieving the ornament are mentioned: induction and distinction of things closely akin (διαίρεσις τῶν συγγένων). Aristotle takes the meaning of induction for granted and explains the meaning of the distinction of things closely akin by giving two examples: "one science is better than another, either because it is more exact or because it is concerned with better objects"[137] and that "some sciences are theoretical, others practical and others productive."[138] Such distinctions obviously do not require the answerer to make a choice and can thus be readily admitted—disputed protaseis scarcely could be used for

---

[133] Θ 1, 156a27-b3; cf. e.g. B 9, 114a26-b5.
[134] Θ 1, 156b10-17; cf. B 10, 114b25-36 and A 18, 108b7-19. I shall deal with the last passage in Chapter Four, pp. 120f.
[135] Θ 2, 157b2-8 vs. B 3, 110a23-111a7; Θ 3, 158b24-159a2 vs. B 4, 111b12-16 and B 2, 109b30-110a9.
[136] Θ 1, 157a12f.
[137] ἐπιστήμη ἐπιστήμης βελτίων ἢ τῷ ἀκριβεστέρα εἶναι ἢ βελτιόνων.
[138] τῶν ἐπιστημῶν αἱ μὲν θεωρητικαὶ αἱ δὲ πρακτικαὶ αἱ δὲ ποιητικαί.

decoration. However, Aristotle does not say much about them and they are clearly of minor importance.

As for the protaseis "to render the argument more clear" (4) Aristotle expresses himself even more briefly (157a14-17). There are two means to achieve clarity: examples (παραδείγματα) and illustrations (παραβολαί). Aristotle specifies the examples slightly: they should be to the point and familiar, such as are those from Homer, not those from Choirilos. With the help of an example another protasis can be rendered clearer (16f.).

Aristotle does not expand any further on these two notions, but he deals with them in *Rhetoric*. Example is defined as a rhetorical induction,[139] which is similar to the standard induction[140] as given in the definition. It differs from induction in that it proceeds from a particular to another particular protasis, rather than from particular protaseis to a universal one.[141] Illustrations are dealt with as a kind of example.[142]

It should be noted that the various means which Aristotle gives for using the four different kinds of protaseis are not necessarily specific to the kind of protaseis—the status of a protasis depends rather on the questioner's intentions. Thus, induction can be used for establishing necessary universal protaseis but also just for ornament. Protaseis which have no function in the syllogism can be used for ornament, as described above, but also for concealment of the final conclusion—one of the instructions for covering up the final conclusion is "to prolong the argument and to introduce into it points which are of no practical good, as do those who construct false geometrical figures; for when the material is less abundant, it is less obvious where the fallacy lies."[143] Illustrations can be used in order to make the argument clearer. However, they can also be used in a different context: the questioner is advised "to formulate the protasis as if it were an illustration (ὡς ἐν παραβολῇ προτείνειν); for people more readily admit a protasis proposed for some other purpose and is not useful for its own sake."[144]

2. *The part of the answerer*

The part of the answerer is of less interest in the framework of this book. The topoi listed in the central books of the *Topics* where written for the part of the questioner and thus it is most important to understand his part in the gymnastic game. Thus, I shall deal with the answerer's part comparatively briefly. Aristotle mainly deals with it in Θ, 5-8 and 10. Θ, 5-7 deal with the

---

[139] *Rhet.* A 2, 1356a4¹.
[140] *Rhet.* B 20, 1393a26.
[141] *Rhet.* A 2, 1357b25-36.
[142] *Rhet.* B 28, 1393a27-30. In 1393b4-8 an example of a Socratic illustration is given: "Public officials should not be chosen by lot. That is like using the lot to choose athletes, instead of choosing those who are fit for the contest; or using the lot to choose a steersman from among a ship's crew, as if we ought to take the man on whom the lot falls, and not the man who knows about it."
[143] Θ 1, 157a1-3.
[144] Θ 1, 156b25-27.

question of how to answer protaseis, whereas 8 and 10 deal with the so-called objections and solutions.

In Θ 5, 159a38ff. Aristotle advises the answerer what sort of protaseis put by the questioner to accept, depending on whether the answerer's thesis is endoxical or adoxical or neither of the two. The answerer's strategy is guided by the requirement that the questioner "who syllogizes well proves his thesis from more endoxical and more known protaseis"[145] than the conclusion, which equals the questioner's thesis. Thus, if the answerer's thesis is adoxical and hence the questioner's thesis and the intended conclusion is endoxical, the answerer should not accept any protaseis which are less endoxical than the conclusion let alone adoxical protaseis.[146] The cases where the answerer's thesis is endoxical[147] or neither endoxical nor adoxical[148] work accordingly. The answerer here obviously has the function of making sure that the questioner "syllogizes well", i.e. that he reasons from premisses which are more endoxical than the conclusion, and not to hinder him at achieving the conclusion.

In Θ 6 Aristotle gives advice on how to deal with protaseis, specifying them not only as endoxical or adoxical or neither of them, but combining this specification with the question as to whether the protasis is relevant to the argument (πρὸς τὸν λόγον) or not. As it is clear from the context, "relevant to the argument" is meant in a very strong sense, meaning that if the protasis is conceded, the answerer's thesis becomes refuted. Aristotle lists all the six combinations of these two aspects. I shall cite the first three cases for illustration:

> If the protasis is endoxical and irrelevant, the answerer should grant it saying that it seems to be true.
> If, however, the protasis is adoxical but irrelevant to the argument, the answerer should concede it but put in a remark (ἐπισημαντέον) that it does not seem to be true, so that he does not appear to be simple-minded.
> If the protasis is relevant and endoxical, he should remark that it seems to be true, but that it is too near to his original thesis and say that, if this is conceded, the thesis becomes destroyed.[149]

Whereas the instructions given in fifth chapter to the answerer had the purpose that the questioner "syllogizes well", the sort of rules given in the sixth chapter cited above make sure not only that the questioner syllogizes well, but that the answerer does not lose face even when his thesis is refuted. In the additional remarks Aristotle advises him on, the answerer always makes clear that he sees what is going on in the debate and if he is refuted, having foreseen it as the result of his various confessions, he will not be thought to suffer through his own fault.[150]

---

[145] Θ 5, 159b8f.
[146] Θ 5, 159b9-16.
[147] Θ 5, 159b16-20.
[148] Θ 5, 159b20-23.
[149] Θ 6, 160a1-6. The remaining three cases are described in ll. 6-11.
[150] Θ 6, 160a11-14.

In Θ 7 Aristotle advises the answerer on how to answer unclear or ambiguous questions. Unclear questions should simply be met with the remark "I do not understand", since answerers often encounter some difficulty if they simply answer "yes" or "no".[151] The strategy on ambiguous questions depends on whether the protasis is true or false in all senses, or true in some, false in some other sense. The former should simply be answered by "yes" or "no", whereas in the latter case the answerer should simply add the remark (ἐπισημαντέον) that the protasis is ambiguous and that in one meaning it is true, in the other it is false.[152] If he did not foresee the ambiguity, but grants the protasis having one meaning in view and the questioner leads on to the other, he should say: "It was not that meaning that I had in view, when I gave my assent, but the other one."[153]

2.1. Solutions (λύσεις) and objections (ἐνστάσεις)

The answerer's function in the gymnastic is not restricted to answer questions by "yes" or "no". Sometimes, if he does not accept a certain protasis, he is supposed to give an objection (ἔνστασις). If a syllogism has been deduced and the answerer does not accept it he is expected to give a solution (λύσις). The notion of objection is much more important in this book since it also occurs in the central books (in B, Γ and Δ). Solutions are concerned with false reasonings which is the subject-matter of the second half of the *Sophistici Elenchi* (chapters 16-33). Objections in a broad sense also include solutions. Thus, in Θ 10, 161a1-12 four kinds of objections are distinguished:

(1) demolishing that on which the falsehood depends (ἀνελόντα παρ' ὃ γίνεται τὸ ψεῦδος)
(2) bringing an objection against the questioner (πρὸς τὸν ἐρωτῶντα)
(3) objection against premisses (πρὸς τὰ ἠρωτημένα)
(4) objection which relates to the time available (πρὸς τὸν χρόνον).

Aristotle only calls the first objection a solution (161a14).[154] This agrees with the definition of the "correct solution" (ὀρθὴ λύσις)[155] in *Soph. El.* 18, 176b29f. as "an exposure of false syllogism, indicating the nature of the question on which the falsehood hinges."[156] A nice example[157] of the solution of a false syllogism is found in Θ 10, 160b26-28 which I have previously cited: "He who sits writes; Socrates is sitting; hence, Socrates is writing." The falsehood lies here of course in the first premiss, "for not everyone who

---

[151] Θ 7, 160a17-23.
[152] Θ 7, 160a23-29.
[153] Θ 7, 160a29-33.
[154] In the *Sophistici Elenchi* the notion of solution seems to have the scope of the word objection in *Top.* Θ. In *Soph. El.* 33, 183a21-23 there is nearly exactly the same list of four objections which are called here solutions; cf. also 9, 170b4f.
[155] There are also the so-called 'seeming solutions', cf. 176a19-23, 175a31-35.
[156] ἡ μὲν ὀρθὴ λύσις ἐμφάνισις ψευδοῦς συλλογισμοῦ, παρ' ὁποίαν ἐρώτησιν συμβαίνει τὸ ψεῦδος. On different ways in which a syllogism can be false and the corresponding ways of solving it see the rest of chapter 18.
[157] It is a nice example because the name "Socrates" is used as an individual constant, just as we find it later in handbooks of classical logic. We find example-sentences with "Socrates" as their subject by the way earlier in Plato, see *Theaet.* 159bff.

sits is writing" (b33). "The man who has demolished that on which the falsehood depends has provided a complete solution" (b33f.).

2.2. *Objections (ἐνστάσεις)*
Of the four kinds of objections (in the broad sense) the first has been singled out as a solution. The main difference between a solution and the remaining three objections is that solution refers to a falsehood which is recognized as such only after the conclusion has been reached: either the answerer failed to recognize that one of the premisses was wrong or, if the syllogism has been incorrectly deduced, he could not even have realized this before the conclusion was reached. In contrast, the other objections are being used before the conclusion has been reached. In fact, their purpose is to prevent the questioner from reaching the conclusion; as Aristotle says, they are "hindrances and impediments in the path to conclusions."[158] Thus, if the answerer realized that the protasis "he who sits writes" is wrong at the time when he was asked, or at any rate before the conclusion was reached, and has objected to it, this would not be a solution but an objection in a narrow sense. The objections ad hominem (2) and playing for time (4) are rather sophistical and are not mentioned as objections at any other place in the *Topics*. Thus, by an objection in the narrow sense I primarily mean the third kind of objection, i.e. objection against a protasis—it is this meaning which Aristotle normally has in mind when mentioning it in Θ and the central books. In this strict meaning ἔνστασις is best understood as "counter-example."

As I have already said, counter-examples occur in a few places in the central books[159] and also in Θ Aristotle speaks at greatest length about them from the standpoint of the questioner, namely in Θ 2, 157a34-b33, which comes immediately after the discussion of induction in 157a18-33.

> If the questioner makes an induction on the basis of a number of particular cases and the answerer refuses to grant the universal proposition, then it is fair to demand his objection.[160]

In fact, a good answerer should not even have to wait for the questioner to demand an objection, but he is expected to give an objection, be it a true or be it an apparent one (ἐνστάσεως ἢ οὔσης ἢ δοκούσης); otherwise he is thought to behave peevishly (δυσκολαίνει).[161] If the answerer cannot provide an objection, he has to admit the universal proposition;[162] if the answerer refuses to do so, again, he behaves peevishly.[163]

The enstasis is formally *an instance of the contradictory of the universal protasis*[164] it objects to, or, expressed differently, it is a protasis expressing a

---
[158] κωλύσεις τινὲς καὶ ἐμποδισμοὶ τῶν συμπερασμάτων (161a15).
[159] There are around fifteen occurrences.
[160] ὅταν δ' ἐπάγοντος ἐπὶ πολλῶν μὴ διδῷ τὸ καθόλου, τότε δίκαιον ἀπαιτεῖν ἔνστασιν, 157a34f.
[161] Θ 8, 160b1-3.
[162] Θ 2, 157b34f.
[163] Θ 8, 160b4f.
[164] The scope of the contradiction is the entire universal protasis. Of course, this does not mean that the enstasis can only have one form: it depends on which part of the problema one looks at to produce the enstasis. Let us take the universal protasis "The angry man desires

counter-example to a universal protasis.[165] Thus it is a particular protasis;[166] Aristotle actually does not say this anywhere explicitly in the *Topics*, but it is clear from their functioning which is analogous to the particular protaseis in induction of the universal protasis. The particular protaseis used in the inductive reasoning express which cases the universal protasis applies in (ἐπὶ τίνων οὕτως), the objections express which cases the universal protasis does not apply in (ἐπὶ τίνων οὐχ οὕτως).[167] The difference between a particular protasis used in induction and the particular protasis used as a counter-example is that with the help of the former a universal protasis is established, whereas with the latter the answerer does not wish to establish the contradictory of the protasis, but only to destroy the universal protasis as it stands. Thus, say, the objection to the protasis "The angry man desires vengeance on account of an apparent slight", namely "We become angry with our parents, but we do not desire vengeance on them" is of course not intended to prove that the contradictory is true, but rather that the universal protasis is *not always* true.

The objection should not be directed at the subject of the particular protaseis used for establishing a universal proposition by induction, but should produce an objection with reference to a different subject.[168] An exception to this rule occurs if the only objection available against the universal protasis is among the particular protaseis enumerated to establish the universal one. As an example of an instance Aristotle names the number "two" which is the only even prime number. The universal proposition the questioner was trying to establish was clearly 'No even numbers are prime' and as evidence for it he named say '14, 8, and 2 are even numbers and not prime'. Now, the only way the answerer can object to the universal thesis is of course by saying that number two is in fact even and prime; he has no other option than using as an objection to the universal protasis one of the protaseis which the questioner has used.[169]

---

revenge on account of a fancied slight" (Θ 1, 156a31f.). The objection to it, "(The angry man does not desire vengeance), because we become angry with our parents, but we do not desire vengeance on them" (a36-38), clearly contradicts "is desirous of revenge". However, one might of course envisage an objection contradicting "for a fancied slight".

[165] Later in *APr.* B 25, 69a37 Aristotle still defines an objection as "a protasis contrary to a proposition" (ἔνστασις δ' ἐστὶ πρότασις προτάσει ἐναντία). The entire chapter 25 is on objection which Aristotle tries to explain within his syllogistic, which is not very helpful in the present context.

[166] *Rhet.* B 25, 1402b1-4 also allows universal protaseis as objections.

[167] Cf. Θ 2, 157a35f.

[168] Θ 2, 157a37-b2.

[169] Aristotle expresses himself very succinctly and the passage in Θ 2, 157a37-b2 can easily be misunderstood: "Also, one ought to demand that objections should not be brought against the actual thing proposed unless it is the only one thing of its kind, as, for example, two is the only even number which is a prime number; for the objector ought either to make his objection with regard to another instance or else assert that the instance in question is the only one of its kind."

One might have the impression that the objection we utter is "Two is the only even number which is a prime number", which would clearly be an objection to the positive universal proposition 'All even numbers are prime', established by induction on the basis of one example only namely 'Two is even and prime'; this would confirm the thesis of von Fritz (1964), that we often find in Aristotle inductions established on the basis of one example only.

However, this interpretation is clearly wrong. The main rule given above by Aristotle is not to dispute the particular protasis given, but to find another instance against the universal

I have mentioned real and apparent objections above and there is a passage which gives concrete examples of apparent objections.[170] An apparent objection here is the objection to a universal proposition not with respect to the thing itself, but with respect to some homonym of it. One of the universal propositions here is: "No man has a foot other than his own" and the corresponding objection is that "A cook can have a foot which is not his own", e.g. the foot of a pig he is going to cook. The answerer obviously took advantage of the expression "to have" being homonymous and took it not in the intended meaning of 'to have as part of one's body' but in the meaning 'to have at one's disposal'. The questioner should meet such an objection by making a distinction (διαιρεῖσθαι), i.e. expose the homonymy making clear which sense is meant and then ask the question again.

If however the opponent makes a correct objection to the universal proposition with respect to the thing itself and not its homonym, the questioner should "withdraw the point objected to and bring forward the remainder putting it in the form of a universal proposition". Aristotle describes such protaseis as "partly false and partly true" (ἐπὶ τὶ μὲν ψευδεῖς

---

protasis. In the case given above this would be extremely easy: one could take any even number apart from 'two' pointing out that it is not prime; there is no necessity to refer to the singular proposition given.

Besides, in the present passage (cf. 157a34) and in fact in all passages in the *Topics* which deal with induction, Aristotle clearly says that we need more than one singular proposition for an induction. I am not sure how well von Fritz succeeds in verifying his thesis with respect to the claim that we have cases of induction based on only one example. The reader of his book will be surprised that he does not give even one example of an induction on the basis of one example only. On p. 63, point 3, he writes that especially in mathematics it is often enough to proceed from a single case to a general proposition. In the above example such generalization would certainly have quite disastrous consequences, establishing the universal protasis 'All even numbers are prime'. The geometrical example von Fritz (1964), p. 23 gives, *APst.* A 71a20f., the word ἐπάγειν is clearly used in its non-technical sense, on which the standard commentaries agree (cf. Ross (1949), p. 506 and Barnes (1994[2]), p. 85, ad 71a17); v. Fritz himself says that we have here the case of an application of a general insight to a specific case („Anwendung einer allgemeinen Erkenntnis auf einen Einzelfall")—clearly not a standard case of induction.

An interesting example can be found in *Top.* B 3, 110b5-7 which von Fritz could have cited. Aristotle says here that it is enough for a geometer to show for one triangle that the angles of a triangle are equal to two right angles in order to show that this is the case with all triangles. This was a common method with which geometers proceeded, as can be seen in Euclid's elements. He often begins his proofs by saying "Let ABC be a triangle", then he proves that some property belongs to this triangle and finally he concludes that *all* triangles have this property. The trick here is, of course, that ABC is an *arbitrarily* chosen triangle. If we can prove something of an arbitrarily chosen triangle we can with good conscience claim that all triangles have this property. *APst.* A 4, 73b32f. shows that Aristotle was well aware of this (Aristotle here also stipulates some other conditions which are not of interest in the present context): "Something holds universally whenever it is proved of a *chance case* (ἐπὶ τοῦ τυχόντος) and primitively". However, Aristotle does not mention induction here.

Theoretically it is conceivable that Aristotle might use an especially illustrative example to make a general point just as he often uses enthymemes (rhetorical syllogisms) rather than fully stated syllogisms, since example (παράδειγμα) is defined as a rhetorical induction (*Rhet.* A 2, 1356a34-b15); however, in some passages—*Rhet.* A 2, 1357b25-30, *APr.* B 24, 69a13-19— example is distinguished from induction as an inference from a particular to a particular; for some possible candidates cf. Wieland (1970[2]), pp. 96ff. The issue would require further investigation. In any case, in dialectical debates induction appears to require more than one particular.

[170] Θ 2, 157b2-8.

ἐπὶ τὶ δ' ἀληθεῖς).[171] For example the universal protasis "The man who has lost the knowledge of something has forgotten it" can be objected by "If the thing changes, he has lost knowledge of it but has not forgotten it". The corrected universal protasis would then be: "If a man has lost the knowledge of a thing *while it still remains*, he has then forgotten it".[172]

Making propositions and objections (προτείνεσθαι and ἐνίστασθαι) are the most important activities of a dialectician; the former is making many things into one (ἓν τὰ πλείω), the latter turning one thing into many (ἓν πολλά) (164b2-7). The former obviously refers to induction, the latter to the producing of instances of the universal proposition and finding an instance in which the universal proposition is not true.

The main task of this chapter has been to clarify the general dialectical situation in which the topoi were used. Knowing the dialectical context—i.e. understanding the rôles of the questioner and answerer, the meaning of problema, thesis and protasis, syllogism and prosyllogism, etc.— will make it easier to understand the workings of the topoi. Topoi themselves do not occur in Θ, but there are some predecessors. Of special importance are the universal protaseis which are established by induction and objected to by objections—we shall see that topoi work in an analogous way.

---

[171] Θ 2, 157b28-31.
[172] Cf. Θ 2, 157b8-16; for other examples cf. ll. 17-22.

CHAPTER TWO

WHAT IS A TOPOS?

Having discussed the structure of dialectical debates I shall now turn to the central question of this book: What is a topos? I shall first concentrate on passages in which Aristotle says something *about* the topoi. These passages are to be found mainly in the *Rhetoric*, Aristotle's only other work which partly also deals with topoi and in which a short list of topoi is given (B 23-24); in the inner books of the *Topics* (B-H) where the list of topoi is given Aristotle scarcely says anything explicit about them. I shall also discuss a passage in book Θ in which the origin of the notion of the topos seems to be found. Then I shall concentrate on passages in which Aristotle lists the topoi, and analyse them; the insights on the context of dialectical debates achieved in the previous chapter will be important here. Finally, I shall deal with Theophrastus' definition of the topos.

A. *Definition of the topos*

Aristotle does not define the notion of a topos anywhere in the *Topics*. Presumably, he took it for granted that his audience knew what a topos was. However, we do find a definition in *Rhetoric*, B 26, 1403a18f.:

> By an element I mean the same thing as a topos, for an element and a topos is something under which many enthymemes fall.[1]

Unfortunately, within this definition we encounter the problematic notion of *enthymeme*. Aristotle defines this as a "rhetorical demonstration" (ἀπόδειξις ῥητορική),[2] "a kind of syllogism" (συλλογισμός τις)[3], "the materials being probability and signs" (ἐξ εἰκότων καὶ σημείων).[4] In *Rhet.* B 20, 1393a24 he also specifies it as one of the two common oratorical arguments (πίστεις), the other one being the example. The enthymeme in rhetoric corresponds to the syllogism in dialectic, whereas example corresponds to induction.[5] It is easiest, perhaps, to understand the definition of the enthymeme by looking at specific instances. Let us look at three enthymemes together with their corresponding topoi listed in *Rhet.* B 23-24: topos from the contraries (ἐκ τῶν ἐναντίων), from the inflections (ἐκ τῶν ὁμοίων πτώσεων) and from the greater and lesser degree (ἐκ τοῦ μᾶλλον καὶ ἧττον). The example of the enthymeme which is constructed

---

[1] τὸ γὰρ αὐτὸ λέγω στοιχεῖον καὶ τόπον· ἔστι γὰρ στοιχεῖον καὶ τόπος εἰς ὃ πολλὰ ἐνθυμήματα ἐμπίπτει.
[2] *Rhet.* A 1, 1355a6.
[3] *Rhet.* A 1, 1355a8.
[4] *Rhet.* A 2, 1357a32f. The last two descriptions are unified in the definition in *APr.* B 27, 70a10: ἐνθύμημα δὲ ἐστὶ συλλογισμὸς ἐξ εἰκότων ἢ σημείων.
[5] *Rhet.* A 2, 1356a35-b5.

according to the topos from the contraries, which is the very first topos in the list in B 23, runs:

> Self-control is good, for lack of self-control is harmful.[6]

Aristotle does not state the corresponding topos from contraries explicitly,[7] but it can be stated in the following way:

> 'If a predicate is predicated of a subject, then the contrary of this predicate is predicated of the contrary of this subject (if the predicate and subject have contraries)'

The example of the enthymeme constructed according to the topos from the inflections (1397a22f.), which is the second topos in the list, runs:

> The just is not always good, otherwise justly would always be good, whereas it is not desirable to be put justly to death.

The corresponding topos is:

> [Inflexions] have to belong or not belong in the like manner (ὁμοίως).[8]

I shall give two enthymemes corresponding to the topos of the greater and lesser degree, one with a negative and one with a positive conclusion (B 23, 1397b12-27). The first example runs:

> If even the gods are not omniscient, certainly human beings are not.

The corresponding topos is, he says:

> If a predicate, which is more probably affirmable of one thing, does not belong to it, it is clear that it does not belong to another of which it is less probably affirmable.[9]

The second example of the enthymeme reads:

> A man who strikes his father also strikes his neighbours.

The corresponding topos is:

> If the less likely thing is true, the more likely thing is true as well.[10]

The enthymemes seem to be arguments with one premiss and one conclusion, having the form of 'P; hence, Q', where 'P' and 'Q' stand for propositions. This argument-form can be expressed in different ways, for example as 'Q, because/for P', as is the case in the very first example of the enthymeme cited above, or as 'If P, then Q'. The topoi here usually do not actually have the

---

[6] *Rhet.* B 23, 1397a10f.

[7] Aristotle gives here only an investigation-instruction "One probative topos is from the contraries. Observe whether the contrary (predicate) belongs to the contrary (subject), as a means of destruction, if it is not, as a means of construction, if it is" (1397a7-9). How the above formulation of the topos can be derived from this instruction will be explained later. I shall deal with the topoi from contraries in detail in Chapter Five, pp. 142-145.

[8] *Rhet.* B 23, 1397a20-23.

[9] τοῦτο γάρ ἐστιν, εἰ ᾧ μᾶλλον ἂν ὑπάρχοι μὴ ὑπάρχει, δῆλον ὅτι οὐδ' ᾧ ἧττον (*Rhet.* B 23, 1397b13-15).

[10] ἐκ τοῦ, εἰ τὸ ἧττον ὑπάρχει, καὶ τὸ μᾶλλον ὑπάρχει (*Rhet.* B 23, 1397b16f.).

form of a rule 'P; hence, Q', but rather that of a law, or a principle as Aristotle would have said, often in the form 'If P, then Q'. The topoi differ in that they express various relations which exist between P and Q; e.g. in the first example, the predicate and subject of P are contraries of the predicate and subject of Q respectively.[11]

The enthymemes seem to be instances of topoi; or, expressed differently, enthymemes are arguments which are warranted by the principle expressed in the topos. Aristotle simply says that enthymemes *fall under* a topos. Now, since enthymemes in rhetoric correspond to syllogisms in dialectic, the relevant definition for the *Topics* may be inferred by replacing enthymeme by syllogism: '*a topos is that under which many syllogisms fall*'.

Topoi as well as enthymemes usually[12] consist of only two parts. In what way should a syllogism which consists of at least two premisses and a conclusion fall into a topos? How should we produce a dialectical syllogism out of the enthymeme 'P; hence Q'? An enthymeme is a syllogism in which a premiss has been suppressed since it is so trivial that the hearer can add it himself in his mind.[13] All we have to do is simply add the premiss 'If P, then Q'. In this way we get the hypothetical syllogism 'If P, then Q; P; hence, Q'. Thus hypothetical syllogism would fall under a topos insofar as it falls under its major premiss in which the essence of the hypothetical syllogism is expressed. In the following section I shall show places in which Aristotle explicitly calls topos a protasis which has the function described above.

B. *Topos as a principle and a protasis*

In what follows I shall point to places in which Aristotle seems to maintain that topoi are *principles* and *protaseis*. I shall show that we can understand them as *hypotheses* of hypothetical syllogisms and that this is how we can understand a topos to be *that under which many syllogisms fall*.

First, a preliminary remark: It is somewhat problematic that Aristotle often seems to have topoi in mind but does not say so explicitly or he uses other expressions. There are a few passages in the *Topics*[14] where he uses the word

---

[11] Thus, enthymemes work in the same way as I have previously characterized the predecessors of topoi in book Θ; Cf. Chapter One, pp. 34f. The difference is that the enthymeme is uttered in one sentence, whereas using the predecessors of topoi one would first state the premiss (or premisses) and then in the following step the conclusion.

[12] There are topoi which consist of more than two parts and the arguments constructed according to them can have more than one minor premiss, as e.g. the topos of the greater and lesser degree given above.

[13] This is the definition given by historical logic textbooks. It is often maintained that this characterisation is un-Aristotelian. It is true that Aristotle does not say this anywhere in these very words. But he comes very close to saying it in *Rhet*. A 2, 1357a16-19: "The enthymeme must consist of few propositions, fewer often than those which make up a primary syllogism. For if any of these propositions is a familiar fact, there is no need even to mention it; the hearer adds it himself." The textbooks usually have categorical syllogisms in mind, but obviously we can have enthymemes which stated in full are hypothetical syllogisms. On the notion of enthymeme cf. Burnyeat (1994), who actually criticises the traditional definition.

[14] Δ 1, 120b13; 3, 123a27; Z 5, 143a13; 9, 147a22; 14, 151b18.

"element" (στοιχεῖον), evidently meaning topos. However, it is not until we read *Rhet.* B 22, 1396b22 or 26, 1403a18f. that he states explicitly that the two expressions are meant in the same way. The same is true for the word "mode" (τρόπος). Matters here are slightly more complicated. The codices often disagree as to whether τόπος or τρόπος should stand in the text[15] and Aristotle does not state anywhere explicitly that they are the same. There are however a few places where we indisputably find τρόπος at places where one would expect to read τόποι.[16] When interpreting what a topos is I shall of course also take into account passages in which Aristotle has topoi in mind.

Having read several passages in which Aristotle says something about the topoi one is left with the impression that he considers topoi to be principles (ἀρχαί) and protaseis (προτάσεις):

1. *The passage in Top. Θ 14, 163b22-33*

> One should also try to master the heads under which the arguments mostly tend to fall (πειρατέον δὲ καὶ εἰς ἃ πλειστάκις ἐμπίπτουσιν οἱ λόγοι κατέχειν). For just as in geometry it is useful to be practised in the elements (τὰ στοιχεῖα[17]), and in arithmetic having the multiplication table up to ten at one's fingertips (κεφαλισμούς[18]) makes a great difference to one's knowledge of the other numbers too, likewise also in arguments (ἐν τοῖς λόγοις) it is a great advantage to be well up in regard to first principles (τὰς ἀρχάς), and to have a thorough knowledge of protaseis (προτάσεις) by heart. For just as to a trained memory, the mere reference to the places (τόποι) in which they occur causes the things themselves to be remembered, so the above heads (ταῦτα, referring to ἃ in b22) will make a man readier in reasoning because he sees them (αὐτάς, referring to ταῦτα, i.e. ἃ) defined and numbered. A universal protasis (πρότασίν τε κοινὴν) should be committed to memory rather than an argument (λόγον), since it is difficult enough to have a first principle or hypothesis (ἀρχῆς ... καὶ ὑποθέσεως) ready to hand.

---

[15] In the edition of Brunschwig (1967) we find six passages in book B where the codices disagree: 109a34, b25, 111a24, 115a33, b7 (all found in Vaticanus 207, saec.XIII (P)) and 114b13 (Boethii translatio (L)); none in Γ and Δ. Ross (1958) does not indicate these variants in his apparatus except in 114b13 (Boethii translatio). In the case of books E-Θ we have to rely on his less thorough edition: we find two variants in Z which is a considerable number since the word τόπος occurs only 4 times in this book: 139b19 (Wallies) and 142b20 (Marcianus 201, anni 955 (B) and Vaticanus 1024, saec. X exeuntis vel XI ineuntis (c)). We have the same problem in *Soph. El.* (6, 169a18; 12, 172b25) and the *Rhetoric* (e.g. *Rhet.* B 23, 1399a19; Γ 15, 1416a6, 13).

[16] B 5, 111b32 (Ἔτι ὁ σοφιστικὸς τρόπος), Z, 4 142a17 (Εἷς μὲν οὖν τρόπος τοῦ μὴ διὰ γνωριμωτέρων (referring to 141a26ff.)) and 142a22 (Τοῦ δὲ μὴ ἐκ προτέρων τρεῖς εἰσι τρόποι). The latter two could be interpreted as indicating kinds of one topos.

We often find τρόπος as referring to a preceding topos, especially in the phrase τὸν αὐτὸν δὲ τρόπον (σκεπτέον), meaning that one should investigate something in the same way as shown in the previous topos (B 5, 112a10; 7, 113a17; 11, 115b11, 19, 22, Δ 6, 128a35, 37, E 3, 131a12; 7, 137a27, 37; 8, 138a2). However, the expression here seems to have a perfectly common everyday-language sense.

[17] Elements in geometry are e.g. line and circle (*Top.* Θ 3, 158b35).

[18] We know the meaning of this word from Alex. *in Top.* 586, 3f. and Suidas.

Now it seems to me to be pretty clear that "the heads under which the arguments mostly tend to fall" (εἰς ἃ πλειστάκις ἐμπίπτουσιν οἱ λόγοι) in b22 is parallel to "element or topos is something under which many enthymemes fall" (στοιχεῖον καὶ τόπος εἰς ὃ πολλὰ ἐνθυμήματα ἐμπίπτει) in *Rhet.* B 26, 1403a18f., i.e. that "the heads under which", which translates the Greek relative pronoun in the plural ἃ, refers to *topoi*.[19] We have exactly the same expression "to fall under" (ἐμπίπτειν εἰς). The arguments (λόγοι) in rhetoric are called enthymemes, those in dialectic syllogisms. Both correspond to each other[20] and both are derived from topoi.[21] Now, the expressions "principles and protaseis" (τὰς ἀρχάς, τὰς προτάσεις) (163b27f.), "universal protasis" (πρότασιν κοινὴν) (b32) and "principle or hypothesis" (ἀρχῆς ... καὶ ὑποθέσεως) clearly refer, directly or indirectly, to "the heads" (ἃ), i.e. to topoi. Thus, topoi are *principles, universal protaseis,* and *hypotheses*.

Matters become somewhat tricky here since in this passage we actually have the origin of the term topos and element. Aristotle compares the general protaseis and principles of arguments (λόγοι) with principles in other areas: topoi in mnemonics,[22] elements in geometry and multiplication table up to ten at one's fingertips in arithmetic. In any event Aristotle here has topoi *in mind* and describes them as principles[23] and general protaseis.

2. *The passage in Rhet. A 2, 1358a10-20 & 29-33*

> I mean that the proper subjects of dialectical and rhetorical syllogisms (συλλογισμοὺς) are the things with which we say the topoi are concerned, that is to say those that apply equally to questions of right conduct, natural science, politics, and many other things that have nothing to do with one another. Take for instance, the topos of the greater and lesser degree. On this it is equally easy to base a syllogism or enthymeme (ἐκ τούτου

---

[19] Those commentators who actually comment on this passage agree on that: Alex. Aphr. *in Top.* 585, 24 (κοινοὶ τόποι), Pacius (1597), Lib. VIII, Cap.XIV, 7 (locos illos communes dialecticos), Waitz (1844-46), p. 527 in 163b22 (locos intell. quos in prioribus libris exposuit), Bonitz (1870), 377a14-16.

[20] *Rhet.* A 2, 1356a35-b5.

[21] Cf. e.g. 1358a12-17. In *Rhet.* B 23-24 topoi are listed from which enthymemes can be derived, similarly as in *Top.* B-H 3 topoi are described from which syllogisms are derived.

[22] Solmsen (1927), p. 173f., is right in seeing in mnemonics the origin of the notion of the topos. In all other respects, however, he misinterprets the passage entirely. Aristotle does not compare arguments (λόγοι) with topoi, as Solmsen maintains, but with protaseis. He does not copy the Sophists whose practice he describes in *Soph. El.* 34 183b38-184a2—he clearly criticises them here: "For some of them gave their pupils arguments (λόγους) to learn by heart which were either rhetorical or consisted of questions and answers under which both parties thought that the rival arguments fell. Hence, the teaching which they gave to their pupils was rapid but unsystematic." It is correct that in 163b17f. Aristotle advises us to learn thoroughly entire arguments (λόγους), but only for problemata of *most frequent occurrence.* In b22ff. however, which is the passage above, a new argument starts (*one should also ...*) and here Aristotle advises the student to learn the *topoi* or *protaseis* into which arguments most often fall. It is, as he states at the end of the passage, difficult enough to have a general protasis to hand, never mind an entire argument.

[23] That there is a connection between topoi and principles is not new; cf. Maier (1896-1900), II, 1, pp. 495ff.; Throm (1932), p. 43. Wieland (1970²), p. 203, maintains that principles are similar to topoi, although he remarks, Aristotle never expressly calls his principles topoi. We could add here that he does it the other way around, i.e. he calls topoi principles.

συλλογίσασθαι ἢ ἐνθύμημα εἰπεῖν) about any of what nevertheless are essentially disconnected subjects—right conduct, natural science, or anything else whatsoever. But there are also those special topoi (ἴδια) which are based on such protaseis (προτάσεις) as apply only to particular groups or classes of things. Thus there are protaseis about natural science on which it is impossible to base any enthymeme or syllogism about the ethics, and other protaseis about ethics on which nothing can be based about natural science. [...] As in the *Topics*, therefore, so in this work, we must distinguish the kinds (εἴδη) and the topoi (τοὺς τόπους) from which enthymemes may be constructed (ἐξ ὧν ληπτέον). By kinds I mean the protaseis peculiar (ἰδίας προτάσεις) to each several class of things, by topoi those common to all classes alike.

This is a well-known passage where Aristotle divides topoi into common topoi (κοινοὶ τόποι) which can be applied to all possible problems (right conduct, natural science, etc.), i.e. which have no particular subject matter (a22), and into specific topoi[24] (ἴδια) or kinds (εἴδη), which can only be applied to specific problems (a12-22).

Syllogisms are drawn from both specific and common topoi.[25] Syllogisms are always drawn from protaseis,[26] which are in the case of dialectical syllogisms endoxical or reputable (ἔνδοξα).[27] Now, specific topoi (or kinds) are protaseis as one would expect from the object of "to draw a syllogism *from*" (συλλογίζεσθαι ἐκ). It would be strange if topoi were not protaseis, since otherwise "from" (ἐκ) would have to have a different meaning with respect to topoi. But he clearly uses "from" with respect to both topoi and kinds;[28] in a30, "from which" (ἐξ ὧν) actually refers to both. In a31f. τόπους must be supplemented by προτάσεις, and I have found no translator

---

[24] Aristotle calls only the common topoi τόποι, not the specific ones, i.e. we do not find the expression 'ἴδιοι τόποι' in Aristotle. However, there are good reasons to call them specific topoi. Aristotle often juxtaposes τόποι and ἴδια; enthymemes and syllogisms can be derived from both (1358a10f., 19; also a27f.). It also makes sense that since Aristotle often speaks of κοινοὶ τόποι (e.g. 1358a28, 32, et al.) he obviously wants to distinguish them from some other kind of topoi. Usually, if Aristotle distinguishes some thing which he calls κοινός from some other thing, he uses the word ἴδιος (cf. κοιναὶ ἀρχαί-ἴδιαι ἀρχαί (*APst*. A 32, 88b27-29), κοιναὶ πίστεις-ἴδιαι πίστεις (*Rhet*. Β 19, 1393a22f.)). Instead of ἴδια Aristotle also often uses the word εἴδη (e.g. 1358a31, 1403b14f.); he seems to have used the term ἴδια in 1358a17 in order to distinguish them from κοινοὶ τόποι in a12. In 1396b30 and 32 we find protaseis which are clearly recognizable as ἴδια or εἴδη (in the sense of 1358a17ff.) and which Aristotle explicitly calls τόποι: b30 προτάσεις περὶ ἕκαστον, b32 (τόποι) περὶ ἀγαθοῦ ἢ κακοῦ ἢ καλοῦ ἢ αἰσχροῦ ἢ δικαίου ἢ ἀδίκου, καὶ περὶ τῶν ἠθῶν καὶ παθημάτων καὶ ἕξεων, ὡσαύτως εἰλημμένοι ἡμῖν ὑπάρχουσαι πρότερον οἱ τόποι. Solmsen (1929), p. 170n.20, who considers εἴδη not to be topoi has to concede: „Es liegt aber in dieser Geschichte des τόπος-Begriffes begründet, daß Aristoteles—prinzipwidrig— auch die προτάσεις περὶ παθῶν, περὶ ἀρετῆς, ἀγαθοῦ usw. gelegentlich τόποι nennen kann (Rhet Β 22, 1396b30, 34; Γ 19, 1419b18, 23, 27)."

All the topoi in the *Topics* are clearly κοινοὶ τόποι (cf. e.g. *Top*. A 1, 100a19f., *Soph. El*. 9, 170a34-36), with the possible exception of *Top*. Γ 1-4 where ethical problems are described, as de Pater (1965), p. 164 points out. However, in principle arguments of "what is better" can also be applied in non-ethical contexts (cf. e.g. the arguments in APst. A 24).

[25] *Rhet*. A 2, 1358a15, 18, 27, 28, 30 (συλλογίζεσθαι ἐκ..., συλλογισμός ἐκ...)
[26] *Top*. A 4, 101b14-16.
[27] *Top*. A 1, 100a30, defined in b21-23 and in A 10.
[28] *Rhet*. A 2, 1358a15 vs.19, 20; a27 vs. 28.

who sees it otherwise: "By kinds I mean the propositions peculiar to each several class of things, by commonplaces *those* common to all classes alike" (Rhys Roberts (1984)), "By specific topics I mean the propositions [...], by universal *those* common to all alike" (Freese (1926)) (my italics), to cite two English translations. The example at a18-20 for specific topoi, which are opposed to common topoi—"protaseis about natural science on which it is impossible to base any enthymeme or syllogism about the ethics, and other protaseis about ethics on which nothing can be based about natural science"— implies what topoi might be: protaseis from which one can derive enthymemes and syllogisms not only in natural science, but also in ethics and in fact in any other discipline.

3. *The passage in Rhet. B 26, 1402a32-34*

> It is clear that counter-syllogisms (ἀντισυλλογίζεσθαι) can be built up from the same topoi (ἐκ τῶν αὐτῶν τόπων); for the materials of syllogisms are endoxical opinions (συλλογισμοὶ ἐκ τῶν ἐνδόξων) and such opinions often contradict each other.

Obviously, topoi are counted among endoxical opinions which are expressed in the form of protaseis; the property of being endoxical always refers to protaseis.

4. *The synonymous use of "element" and "topos"*

The very fact that Aristotle uses the word "element" (στοιχεῖον) synonymously with topos, and element is often synonymously used with "principle" (ἀρχή),[29] leads one to believe that a topos is some sort of principle. In fact, we find topoi which are very similar to Aristotle's highest principles (κοιναὶ ἀρχαί). In B 7, 113a22f. we find a topos which clearly points in the direction of the Principle of Contradiction:[30] "for it is impossible that contrary predicates should belong at the same time to the same thing." In B 6, 112a24 we find a topos which clearly points in the direction of the Principle of the Excluded Middle:[31] "in regard to subjects which necessarily have only one of two predicates, ..."; I shall discuss these two topoi in Chapter Four, pp. 103-105. In H 1, 152b11-15 we find a topos which points in the direction of the principle "If equals are taken from equals equals remain";[32] it runs: "see if the subtraction of the same thing from each leaves a different remainder."[33]

---

[29] Cf. Bonitz (1870), 702a26-39.

[30] The Principle of Contradiction is discussed in *Met.* Γ 3-6. One of its forms is: "the same attribute cannot at the same time belong and not belong to same subject in the same respect" (Γ 3, 1005b19f., contrast e.g. b26f.).

[31] The Principle of the Excluded Middle is discussed in *Met* Γ 7. One of its forms is: "Everything is asserted or denied" (*APst.* A 11, 77a22).

[32] Τὸ ἴσα ἀπὸ ἴσων ἂν ἀφέλῃ, ὅτι ἴσα τὰ λοιπά, *APst.* 76a41. On the view that this principle is "strictly speaking of a sort between κοιναὶ and ἴδιαι ἀρχαί" cf. Ross (1924), vol. 1, p. 262.

[33] εἰ τοῦ αὐτοῦ ἀφ' ἑκατέρου ἀφαιρεθέντος τὸ λοιπὸν ἕτερον. This topos actually represents an investigation instruction from which however a principle can be derived, cf. 54-58 below.

C. Other interpretations of topoi and how they square with the interpretation of topoi as protaseis and principles

1. Topoi as rules of inference

Topoi are often taken to be inference rules.[34] Indeed, reading certain topos-entries in the *Topics* one might get the impression that topoi are rules of inference. Now, without commenting on the question of whether it is right or wrong to interpret topoi in this way, I shall firstly ask the question of whether this interpretation contradicts my interpretation. *Can an inference-rule be a protasis?* This difficulty, it would appear, is easy to solve. An inference rule can be expressed in a sentence, i.e. in our case a protasis. Let us take the first topos of the greater and lesser degree. In a simplified and slightly formalized form it runs: '*If being more A belongs to what is more B, then A belongs to B.*'[35] One might say that here, a rule is expressed in an if-then-sentence, i.e. in our case an instruction which allows us to pass from sentences of the form 'being more A belongs to more B' to 'A belongs to B'.

Before answering the question of whether an inference-rule can be a protasis or not, another question must be answered first, namely: Can a proposition of the form 'If being more A belongs to more B, then A is B' be called a protasis at all? In the *Prior Analytics* the usual form of a protasis is 'A is B'. It is not necessarily single words that correspond to the terms A or B, but also complex words, as Aristotle asserts in *APr.* A 35, but in any case we always have one subject and one predicate only. Thus, in *Soph. El.* 6, 169a7f. Aristotle defines protasis as "a single predication about a single subject" (ἓν καθ' ἑνός). According to this definition we would have two protaseis here (one expressed in the antecedent, the second in the apodosis). Does this definition strictly hold, or does Aristotle sometimes consider more complicated sentences as protaseis? I believe the latter, and the common principles (κοιναὶ ἀρχαί) which can function as protaseis in proofs are an example of it.[36] We also find explicit examples in the *Topics* which are called protaseis: "Sensation differs from knowledge, because it is possible to recover the latter when one has lost it but not the former" (*Top.* A 13, 105a28-30) "Should one rather obey parents or the laws, if they are at variance?" (*Top.* A

---

[34] Cf. e.g. Sainati (1968), p. 41. The Oxford and Loeb translators often translate τόπος by "a commonplace rule" or simply "a rule" (Pickard-Cambridge (1984), e.g. 109a34, b13.; Forster (1960), e.g. 109b13).

[35] This is the first of the four topoi of the greater and lesser degree which Aristotle enumerates in *Top.* B 10, 114b37-115a14; in both parts of the compound proposition the predicate and subject are the same. Thus it is different from the topos cited at the beginning of this chapter, p. 44, which corresponds to the second topos in *Top.* B 10 and in which the subjects change while the predicate remains the same in both parts of the proposition. I shall deal with the topoi of the greater and lesser degree in more detail in Chapter Five, pp. 146-149.

[36] As does for example the principle "if equals are taken from equals the remainder is equal" (τὸ ἴσα ἀπὸ ἴσων ἂν ἀφέλῃ (...) ἴσα τὰ λοιπά), *APst.* A 10, 76a41; cf. also A 11, 77a27, 76b14. In *Met.* B 3, 996b29-31 the Principle of the Excluded Middle and the Principle of Contradiction are explicitly called προτάσεις and Aristotle makes clear that there are other protaseis of this kind; cf. also *Met.* Γ 3, 1005b26-28.

14, 105b22f.).³⁷ These examples adequately demonstrate that protaseis do not have to have the form 'A is B', but can have more complicated forms, including even if-then-sentences.

Thus, rules of inferences can be, and in fact usually are, expressed in a sentence. So if we just simply assert that topoi are protaseis,³⁸ and Aristotle could just as well have called them λόγοι (in the meaning of sentences), our interpretation would not seem to be in opposition to the interpretation of topoi as inference-rules.

However, Aristotle uses "protasis" in a certain context, namely that of reasoning (συλλογίζεσθαι, λογίζεσθαι), and he unambiguously says that we derive syllogisms from topoi.³⁹ Thus topoi are protaseis of a syllogism. But if topoi are rules of inference of such reasonings as are described in the *Topics*, and when we take these reasonings to be syllogisms we might very well be puzzled. A rule of inference of a syllogism cannot at the same time be a premiss of the syllogism. A syllogism in the *Topics* would seem then rather to be the rule of the following reasoning:

Doing greater injustice is a greater evil
―――――――――――――――――――――――――   from 'what is more A is more B',
Doing injustice is an evil⁴⁰   you may infer: 'A is B'

We can clearly see that the rule does not belong to this syllogism as a protasis, but as an external rule. Thus the word *from* in "to draw a syllogism *from*" (συλλογίζεσθαι ἐκ), where it refers to topoi, exceptionally, so it seems, would not refer to protaseis, but to rules. The alleged syllogism above does not fit the definition of the syllogism Aristotle gives several times⁴¹ since the conclusion clearly does not necessarily follow from the *premisses*—there is only one premiss. Thus it would appear that we have here *another* sort of syllogism. Solmsen (1929), p. 20 calls them „die aus τόποι gebildeten Syllogismen"—*syllogisms derived from topoi*.

However, I do not think that Aristotle had any earlier version of a syllogism in the *Topics*. In *Top.* B-H, and in the places where he speaks about them referring to topoi, he clearly has a notion of the syllogism as

---

³⁷ Cf also the complex universal protaseis in book Θ discussed on p. 23f. above and the protaseis on p. 56 below.

³⁸ Grimaldi (1958), p. 12 is happy with that and goes no further. He simply states that common topoi (κοινοὶ τόποι) are "general axiomatic propositions" without giving any explanation. I suppose that since he interprets εἴδη as ἴδιοι τόποι, which are προτάσεις (*Rhet.* A 2), he takes it for granted that κοινοὶ τόποι are προτάσεις as well.

³⁹ *Rhet.* A 2, 1358a15, B 26, 1402a32, et al.

⁴⁰ Indeed, Sainati (1968) does represent the topoi as rules in such a way; cf. e.g. p. 54, the topos from the contradictories:

A ⊂ B
―――――
- B ⊂ - A

He does not ask himself the question of how this argument should fit the definition of the syllogism.

⁴¹ E.g. *Top.* A 1, 100a25-27.

defined by him in several places.⁴² In these definitions it is always stated that the conclusion follows from premisses *through* the premisses alone (διὰ τῶν κειμένων),⁴³ by reason of them, by their being so (τῷ ταῦτ' εἶναι),⁴⁴ and not because of any external rule.

I would also note that the reasoning as it stands above is not very convincing. We are supposed to show that "to do injustice is an evil" (a thesis which the opponent contests). In order to show this we say that "to do more injustice is a greater evil", and if the opponent says "Yes", we infer, having our topos-rule *in mind,* that it follows "to do injustice is an evil". It is quite improbable that the answerer who disputes that "to do injustice is an evil" should grant the protasis that "to do greater injustice is a greater evil". Taking the implication the other way around, which Aristotle also asserts (B 10, 114b39f.), the inference clearly could be wrong: we cannot always infer from the protasis that 'A is B' that 'being more A is more B'—doing sport, say, or eating might be a good thing, but not in excess. Thus the answerer could justifiably dispute that the one protasis follows from the other. To make our argument more cogent we have to do something very simple: *We have to utter the rule we used and convince the opponent of the correctness of this rule.* So, how might the latter be achieved? Aristotle tells us in 115a5f.: "this has to be established by induction" (τοῦτο δ' ἐπαγωγῇ ληπτέον).⁴⁵ This means we should provide examples (in protaseis) where this rule is clearly at work and then state the rule generally. Indeed, if the opponent admits the rule and that "doing more injustice is a greater evil", he cannot deny the conclusion: it follows necessarily (ἐξ ἀνάγκης). The same is of course true of the occurrences of "induction" (ἐπαγωγή) in 113b17 and b29 with respect to the corresponding topoi. In 113b22 Aristotle says of the result of induction here, which is the Law of Contraposition, that "in all cases a claim of this sort should be made" (ἐπὶ πάντων οὖν τὸ τοιοῦτο ἀξιωτέον). From *Soph. El.* 11, 172a17-21 it is clear that even "primary things and principles" (πρῶτα and οἰκεῖα ἀρχαί) must be granted by the answerer.⁴⁶

---

⁴² *Top.* A 1, 100a25-27, *Soph. El.* 1, 165a1f., *Rhet.* A 2, 1356b15-17, with slight differences.

⁴³ *Top.* A 1, 100a26f., *Soph. El.* 1, 165a2.

⁴⁴ *Rhet.* A 2, 1356b16, *Soph. El.* 6, 168b24.

⁴⁵ The Greek word λαμβάνειν, which can be translated as "to establish", "to secure" or "to assume", often refers to protaseis. Cf. *Top.* A 3, 105a23; 14, 105a34, *Rhet.* A 9, 1366b32, *Top.* H 3, 153a9; cf also the Greek word λῆμμα *Top.* Θ 1, 156a21, *Top.* A 1, 101a14 (and many other instances in the *Analytics*) that is derived from λαμβάνειν and simply means "premiss". *Met.* Δ 29, 1025a6-13 seems to confirm this: "This is why the proof in the *Hippias* that the same man is false and true is misleading. For it assumes (λαμβάνει) he is false who can deceive (i.e. the man who knows and is wise); and further that he who is willingly bad is better [*Hip. Min.* 375d1f.]. He secures this falsehood by induction (λαμβάνει διὰ τῆς ἐπαγωγῆς); for a man who limps willingly is better than one who does so unwillingly; by 'limping' Plato means 'mimicking a limp'." I.e. Plato arrived at the statement by a misleading induction; cf. *Hip.Min.* 373-375. I therefore conclude that ἐπαγωγῇ ληπτέον tells us to infer a general rule by giving examples and stating the inherent rule as a protasis, and not to make the rule clear to us in our mind—this is already presupposed. Thus we should translate the phrase as "establish by induction", not as "grasp by induction", as Pickard-Cambridge (1984) does. I shall deal with this topos again in Chapter Five, pp. 146f.

⁴⁶ The term induction occurs only in B (5 occurences) and Δ (2 occurrences). Three of the occurrences in B are clearly meant to establish a topos: 113b17, 29 and 115a5, as already

Thus we create our syllogism by adding to the reasoning above *the rule of the reasoning itself* as a premiss. The new reasoning, which we may in the true sense call a syllogism, here a hypothetical one, is of course not ruled any more by this rule. We have then:

(I) If being more A is more B, then A is B.
(II) Doing greater injustice (A) is a greater evil (B).

Doing injustice (A) is an evil (B)

When the major premiss is admitted as a generally applicable rule by the opponent, it contains of course as an axiom-instance so to speak the proposition: (Ia) If doing greater injustice (A) is a greater evil (B), then doing injustice (A) is an evil (B). Thus, with the instantiated premiss we would have the following argument:

(Ia) If doing greater injustice (A) is a greater evil (B), then doing injustice (A) is an evil (B).
(II) Doing greater injustice (A) is a greater evil (B).

Doing injustice (A) is an evil (B)

However, according to Aristotle the first argument is certainly just as valid as the second one with the instantiation of the topos-principle. In fact the first argument was certainly more common in dialectical debates since the answerer was supposed to realize as little as possible that the questioner was coming nearer to refute him. The fact that in several passages cited above he calls topos a protasis shows that he considered topos to be part of the syllogism despite its being a premiss-form which has many instances. Aristotle was well aware of the distinction which he usually expresses with the help of the notions "universal" and "specific". In *APst.* A 10, 76a37-b2 he in fact says explicitly that it does not matter whether a common or a proper principle is used as a premiss in the general or a specific form.[47] In this book I shall follow Aristotle in his nonchalant treatment of general and specific hypotheses and shall sometimes write the argument with the general

---

shown above; both occurrences in Δ have this function: 122a19 and 123b7. However, Aristotle does not always explicitly state that something has to be established by ἐπαγωγή. We more often find the phrase "likewise also in other instances" (ὁμοίως δὲ καὶ ἐπι τῶν ἄλλων; sometimes τῶν τοιούτων is added or τῶν λοιπῶν is in place of τῶν ἄλλων): B: 113b18, 34, 114b27, 115a31; Γ: 116a27, 119a6; Δ: 121a9, 122b30, 123b33, 126a20, 127a8; Z: 146b30, 147a13, 149b11; H: 152a10, b5, 153b33f. I shall analyse a few more examples of topoi established by induction in Chapter Five, pp. 140-144.

[47] "Of the items used in the demonstrative sciences some are proper to each science and others common [...]. Proper: e.g. that a line is such-and-such, and straight so-and-so. Common: e.g. that if equals are removed from equals, the remainders are equal. It is sufficient (ἱκανὸν) to assume each of these in so far as it bears on the kind; for it will produce the same results (ταὐτὸ γὰρ ποιήσει) even if it is assumed as holding not of everything but only for magnitudes or, for arithmeticians, for numbers." The word "sufficient" makes it clear that the principles can also be assumed in its general form, although it is sufficient to assume them in the form appropriate to the subject-matter ("in so far as it bears on the kind").

hypothesis and sometimes with the appropriate instantiation of the general hypothesis, depending on what suits Aristotle's text most.

2. *Topoi as laws*

Topoi have also been defined as certain types of non-analytical laws.[48] The interpretation of topoi as laws clearly does not contradict my interpretation of topoi as protaseis, since laws are expressed in sentences. It is again a question of which context within the argument one sees the rôle of the law in. De Pater (1965), p. 231 interprets the topos as "une loi logique" which serves as a "formule d' inference" (p. 133) in the framework of a modified argument-schema developed by Toulmin (1964). The modified argument-schema, though interesting, is certainly slightly anachronistic; Aristotle himself provides a logical system in which topoi can be accommodated and in the framework of which topoi are best understood. Bocheński (1951a), pp. 70f. is one of very few authors who brings the laws into connection with the hypothetical syllogism; however, he does not expand upon it.

Lastly, a note on the distinction between rules and laws. Aristotle had no word for either of the two notions. The notion of a principle (ἀρχή), and thus that of a topos, seems to encompass both notions. One tends to think of the principles as laws—e.g. we speak about the Principle or Law of Contradiction. However, a law or topos which is explicitly stated as a premiss of a hypothetical syllogism does *rule* the hypothetical syllogism in a certain way. Thus, we can call topos a rule, as long as it is clear that it is explicitly stated as a premiss.[49]

3. *Topoi as investigation-instructions*

3.1. *Organa*

If one looks at the topoi-entries in the central books they appear first of all to be investigation-instructions.[50] The topoi-entries very often begin with the phrase 'another topos is to look/investigate/examine/etc.[51] whether, with respect to a certain aspect[52] of the thesis, such and such is the case'. Let us look at the beginnings of the very first four topoi in book B:

> Now one topos is to investigate whether (εἶς μὲν δὴ τόπος τὸ ἐπιβλέπειν εἰ) the opponent has assigned as an accident something which belongs in some other way [...]. (1) [B 2, 109a34f.]
> Another topos is to examine (ἄλλος (sc. τόπος) τὸ ἐπιβλέπειν) all cases where a predicate has been said to belong to all or none of something. Look

---

[48] Cf. Bocheński (1951a); de Pater (1965), p. 141.

[49] Aristotle in fact seemed to have reservations about hypothetical syllogisms on the grounds that their way of working is expressed in the hypothesis, as is clear from *APst.* B 6, 92a11-19; I shall discuss this passage on p. 117n.82 below.

[50] De Pater (1965), p. 231, apart from "loi logique", also understands topos as a "formule de recherche"; similarly, Stump (1989), p. 22.

[51] ἐπιβλέπειν/σκοπεῖν/ὁρᾶν εἰ or some infinitive having the meaning of an imperative.

[52] In fact, topoi have sometimes also been defined as "points of view" („Gesichtspunkte"): e.g. Hambruch (1904), p. 31; Wieland (1970²), p. 203. Such a specification is correct but far from exhaustive.

at them (σκοπεῖν δὲ) species by species [...]. E.g. if a man has said that the knowledge of opposites is the same, you should look and see whether (σκεπτέον εἰ) [...].(2) [B 2, 109b13-18]
Another topos is to make definitions (ἄλλος (sc. τόπος) τὸ λόγους ποιεῖν) both of the sumbebekos and of that to which it belongs as a sumbebekos (i.e. of its subject) [...] and then see if (σκοπεῖν εἰ) anything untrue has been assumed as true in the definitions. [...] (3) [B 2, 109b30-32]
Moreover, one ought to turn the problem into a protasis for oneself [...]. This topos is very nearly the same as the topos to investigate (ὁ τόπος οὗτος σχεδὸν ὁ αὐτὸς τῷ ἐπιβλέπειν) all cases where a predicate has been said to belong to all or none of something; but it differs in method. (4) [110a10-13]

Now, the fact that topoi are investigation-instructions does not conflict with my interpretation of topoi as protaseis and principles since *in the investigation-instruction a certain protasis and principle is expressed*. This can be readily seen in the concrete topoi in the central books. For example from the investigation-instruction of the very first topos the principle could be derived that 'what belongs in some other way than accident (i.e. belongs as definition, proprium or genus) does not belong as an accident'. I shall investigate all the four topoi cited above in Chapter Five[53] and show in detail how the topos-principle can be derived from the investigation-instruction.

However, the investigation of the so-called organa which are found in *Top.* A 13-18 gives us another impressive confirmation of the fact that in the investigation-instruction a protasis is expressed. The organa are not only investigation-instructions,[54] but have a very similar structure to topoi, and are explicitly said to be "in a way" protaseis. Organa are "means by which we will be well supplied with syllogisms" (δι' ὧν εὐπορήσομεν τῶν συλλογισμῶν).[55] In A 13, 105a21-24 Aristotle enumerates the four organa under which all the other organa in A 14-17 fall:

1. provision of propositions (τὸ προτάσεις λαβεῖν) (treated in A 14)
2. the ability to distinguish in how many senses a particular expression is used in (τὸ ποσαχῶς ἕκαστον λέγεται δύνασθαι διελεῖν) (treated in A 15)
3. the discovery of differences (τὸ τὰς διαφορὰς εὑρεῖν) (treated in A 16)
4. the investigation of likeness (ἡ τοῦ ὁμοίου σκέψις)[56] (treated in A 17)

Aristotle then (105a25f.) says something of major interest:

---

[53] Cf. pp. 150-155.
[54] Cf. e.g. expressions like διὰ τῶνδε θεωρητέον ..., σκοπεῖν εἰ ... (A 15, 106a10f.), σκοπεῖν εἰ ... (106b13), ... ἐπισκοπεῖν (b22), etc.
[55] *Top.* A 13, 105a21f.; cf. 108b32.
[56] Likeness is meant in a broad sense and can include analogy.

> The last three of these are also [i.e. as the first organon] in a sense protaseis; for it is possible to make a protasis in accordance with each of them.[57]

Examples of the corresponding protaseis are:

1. "The perception of contraries is the same (for the knowledge of them is also the same)" (105b5f).
2. "An object of choice is the honourable or the pleasant or the expedient" (105a27f.).
3. "Sensation differs from knowledge, because it is possible to recover the latter when one has lost it but not the former" (105a28-30).
4. "The healthy stands in the same relation to health as the sound to soundness" (105a30f.).[58]

These protaseis seem to be the result of *organa* applied to *concrete terms*. Thus the *third* protasis is the result of applying "the discovery of differences" to the terms "perception" and "knowledge". This does not simply consist in stating that there is a difference, but also in defining the difference, i.e. in stating the reason why two terms differ, thus giving the answer to the question "in what (τινί) does perception differ from knowledge?" stated in 108a4. This is found in the because-sentence (105a29). Aristotle lays stress upon it in A 15, 106a1-8, with respect to the *second* organon:

> As regards the number of ways in which a term can be used, we must not only deal with those terms which are used in another way but also try to give reasons for their being used in different ways (λόγους). For example, we must not merely say that justice and courage are called good in one way, and that what conduces to vigour and what conduces to health are called so in another, but also that the former are so called because of a certain intrinsic quality they themselves have, the latter because they are productive of a certain result and not because of any intrinsic quality in themselves.

Thus the *second* protasis (105a27f.) is actually defective, because it merely states that "an object of choice" (being homonymous) is used in a different way with respect to each of the three terms—no reasons for this are given. Also in the case of the fourth protasis, Aristotle does not tell us what the sameness of the relation consists in. However, ideally, it might be assumed that it should always be stated what the homonymy, difference or likeness consists in. Thus, in A 18, 108b24-27 Aristotle gives two examples of protaseis of the fourth organon which state the reason for the likeness: "calm at sea and windlessness in the air are the same thing *(for each is a state of rest)*" and "a point on a line and a unit in number are the same thing *(for each is a principle)*". The statement of reasons establish the organon-protaseis in a similar way as induction establishes the topos-protaseis.

---

[57] ἔστι δὲ τρόπον τινὰ καὶ τὰ τρία τούτων προτάσεις· ἔστι γὰρ καθ' ἕκαστον αὐτῶν ποιῆσαι πρότασιν.

[58] It is worthy of note that the protaseis 2-4 above are fairly complex: the second protasis, for example, is a disjunctive proposition, the fourth one expresses an analogical relation.

3.2. *Structure of the organa (and topoi)*

The question now arises of how homonymy, differences and similarities are investigated and established? A clear answer is to be found in chapters 15-17 where Aristotle investigates those notions with the help of what are usually called topoi in *Top.* B-H[59] and which are obviously meant to be organa here.[60] Roughly, the same structure can be found in both cases[61]:

1a (in the case of...) (ἐπι; ..)   (not always stated explicitly)
  b investigate (σκοπεῖν) if something is the case
2 reason given for the investigation, usually indicated by "since" (γάρ)
3 an example (οἷον)[62]

Let us cite once again the very first topos in B, in a slightly fuller form, as an example for such a topos (B 2, 109a34-38):

> Now one topos is to investigate (ἐπιβλέπειν εἰ) whether the opponent has assigned as an accident something which belongs in some other way. This mistake is commonly made with respect to the genera of things, e.g. (οἷον) if someone were to say that being a colour is an accident of white—for (γὰρ) being a colour is not an accident of white, but colour is its genus. [...]

As an example of an organon let us cite the very first one in A 15, where organa of the second kind (detection of ambiguity of meaning) are listed:

> First, examine (σκοπεῖν) the contrary of a term (ἐπὶ τοῦ ἐναντίου) and see if it is used in several senses, whether the difference be one of kind or one of names. For (γὰρ) in some cases a difference is immediately apparent even in the names. For example (οἷον), the contrary of sharp in the case of a note is flat, while in the case of a body it is dull. The contrary of sharp, therefore, obviously has several meanings, and this being so, so also has sharp; for (γὰρ) the contrary will have different meanings, corresponding to each of those meanings. For sharp will not be the same when it is the contrary of flat, though sharp is the contrary in both cases.[63]

Aristotle only gives a few organa for the investigation of differences (third organon) and similarity (fourth organon) in chapters 16 and 17, but quite a number, namely seventeen, for the investigation of ambiguous terms (second organon) in chapter 15.

The main difference between topoi in *Top.* B-H and organa in A 15-17 is that the aim of the former is to find out whether something is accident (*Top.*

---

[59] Cf. 107b38 and e.g. 128b14: διὰ τῶνδε σκεπτέον.

[60] Aristotle does not say here that these investigation-instructions are organa; one might take them to be topoi of the four organa, as in fact Alexander does (cf. e.g. *in Top.* 100, 17; 101, 18, et al.). However, Aristotle does not mention topoi here either and at the very end of book A he says of the previous investigation-instructions: "Such then are the organa through which syllogisms are carried out. The topoi for the application of which the aforesaid organa are useful are as follows." Thus, the investigation-instructions listed in A 14-17 are obviously organa which are subsumed under the four kinds of organa, only the latter ones being explicitly called "organa".

[61] For topoi cf. e.g. B 8, 113b15ff., 27ff. 114a7ff., etc.; for organa e.g. A 15, 106a10ff., 23ff., 36ff., etc.

[62] (2) is often stated after (3).

[63] A 15, 106a10-17.

B-Γ), genus (Δ), proprium (E) or definition (Z-H, 3), whereas the aim of the latter is to find out whether something is homonymous, different or similar.[64] The aspect which one is advised to look at[65] in A 15-17 can usually be found in B-H as well.[66] In A 18 Aristotle deals with the utility of the three organa. The detection of ambiguity is useful, in the main, "in order that the syllogisms may be directed to the actual thing and not to the name by which it is called" (A 18, 108a20-22). The discovery of differences is useful for the syllogisms about sameness and difference (A 18, 108a38-b6)—I shall deal with them in Chapter Five.[67] The discovery of likenesses is useful for hypothetical syllogisms based on likeness, for induction and definitions (A 18, 108b7-31). Thus organa have their function within the main syllogism, the latter being formed by a topos.

3.3. Conclusion

The same structures are found in investigation-instructions in A 15-17 as in B-H, where they are called topoi. The structures we find in A 15-17 are not called topoi, and are obviously meant to be organa. Such a protasis as "sensation differs from knowledge, because it is possible to recover the latter when one has lost it but not the former" is clearly the result of an organon of the sort which is described in A 15-17. The difference between "sensation" and "knowledge" can be found with the help of an organon which can be described in the following way: 'In the case of two things, see if when one loses them it is possible to recover them both; for if it is only possible with one of them, it is clear that they are different'; the difference itself is implicitly expressed in the organon. Thus to all organa corresponding protaseis can be produced; these organa are therefore in a way protaseis. We have seen that organa are investigation-instructions of a similar structure to the topoi. *It might thus be inferred that to topoi too, corresponding protaseis can be produced and that topoi are in a way protaseis.*

D. *Objection and induction in Θ and in the central books*

In section B above I have demonstrated several passages in the *Rhetoric* from which it was clear that topos is a protasis and one passage in Θ 14 where the notion of the topos seems to be in the making. In section C I have shown how other interpretations of a topos square with this interpretation and in the course of this I have shown how a topos works. With this rough knowledge of the workings of the topos as the hypothesis in a hypothetical syllogism we can turn briefly to the central books. Can an explicit indication in the central books be found to the effect that topoi are protaseis, apart from the concrete

---

[64] Aristotle says so about the organa at A 18 and after each topos in B-H, specifying whether the topos is useful for construction or for destruction or for both. I shall deal with the notion of the predicables in detail in Chapter Three.

[65] I.e. what follows the phrase "in the case of" (ἐπί).

[66] So "terms that are opposed as privation and possession" (ἐπὶ τῶν κατὰ στέρησιν καὶ ἕξιν) (106b21) e.g. in *Top.* B 8, 114a13ff., "inflections" (ἐπὶ πτώσεων) (106b29) e.g. in B 9, 114a26ff., "definition" (ἐπὶ τὸν ὁρισμόν) (107a35) e.g. in B 4, 111b13ff., et al.

[67] Cf. pp. 157-160 below.

arguments found there which clearly show that topoi work as hypotheses of hypothetical syllogisms, as I shall demonstrate in detail in Chapter Four?

Indeed, there is a clear confirmation that topoi are protaseis—in the passage that I cite below Aristotle explicitly says that a topos is put forward as a protasis. Also, we find an important indirect confirmation: in several passages in the central books of the *Topics* Aristotle specifies that a certain topos has to be established by induction and in several passages he also mentions that an objection can be raised against a topos. In the dialectical debate described in Θ the universal protaseis play the most important rôle, being the major necessary premises of a syllogism. These protaseis are established by induction and can be objected to by objections, i.e. counter-examples. From this one can infer that topoi are universal protaseis as well. A topos established by induction has already been shown in the last section. As for objections, the most impressive passage seems to be found in Δ 6, 128a38-b9. The passage runs:

> Moreover, seeing that it is difficult to distinguish that which always follows a thing, and is not convertible with it, from its genus, if this (A) always follows that (B), whereas that (B) does not always follow this (A)—as e.g. calm always follows windlessness and divisible follows number, but not conversely (for the divisible is not always a number, nor windlessness calm)—you may yourself argue as though *the one which always follows a thing is the genus, whenever the other is not convertible with it*; if on the other hand, someone else *puts forward the protasis* (προτείνοντος), you should not accept it universally. An objection to this is that not-being always follows that which is coming into being (for that which is coming into being does not exist) and is not convertible with it (for what does not exist is not always coming into being), but nevertheless not-being is not the genus of coming into being; for not-being has no species at all.

The topos here is clearly expressed by the proposition set out in italics and can be more easily described with the help of letters: 'If A always follows B, but B does not always follow A (i.e. A is not convertible with B), then B is a genus of A'. Aristotle gives one example to confirm the topos; in real debate of course more than one example would have to be given in order to establish it inductively. A syllogism constructed with the help of this topos could look as follows:[68]

> If A always follows B, but B does not always follow A, then B is a genus of A
> Divisibility always follows number, but not vice versa.
> ---
> Hence, divisibility is a genus of number.

The objection is obviously an instance in which the topos is not true: "not-being always follows that which is coming into being (for that which is coming into being does not exist) and is not convertible with it (for what does not exist is not always coming into being), but nevertheless not-being is not

---

[68] In a real debate the questioner would certainly avoid giving an example as a confirmation of the hypothesis which contains the desired conclusion.

the genus of coming into being; for not-being has no species at all." This passage is most impressive because Aristotle explicitly says here that the topos is stated as a protasis (προτείνοντος).[69]

There are five other occurrences of objections in book Δ; I shall content myself by giving just one other example, Δ 4, 124b35-125a4:[70]

> Again, you must see whether the genus and species are used in the same manner in respect of the inflections which they take, for example datives (τινί) and genitives (τινός)[71] and all the rest. For, as the species is used, so also is the genus, as for example in the case of the double and its higher genera; for both the double and the multiple take a genitive. [...] An objection may be raised that in some cases it is not so; for alien and contrary take a dative, but different, which is a genus of these terms, does not take a dative but a genitive—for we say different from something (τινός).

The topos here could be expressed in the following way: 'If A is genus of B, then A and B take the same casus'. The objection clearly is directed against this topos giving an instance in which the topos is not true: "different" is genus of "alien" and "contrary", but takes a different casus from them.

Many examples of objections are also found in book Γ. The hypotheses here have the form 'X is more worthy of choice than Y'.[72] I shall just cite one of them, 2, 117a16-24:[73]

> Moreover, a greater number of things is more worthy of choice than a smaller, either absolutely or when the one is included in the other, viz. the smaller number in the greater.
> An objection may be raised if in some particular case the one is for the sake of the other; for then the two together are not more desirable than the one; e.g. recovery of health and health, than health alone, inasmuch as we desire recovery of health for the sake of health.

The hypothesis here is "a greater number of things is more worthy of choice than a smaller (either absolutely or if one is included in the other);" the objection that recovery of health and health are not more worthy of choice than health alone is clearly directed against the topos-hypothesis.

---

[69] There are some other passages in the *Topics* in which Aristotle expresses himself in a way which clearly indicates that he takes topoi to be protaseis. E.g. in Γ 6, 119a38f. he compares the universal (containing the universal quantifier) and particular (containing the particular quantifier) forms of the so-called "most opportune" topoi and says of them that it is "equally endoxical to claim them/ask the opponent to admit them" (ὁμοίως γὰρ ἔνδοξον τὸ ἀξιῶσαι). The expressions "endoxical" and "claim" of course apply to protaseis as has been shown on pp. 19f. and 52.

[70] The four remaining occurrences in Δ are: 3, 123b17, 27, 34; 4, 124b32.

[71] The grammatical terms 'genitive' and 'dative' do not actually appear in the Greek, but only what we would now call the dative and genitive of indefinite pronouns: "to something/someone" and "of something/someone". The grammatical names for the various casus were developed only later.

[72] I shall deal with this kind of syllogism in Chapter Five, pp. 156f.

[73] Other examples in Γ: 2, 117b12-17; b19-25.

I shall give a few more examples of topoi established by induction and objected to by objections in Chapter Five, section B (on the so-called "most opportune" topoi).[74]

E. *The evidence of Theophrastus*

1. *Tradition of the interpretation of the topos as a protasis*

The interpretation of the topos as a protasis is not new. Theophrastus defined a topos as a principle (ἀρχή)[75] and also as a "premiss derived from a precept" (ὁ γὰρ τόπος πρότασις ἤδη τις ἀπὸ τοῦ παραγγέλματος γεγονυῖα).[76] I shall deal with his definition shortly. Alexander himself also takes topoi to be protaseis.[77] Boethius, in *De topicis differentiis*, II, 1185A, takes topoi to be maximal and principal propositions which are "propositions which are not only known per se but also have nothing more fundamental by which they are demonstrated".[78] Of more modern scholars, Thionville (1855), p. 32 states that "les lieux communs sont des *propositions* exprimant les vérités probables les plus universelles". Grimaldi (1958), p. 12 simply maintains that common topoi (κοινοὶ τόποι) are "general axiomatic *propositions*" without giving any explanation. Solmsen (1929), p. 20, strongly opposes the view that topoi are protaseis. With respect to a problem which would be solved by taking common topoi as protaseis he says:

> Man müßte schon zu einem Verzweiflungsmittel greifen und die τόποι selbst als προτάσεις ansehen; aber diese völlig unaristotelische Auffassung, die meines Wissens auch bisher nie vertreten worden ist, würde schon an der ins Licht gerückten Antithese zwischen τόποι und προτάσεις 1358a10ff. scheitern.

Solmsen's argument with the „Antithese" in 1358a10ff. is not particularly impressive, since just the opposite may be concluded from it, as I have shown (and as Grimaldi takes for granted), i.e. that topoi themselves are protaseis. It is also striking that Solmsen does not deal with the passages which have led to my suggestion that topoi are protaseis,[79] which also means that he does not give us an explanation for these seemingly puzzling passages.

---

[74] Pp. 140-150.

[75] Alex. *in Top.* 5, 21-23; 25f.; again in 126, 14-16.

[76] Alex. *in Top.* 135, 10f. There is no dispute as to whether the former definition is that of Theophrastus, since it is cited twice in the same form. I see no reason therefore to doubt the second specification. That we can derive protaseis from the topos is explicitly stated in 5, 26f., a passage which quite probably belongs to the definition. Now, whether or not it is an exact citation, I think that Alexander has certainly paraphrased this according to Theophrastus' text which he had before him. Besides, a principle can of course be expressed in a protasis, and Aristotle himself sometimes uses principles as premisses even in categorical syllogisms, cf. e.g. A 31, 46b29-32.

[77] Cf. *in Top.* 126, 16ff.; 135, 10; 586, 23f.

[78] "*Propositiones* quae per se notae sint, tum nihil ulterius habeant quo demonstrentur, hae maximae et principales vocantur." Boethius also takes the topos to be the differentia of a maximal proposition, on which cf. Stump (1978), p. 204.

[79] Θ 14, 163b22-33 (Solmsen treats this passage merely from one angle), *Rhet.* B 26, 1402a32-34, *Top.* A 13-18, et al.

Let us now come to Theophrastus' definition of the topos.

2. *Theophrastus' distinction between parangelma and topos and his definition of the topos*

Theophrastus was Aristotle's most important pupil and seems to have *commented or developed* his teacher's theories rather than breaking wholly new paths. He also wrote a treatise called the *Topics*.[80] It is not far off to speculate that Theophrastus, by calling the topos a principle and protasis, merely adopted Aristotle's later definition of the topos. I shall now turn to the first relevant text in Alexander's commentary.

2.1. *Distinction between parangelma and topos & definition of the topos with respect to its rôle in the hypothetical syllogism (in Top. 135, 2-23)*

Theophrastus, according to Alexander, calls the investigation-instruction a *parangelma* (precept, instruction) and only the principle a *topos*.[81] If only the parangelma is listed however[82] he calls it "parangelma" (παράγγελμα) or "parangelmatic topos" (τόπος παραγγελματικός).[83] Alexander gives examples of Theophrastus' distinction in the strict sense.

Examples of parangelma are:[84] "one has to attack from the contraries, from the co-ordinates" (δεῖ ἐπιχειρεῖν ἀπὸ τῶν ἐναντίων, ἀπὸ τῶν συστοίχων).

Examples of topoi are:[85] "If the one contrary has several senses, the other has too",[86] "If the one contrary (of a pair) belongs to the one contrary (of another pair), the other contrary also belongs to the other contrary",[87] or "As is one of the co-ordinate terms, so are the rest".[88]

The topos stands in the following relation to the parangelma according to Theophrastus:

> For an investigation-instruction is what is said in more common, universal and simple terms, and from it the topos is found; for the principle of the

---

[80] Alex. *in Top.* 55, 24-27; for further evidence see Fortenbaugh, Huby, Sharples, Gutas (1992), vol. I, p. 118f.
    It consisted of two books (Τοπικῶν α' β') (Diog. Laert. V 45), possibly introduced by an "Introduction to the *Topics*" (Τὰ πρὸ τῶν τόπων α') (Diog. Laert. V 50), cf. Sollenberger (1984), p. 288 (l.171) and p. 363 (l. 282). Another book on the topoi by Theophrastus might have been 'Ανηγμένων τόπων, where, however, many scholars assume that τόπων is corrupt for λόγων, cf. Sollenberger (1984), p. 222f. (l.83) or (1985), p.46 (l.83).

[81] According to Green-Pedersen (1984), p. 63f. "Boethius' description of the distinction between the differentia and the maxim is so closely similar to Alexander's reproduction of Theophrastus' distinction between parangelma and topos that it is obviously the same distinction they are explaining."

[82] As e.g. in B 2, 109a34f. (Alexander gives this topos as an example *in Top.* 135, 13-15).

[83] Alex. *in Top.* 135, 13.

[84] Alex. *in Top.* 135, 6f.

[85] Alex. *in Top.* 135, 7-10.

[86] εἰ τὸ ἐναντίον πολλαχῶς, καὶ τὸ ἐναντίον.

[87] εἰ τῷ ἐναντίῳ τὸ ἐναντίον ὑπάρχει, καὶ τὸ ἐναντίον ὑπάρχει τῷ ἐναντίῳ.

[88] ὡς ἓν τῶν συστοίχων, οὕτως καὶ τὰ λοιπά.

topos is the investigation-instruction, just as the topos is the principle of epicheireme.⁸⁹

Topos is defined (characterizing its rôle in a hypothetical syllogism) as "a premiss derived from a parangelma (i.e. investigation-instruction)".⁹⁰ This is in line with what I said above (p. 55): *in the investigation-instruction a certain protasis and principle is expressed.*

Alexander remarks that Aristotle also calls parangelmatic topoi topoi as well. His explanation is that we give specific rather than generic names to things, and topos is more specific than parangelma, which is more generic.⁹¹ This shows that he agrees with Theophrastus' distinction, i.e. most importantly: a topos in the strict sense is the principle (or hypothesis).⁹²

Alexander gives us another Theoprastean definition of the topos in two other places. After these definitions he gives examples in both cases of *dialectical syllogisms*, as we derive them from topoi,⁹³ and in which topoi function as major premisses. These syllogisms are clearly hypothetical syllogisms with one hypothetical premiss in which the conclusion is obtained from the premisses by a rule similar to the Modus ponens rule.⁹⁴

Alexander gives these examples as if explaining Theophrastus' definition which he obviously believes to be a true account of Aristotle's text, and as it is known that Theophrastus worked on hypothetical syllogisms,⁹⁵ I see no reason to disbelieve that it is Theophrastus' own account. I shall now have a closer look at the Theophrastean definition of topos.

---

⁸⁹ παράγγελμα μὲν γάρ ἐστι τὸ κοινότερον καὶ καθολικώτερον καὶ ἀπλούστερον λεγόμενον, ἀφ' οὗ ὁ τόπος εὑρίσκεται· ἀρχὴ γὰρ τόπου τὸ παράγγελμα, ὥσπερ ὁ τόπος ἐπιχειρήματος (135, 3-6), ἐπιχείρημα being συλλογισμὸς διαλεκτικός (*in Top.* 126, 12; 541, 11) in accordance with *Top.* Θ 11, 162a16.
⁹⁰ πρότασις ἤδη τις ἀπὸ τοῦ παραγγέλματος γεγονυῖα
⁹¹ Alex. *in Top.* 135, 4; also 276, 7; cf. *Cat.* 2b7-14.
⁹² This interpretation is in line with de Pater's distinction of the same two aspects of a topos, namely a «formule de recherche» or «règle» (corresponding to παράγγελμα) and «formule probative» or «loi logique» (corresponding to the topos). De Pater (1965), p. 116, is also of the opinion that «...le caractère le plus fondamental, le plus central du lieu est son caractère probatif» and that topoi without that «caractère probatif» are only «lieux en un sens faible» (as the τόποι παραγγελματικοί). In his article (1968), p. 174, he states: «Il semble donc que Théophraste a eu raison en réservant le terme τόπος pour ce que nous appelons la loi» (cf. also (1968), p. 167).
⁹³ *In Top.* 6, 1-11 and 126, 25-30 and 127, 6-16.
⁹⁴ To cite one of these examples (6, 1-5): τὸ γὰρ ὅτι /ἡ ἡδονὴ ἀγαθὸν τέλος/(=conclusion) δι' ἀληθῶν μὲν οὐχ οἷόν τε δεῖξαι, ὅτι μηδὲ ἀληθές ἐστι τὸ δεικνύμενον, δι' ἐνδόξων μέντοι οἷόν τε· ἂν γὰρ λάβωμεν ὅτι /πᾶν, ὃ αἱρετὸν ὄν μὴ δι' ἄλλο τι ἀλλὰ δι' αὑτὸ τοιοῦτόν ἐστι, τελικὸν ἀγαθόν ἐστι/ (=hypothetical premiss, i. e. τόπος or ἀρχή or ὑπόθεσις, cf. 587, 4f. in the context of his interpreting ἀρχή and πρότασιν κοινήν as τόπος), καὶ προσλάβωμεν τὸ /'ἡ δὲ ἡδονὴ τοιοῦτον'/(=second premiss) ἔνδοξον ὄν, συνάξομεν τὸ προκείμενον. Alexander, as well as many other Peripatetics, believed that hypothetical premisses are potentially equivalent to categorical premisses and states the hypothetical premiss in a categorical quantified form.
⁹⁵ Alex. *in APr.* 390, 2f.; Philop. *in APr.* 242, 18-21, et al.

2.2. Theophrastus' definition of the topos with respect to its internal structure (in Top. 5, 21-27 and 126, 11-127, 16)

The passage in italics cited below represents without doubt the exact wording of Theophrastus' definition. Both passages in Alexander's commentary on the *Topics* (*in Top.* 5, 19-27 and 126, 14-16) agree on it and it is stated in its pure form at 126, 14-16, where it is put into quotation marks by Wallies. Here I shall cite the passage in 5, 21-27. The contents of the brackets and possibly the last passage numbered (4) appear to be Alexander's own explanations. I assume that Alexander gives these explanations according to Theophrastus' text as they fit in very well with Aristotle's *Topics* and we might thus expect to find them in his pupil's book about topoi:

> *A topos is a principle or element* (τόπος ἐστὶν ἀρχή τις ἢ στοιχεῖον), *from which we take the appropriate principles* (ἀφ' οὗ λαμβάνομεν τὰς περὶ ἕκαστον ἀρχάς) (1), *determined in its compass* (τῇ περιγραφῇ μὲν ὡρισμένος) (for either it includes common and general terms, which govern the syllogisms (ἢ γὰρ περιλαμβάνει τὰ κοινὰ καὶ καθόλου, ἅ ἐστι τὰ κύρια τῶν συλλογισμῶν), or from them such terms can be shown and taken (ἢ δύναταί γε ἐξ αὐτῶν τὰ τοιαῦτα δείκνυσθαί τε καὶ λαμβάνεσθαι)) (2), *indeterminate with regard to particulars* (τοῖς δὲ καθ' ἕκαστα ἀόριστος) (3): for starting from these it is possible to obtain plenty of endoxical protaseis for the problem in hand (ἀπὸ τούτων γὰρ ἔστιν ὁρμώμενον εὐπορεῖν προτάσεων ἐνδόξων[96] πρὸς τὸ προκείμενον); for this is the principle (τοῦτο γὰρ ἡ ἀρχή) (4).

In the following I shall deal with the sections numbered (1)-(4) of the passage one after another.

(1) the appropriate principles (τὰς περὶ ἕκαστον ἀρχάς):

The question of what the word "appropriate" (περὶ ἕκαστον) in "the appropriate principles"[97] refers to arises here. In this instance, it clearly seems to me to refer to the *problema*. We can see this e.g. at 126, 21-23 where in the first part of the passage Alexander states the problema: "if we want to investigate whether *the good is useful*."[98] He then goes on to say:

> We should secure (ληψόμεθα), starting from the topos in hand (ἀπὸ τοῦ προκειμένου τόπου ὁρμώμενοι), the protasis appropriate to the prob-

---

[96] It seems to have escaped the notice of Graeser (1973), F 38 p. 37, Repici (1977), p. 169n.16 (frgm 54a) and Fortenbaugh, Huby, Sharples, Gutas (1992), p. 260 frgm. 122A that Wallies from whose edition they expressly extract their text decides in Corrigenda et Addenda (p. 711; cf. XXVI and VIf.) to give preference in 5, 26 to the reading of Paris. 1832 (against that of the Aldina edition, on which his edition is mainly based) and to read προτάσεων ἐνδόξων instead of προτάσεως ἐνδόξου. His decision I think is correct because εὐπορεῖν with a genetivus rei only seems to make sense with the genetivus in plural; also cf. 127, 6-8: ἔστι μέντοι περὶ ἕκαστον τῶν τῷ μᾶλλον τε καὶ ἧττον προσχρῆσθαι δυναμένων προβλημάτων ὁρμωμένους ἀπὸ τοῦ προειρημένου τόπου οἰκείων εὐπορεῖν προτάσεων.

[97] In Aristotle it usually means "principles appropriate to each discipline (astronomy, medicine, etc.)". Cf. e.g. *APr.* A 30, 46a18; similarly in *Rhet.* A 2, 1358a17. They are often called αἱ οἰκεῖαι ἀρχαί as well, cf. e.g. *De Gen. Anim.* B 8, 747b30, 748a8, *Top.* A 2, 101a37.

[98] εἰ μὲν γὰρ ζητοῖτο περὶ ἀγαθοῦ εἰ ὠφελεῖ

lema in hand (προσεχῆ πρότασιν τῷ προκειμένῳ προβλήματι): *if the evil is harmful, then the good is useful.*

The "appropriate protasis"[99] clearly corresponds to the "appropriate principles"—both are derived from a topos. The topos in hand here is the topos from the contraries: "If the one contrary (of a pair) belongs to the one contrary (of another pair), the other contrary also belongs to the other contrary."[100] Now, the principle or protasis "if the evil is harmful, then the good is useful" is clearly derived from the topos from the contraries and is appropriate to the problema "the good is useful".[101] In *APst.* A 2, 71b23 the notion of the principle in precisely this meaning is found: *principles appropriate to what is being proved* (αἱ ἀρχαὶ οἰκεῖαι τοῦ δεικνυμένου).[102] The principle in the context of the syllogism is of course the hypothesis.[103]

(2) determined in its compass (τῆ περιγραφῆ ὡρισμένος):

The way Alexander understands "determined in its compass" is clarified in 126,16-20:

> For example, "If the one contrary (of a pair) belongs to the one contrary (of another pair), so will the other contrary belong to the other contrary" is a topos. For this sentence and protasis is determined with respect to the universal (for it is clear that it is stated about contraries universally), but it is not determined in it whether it is said about these or these particular contraries.[104]

Alexander seems to think that the topos is determined in its compass[105] by the general character of the terms it contains, i.e. a topos contains contraries, co-

---

[99] Alexander uses the word προσεχῆ here to convey the meaning of "appropriate". At times he also uses the word οἰκεῖος, cf. *in Top.* 127, 8 (οἰκείων ... προτάσεων).

[100] Alex. *in Top.* 126, 16f.

[101] Alex. *in Top.* 126, 27f. and 30 gives two other examples of appropriate principles derived from the topos from contraries which differ from each other only with respect to the problema to which they are appropriate.

[102] Alexander, like Aristotle, usually uses problema in the meaning of the thesis to be proved which equals the conclusion (cf. e.g. *in Top.* 127, 21). In 6, 1-11 he simply states propositions which are to be proved (in l. 2 he calls one of them τὸ δεικνύμενον) and says in l. 13f., clearly referring to these propositions: συλλογιεῖται τὰ τοιαῦτα τῶν προβλημάτων.

[103] Bocheński (1947), p. 122 and de Pater (1965), p. 167n.1 render τὰς περὶ ἕκαστον ἀρχάς as "principes regardant le singulier" which seems to me to be an incorrect interpretation. The word ἕκαστον is of course not the same as καθ' ἕκαστον. Περὶ ἕκαστον ἀρχή is a technical term in Aristotle and always needs a supplement, which we readily find in πρόβλημα. It is indeed the topos-principle which contains the particlulars (or singulars) (καθ' ἕκαστα). But Theophrastus obviously expresses it by referring to the problema which contains the καθ' ἕκαστα, not to the καθ' ἕκαστα themselves. Fortenbaugh, Huby, Sharples, Gutas (1992), p. 261 are more correct in translating it as a "starting point about each matter"; the "matter" is of course expressed by the problema.

[104] οἷον τόπος ἐστὶν εἰ τὸ ἐναντίον τῷ ἐναντίῳ ὑπάρχει, καὶ τῷ ἐναντίῳ τὸ ἐναντίον· οὗτος γὰρ ὁ λόγος καὶ ἡ πρότασις αὕτη τῷ μὲν καθόλου ὥρισται (ὅτι γὰρ περὶ ἐναντίων καθόλου λέγεται, δηλοῖ), οὐκέτι μέντοι, εἰ περὶ τῶνδε ἢ τῶνδε τῶν ἐναντίων λέγεται, ἔστιν ὡρισμένον ἐν αὐτῷ.

[105] This seems to me to be a good translation for περιγραφή ("domain" would be another alternative). We find περιγραφή in the meaning of "compass of an expression" in the rhetors of the first and second century AD, in other words several centuries after Theophrastus. But

ordinates (ἐναντία, σύστοιχα), etc., as opposed to specific contraries, e.g. good-bad, specific co-ordinates, e.g. just-justly, etc. These general terms admit of all particulars (καθ' ἕκαστα) of these terms.[106]

Now, it would be highly surprising if this were really so. One would rather expect that the compass of a topos is determined by its general terms themselves, not their generality which is evident and common to all topoi. Thus contraries (ἐναντία) for example would determine the compass of a topos insofar as only contrary particulars, not say co-ordinate particulars, can be put in for them.[107]

Alexander gives a further explanation in brackets: "either it includes common and general terms, which govern the syllogisms, or from them (ἐξ αὐτῶν) such terms (namely common and general) can be shown and taken." The second part of the sentence is not entirely clear. The plural αὐτῶν seems to refer to τόπος in singular. What is meant is, I take it, the following: From a topos which contains general terms (say opposites) another topos containing less specific terms, i.e. less specific opposites (say contraries) can be deduced; again, from the topos containing contraries another instance of a topos can be derived containing less specific contraries (e.g. good and bad).

(3) undetermined with respect to particulars (καθ' ἕκαστα ἀόριστος).

This is entirely clear from the above. In place of such general terms as contraries, co-ordinates, more and less something etc. we can put in particular contraries, co-ordinates, etc., i.e. instances of them. These general terms of course admit of many various instances, e.g. in the case of contraries we can put the pairs good-bad, harmful-useful, black-white, etc. Expressed in modern terminology, we could say that topoi contain very high-level general terms.

Let us turn to the last sentence which is found at 5, 26f. and comes after the definition.

(4) for starting from these it is possible to obtain plenty of endoxical protaseis for the problem in hand (ἀπὸ τούτων γὰρ ἔστιν ὁρμώμενον εὐπορεῖν προτάσεων ἐνδόξων πρὸς τὸ προκείμενον); for this is the principle (τοῦτο γὰρ ἡ ἀρχή).

---

the meaning of "compass" is contained in that of "outline" (in the sense of "contour") which can already be found in Plato (cf. LSJ).

[106] Cf. the somewhat similar terminology in a different context in *De Gen. Anim.* B 6, 743b20-22: "All the parts are first marked out in their outlines (ταῖς περιγραφαῖς διορίζεται) and acquire later on their colour and softness and hardness."

[107] Solmsen (1929), p. 68, assumes that Alexander interprets the *determination in compass* as deriving from the generality of the terms the topos contains. Thus, he writes: „so werden wir den ersten Teil dieser Charakteristik nicht auf die begriffsinhaltliche Bestimmung beziehen dürfen, die beim τόπος in dem sogenannten παράγγελμα, der eigentlichen differentia specifica des τόπος (z.B. ἀπὸ τῶν ἐναντίων, ἀπὸ τῶν συστοίχων) liegen würde." However, in fn. 6 he points out that he believes, correctly, I think, this interpretation to be correct anyway, but that he does not dare hold it against that of Alexander. If Alexander really wanted to make this unusual assertion, he might have been misled by taking τῇ περι-γραφῇ ὡρισμένος, which he read in Theophrastus' text, as a dativus instrumenti (determined *by* its compass), not as a dativus respectu (determined *with respect to* its compass), as I have translated it above.

This sentence is slightly difficult. Reading the entire passage for the first time one would automatically refer "from these" (ἀπὸ τούτων) to one of the two words which are in the plural in the previous sentence: "particulars" or "appropriate principles". Similarly, one would automatically refer "this" (τοῦτο) to "the problema in hand".[108] However, this would not make any sense—both words clearly refer to topoi.[109] The endoxical protaseis (προτάσεις ἔνδοξοι) which one obtains are topoi in which the general terms have been substituted by particular terms (τὰ καθ' ἕκαστα) needed for the problema in hand: this is clear from several passages in Alexander's commentary.[110]

I have shown that in some passages Aristotle speaks of the topoi as of protaseis, which obviously work as hypotheses in hypothetical syllogisms. I have also shown how other interpretations of the topos are compatible with my interpretation, pointing out different aspects of the topos. The investigation of organa which are very similar entities to the topoi and which are "in a way" protaseis, confirms my interpretation of the topoi as protaseis. In one passage in the central books Aristotle explicitly says that the topos is uttered as a protasis. Topoi in the central books are established by induction and objected to by objections, just as the universal propositions in book Θ; this also confirms the interpretation of topoi as universal protaseis. Theophrastus' definition of the topos, in which he calls topos a principle from which protaseis can be derived, confirms my interpretation of the topos as a principle and hypothesis of a hypothetical syllogism as well. Additionally, Theophrastus' definition also specifies further the structure of the topos as a principle: it contains general terms which can be substituted by more specific terms according to the problema in hand—one might call the former specification a formal one, the latter a material one.

---

[108] From *in Top.* 127, 6-8; 6, 1-5, and 126, 22f. it is clear that "for the thing in hand" (πρὸς τὸ προκείμενον) has to be supplemented by "problema". As for the plural "from these" (ἀπὸ τούτων) referring to the "topos" in the singular, it is already the second instance of this peculiarity in this short passage, since "from them" (ἐξ αὐτῶν) picked up "topos" as well.

[109] "Starting from" (ὁρμᾶσθαι ἀπὸ τούτων) in this commentary nearly always—and in our passage without exception—refers to topoi; cf. *in Top.* 126, 20, 22; 127, 7. 10; also 28, 6; 181, 16; 300, 29; 517, 16.

[110] Cf. Alex. *in Top.* 127, 6-8; 126, 22f. 26f., 6, 2-5.

CHAPTER THREE

PREDICABLES AND THE SPECIAL STATUS OF SUMBEBEKOS

In Chapter One I discussed the notions of problema and protasis. An important result was that the problema or its negation equals the conclusion of the questioner's syllogism with the help of which he refutes the answerer, drawing his conclusion from the protaseis answered by the answerer. In *Top.* A 4 Aristotle specifies problemata and protaseis further by subdividing them into the four so-called predicables:

> Every protasis and every problema indicates (δηλοῖ) either a definition (ὅρον) or a proprium (ἴδιον) or a genus (γένος) or an accident (συμβεβηκός).[1]

This classification is of the utmost importance, because all the topoi presented in the central books are divided according to the predicables. Not only do conclusions of the syllogisms indicate the predicables but also, more importantly, the topoi-protaseis. It is essential to understand the meaning of the predicables in order to understand the working of the topoi, since the principles expressed by the latter presuppose the properties of the former.

A. *Definition of the predicables*

1. *The passages in Top. A 5 and 8*

In *Top.* A 5 Aristotle gives the following definitions of the predicables.

> *Definition* (ὅρος) is a phrase (λόγος) indicating (σημαίνων) the thing's very essence (τὸ τί ἦν εἶναι).[2]

The last two central books, Z and H, deal with the topoi of definition. Book Z deals with the destruction, H 3-5 with the construction of definitions; H 1-2 actually deals with topoi concerning problemata of the form 'Is A the same as B, or not?', where A and B stand for terms; an example is "Is perception the same as knowledge, or different?"[3] Aristotle calls such problemata "definitory" (ὁρικά), "for argument about definitions is mostly concerned with questions of sameness and difference."[4]

A common example for a definition of "man" is "two-footed terrestrial animal".[5]

> *Proprium* (ἴδιον) is something which does not indicate the very essence (τὸ τί ἦν εἶναι) of a thing, but belongs to it alone (μόνῳ δ' ὑπάρχει) and is predicated convertibly of it (ἀντικατηγορεῖται).

---

[1] A 4, 101b17 combined with b25.
[2] A 5, 101b38.
[3] A 5, 102a6f.
[4] A 5, 102a5-9.
[5] A 4, 101b30f.

> Thus it is a proprium of man to be capable of learning grammar (τὸ γραμματικῆς εἶναι δεκτικός); for if he is a man, then he is capable of learning grammar, and if he is capable of learning grammar, then he is a man.[6]

Book E deals exclusively with the topoi of proprium.

> *Genus* (γένος) is that which is predicated in the category of essence (ἐν τῷ τί ἐστι) of several things which differ in their species (κατὰ πλειόνων καὶ διαφερόντων τῷ εἴδει).
> Predicates in the category of the essence may be described as such things as are fittingly contained in the reply of one who has been asked "What is the object before you?" For example, in the case of man, if someone is asked what the object before him is, it is fitting for him to say "An animal."[7]

Book Δ deals with the topoi of genus.

As far as accident is concerned, there are two definitions:

> *Accident* (συμβεβηκός) is that which is none of the foregoing things—i.e. neither a definition nor a property nor a genus—yet belongs to the thing.
> *Accident* (συμβεβηκός) is something which may either belong or not belong to any one and the self-same thing.
> For example, being seated may belong or not to some one particular thing. This is likewise true of whiteness; for there is nothing to prevent the same thing being at one time white and at another not white.
> The second of these definitions of accident is the better; for when the first is enunciated, it is necessary, if one is to understand it, to know beforehand what is meant by definition and genus and proprium, whereas the second suffices of itself to enable us to know what is meant without anything more.[8]

I shall designate accident as it is defined by the first and second definition as accident-(1) and accident-(2) respectively.

The topoi of the accident are dealt with in the first two of the central books, B and Γ. In book Γ problemata of the specific form 'Is A or B more worthy of choice?' are found, where A and B stand for terms; e.g. "Is the honourable or the expedient more worthy of choice?" Aristotle subsumes topoi dealing with this sort of problemata under the topoi of the accident because "in all such cases the question is to which of the two does the predicate[9] more properly belong as an accident."[10]

Aristotle obviously considers this division of the predicables to be complete and even gives two proofs (πίστεις) for it: one by induction, the other by syllogism.[11] Induction and syllogism do not have here their regular meaning as discussed in Chapter One. Proof by induction of the classification of predicables consists here in the alleged fact that "if any one were to survey

---

[6] A 5, 102a18-22.
[7] A 5, 102a31-35.
[8] A 5, 102b4-14.
[9] Clearly the predicate "being worthy of choice" (αἱρετόν) must be meant.
[10] A 5, 102b14-20.
[11] A 8.

protaseis and problemata one by one", he would always have to classify them as expressing one of the four predicables.[12] Proof by syllogism refers here to a diairetic division common in late Platonic dialogues. The notion of the predicate is subdivided into four different branches with the help of two distinctions (being predicated convertibly of each other and being part of a definition); these two different branches yield the four predicables.[13]

2. The clash between the definition of the predicables and the explanation of their use in Top. H 5, Z 1 and A 6

The definitions of the predicables given in book A, except A 6, has the appearance of clashing in certain respects with passages describing the construction and destruction of predicables in A 6, Z 1, and H 5 and the practice in the central books. With respect to genus, proprium and definition this appearance is only seeming; with respect to accident, the clash is real. For the meaning συμβεβηκός has in these passages I shall use the transliteration *sumbebekos* (pl. sumbebekota). Let us look at H 5, 155a3-18 & 28-31 to illustrate the clash. This is a passage at the very end of the central books where the difficulty of destroying and constructing the predicables is compared: definition is most difficult to establish and easiest to destroy whereas sumbebekos, at the other end of the spectrum, is the most easy to construct and the most difficult to destroy. The passage runs in full:

> It is clear also that the easiest thing of all is to destroy a definition. [...] Moreover, the other topoi (διὰ τῶν ἄλλων)[14] may be used as means for attacking (ἐπιχειρεῖν) a definition; for if either the account is not peculiar (ἴδιος), or what is rendered is not the genus, or something included in the account does not belong (μὴ ὑπάρχει), the definition is thereby destroyed. On the other hand, against the others it is not possible to use all the topoi drawn from definitions (τὰ ἐκ τῶν ὅρων), nor yet of the rest; for only those directed against sumbebekota (τὰ πρὸς τὰ συμβεβηκότα) apply generally (κοινὰ) to all the aforesaid kinds of attribute. For each of the aforesaid predicables must belong to the subject, but if the genus does not belong as a proprium, the genus is not yet thereby destroyed; likewise also

---

[12] A 8, 103b3-6.

[13] A 8, 103b6-19. In APr. A 31, 46a33 Aristotle calls division a "weak syllogism".

[14] Other than those of the definition. The word topos is not actually used here and it in fact does not occur in H 5 explicitly, except in the transitional passage at the end. But it is clear that this is meant, since in the following line (155a8f.) the results achieved by destructive topoi with respect to the three predicables are enumerated. The expression "to attack by means of" (ἐπιχειρεῖν διὰ) which is used throughout H 5 typically has topoi as the object of "means of"; cf. H 5, 155a37, which is the very end of H 5: τόποι δι' ὧν εὐπορήσομεν πρὸς ἕκαστα τῶν προβλημάτων. There are other expressions coming up later in the passage which are used of topoi: "(sc. topoi) drawn from definitions" or "(sc. topoi) directed against (or relating to) sumbebekota" and "common" or "general" (κοινός); the latter occurs in 119a37, 154a16, 125b11, et al. to express that the described topoi can be used for other or all predicables.

We have exactly the same situation in B 1 where the word topos does not occur explicitly either, cf. B 1, 109a1-3: πρὸς ἀμφότερα τὰ γένη τῶν προβλημάτων κοινὰ τὰ καθόλου κατασκευαστικὰ καὶ ἀνασκευαστικά; cf. also Γ 6, 119a33f, 120b7f., H 2, 152b37f; 153a1f. In Δ 1, 120b11f. τὰ πρὸς τὸ γένος καὶ τὸ ἴδιον are explicitly described as "elements" (στοιχεῖα), i.e. topoi.

the proprium need not belong as a genus, nor sumbebekos as a genus or proprium, but they may merely belong (ὑπάρχειν μόνον). So that it is impossible to use one set as a basis of attack upon the other except in the case of definition. Clearly, then, it is the easiest of all things to destroy a definition, while to construct one is the hardest. [...]
The easiest thing of all to construct is sumbebekos; for in the other cases one has to prove not only that the predicable belongs, but also that it belongs in such and such a way (οὕτως); whereas in the case of the sumbebekos it is enough to prove merely that it belongs (ὑπάρχει μόνον). On the other hand, a sumbebekos is the hardest thing to destroy, because it affords the least material; for in stating a sumbebekos one does not add any indication (προσσημαινείνει) of how it belongs (πῶς ὑπάρχει); and accordingly, while in the other cases it is possible to destroy what is said in two ways, by proving either that it does not belong, or that it does not belong in the particular way stated (οὕτως), in the case of a sumbebekos the only way to destroy it is to prove that it does not belong at all.

In order to establish a thesis claiming that a sumbebekos belongs to a subject we simply have to prove that it belongs; in order to destroy such a thesis we simply have to prove that it does not belong. Sumbebekos does not have to belong in a particular way.

The meaning of sumbebekos assumed here is obviously not the one of accident-(1) or accident-(2). In the case of accident-(1) the belonging obviously has a particular specification. In order to establish it one has to show that it belongs *and* that it is neither of the three other predicables; in order to destroy it we have to show that it does not belong *or else* that it belongs as one of the other predicables.[15] In the case of accident-(2) the belonging is specified insofar as it does not necessarily hold, but only contingently (ἐνδέχεται ὑπάρχειν καὶ μή). In order to construct it one has to show that it can belong and not belong; in order to destroy it one has to show that either it does not belong at all or else that it necessarily belongs.[16]

One certainly could not refute the other predicables by proving that they do not belong as accident-(1) or accident-(2), rather the opposite: one could prove that a predicate *does* belong as an accident and thereby refute that it belongs as any other predicable. In the case of accident-(1) it would in fact have to be part of the proof to show that it does not belong as genus, proprium or definition.

Before discussing sumbebekos further let us first look at the other predicables and see whether there are any discrepancies between the two groups of passages as there are in the case of sumbebekos. To put the question more concretely: Is it possible to destroy a definition with the help of the topoi of proprium or genus as described in H 5 assuming the definition of genus, proprium and definition in A 5, or not? The answer is yes, but it is easy to be misled into thinking that this is not so, as was in fact the case with Brunschwig (1967), pp. LXXVI-LXXXIII who gives an interpretation of the predicables which distinguishes two different «interprétations», the «exclusive» and the «inclusive» one, and maintains that only within the

---

[15] As Aristotle in fact does in B 2, 109a37f.
[16] Aristotle only uses accident-(2) in two places in the central books: Δ 1, 120b30-35 and Z 6, 144a23-27.

inclusive interpretation the definition can be destroyed with topoi other than those of the definition. Subsequently, Brunschwig (1986) partly revised his interpretation for the better, but certain errors remain. Most importantly, Brunschwig decided to adhere to his distinction between exclusive and inclusive interpretation—a distinction which I think would be best abandoned. Every serious student of the first four books of the *Topics* will be using Brunschwig's edition of the text including the introduction in which his interpretation is contained and which had some influence. This alone provides reason enough to deal with it extensively and to say exactly what is actually wrong with it;[17] apart from that, the errors seem to me to be fairly instructive and can show the student pitfalls to avoid. In the next few pages I shall describe Brunschwig's interpretation and show that it is wrong with respect to genus, proprium and definition and within the critique I shall deliver at the same time a positive interpretation.

B. *Brunschwig's interpretation*

Exclusive interpretation:
According to the exclusive interpretation, found mainly in A 4, 5 and 8 and in a few places in the central books,[18] the predicables are an instrument with the help of which the set («ensemble») of propositions is divided into four subsets («sous-ensembles») of propositions which exclude each other: a proposition belongs to only one of the four subsets, i.e. a proposition indicates, in its predicate, *either* a definition *or* a proprium *or* a genus *or* an accident.

Inclusive interpretation:
The inclusive concept is used in the central books except in a few places, and is especially well recognisable in A 6, Z 1, and H 5. Here, the predicables are included in each other in the following way: a proposition can belong to more than one of the subsets, if it belongs to one subset which is included in another.

Thus, in the case of the *proprium* it is enough to show of a predicate that it is coextensive; whether it is essential as well, and thus a definition, is left undetermined. I.e. it is possible for a proprium to be a definition. In order to determine that it is a proprium (in the exclusive interpretation) it has also to be shown that it is not essential.

A *genus* is essential and can be coextensive, i.e. it can also be a definition.

A *sumbebekos* can also be essential and coextensive, i.e. a genus or a proprium or both of them, i.e. a definition.

---

[17] Brunschwig (1986), p. 146 does not actually render the interpretation given in (1967) exactly.
[18] B 2, 109a34-b12, Δ 1, 120b21-35 and a considerable number in E: 3, 131b37-132a9; 4, 132b35ff., 133a18ff.; 5, 135a9-19. Brunschwig considers this exclusive concept to be a later development and the passages in B and Δ later insertions.

1. Critique of Brunschwig's interpretation

1.1. Genus

Brunschwig says that, in the inclusive interpretation, when a genus, which is essential and allegedly undetermined with respect to coextension, turns out to be coextensive it becomes a definition; i.e. genus is undetermined as to whether it is a definition or not. I disagree with this for two reasons.

Firstly, Brunschwig fails to see that a definition is a complex expression of which the genus is a part only, being itself a simple term. Aristotle explicitly says that definition is a phrase (λόγος) in place of a term (ὄνομα) or another phrase.[19] What Aristotle says of propria in H 5, 154b15f. is a fortiori true of definitions: "for the proprium is for the most part rendered in a complex phrase (ἐν συμπλοκῇ)". Thus, the expression "what is rendered" (τὸ ἀποδοθέν) in the phrase "if [...] what is rendered (τὸ ἀποδοθέν) is not the genus, [...] the definition is thereby destroyed" cited above (155a8-10) refers to the *part* in the definition which is claimed to be genus, not to the whole definition, as Brunschwig obviously takes it to be by assuming that genus is undetermined as to whether it is a definition. Aristotle's way of expressing himself is misleading here, but there are other passages where he is absolutely clear. Thus, in A 6, 102b29-33 he writes: "For when we have shown that [...] what is assigned *in the definition* is not the true genus (ὅτι οὐ γένος τὸ ἀποδοθὲν ἐν τῷ ὁρισμῷ), we shall have destroyed the definition."[20]

Secondly, Brunschwig fails to see that a genus is predicated in the essence (ἐν τῷ τί ἐστι) whereas a definition expresses what I shall translate as "the *very* essence" (τὸ τί ἦν εἶναι) of a thing. Thus, it is not the case that when a genus, which is «essentiel», turns out to be «coextensive» as well, then it signifies a definition (definition being «essentiel» and «coextensive») since a definition expresses the *very* essence (τὸ τί ἦν εἶναι), not just the essence. Now, when Brunschwig says of both the definition and the genus that they are «essentiel» (the only difference between definition and the genus being that the former is also coextensive), he seems to confuse the essence (τὸ τί ἐστι) with the very essence (τὸ τί ἦν εἶναι).[21] There is a connection between these two terms, but they are of course not equal. In Z 1, 139a29-31 Aristotle says: "for the genus seems to indicate more than any other component part of a definition (μάλιστα γὰρ τῶν ἐν τῷ ὁρισμῷ) the very essence (οὐσίαν) of the subject which is defined."[22] Thus

---

[19] A 5, 102a1. It is clear from several passages that this λόγος is supposed to be a complex expression: H 5, 154a26-29, 32-36, A 6, 102b29-34, H 3, et al.

[20] Cf. e.g. also Z 1, 139a27-31.

[21] It must be said that Aristotle himself is not always consistent in his usage of τὸ τί ἐστι. Usually it stands for what is expressed by the genus, sometimes, however, it stands for what is expressed by the definition as a whole (where one would expect τὸ τί ἦν εἶναι), as is e.g. the case in H 3, 153a21f. Aristotle's inconsistency is not confined to the *Topics*; cf. Barnes (1994²), 174f.

[22] I take οὐσία to be the same as τὸ τί ἦν εἶναι, as Z 3, 140a34 shows, where a phrase (λόγος) which is peculiar (ἴδιος) and indicates the ousia (δηλοῖ τὴν οὐσίαν) is supposed to be a definition. This corresponds to the characterization of the definition in A 4, 101b21-23 where the only difference is that here Aristotle uses the expression τὸ τί ἦν εἶναι.

Aristotle does not simply say that genus expresses the very essence (οὐσία), but only that it does so more than any other component part of the definition; in E 4, 132b35-133a3 we learn in fact that the differentia contributes (συμβάλλεται) to the very essence (τὸ τί ἦν εἶναι). In H 5, 155a18-22 Aristotle says that in order to establish the definition one has to show, among other things, that "what is rendered is the genus" and, apart from that, that "the account expresses the very essence (τὸ τί ἦν εἶναι) of the thing"—the latter is obviously something which is not entirely expressed by the genus.[23]

Thus, the system of predicables Aristotle gives in A 4 is not exclusive in the way Brunschwig takes it to be with respect to genus and definition. Each sentence expresses one predicable only: either a definition or a proprium or a genus or an accident (101b16 combined with b25). Thus the sentence "man is a terrestrial two-footed animal" expresses a definition; the sentence "man is an animal" expresses a genus. Clearly, a definition is not a genus and a genus is not a definition and as such they exclude each other. However, the definition "terrestrial two-footed animal" consists of the genus "animal" and the differentia "terrestrial two-footed",[24] i.e. the definition *includes* the genus. Thus it is clear that with the help of the topoi of genus we can destroy the definition. What Aristotle says in H 5, Z 1, and A 6, where the inclusive interpretation is alleged to be found, is also true of the definition and the genus as they are defined in A 4 and 5, where the exclusive interpretation is alleged to be found, and not only in the places where we have the «inclusive interprétation»: When the genus, which is a part of the definition, is destroyed, the whole definition is destroyed—both in the inclusive and the exclusive interpretation.[25]

---

[23] Interestingly, Brunschwig seems to be aware of a difference between τὸ τί ἐστι and τὸ τί ἦν εἶναι, by translating the former by «essence», the latter by «l'essentiel de l'essence» and giving some explanations for this, p. 5n.3. But he obviously does not distinguish these things in his interpretation here, p. LXXVII, when assuming that a genus which is essential and coextensive would make a definition.

[24] In E 4, 132b35-133a5 Aristotle explicitly says that "terrestrial two-footed" is a differentia and not a proprium. In E 4, 133b8 however he says that it is a proprium of man ; the same in 136b20-22. In A 4, 102a27f. he tells us that "two-footed" (δίπουν) is a relative property (πρός τι ἴδιον) (man is two-footed with respect to the horse and the dog). Now, is this a proprium or a differentia? The solution seems to be found in E 1, 129a6-10 where Aristotle explicitly says that differentia (διαφορά) is a relative property (τὸ πρὸς ἄλλον ἴδιον) and gives two-footed (δίπουν) as an example. The fact that in the two latter passages "terrestrial" is left out might be explained in that Aristotle is comparing the man with the horse or the dog which are both terrestrial as well.

[25] Brunschwig (1986), pp. 151 and 153 realized that genus is only a part of definition. However, he still seems to assume that the genus in the definition expresses the entire essence (i.e. the very essence) of a thing, as his (I think unsatisfactory) definition of the definition, p. 154, suggests. Thanks to his insight that genus is only part of the definition, Brunschwig does not distinguish any more between genus in the exclusive and inclusive sense (p. 154); but then I do not see the point in his upholding the difference between the exclusive and inclusive interpretation altogether, which is misleading. One might still speak of an inclusive and exclusive sense of συμβεβηκός and proprium but not of an exclusive and inclusive sense of *all* predicables, since it only applies to two of them.

1.2. *Proprium*

In order to show that a predicate is a proprium one should according to A 4 not only show that it is coextensive but also that it is not essential, or one should rather say, that it does not express the very essence (τὸ τί ἦν εἶναι). In H 5, 154b13-23 and 155a23-27, Brunschwig argues, Aristotle does not find it necessary to establish that the proprium does not indicate the very essence, but finds it enough to establish it by showing the coextensivity. The same allegedly is true of the topoi establishing proprium in book E. How can it be excluded that what is established as a proprium in this way also indicates the very essence and is thus actually a definition? Brunschwig resolves the problem by saying that proprium here is undetermined as to whether it expresses the very essence or not, i.e. whether it is a definition or not.

Now, what Aristotle actually says in connection with the construction of the proprium is the following:

> Of the rest, the proprium most merely resembles the definition; for it is easier to destroy, because it is usually composed of a number of terms, and most difficult to confirm, because a number of points must be brought together (πολλὰ δεῖ συμβιβάσαι), and, besides this, because it belongs to the subject alone and is predicated convertibly with it (μόνῳ ὑπάρχει καὶ ἀντικατηγορεῖται).[26]

Here indeed Aristotle does not mention the negative characterization of the proprium as not expressing the very essence of the subject. However, by saying that "the proprium most merely resembles the definition" he obviously says that the two are not equal. As for topoi in book E, Aristotle usually neither establishes that the proprium does not express the very essence of the subject nor that it is coextensive with it, but relies on yet some other criteria; it is not possible to determine whether proprium is meant here to express the very essence or not.[27] There are a few passages where it is required that the very essence is not expressed[28] and a few passages where proprium clearly has the wider sense.[29]

In general it must be said that things seem to be especially difficult in E.[30] In the definitions of proprium in E 1 it is not stipulated that a proprium should not express the very essence, but the stipulations given are different from those given in A 5 and H 5. In E 1, 129a34f. Aristotle tells us that the topoi in E are concerned with essential (τὰ καθ' αὑτό) and permanent (τὰ ἀεί) propria. The essential proprium is defined as "one which is ascribed to a thing in comparison with everything else (ὃ πρὸς ἅπαντα ἀποδίδοται) and distinguishes it from everything else (παντὸς χωρίζει), for example the proprium of man as 'a mortal living being capable of receiving knowledge'." (128b34-36). The definition of the essential proprium seems to express the same as the weak sense of proprium in A 5 and H 5, i.e. to

---

[26] H 5, 155a23-27; cf. also 154b13-23.
[27] Barnes (1970), p. 141 counts 27 out of 36 topoi in which the meaning cannot be determined.
[28] E 3, 131b37-132a9; 4, 132b35-133a11; 133a12-23 and 5, 135a9-19.
[29] E 4, 132b8-18; 132b19-34; 5, 134a18-25; 5, 134a18-25 and 7, 137a21-b2.
[30] Pflug (1908) has in fact questioned the authenticity of this book.

belong to a subject alone (μόνῳ ὑπάρχειν) or being convertibly predicated of it (ἀντικατηγορεῖσθαι). The permanent proprium is defined as "one which is true at every time (ὃ κατὰ πάντα χρόνον ἀληθεύεται) and never fails (μηδέποτ' ἀπολείπεται), for example that of a living creature that it is 'composed of soul and body'." (128b39-129a2). The permanent proprium seems to express something that is not found in A 5.[31]

In any case, a definition can be destroyed with the help of topoi of the proprium as it is defined in A 4 in the broad sense. In A 4, 101b17-25 Aristotle first introduces the notion of proprium in a broad sense and subsequently subdivides it into that which signifies the very essence (τὸ τί ἦν εἶναι), calling it the definition, and that which does not signify the very essence, giving it the same name as the generic term, namely proprium. Aristotle here does not specify what the proprium in the broad sense means, but it can be easily inferred from the definition of the proprium in the narrow sense by taking away the stipulation of not indicating the very essence. The proprium in the narrow sense is defined as "something which does not indicate the very essence (τὸ τί ἦν εἶναι) of a thing, but belongs to it alone (μόνῳ δ' ὑπάρχει) and is predicated convertibly with it (ἀντικατηγορεῖται)" (A 5, 102a18f). Thus, the proprium in the broad sense obviously is defined as an attribute that is convertibly predicated of the subject, that is to say, that belongs to the thing alone.

Now, with the help of the topoi of proprium we can show that a predicate is not *peculiar* to the subject. Hence, we can use these topoi in order to destroy the definition in the framework of the alleged exclusive interpretation found in A 4 as well. There is no need to assume two interpretations here; Aristotle in A 4 explicitly distinguishes between a broad and narrow sense of proprium.

Brunschwig (1967), p. LXXVIII seems to think that Aristotle says of definition in H 5 that it is a proprium, and that this contradicts the definitions in A 4 and 5: «en effet, affirmer que la définition est a fortiori le propre de son sujet, c'est nier tout ensemble l'idée qu'une définition ne peut pas être un propre et l'idée qu'un propre ne peut pas être une définition».[32]

It seems to me that Brunschwig does not distinguish the predicable proprium and the property of being *peculiar*; a definition is peculiar to its subject, but it is not its proprium (in the narrow sense). In H 5 Aristotle only says that we can use the destructive topoi about propria for showing that the definition is or is not peculiar,[33] i.e. he does not say that the predicable definition or the definitory phrase (λόγος) is at the same time the predicable

---

[31] On the notion of proprium cf. Barnes (1970). With respect to the notion of per se accidents (καθ' αὑτὰ συμβεβηκότα), the latter article stimulated several articles: Wedin (1973), Graham (1975) and Hadgopoulos (1976). Hagdopoulos' suggestion that per se accidents are permanent properties seems to be fairly appealing to me.

[32] Brunschwig (1986) is still of the same opinion. He writes, p. 155: «Concernant le propre, Aristote est plus explicite: il déclare sans réticence que la définition doit être propre [...], ce qui n'est à nouvaux possible que dans l'interprétation inclusive [...]. Concernant le genre, en revanche, il ne dit rien d'analogue [...]: tout ce qu'il demande à la définition, c'est de contenir le genre, non d'être le genre de son sujet [...].»

[33] (μὴ) ἴδιος ὁ λόγος, 155a8 (a20).

proprium, for which he would have to use the noun "the proprium" (τὸ ἴδιον); rather he uses the adjective "peculiar" (ἴδιος), dependant in form on phrase (λόγος), here clearly derived from the broad meaning of the proprium in A 4. Cf. also the first passage of H 5 (154a23-b12), where Aristotle shows that it is more difficult to construct a definition than to destroy one:

> For the definition [...] must be convertible (ἀντιστρέφειν), if the definition assigned is to be peculiar (ἴδιος) to the subject.[34]

The definition has to be peculiar, i.e. it has to belong to the subject only. This is clearly expressed in A 6, 102b29f.:

> For when we have shown that some attribute does not belong to the subject of the definition only (οὐ μόνῳ ὑπάρχει), *as we do also in the case of a property* (ὥσπερ καὶ ἐπὶ τοῦ ἰδίου), [...] we shall have destroyed the definition.

Cf. also 154b18-23:

> Also, almost all the other things which can be said of the definition can be fittingly said of the proprium as well [...]. Even if it belongs to everything falling under the term, but not to that only (παντὶ ὑπάρχει μὴ μόνῳ δέ), in these circumstances too the proprium is destroyed, as was explained in the case of the definition (καθάπερ ἐπὶ τοῦ ὁρισμοῦ ἐλέγετο).

Thus we have seen that Brunschwig is mistaken in his strict distinction between the exclusive and inclusive interpretation with respect to genus and also with respect to proprium. What Aristotle says in H 5, 155a8-10 also applies to definition, proprium and genus as they are defined in A 4: definition can be destroyed not only with the topoi of definition, but also with the topoi of genus and proprium.

With respect to sumbebekota however Brunschwig seems to be correct in distinguishing two «interprétations»; sumbebekos in the central books seems to have the meaning it has in the «inclusive interprétation»: it can also be genus, proprium, and definition, but not determined as such. In contrast to proprium Aristotle does not give any explicit characterization in A 4 or elsewhere of what a sumbebekos in the broader sense means. Thus, it is necessary to find this out for oneself.

C. *Sainati's interpretation*

Brunschwig (1967) does not expand further on the meaning of sumbebekos. Sainati (1968),[35] pp.70-78 also offers an interpretation on the predicables in the *Topics* and concentrates on an analysis of the sumbebekos. Sainati maintains that sumbebekos in B usually has the meaning of that which belongs to something (or is predicated of something) and means thus simply "predicate", without any modal determination in the sense of contingent or necessary belonging. Sainati interprets the occurrences of sumbebekos as

---

[34] H 5, 154a37-b3.
[35] Sainati was not familiar with Brunschwig's book, published only a year earlier.

meaning "accident" in A, in a few places in B[36] and in Δ-Z[37] as later additions. He arrives at this interpretation by showing that συμβεβηκός in several books of B and Γ[38] has the meaning of "predicate", not of "accident".

Sainati assumes the main difference between the sumbebekos and the other predicables to be that sumbebekos expresses just an extensional predication (inclusion of classes), whereas the predication in the case of other predicables is additionally specified modally, namely as necessary predication. He believes this interpretation is confirmed in H 5, 155a28-36 where he interprets the particular way of belonging (οὕτως ὑπάρχειν) as indicating modal determination. Thus Sainati divides the central books into extensional (B-Γ) and intensional (Δ-Z) books; in the former we find extensional rules, in the latter intensional rules (p.73). He concludes, p.74: «[M]entre ogni γένος o ἴδιον o un ὅρος è anche, inevitabilmente, un συμβεβηκός, quest'ultimo non è necessariamente anche un γένος o un ἴδιον o un ὅρος, potendosi presentare come semplice determinazione predicativa, priva di qualsiasi dimensione o connotato modale.»

I agree with both Sainati and Brunschwig, that συμβεβηκός in central books usually conveys the meaning defined in H 5 as opposed to that defined in A 5. Sainati's interpretation of συμβεβηκός as "predicate" however seems to me, though tempting, not entirely correct. I shall show that it is best understood as an 'attribute' and that the difference between sumbebekos on the one hand and the other predicables on the other indicated in H 5 does not refer to modal determinations—sumbebekos could actually be a genus, proprium or definition and thus express a necessary predication—but to explicit statement of the other predicables in the problema. I shall verify these claims below.[39]

D. *My interpretation*

Turning now to Aristotle's text itself, I shall first investigate thoroughly H 5 and Z 1 in order to try to determine what συμβεβηκός means here. Only then shall I proceed to B.

1. *The passage in Top. H 5, 155a3-36*

Let us look again at a28-36 and in particular at a28-31 which I shall cite again:

> The easiest thing of all to construct is a sumbebekos; for in the other cases one has to prove not only that the predicable belongs, but also that it

---

[36] E.g. B 2, 109a34-b12, 4, 111a14-b16.

[37] Δ, 1, 120b21-23; 4, 125b11; 5, 126a14-16; E 4, 133b17-19 & 31-36; Z 6, 144a23-27.

[38] B 2, 109b30-32, 6, 112b21-26, 7, 113a20-23, B 7, 113a33ff., 10, 115a3ff., Γ 6, 120a38-39, 120b7.

[39] Also, the topoi cannot be so easily divided into intensional and extensional rules; for example the "most opportune" topoi, which I shall deal with in Chapter Five, occur in *all* books and have the same basic structure. Sainati's interpretation of the workings of the topoi in general (pp. 51-70) seems to me to be mistaken.

belongs in such and such a way (οὕτως); whereas in the case of the sumbebekos it is enough to prove merely that it belongs (ὑπάρχει μόνον).

Aristotle states here that of all the predicables sumbebekos is the easiest to establish, since with the other predicables it is necessary to show not only that they *belong* (οὐ μόνον ὑπάρχον), but also that they belong *in a particular way* (καὶ ὅτι οὕτως ὑπάρχει).

How this double requirement of belonging *and* belonging in a particular way is to be understood in the case of definition, proprium and genus can be easily demonstrated from the preceding passages in H 5 where Aristotle tells us what we have to do in order to construct each of the predicables. Thus, in order to construct a definition the following has to be achieved (155a18-22):

> For there one both has to establish all those other points by syllogism (i.e. that the attributes asserted belong, and that what is rendered is a genus, and that the account is peculiar), and besides this, that the account indicates the very essence of the thing; and this has to be done correctly.

In the case of definition it has to be established that the attributes belong, or, put differently, "it has to be syllogized that all the parts in the definition belong."[40] Aristotle also stresses that the predication has to be universal: "the definition has to be predicated of all of what the definiendum is predicated."[41] This characterizes the pure predication.

Besides it is necessary to show that what has been rendered as part of the definition, is the genus, that the account is peculiar,[42] and that it indicates the very essence (τὸ τί ἦν εἶναι). This characterizes the specified predication in the case of the definition. A phrase belongs to a subject as (ὡς) definition when all these requirements are satisfied.

In the case of proprium again it is necessary to establish that the proprium belongs universally to the subject.[43] This is the requirement for pure predication. Apart from that it has to belong as proprium (ὡς ἴδιον), i.e. it belongs to the subject only or[44] it is convertibly predicated of the subject.[45] This characterizes the specified predication in the case of proprium.

In the case of genus it has to be shown that it "belongs universally to the subject" (b24f.). Further, "it is not enough to show that it belongs, but you must also show that it belongs as a genus (ὡς γένος)" (b27f.).[46] Aristotle

---

[40] πάντα ἀνάγκη συμβιβάζειν ὅτι ὑπάρχει τὰ ἐν τῷ ὅρῳ (H 5, 154a35f.). The parts are of course genus and differentia, cf. H 5, 154a26f.; 3, 153a18, b3, 14f., et al.

[41] δεῖ γὰρ κατὰ παντὸς οὗ τοὔνομα <κατηγορεῖται> κατηγορεῖσθαι τὸν ὅρον (154a36-b1).

[42] I.e. that the definition and the definiendum are convertibly predicated of each other (this is the meaning of ἀντιστρέφειν, 154b1-3), or, what I take to be equivalent, that the definition is predicated of those things only (μόνῳ) of which the definiendum is predicated (b10, implicitly).

[43] H 5, 154b19-21.

[44] Thus, I take the καὶ in B 5, 102a19 to be explicative. This seems to be confirmed by the fact that Aristotle usually mentions either only ἀντιστρέφειν (e.g. 154b2) or only ὑπάρχειν μόνῳ (e.g. b11). Thus Aristotle seems to say that 'x belongs to y only' where we would say that 'x belongs to y and only to y'.

[45] H 5, 154b22; 155a13; 155a25-27.

[46] H 5, 154b23-28

does not specify further in which way "as a genus" has to be understood, but it is of course clear from the definition given in A 5, 102a31f. that genus is that which is predicated in the category of essence of several things which differ in their species. This is the characterization of the specified belonging.

Let us now return to the passage in 155a28-31. I have shown how to understand the assertion that in constructing definition, proprium, or genus we have to show *that* they belong and additionally *how* they belong. Now Aristotle tells us that the construction of sumbebekos is the easiest, since "in order to construct it we only have to show *that* it belongs". The destruction of it, on the other hand, is the most difficult of all predicables, since "the only way to destroy it is to show that it does not belong" (a35f.). Thus the sumbebekos can be defined in the following way:

'*Sumbebekos is that which belongs to (or is predicated of) a subject.*'

There is no further specification as in the case of the other predicables or in the case of accident-(1) or accident-(2) as defined in A 5. However, since the other three predicables have to belong to their subject as well, just as sumbebekos, the case that sumbebekos might actually be a genus, proprium, or a definition, but not determined as such, is obviously not excluded. How then do we know whether, say, the predicate "is an animal" in the sentence "man is an animal" is a sumbebekos or a genus? Or is it both at the same time, as Sainati (1968), p.74 and Brunschwig (1967), p. LXXVIII maintain? Interestingly however, Aristotle never says so. All he says is that with the help of the topoi of sumbebekos we can destroy and (partly) construct other predicables, because all predicables have to belong to the subject.[47] Even if "is an animal" can in a way be a sumbebekos and a genus of "man", on which cf. p. 92 below, this does not yet explain how the disputants should know whether a genus- or a sumbebekos-predication is to be established.

The solution to the problem can be found in H 5, 155a32f., which I shall cite again:

> On the other hand, a sumbebekos is the hardest thing to destroy, because it affords the least material; for in stating a sumbebekos one does not add any indication (προσσημαινείνει) of how it belongs (πῶς ὑπάρχει).

Aristotle says that in contrast to the other predicables "in stating a sumbebekos one does not add any indication (προσσημαίνεται) of how it belongs". How is this "adding an indication" (προσσημαίνεται) to be interpreted? Does it mean that the predicable sumbebekos is itself such that it does not indicate how it belongs whereas genus and other predicables do? Thus in a passage in *De Interpretatione*[48] the verb "is healthy" (ὑγιαίνει) is distinguished from the noun "health" (ὑγιεία), because the former "indicates additionally" (προσσημαίνει) the time. In a passage in *Rhetoric*[49] words

---
[47] Cf. H 5, 155a11-13: μόνα γὰρ τὰ πρὸς τὸ συμβεβηκὸς κοινὰ πάντων τῶν εἰρημένων ἐστίν. ὑπάρχειν μὲν γὰρ δεῖ ἕκαστον τῶν εἰρημένων.
[48] *De Int.* 3, 16b6-10.
[49] *Rhet.* A 13, 1374a12f.

such as "outrage" or "theft", apart from the mere action, "indicate additionally" (προσσημαίνει) also the choice (προαίρεσις); if an action is called a theft it is understood implicitly that this action has been committed intentionally. There is a passage in the *Topics* itself where the word "to indicate additionally" is clearly meant in the meaning of *implicitly* indicating something in addition: *Top.* Z 2, 140a19f. Aristotle says here that correctly assigned definitions "indicate additionally" (προσσημαίνουσιν) their contraries.[50] What Aristotle means here is that given the definition of a term it should be possible to give the definition of the contrary of this term, if existent, simply by converting one of the parts of the definition, i. e. genus or differentia, into the contrary. For example having the definition of "justice" as "a virtue of the soul" one should be able to derive the definition of the contrary of justice, i.e. "injustice", simply by converting the genus of the given definition, which is "virtue", into its contrary, i.e. "vice". The definition one then gets of "injustice" is "vice of the soul".[51]

In all the examples given "to indicate additionally" (προσσημαίνειν) seems to mean "to *implicitly* indicate something in addition". But how can "is animal" in the sentence "man is an animal" indicate implicitly that it is a genus and say "is white" in "man is white", to take an example of sumbebkos as defined in A 5, i.e. an accident, not indicate that it is a sumbebekos? Given the way sumbebekos is defined here, it in fact seems that "is animal" in "man is animal" is a sumbebekos, since it belongs, just as it is a genus, since "animal" is genus of "man". In what sense should "is animal" in the sentence "Man is an animal" implicitly indicate that apart from belonging it is also a genus but not indicate that it is a sumbebekos, even though it belongs?

The last example shows quite clearly that "to indicate additionally" cannot be understood as signifying an *implicit* indication and the solution is that we have to understand it as an *explicit* indication, i.e. the way of belonging is explicitly specified in the problem by the questioner who poses it.[52] Indeed, the expression "to indicate additionally" occurs in the *Topics* most often in this meaning; Aristotle does not necessarily use the Greek word προσ-σημαίνειν, but also other connate words (ἐπισημαίνειν, προστιθέναι, etc.). There are a few passages in book Θ which I have already mentioned in Chapter One. In Θ 6, 160a3 for example the answerer is advised that in the case of a true, but irrelevant protasis he should grant it "but add a remark (ἐπισημαίνειν) that it does not seem to be true".[53] More interestingly, in E

---

[50] Of course, one should specify : *if the definition has a contrary*.

[51] Cf. H 3, 153b14-24; the example given above is extracted from b7-9, which is used here in a different context.; for an example where the differentia changes see a39-b1. Cf. also Z 9, 147a15-22.

[52] In fact, I see no reason why we should not adhere to the active form προσσημαίνει ("the opponent does not indicate additionally") attested by all codices including Boethius' translation and adopted by Waitz (1844-46) and Strache, rather than to the passive form προσσημαίνεται ("is additionally indicated"), emended by Wallies (1923), who edited Strache's version, and accepted by Ross (1958). Wallies' emendation is simply unnecessary. In general, however, it does not actually make any difference whether we use the active (seen from the perspective of the dialectician who poses the problema) or the passive form (seen from the perspective of how predicables are expressed in the problema), as long as it is clear that the specification is made in some way explicit and is not inherent in the predicates as such.

[53] For other examples cf. Θ 6, 160a10, B 3, 110b13f., Θ 1, 156b20; cf. pp. 37f. above.

5, 134a26-135a8 errors are discussed when certain qualifications are not stated explicitly in problemata. More specifically, these errors arise from lack of a definite statement of "how (πῶς) and of what (τίνων) the property is stated" (a27f.). Aristotle first explains in which sense the assignation of a property can be meant listing ten possibilities (134a28-b4); then he explains why the opponent makes an error when he does not explicitly state in which sense he assigns the property (b5-135a5). The first example of an error runs:

> A man, therefore, errs if he does not add the word (προσθείς) "by nature", for it is possible for that which belongs not actually to belong to that to which it belongs by nature; for example, it belongs to man by nature to possess two feet.[54]

In the other examples in this passage Aristotle uses various other words apart from "adding the word" (προστιθέναι) including "indicate additionally" (προσσημαίνειν).[55]

Thus in the case of genus, proprium and definition the questioner explicitly claims that the predicable belongs as such to the subject, in the case of sumbebekos he leaves it open whether an attribute belongs to the subject as a definition, proprium, genus, or as something altogether different from them; all that is asserted in the case of a sumbebekos is the predication between the subject and a predicate. Thus, to take the example given above, in the problema "Animal is the genus of man" or "Animal belongs as genus to man", "is animal" is claimed to express the genus of man, i.e.: "being animal" belongs to "man" and it belongs as genus. In the problema "Man is animal" or "Animal belongs to man" "is animal" is claimed simply to be predicated of man and is just a sumbebekos.

Indeed, Aristotle formulates problemata exactly in this way in A 4, 101b30-33 where they are introduced for the first time:

> Is two-footed terrestrial animal the *definition* of man, or not?[56]

This is the only explicit example of a problema Aristotle gives in A 4, but it is clear from the context that problemata containing the other predicables are to be formulated accordingly:

> 'Is terrestrial two-footed the *proprium* of man, or not?"

and

---

[54] E 5, 134b5-7. Thus, if the problema of the answerer is "Two-footed is a proprium of man", the questioner can argue that "two-footed" is not a proprium of an invalid man who lacks one or both legs, and that hence it is not a proprium of man, because it cannot be predicated of all men.

[55] E 5, 134b18 (μὴ προσσημήνας). Aristotle also uses the following expressions: "state definitely" (μὴ διορίσας, b6), "make clear" (μὴ δηλώσας, b10), "indicate beforehand" (μὴ προείπας, b13), "expressly distinguish" (μὴ διαστείλας, b22).
Also of interest is the occurrence of "to indicate additionally" in *Soph. El.* 7, 169b9-12. Applied to 167a10ff. it means that in the sentence "the Ethiopian is white with respect to his teeth" we may regard the addition "with regard to his teeth" as not "indicating additionally" (προσσημαῖνον) anything and thus we concede that "the Ethiopian is white". I shall discuss this passage in another context in Chapter Five, pp. 136f.

[56] Πότερον τὸ ζῷον πεζὸν δίπουν ὁρισμός ἐστιν ἀνθρώπου ἢ οὔ.

'Is animal the *genus* of man, or not?'

Since in A 4 Aristotle defines the predicables as excluding each other, the sumbebekos is obviously meant to have the meaning of the accident here. The problema containing the accident-(1) or accident-(2) would run correspondingly:

'Is being white an *accident* of man, or not?'

In contrast, the problema containing the sumbebekos would simply run:

'Is man an animal, or not?'

That a sumbebekos may express what can be further determined as genus is also clear from the previously cited passage in Δ 4, 125b10-14, which belongs to the group of theses in which a definition is expressed and the opponents seem to agree on what has been asserted as a genus. With respect to the topos in 125a33-b10[57] Aristotle says in 125b10-14:

> The aforesaid topos is common to the subject of sumbebekos as well; for it makes no difference whether you say that persisting is the genus of memory, or allege that it is a sumbebekos of it.[58] For if in any way whatever (ὁπωσοῦν) memory is a persisting of knowledge, the same argument in regard to it will apply.

The expression "in any way whatever" (ὁπωσοῦν) clearly indicates that in the case of sumbebekos the way of belonging (πῶς) is undetermined, i.e. not explicitly specified, as indicated in H 5, and that this is what makes the difference between the two problemata.[59]

---

[57] Aristotle distinguishes three kinds of relative terms (a33-37; a37-b1; b1-4); as is clear from the instruction (b4-6), both the subject and the predicate which belongs as the genus (subject and predicate being relative terms) have to belong to one and the same kind of relative terms.

[58] It is slightly odd that Aristotle says that "it makes no difference whether one says that 'persisting' is the genus of 'memory' or allege that it is a sumbebekos of it.", as it clearly does make a difference. What Aristotle presumably meant to say, but worded it misleadingly, is that whether the predicate is asserted as a genus or as a sumbebekos, the same argument applies in each case. This is clearly confirmed by the passage following on from b12-14: εἰ γὰρ ὁπωσοῦν ἐστιν ἡ μνήμη μόνη ἐπιστήμης, ὁ αὐτὸς ἁρμόσει περὶ αὐτῆς λόγος

[59] Thus, Sainati (1968), p. 74 is wrong in interpreting the expression «to indicate in addition the way in which it belongs» (προσσημαίνειν πῶς ὑπάρχειν) in H 5 as indicating modal determinations («determinazioni modali»): in the case of a definition, proprium and genus necessary character of the relation («carattere necessario della relazione»), in the case of sumbebekos lack of any modal dimension or connotation («qualsiasi dimensione o connotato modale»). I have shown above that what is indicated additionally is the explicit statement of how a predicate belongs and that this means, e.g. in the case of definition, that it has to express the very essence (τὸ τί ἦν εἶναι), etc. A short look at the topoi in B shows that modality, as well as quantification, was included in the treatment of sumbebkos. *Top.* B 6, 112b1-20 deals with different kinds of modality. In 111b25 the problema contains the modal operator "necessarily" (ἐξ ἀνάγκης), in 109b33 the modal operator "possibly" (ἔστι), in 113b13 the conclusion contains, again, "is possible" (ἐνδέχεται ὑπάρχειν). In general, a geometrician, say, necessarily is a biped terrrestrial animal, even though this is not the definition of a geometrician—definition-, proprium-, and genus-predications are not the only necessary predications.

2. The form of problemata/theses in Top. Δ-Ζ

It is now time to look at examples in the central books in the *Topics* and see whether the problemata found are in harmony with the findings made above. The result will be that indeed in books Δ, Ε and Ζ the genus, proprium and definition are explicitly stated; in book Β, on the other hand, except in one case[60] problemata express a simple predication.

2.1. The form of problemata in Δ

The first example of an argument in Δ runs (1, 120b17-19):

> For example, if it is laid down (κεῖται) that good is a *genus* of pleasure, see whether some pleasure is not good; for, if so, clearly good is not the *genus* of pleasure.

Here, the thesis is obviously "good is a genus of pleasure" and the word "genus" has explicitly been stated in the thesis as well as in the conclusion which refutes the thesis. By refuting good to be a genus of pleasure it is of course not yet refuted that pleasure is not good. This could only be refuted or proved by a topos of sumbebekos; Aristotle in fact explicitly refers to a corresponding topos of sumbebekos which works in an analogous way.[61] The difference between pure predication is especially clear in a passage in which with respect to a certain topical investigation procedure Aristotle specifies:

> For constructive purposes, if the asserted genus is admitted to belong (ὁμολογουμένου μὲν ὑπάρχειν) to the species but it is a matter of dispute whether it belongs as a genus (ὡς γένος ὑπάρχει), then [...]
> But, if it is disputed whether the assigned genus belongs at all (ἁπλῶς ὑπάρχειν), [...][62]

Obviously, pure belonging and belonging as a genus are different things. There are many other places in which genus is stated explicitly.[63] However, Aristotle does not always use the very word genus to indicate that a genus-predication is meant but sometimes also uses the expression "that which" (ὅπερ) instead: 'S is *that which* P' has the same meaning as 'P is the genus of S'.[64] Accordingly, there are several places where problemata are expressed in this way. There are also a few examples of theses in which the predication

---

[60] Β 2, 109a39-b1; I shall deal with this topos in Chapter Five, pp. 150-153.

[61] καθάπερ ἐπὶ τοῦ συμβεβηκότος, 120b17. The topoi Aristotle refers to are clearly those in Β 2, 109b13-29 and Γ 6, 120a32-b6.

[62] Δ 2, 122a10-12; 19f.

[63] Other examples (in which genus is usually stated in the conclusion): 120b33. 39; 121a2f.; 121b3 (εἶδος) 121b19 (οἷον εἴ τις ἀτόμους τιθέμενος γραμμὰς τὸ ἀδιαίρετον γένος αὐτῶν φήσειεν εἶναι; Δ 2, 121b26-28; 122a2; 124a17f.; 4, 125a26 (sc. γένος); 5, 125b28-30 (sc. γένος); 6, 127a26 (εἰ τὸ πᾶσιν ἀκολουθοῦν γένος ἢ διαφορὰν εἶπεν), 128a26, et al.

[64] Cf. Γ 1, 116a23-27: "for nothing is said to be that which is the genus, which does not actually belong to the genus" (οὐδὲν γὰρ λέγεται ὅπερ τὸ γένος ὃ μὴ τυγχάνει ἐν τῷ γένει ὄν) (25f.); cf. also *APr.* Α 39, 49b6-8, Δ 1, 120b21-24. The last passage seems to suggest that S ὅπερ P indicates that P is predicated in the essence of S (ἐν τῷ τί ἐστι κατηγορεῖται), which expresses the most important part of the definition of the genus (cf. Α 5, 102a3f.; Δ 1, 120b29f., al.). On the Platonic origin of ὅπερ cf. De Strycker (1968b), p. 155.

For examples of theses containing "that which" cf. Δ 2, 122a18-24; 4, 125a28.

asserted is that of species (εἶδος).⁶⁵ Of course, to say that 'P is a species of S' is just the converse of saying 'S is the genus of P'.⁶⁶

There is also another sort of problemata in which a differentia (διάφορα) is asserted to belong to a subject. This is not just another way of expressing genus-predication, but represents something different.⁶⁷ In A 4, 101b18f. Aristotle expressly subsumes problemata indicating the differentia under those indicating the genus.⁶⁸

There is also a small number of examples of theses in which the genus seemingly is not explicitly indicated as such.⁶⁹ However, it seems that Aristotle expresses himself succinctly leaving out the full form of the thesis, taking it as read that the thesis in full explicitly mentions the genus. I shall cite an example which illustrates the point well (I am only citing the thesis and the final conclusion):

> If, therefore, anyone says that shame is fear or that anger is pain, [...]. Hence the terms assigned are not genera (οὐ γένη τὰ ἀποδοθέντα).⁷⁰

The conclusion shows that the full form of the theses was not just "Shame is fear" or "Anger is pain", but "Fear is the genus of shame" and "Pain is the genus of anger".

There are also theses in which a purported definition is stated and the genus is not explicitly mentioned,⁷¹ e.g.:

> Sometimes also people unobservedly put the whole inside the part, e.g.: "Animal is an animated body". But the part is not in any way predicated of the whole, so that body cannot be the genus of animal, for it is a part only.⁷²

It seems that the opponents agree on the fact that the thesis has been asserted as a definition and on what has been asserted as a genus in the definition, since the refutation simply consists in stating that the assigned genus is not correct.⁷³ All these examples occur in the framework of destructive topoi in which it is shown that the genus is not correct and thus the thesis is refuted. The situation is similar in book Z where it seems to be taken for granted that the theses deal with definitions even though they have not been explicitly specified as such; I shall discuss book Z shortly.

---

⁶⁵ Δ 3, 123a23-26; 6, 128a9-12.

⁶⁶ Aristotle, in one and the same topos-entry, sometimes switches between saying 'P is genus of S' and 'S is the species of P': cf. 121a30-39 (30f. thesis with genus, 35f. refutation with species).

⁶⁷ Δ 2, 123a3-5; 6, 127a26.34.

⁶⁸ "For the differentia too, being generic, should be ranked together with the genus" (καὶ γὰρ τὴν διαφορὰν ὡς οὖσαν γενικὴν ὁμοῦ τῷ γένει τακτέον).

⁶⁹ Δ 3, 123a34, 4, 124a12f., 5, 126a6.

⁷⁰ Δ 5, 126a6.10f.

⁷¹ Δ 2, 122b26-36; 4, 125b6-14; 5, 125b15-19, b20-27, 126a26-29, a30-36, b13-19, b34-127a2, 127a3-19 (a4, 13f., 14f., 18f.).

⁷² Δ 5, 126a26-29.

⁷³ An interesting example is found in Δ 4, 125b6-14 where the thesis seems to be "Memory is the permanency of knowledge" (b6), but is later quoted as "Permanency is the genus of knowledge" (b11f.).

2.2. *The form of problemata in E*

Book E is the most orderly of all the central books (B-H) and all the examples of theses and problemata show that the predicable was explicitly specified. In E 1 Aristotle gives many examples of problemata[74] to illustrate various kinds of propria; in all of them the word proprium (ἴδιον) is explicitly stated. The example for a relative proprium is:

> It is a proprium (ἴδιον) of man, in relation to a horse, to be a biped.[75]

In E 2-3 in nearly every topos the formula "for then the proprium will not be rightly stated"[76] occurs as the conclusion of the destructive part of the argument; the same with the formula "for then that which is stated to be proprium is not proprium" in E 4;[77] correspondingly the positive formulae in the constructive arguments. In the problemata themselves the predicables are explicitly stated.[78] I cite three examples:

> E.g. anyone who has stated (θείς) that it is a *proprium* of fire to bear a very close resemblance to the soul [...].[79]
> E. g. a man who has said (εἴπας) that the possession of perception is a *proprium* of animal [...].[80]
> E. g. when he renders (ἀποδοίη), as a *proprium* of fire, the body which is the lightest of bodies [...].[81]

In E 6-8 the word proprium is regularly explicitly stated in the conclusion.[82]

2.3. *The form of problemata in Z*

In book Z there are scarcely any examples of problemata in which the predicable definition would be explicitly stated as found in books Δ and E. The situation here is similar to that of the definition stated in book Δ which I mentioned briefly above. In most cases the examples of definitions are given without explicit mention of the word definition, as for example in the very first topos: "e.g. becoming is a passage into being".[83] However it is always understood that what has been assigned is a definition and that what has to be refuted is the assertion that the predicate is a definition, as the following two examples make clear—I am citing only the thesis and the conclusion:

---

[74] They are explicitly named as such in E 1, 128b22-24; b28f.; 129a19f.; 30.

[75] E 1, 128b24f. In the same way: b29f., b35f., 129a2 (sc. ἴδιον), a4 (sc. ἴδιον), a8f. a11.

[76] οὐ γὰρ ἔσται καλῶς κείμενον τὸ ἴδιον (129b7, 23, etc.).

[77] οὐ γὰρ ἔσται ἴδιον τὸ κείμενον ἴδιον εἶναι (132a30f., 36, etc.).

[78] The act of uttering the predicable is normally expressed by "to say" (εἰπεῖν), "to state" (θεῖναι) or "to render" (ἀποδιδόναι).

[79] οἷον ἐπεὶ ὁ θεὶς πυρὸς ἴδιον εἶναι τὸ ὁμοιότατον ψυχῇ ἀγνωστοτέρῳ, E 2, 129b9-11. For other examples in which the act of uttering is expressed by "to state" cf. E 2, 129b18f.; 3, 131a8f,; 4, 133a8f.; 5, 134b6f.; 9, 139a18f., et al.

[80] οἷον ἐπεὶ ὁ εἴπας ζῴου ἴδιον τὸ αἴσθησιν ἔχειν, E 2, 129b26. For other examples in which the act of uttering is expressed by "to say" cf. E 2, 130b8.; 4, 132b31f.; 5, 134a8f.; 9, 138b30f., et al.

[81] καθάπερ εἴ τις ἴδιον ἀποδοίη πυρὸς σῶμα τὸ λεπτότατον τῶν σωμάτων, E 2, 130a36f. For other examples in which the act of uttering is expressed by "to render" cf. E 2, a39-b1; 4, 132b21f.; 5, 134a14f; 9, 139a4f., et al.

[82] E 6, 135b12. 16. 21f., etc.

[83] Z 2, 139b20f.; cf. 139b32f., 140a7f., and many others

For example, when he says that an odd number is a number which has a middle, [...] so that this could not be a *definition* (ὁρισμός) of 'odd'[84]

For example, if he says that medicine is a science of reality. [...] Obviously, therefore, such a definition is not a *definition* (ὁρισμός) of any science; for the definition ought to be peculiar to one thing, not common to many.[85]

Whereas the word "definition" does not seem to have been explicitly mentioned in the thesis, it is explicitly stated in the conclusion and this makes clear that it had to be in some way indicated that the predicate in the thesis is asserted as a definition. The fact that the thesis is refuted by establishing for instance that it is not peculiar to the subject (as in the second example) only makes sense, if the opponent explicitly says that his thesis is meant to be a definition. Otherwise the opponent could simply say that the predication was not meant to be peculiar and would thus not be refuted. One way of specifying that the predication in the thesis represents a definition is to explicitly assert the predicate to be a definition of the subject, as Aristotle formulates problemata in A 4, 101b32f., i.e. 'A is definition of B'. The fact that in the examples of definitions given in Z the word "definition" is not explicitly stated could be explained by interpreting these theses as short forms of full theses. Alternatively, one could speculate that in an Academic debate it could be ruled that during a certain period of time all the theses dealt with have to be definitions. What is at any rate important is that the thesis was claimed to be a definition, in whatever way, and the easiest way to represent it was to name the definition explicitly, as Aristotle does in A 4, which is the systematic part of the *Topics*.

2.4. *The form of problemata in B*

2.4.1. *To belong (ὑπάρχειν)*

Before proceeding with the investigation of concrete examples in book B, I shall first establish further what it means to say that a sumbebekos belongs to a subject and how this belonging can be further specified.

In the case of the predicables of genus, proprium, and definition, their belonging is explicitly specified as such, whereas in the case of sumbebekos it is not. The external specifications indicate the way of predication: a proprium not only has to belong to the subject but it also has to belong convertibly, and correspondingly in the case of genus and definition. A sumbebekos on the other hand only has to belong. The level of the predicate belonging to a subject, i.e. the level of pure predication, is common to all predicables, whereas sumbebekos has this level only.

The question arises whether there are any differences at this very level between a sumbebekos and the other predicables. Indeed, there is a difference. As far as the construction of a sumbebekos is concerned there are two sorts of quantification: universal (τὸ καθόλου) and particular belonging (τὸ ἐπὶ μέρους) (154b33-155a2). In the case of the construction[86] of a definition,

---

[84] Z 12, 149a30f.; 34f.
[85] Z 12, 149b6f.; 21.
[86] I am interested here in the requirements which have to be fulfilled in order for a predicate to be a definition, proprium, etc., and thus in the case of construction. Of course, in

proprium and genus, universal belonging (παντὶ ὑπάρχει) is always required.[87] This seems quite clear: a definition of man has to belong to all men, the same goes for proprium and genus; when we say that animal is the genus of man we imply, on the level of belonging, that all men are animals.[88] In the case of sumbebekos on the other hand it is clearly correct to say that 'Animal belongs to all men' and also that 'Animal belongs to some man'.[89] Universally asserted sumbebekota are easier to destroy, whereas the particularly asserted sumbebekota are easier to construct.[90]

How is the verb belonging (ὑπάρχειν) here, which constitutes entirely the sumbebekos and partly the definition, proprium and genus, to be understood? A clear answer to this is found in Z 1, 139a36-b3, where it is explained how to destroy the definition with the help of the topoi of sumbebekos, which is one of five ways of destroying the definition (139a25-27):

> Whether, then, the definition is not also true (μὴ ἀληθεύεται) of that of which the name is true must be examined with the help of the topoi of the sumbebekos. For there too the investigation is concerned with the question of whether so and so is true or not (πότερον ἀληθὲς ἢ οὐκ ἀληθές). For whenever we argue that a sumbebekos belongs (ὅτι ὑπάρχει τὸ συμ-βεβηκὸς διαλεγώμεθα), we assert it to be true (ὅτι ἀληθὲς λέγομεν), while whenever we argue that it does not belong (ὅτι οὐχ ὑπάρχει), we assert it to be untrue (ὅτι οὐκ ἀληθές).

Thus, when we argue that a predicate is a sumbebekos of a given subject, we assert that the predicate belongs truly; when we argue that a predicate is not a sumbebekos of a given subject, we assert that it is not true that it belongs.[91] In this sense it is also clear that we can say that 'Some men are animals' since it is simply true to say that some men are animals, even though it is not, so to speak, the exhaustive truth, since actually all men are animals.

2.4.2. Sumbebekos in B

Looking at topoi of sumbebekos in book B it is fairly clear that sumbebekos here has the meaning as defined above, and not that of the accident, because with the help of the topoi here we establish that a predicate belongs or does not belong to a subject. There are passages in which to belong as a sumbebekos is specified as an assertion that a predicate belongs truly as defined in Z 1, 139a38-b1 as discussed above. In B 1, 109a27-30 Aristotle gives the

---

the case of destruction of the definition, proprium, or genus we destroy these predicables by proving that they do not belong universally or that they belong only *particularly*. But it is clearly not this belonging which Aristotle means by particular belonging (ἐπὶ μέρους) in 154b36, which can be constructed and destroyed; it refers, as well as the universal belonging (τὸ καθόλου), to the positive part of the problema which claims to constitute a predicable.

[87] The quantification obviously does not count as a specification of ὑπάρχειν ("οὕτως"), since otherwise Aristotle would not assert that for sumbebekos "the way it belongs" (πῶς ὑπάρχει) is not indicated.

[88] In the definitions of the predicables in A 5 Aristotle does not explicitly mention that definition, proprium and genus have to belong *universally*—this is obviously taken for granted.

[89] Aristotle makes this distinction between universal and particular problemata expressing a sumbebekos in B 108b34-109a1.

[90] H 5, 154b33-155a2.

[91] Cf. also *Met.* Δ 7, 1017a31-35.

definition of the contradictory of "to make a true statement" (ἀληθεύεσθαι), namely that of "to make a false statement" (ψεύδεσθαι) as "to say that something belongs to a thing which does not belong to it" (τὸ μὴ ὑπάρχον ὑπάρχειν τινὶ λέγοντες). This obviously indicates the error when sumbebekos has been wrongly assigned. Thus, we read in 109b30-32 and b39-110a1:

> Another topos is to make definitions both of the sumbebekos and of its subject [...] and see if anything untrue has been assumed as true in the definitions.[92]
> Again, to see if [...]; for then it will be obvious whether the statement is true or false.[93]

The problemata are formulated with the help of the verb "to belong"[94] or simply "to be" or some other verb.[95] The concrete examples of problemata confirm that sumbebekos can represent a predicate which actually is a genus, proprium or definition, or neither of them, i.e. an accident as defined in the first definition. The most clear example is "Man is animal" in B 8, 113b17f., because "Animal is the genus of man" is Aristotle's standard example for a genus-predication[96]. Another good example is "Pleasure is good", which often occurs in B[97] and in the form "Good is the genus of pleasure" again in Δ.[98] There are also examples of predications which clearly satisfy the definition of accident-(1), i.e. are neither genus, proprium or definition but still belong to the subject, such as "of opposites the knowledge is the same",[99] "there is correctness and error in perception",[100] "the soul is in motion"[101] or "X is white/good".[102]

The semantical analysis of the word συμβεβηκός in the few passages in which it occurs in B points in the same direction. Thus the occurrence of this word cited in the first line of the passage above clearly means sumbebekos or attribute and not accident, since the investigation-instruction "to see whether anything untrue has been assumed as true" points to the meaning of sumbebekos as defined in H 5. In the topos in B 7, 113a20-23 again συμ- βεβηκός seems to have the meaning of an attribute and not an accident:

---

[92] ἄλλος τὸ λόγους ποιεῖν τοῦ τε συμβεβηκότος καὶ ᾧ συμβέβηκεν (...) εἶτα σκοπεῖν εἴ τι μὴ ἀληθὲς ἐν τοῖς λόγοις ὡς ἀληθὲς εἴληπται.
[93] καὶ εἰ (...) οὕτω γὰρ καταφανὲς ἔσται πότερον ἀληθὲς ἢ ψεῦδος τὸ ῥηθέν.
[94] Cf. e.g. 110a30-b1, 111a14, 112a27-30, 113a23, 113b9-14.
[95] Cf. e.g. 109b34, 37f., 110a4, b11f., 111a15f., b10f.
[96] Cf. e.g. A 4, 101b31; 5, 102a34f.; B 1, 109a16f.
In B 8, 113b15-26 Aristotle does not use the word συμβεβηκός, as he does not in most topoi, but in Δ 4, 124b7f. this topos is explicitly referred to as a topos of sumbebekos.
[97] B 1, 108b34-109a1; Γ 6, 119a39f., 120a6-27; B 10, 114b39-115a5 (construction and destruction); in the last example the expression (οὐ) συμβεβηκέναι (a4f.) is explicitly used.
[98] Δ 1, 120b17-19 (destruction); 4, 124a17-20 (construction); 124b8-14 (destruction and construction).
[99] B 2, 109b17.
[100] B 4, 111a15f.
[101] B 4, 111b5.
[102] B 11, 115a27-29.

Moreover, if the sumbebekos of a thing has a contrary, see whether it belongs to that (subject) to which the sumbebekos has been said to belong; for if the former belongs the latter could not belong; for it is impossible for two contraries to belong to the same thing at the same time.[103]

It would be strange to restrict the principle that two contraries cannot belong to the same thing to accidents alone. Contraries can certainly also stand for contrary genera, propria, and definitions.[104]

The passage at B 6, 112b21-26 seems to be controversial:

> Moreover, look and see if he has stated a thing to be a sumbebekos of itself (αὐτὸ αὐτῷ συμβεβηκὸς ἔθηκεν), taking it to be a different thing because it has a different name, as Prodicus used to divide pleasures into joy and delight and merriment; for all these are names for the same thing, namely pleasure. If therefore any one says that joy is a sumbebekos of merriment, he would be declaring it to be a sumbebekos of itself.

Prodicus' dividing pleasure into three parts could be expressed as the sentence "Pleasure is joy, delight or merriment". Aristotle seems to call joy, delight and merriment sumbebekota of pleasure. These are not accidents of pleasure, but simply attributes which have been claimed to belong to pleasure. The error is that they are just different names of the same thing, namely pleasure, and we predicate them of pleasure as if they were something different, because the name is different. We would of course have the same error when only one of the three names is predicated of pleasure, or when one of the three names is predicated of another one, as is the case in the example Aristotle gives—"joy is sumbebekos of merriment". The error here would be that of unnecessary double predication (δίς τὸ αὐτὸ λέγειν).[105] The person who commits this error makes things less clear and seems to babble.[106]

However, it is also possible to interpret sumbebekos as an accident here and argue that the error committed is the one described in E 5, 135a11-19 of a thing being stated as a predicable of itself by using another word. The error is that "a thing itself always shows its own essence (αὐτὸ γὰρ αὐτῷ πᾶν τὸ εἶναι δηλοῖ), and what shows the essence is not a proprium but a definition"; in the case of the accident the error would be accordingly that that which indicates the essence is not an accident.

---

[103] I shall discuss this topos in more detail on pp. 104f.

[104] Examples for contrary accidents come easily to mind: black and white, cold and warm, etc. An example for contrary genera is: virtue (ἀρετή), being the genus of justice (δικαιοσύνη) and vice (κακία), being the genus of injustice (ἀδικία) (Δ 3, 123b31-33); propria: "object of choice" (αἱρετόν) (proprium of "good" (ἀγαθόν)) and "object of avoidance" (φευκτόν (proprium of "evil" (κακὸν)) (E 6, 135b14-16; also B 8, 113b31-33); definitions: productive of good (τὸ ποιητικὸν ἀγαθοῦ) (definition of beneficial (ὠφέλιμον)) and productive of evil (τὸ ποιητικὸν κακοῦ) (definition of harmful (βλαβερόν)) (Z 9, 147a31ff.). With the help of the above topos we can for example prove that the good (ἀγαθόν) is not an object of avoidance (φευκτόν) by proving that it is an object of choice (αἱρετόν).

[105] As described in Z 3, 140b27-141a14, especially 141a4-14 or in E 2, 130a29-b10, especially a39-b5.

[106] E 2, 130a32-34.

2.4.3. *The meaning of sumbebekos*

Thus it seems that sumbebekos can express anything that may be further specified as genus, proprium and definition as well as attributes which cannot be further specified as genus, proprium and definition. What then is a sumbebekos? Sainati (1968), pp. 70ff. says it signifies "predicate". Such an interpretation is tempting, but I think not entirely correct. It is better to understand it as 'attribute', as I have already rendered sumbebekos in several passages—the justification is set out below.

A predicate P is a sumbebekos of S, if P belongs (ὑπάρχει)[107] to S; Now, if sumbebekos meant simply "predicate", then there would be no difference between it and the standard word Aristotle uses for a predicate (τὸ κατηγορούμενον[108]). However, Aristotle seems to treat sumbebekos on the same level as genus, proprium and definition: Aristotle says of them that these have to belong, not that they have to belong as a sumbebekos. Thus, sumbebekos, being an entity of the same kind as genus, proprium and definition, represents the *content* expressed by the predicate, and this is why I think that it is best understood as 'attribute'.[109] Sumbebekos is not specified in the way it belongs; it can be further specified as genus, proprium or definition or in fact none of the three. The sumbebekos is in fact specified insofar as the way of belonging is not explicitly specified in the problema. This is arguably the reason why Aristotle never calls the other predicables sumbebekota, but only that the other predicables have to belong in the way that sumbebekota have to belong. Sumbebekos is specified by its form in the problema as an *unspecified* attribute.[110] Thus, it would appear that although a sumbebekos might possibly be further specified as genus, proprium, or definition, once it has been specified as one of them it is not a sumbebekos any more,[111] although it is certainly still a predicate. In any case, only if

---

[107] The word "to belong" (ὑπάρχειν) could of course be replaced by some other word expressing predication in the *Topics*: "to be predicated of" (κατηγορεῖσθαι κατά τινος), "to be said of" (λέγεσθαι), "to be truly predicated of" (ἀληθεύεσθαι), etc.

[108] We find this word in many places in the *Topics*: A, 102a31 (participle), b20 (noun), 103b8, Δ 122a13f., 127b29, E, 132b23 (noun), 136a6, 15 (noun), H, 152b25f.(noun), 153a16 (noun) (and some others) (also in the form of τὸ ἀντικατηγορούμενον: A, 103b11, E, 132a4, 7, al.).

[109] Συμβαίνειν as a word of the everyday-language certainly often has the meaning of something's happening accidentally, and Aristotle in fact sometimes invokes this usage when he seeks to make clear what he means by an accident: cf. e.g. *APst.* A 4, 73b11-13 (...συνέβη, φαμέν, τοῦτο). But we also find occurrences of it where nothing accidental seems to be involved: cf. e.g. *Rhet.* B 22, 1396 b15ff.: ἴδια δὲ μηδενὶ ἄλλῳ συμβέβηκεν ἢ τῷ Ἀχιλλεῖ, οἷον τὸ ἀποκτεῖναι τὸν Ἕκτορα ... (Rhys Roberts (1984) translates "...are true of Achilles alone ..."; Freese (1926) translates "...what belongs to Achilles, but to no one else ..."). Or *Cat.* 7, 7a22-25; 34-37: περιαιρουμένων ἁπάντων ὅσα συμβεβηκότα ἐστὶ τῷ δεσπότῃ, οἷον τὸ δίποδι εἶναι, τὸ ἐπιστήμης δεκτικῷ, τὸ ἀνθρώπῳ (a35-37); "being an animal" or "being two-footed" are surely not accidents of master, but simply attributes of him. Cf. also, amongst others, *Soph. El.* 5, 166b28-36 ("being a man" is an attribute, not an accident of Koriskus or Socrates) and *Met.* B 2, 997a25-34 (where Ross (1924), p. 230 correctly translates συμβεβηκότα (ll.26, 29, 33) as "attributes" and equates them with πάθη in 997a7).

[110] In the same way as Aristotle says of a definition that it is peculiar to the subject, not a proprium.

sumbebekos is understood as an attribute, whether specified as unspecified in the above sense or not, rather than a predicate does it become clear how Aristotle could have taken the next step in the meaning of the accident as defined in the first definition, simply by narrowing down the scope of sumbebekos by excluding the other three predicables, and that he did not hesitate simply to add topoi about sumbebekos without any warning, as he does in B 2, 109a34-b12.

2.4.4. Accident

I believe along with Brunschwig and Sainati, that the notion of the accident as defined in the first definition is a later development. The topos in B 1, 109a34-b12 is clearly added later. It is the only topos in B where the first definition of the accident is presupposed. The subject-matter which is the confusion between genus and sumbebekos suggest very much that it belongs to the group of topoi at the very beginning of Δ,[112] where συμβεβηκός (120b21f.) has the meaning of the accident-(1). Συμβεβηκός in this specific meaning can be found in a few places in E and Z.[113] The second definition seems to be an even later 'discovery'. Aristotle mentions it as the second definition of the accident in A 5, 102b6-9 and claims in b10-14 that it is better than the first definition. We find this definition only twice in use in the rest of the *Topics*: Δ 1, 120b30-35 and Z 6, 144a23-27. In the first case it is especially clear that it is a later addition. This topos refutes exactly the same thesis as the preceding one (120b15-29), namely "movement is genus of the soul", with the difference that in this topos the second definition is used whereas in the preceding one the argument is that the asserted genus is not predicated in the essence (ἐν τῷ τί ἐστι), but as an accident (ὡς συμβεβηκός); Aristotle clearly thinks that this is a better topos: "Especially (μάλιστα) you should look at the definition of accident [the second one] ...".

It is striking that the typical examples Aristotle gives for accidents in A 5, "to be white" and "to sit" (λευκόν and καθῆσθαι) scarcely occur in B: the former occurs in the very first topos in B 2 and in B 11. A 11, 105a3-7 in fact says that problemata containing some accidents were too trivial to occur in a dialectical debate and that "people who are puzzled to know whether snow is white or not need perception" (105a7). However, this example is the most

---

[111] This might sound slightly strange. A European whose nationality has been further specified as French or English surely still remains a European. However, the above analogy is misleading in that "being European" is already a specified attribute. A good analogous example of an unspecified attribute would be "of unspecified citizenship": when the citizenship of a man of unspecified citizenship has been further specified, he is not of unspecified citizenship any more (although it might turn out that he is not a citizen of any state, if he is stateless, just as sumbebekos might turn out to be neither definition, proprium or genus, but an accident). In the context of dialectical debates in which sumbebekos in contrast to the other three predicables is not explicitly stated as such in the problema, it seems to me to be reasonable to understand sumbebekos in this way, especially given the fact that in the *Topics* we find expressions of the form 'A belong as (ὑπάρχει ὡς) genus to B', but never 'A συμβέβηκε as genus to B' (ἴδια in *Rhet*. B 22, 1396b15 cited in fn. 109 above does not refer to the *predicable* propria). Συμβεβηκός occuring in other writings such as cited in fn. 109 above simply means of course 'attribute'.

[112] Δ 1, 120b15-121a9.

[113] E 4, 133b15-134a4; Z 5, 142b35-143a8;12, 149b4-23; in the latter two we have the distinction between "essentially" (καθ' αὐτό) and "accidentally" (κατὰ συμβεβηκός).

common instance of an accident-predication in Δ.[114] It seems that Aristotle was mainly interested in such accidental predications insofar as the opponent incorrectly assigned them as a genus i.e. committed the opposite error that Aristotle describes in B 2, 109a34-36, where the genus is incorrectly assigned as an accident, and of which he says that it most often occurs in the case of accident and genus.

In any case, the two definitions of the accident appear to be chronologically later and it certainly does not fit the system of predicables orientated to definition in H 5. In order to destroy the definition we have to show that it (or its parts) does not belong as a sumbebekos; in order to destroy the definition with the help of an accident-(1) or accident-(2) we would actually have to show that the definition does belong as an accident-(1) or accident-(2). In order to construct a definition, we have to show, among other things, that it belongs as a sumbebekos; showing that the definition belongs as an accident would actually destroy the definition.[115]

In this chapter I have shown that in the case of the topoi of genus, proprium, and definition (books Δ, E and Z) the conclusions (and the theses) of the arguments will always read: 'A is /is not the genus/ proprium/ definition of B'. However, in the case of the topoi of sumbebekos, the conclusions will always read 'A is/is not B' (book B); i.e. συμβεβηκός in book B most often carries the meaning of an 'attribute', not of 'accident' as it is always translated. It is very important to see this, since otherwise, i.e. when taking συμβεβηκός as defined in A 5, the topoi in book B might appear incomprehensible. In the very rare cases of topoi of accident-(1) and accident-(2) the conclusion will be 'A is/is not an accident of B'. This also means that one part of the hypothesis of the hypothetical syllogism has one of the forms mentioned. Thus the general terms will not just be terms such as "contrary" and others (contained by the so-called "most opportune" topoi), given as examples by Alexander, but also specified or unspecified predicables. Topoi of sumbebekos are more important than those of the other predicables[116] since they deal with the level of belonging only, which is common to all the other predicables as well. Thus, they can also be used for destruction of the genus, proprium and definition. Topoi of genus and proprium can also be used for the destruction of definitions.

---

[114] Main examples are: "snow/swan is that which is white" (χίων (κύκνος) ὅπερ λευκόν) (120b23; b28; b38f.; 127b2) and "the soul is that which is movement" (ἡ ψυχὴ ὅπερ κινούμενον) (120b24).

[115] Thus, it is not surprising that Theophrastus "separated the accident [certainly in the sense of accident-(2)]from the other predicables, as it was not subsumed under definition (ὡς μὴ ὑπαγόμενον τῷ ὅρῳ)" (Alex., in Top. 55, 25f.): contingent predications have no place in a definition. He seems to have subsumed the topoi under two predicables (definition and accident) (cf. Proclus, in Parm. 635, 2-12). Alexander seems to me to be quite wrong in criticizing him for contravening Aristotle's dictum in Top. A 6, 102b35-38 (in Top. 55, 26f.). Aristotle's system of predicables certainly needed clarification.

[116] The most important topoi are the so-called "most opportune" topoi which can be used in conjunction with all predicables for destruction and construction and which occur in all books of the Topics; cf. Chapter Five, pp. 140-150.

CHAPTER FOUR

HYPOTHETICAL SYLLOGISMS—THE MAIN FORM OF ARGUMENTS
IN THE *TOPICS*

In this chapter I shall make it my task to establish thoroughly that the vast majority of the arguments in the *Topics* work as hypothetical syllogisms. I shall demonstrate this by pointing to particular arguments where structures of hypothetical syllogisms are clearly recognisable, by analysing arguments which Aristotle explicitly calls "hypothetical syllogisms" in the *Analytics* and the *Topics*, and by pointing to the hypothetical syllogisms which are ascribed to Theophrastus and which were clearly largely taken over from Aristotle. It seems to me that no entirely satisfactory account has been given to date of what a hypothetical syllogism actually is. Thus a large part of the chapter will be devoted to answering this question.

A. *Hypothetical syllogisms in the Prior Analytics: A 23, 29, and 44*

In the *Prior Analytics* A 23, 29 and 44 Aristotle makes some remarks about the hypothetical syllogism. It seems to be a general term for many kinds of arguments of which the one he describes in A 44, 50a19-25 and on which scholars writing on hypothetical syllogisms usually concentrate is only one specific type. A further example is the argument (or syllogism) per impossibile, as is explicitly stated in A 23, 40b25f. The common characteristic of the hypothetical syllogism is the following:

> In every case the syllogism leads up to the substituted proposition (πρὸς τὸ μεταλαμβανόμενον), but the required conclusion (τὸ δ' ἐξ ἀρχῆς) is concluded (περαίνεται) by means of an agreement or some other hypothesis (δι' ὁμολογίας ἢ τινος ἄλλης ὑποθέσεως).[1]

The argument per impossibile falls under this classification because the required conclusion here is shown by means of a hypothesis (τὸ δ' ἐξ ἀρχῆς ἐξ ὑποθέσεως δείκνυται) (A 23, 41a34). In A 29, 45b15-20 Aristotle mentions two further examples of hypothetical syllogisms (b17): those which proceed by substitution (κατὰ μετάληψιν) and the qualitative ones (κατὰ ποιότητα).[2] Alexander *in APr.* 324, 19-325, 24 explains that qualitative hypothetical syllogisms are those "from the greater or lesser or same degree" (ἀπὸ τοῦ μᾶλλον καὶ ἧττον καὶ ὁμοίως).[3]

---

[1] A 23, 41a38-b1; similarly in 29, 45b17-19.
[2] Line 17f. and also 41a38-b1 make it clear that in the case of the qualitative hypothetical syllogism (κατὰ ποιότητα) a substitution (μεταλαμβάνειν) also takes place. Thus, the hypothetical syllogism which proceeds by way of substitution (κατὰ μετάληψιν) seems to derive its name from a more specific meaning of substitution (μετάληψις). This is not unusual in Aristotle's terminology, cf. for example the broad and narrow meaning of proprium in *Top.* A 4, 101b19-23.
[3] Cf. also Philop. *in APr.* 301, 11-20.

In A 29, 45b19f. Aristotle writes that the different types of hypothetical syllogisms should be considered and analysed.[4] However, Aristotle does not do this anywhere in the *Analytics*. He only deals briefly with one kind of hypothetical syllogism, which he possibly means specifically by "on the basis of a concession" (δι' ὁμολογίας)[5] and which rests on likeness (ὁμοιότης),[6] and with the argument per impossibile, especially in B 11-14.

We find hypothetical syllogisms which rest on likeness in several places in the *Topics*.[7] The argument per impossibile is mentioned twice in book Θ[8] however we do not find per impossibile arguments in the form that they take in the *Analytics* in the central books of the *Topics* where the topoi are listed (B-H).

It would appear that the origins of the two other hypothetical syllogisms Aristotle mentioned in the *Analytics* are found in the *Topics*. The topos from the greater, the lesser and the like degree (ἐκ τοῦ μᾶλλον καὶ ἧττον καὶ ὁμοίως), most explicitly stated in B 10, 114b37-115a14, tells us how the hypothesis of the qualitative hypothetical syllogism (κατὰ ποιότητα) works. The topoi in B 4, 111b17-23 and 5, 112a16-23, where the term substitution (μετάληψις) occurs, tell us how to construct the hypothetical syllogism proceeding by way of substitution (κατὰ μετάληψιν) and how this works.

B. *Theophrastus' list of hypothetical syllogisms*

There are also some other topoi in the *Topics* which tell us how to construct hypothetical syllogisms which are not mentioned in the *Analytics*, but which Alexander mentions in his commentary on *APr.* A 44, 50a39-b2.[9] Aristotle writes in this passage:

> Many other conclusions are reached by hypothesis (περαίνονται ἐξ ὑποθέσεως), and these require further study and clear explanation.[10] We

---

[4] ἐπισκέψασθαι δὲ δεῖ καὶ διελεῖν ποσαχῶς οἱ ἐξ ὑποθέσεως.

[5] A 23, 41a40f. If he does, then the name is scarcely more fortunate than "proceeding by way of substitution" (κατὰ μετάληψιν), since all hypotheses have to be agreed. Alex. *in Top.* 122, 16f. at any rate calls the hypothetical syllogism in *Top.* A 18 "on the basis of a concession" (ἐξ ὁμολογίας) and *in APr.* 325, 37-326, 1 he enumerates it in a row with diairetic and metaleptic hypothetical syllogisms as a separate kind of hypothetical syllogism.

[6] This becomes clear only in *Top.* A 18, 108b7-19. In B 10, 114b25f. and in Θ 1, 156b10-17 Aristotle used a very similar example to the one he used in *APr.* A 44, 50a19f. and 34f. to illustrate likeness (ὁμοιότης). I shall deal with this in detail on pp. 111 and 120f.

[7] A 18, 108b7-19; B 3, 110a37-b4; Γ 6, 119b35-120a5.

[8] Θ 2, 157b34-158a2; 12, 162b5-7. In the first passge, interestingly, Aristotle advises the questioner to avoid the argument per impossibile, because people often dispute that the conclusion reached really is impossible.

[9] Alex. *in APr.* 389, 31-390, 9. I should stress here that I treat Alexander's passage below insofar as it is of interest to material found in the *Topics* and the *Analytics*. For a more in-depth treatment of the passage, with discussion of problems specific to Alexander's text and references and parallels to other post-Aristotelian writers (I usually content myself with citing what seems to me to be the most important source) I refer to Barnes (1985a). Also, I use the improved text of Barnes (1985a), p. 276.

[10] Cf. also A 29, 45b19f.

shall describe in sequel their differences and the various ways in which hypothetical arguments are formed.

Alexander remarks that no book by Aristotle on the hypothetical syllogisms is in circulation, but that "Theophrastus refers to them in his own *Analytics*, and so do Eudemus and some others of Aristotle's associates" (*in APr.* 390, 2f.). Alexander then (*in APr.* 390, 3-9) enumerates the hypothetical syllogisms that he thinks Aristotle presumably had in mind (λέγοι δ' ἄν). Alexander uses both the Peripatetic and the Stoic terminology when describing the first two hypothetical arguments based on the conditional (συνεχές versus συνημμένον and πρόσληψις) and on the disjunctive premiss (διαιρετικόν versus διεζευγμένον):[11]

> 1. hypothetical arguments which proceed by way of a continuous proposition, which is also called a connected proposition, together with the additional assumption (διὰ συνεχοῦς, ὃ καὶ συνημμένον λέγεται, καὶ τῆς προσλήψεως ὑποθετικούς)
> 2. those which proceed by way of a diairetic or disjunctive proposition (καὶ διὰ τοῦ διαιρετικοῦ τε καὶ διεζευγμένου)
> 3. and maybe also those which proceed by way of a negated conjunction, if they are indeed different from the ones mentioned (ἢ καὶ διὰ ἀποφατικῆς συμπλοκῆς, εἰ ἄρα οὗτοι ἕτεροι τῶν προειρημένων).
>
> In addition to those mentioned above, there will also be (παρὰ τοὺς εἰρημένους εἶεν καὶ)
>
> 4. arguments on the basis of analogy (οἱ ἐξ ἀναλογίας)
> 5. and those which they call "qualitative", i.e. arguments from the greater, lesser or like degree (καὶ οὓς λέγουσι κατὰ ποιότητα, τοὺς ἀπὸ τοῦ μᾶλλον καὶ ἧττον καὶ ὁμοίως,)
> 6. and whatever other varieties of arguments based on a hypothesis there are, which have been discussed elswhere (καὶ εἴ τινες ἄλλαι τῶν ἐξ ὑποθέσεως διαφοραὶ [προτάσεών] εἰσι, περὶ ὧν ἐν ἄλλοις εἴρηται).

C. *The topoi for the construction of corresponding hypothetical syllogisms found in the Topics*

Barnes (1985a) has argued that Alexander clearly implies, although he does not state entirely explicitly, that the hypothetical arguments listed above were dealt with by Theophrastus and his associates, as opposed to many other scholars who insist that Alexander does not state this explicitly, presuming usually that hypothetical syllogisms were developed much later[12]. My investigation confirms Barnes' interpretation and I make the stronger claim that Aristotle himself had already, to a considerable extent, dealt with these hypothetical arguments. Theophrastus, and other early Peripatetics, merely developed them further. My main evidence is of course the arguments

---
[11] On the terminology cf. Frede (1974), p. 80 fn.18 and p.93 fn.20.
[12] Barnes (1985a), p. 564.

themselves found in the *Topics* which clearly correspond to those which Peripatetics described as hypothetical syllogisms;[13] the terminology is often the same or can be clearly traced back to Aristotle. A further argument is that in the *Analytics*, Aristotle formulates the common characteristic of hypothetical syllogisms (*APr.* A 23, 41a38-b1), promises a more thorough treatment of them, and even mentions some of them using specific names.[14] The formulation of a common characteristic of the hypothetical syllogisms and the existence of a terminology seems to me to presuppose that Aristotle had quite a clear notion of what the hypothetical syllogisms were; the terminology was probably settled at the latest by his pupils. The fact that "no book on them is in circulation" is clearly not evidence enough to show that Aristotle did not hold lectures on the subject. In the following sections I shall go through the hypothetical syllogisms found in the *Topics* (and partly in the *Prior Analytics*) which clearly correspond to those listed by Alexander.

1. *Hypothetical syllogisms proceeding by way of a continuous proposition together with the additional assumption*

In his commentary on *APr.* A 29, 45b15-20 where Aristotle mentions the hypothetical syllogism which proceeds by way of substitution (κατὰ μετά- ληψιν) Alexander, *in APr.* 324, 17 tells us that "what the moderns (οἱ νεώτεροι) call 'the additional premiss' (πρόσληψιν) Aristotle's associates (οἱ περὶ 'Αριστοτέλη) [i.e. the Peripatetics] used to call 'substitution' (μετάληψιν)."[15] Thus Alexander certainly refers to this hypothetical syllogism that Aristotle calls "proceeding by way of substitution" (κατὰ μετάληψιν), the origins of which are found in *Top.* B 4, 111b17-23; the destructive part can also be found in B 5, 112a16-23. The topos runs:

> Moreover, investigate with regard to what is set forth (τοῦ προκειμένου), /what is such that if it is the case (τίνος ὄντος) what is set forth is the case (τὸ προκείμενον ἔστι)/ (1), or /what is such that it is necessarily the case (τί ἐστιν ἐξ ἀνάγκης) if what is set forth is the case (εἰ τὸ προκείμενον ἔστι)/ (2).
> For constructive purposes investigate /what is such that if it is the case what is set forth is the case/ (1) (for if the former is shown to hold (ἐκεῖνο δειχθῇ ὑπάρχον[16]), what is set forth will also have been shown (δεδειγμένον ἔσται));
> for destructive purposes investigate /what is such that it is the case if what is set forth is the case/ (2) (for if we show that what follows what is set forth (τὸ ἀκόλουθον τῷ προκειμένῳ μὴ ὄν) is not the case, we shall have destroyed what is set forth (ἀνῃρηκότες ἐσόμεθα τὸ προκείμενον)).

---

[13] The main sources are, apart from Alexander's commentaries on the *Prior Analytics* and the *Topics*: Ammonius *in APr.*, pp. XIf. (Praefatio by Pseudo-Ammonius), Galen's *Institutio logica* and Boethius' *De syllogismis hypotheticis*.

[14] κατὰ μετάληψιν, κατὰ ποιότητα, ἐξ ὁμολογίας.

[15] However, sometimes the associates "also use the word 'additional premiss' instead of 'substitution'" (Alex. *in APr.* 264, 5f.).

[16] The word ὑπάρχον here is obviously used parallel to ὄν in b23 (penultimate line in the text cited above) and in this context simply means "to hold" or "to be the case".

I shall call this argument 'metaleptic hypothetical syllogism' and abbreviate it as (Hm); let (Hm)c stand for the constructive part, (Hm)d for the destructive part of the argument.[17] It can be schematized in the following way:

(Hm)c	(Hm)d
If P, then Q	If Q, then P.
.	.
.	.
P.	not P.
Hence Q	Hence not Q.

P and Q stand for propositions; the points above P/not P stand for a proof.

It is absolutely clear that Aristotle is speaking here about propositions, not predicates. Expressions typical of a hypothetical syllogism are used here (genitivus absolutus in the singular, aorist-future perfect) which will be discussed later in the chapter; cf. also the predecessor of this topos in Θ 1, 156b27-30 which I discussed on pp. 34f. above, where Aristotle also clearly refers to propositions. The exact workings of this hypothetical syllogism will be explained later. The above schematization needs an explanation, particularly the use of letters in place of propositions in the argument-schema. In addition, the argument above has been interpreted by two other scholars who require mention.

Brunschwig (1967), p. 44 n.3 interprets the passage in the same way as I do. He sees in it a clear confirmation of his interpretation of the workings of the topoi according to Modus ponens and Modus tollens given in his introduction, pp. XXXVIII-XLII. However, he does not explain the exact *working* of the topos in the argument.[18] Moreover, although it is true that many

---

[17] 'H' stands for 'hypothetical syllogism', 'm' for 'metaleptic' or 'proceeding by way of substitution' (κατὰ μετάληψιν in Greek), 'c' for 'constructive' 'd' for 'destructive'.

[18] Brunschwig (1967), p. XXXIX defines topos metaphorically as «une machine à faire des prémisses à partir d'une conclusion donée»; similarly, Pelletier (1985), p. 405. Given a thesis P, the topos helps the questioner to find a premiss Q which is either implied by P (in the case of destruction) or which implies P (in the case of construction) (in the former case Q is a necessary, in the latter a sufficient condition of P). I agree with Brunschwig except that I would say that with the help of the topos not just the premiss 'Q' is found, but the hypothetical premiss 'If P, then Q' or 'If Q, then P' (or in fact some other kind of hypothetical premiss), i.e. I take topos to be part of the argument. It seems to me that my interpretation of topos as a principle and compound proposition tells us how the topos manages to 'produce' premisses and the desired conclusion. Topos itself is a complex propositional schema which is explicitly stated as a hypothetical premiss either as a schema or as an instance of the schema, i.e. with concrete terms. Let us take the Law of Contraposition as an example (which is stated in *Top.* B 8, 113b15-26; cf. pp. 141f. below): 'A is B if and only if not-B is not-A.' Given the conclusion 'A is B', the Law or Topos of Contraposition does not just help us to find the premiss 'not-B is not-A', replacing A and B by concrete terms, but, in the case of destruction, the entire implication 'If A is B, then not-B is not-A' is found as a premiss, and, in the case of construction, the implication 'If not-B is not-A, then A is B'. Then, by destroying or constructing 'not-B is not-A' as the minor premiss, we destroy or construct 'A is B' using Modus tollens or Modus ponens respectively. As will become clear, the implication is not the only form the topos can take; e.g., to a given conclusion 'A is B' we can create, with the help of the topos in the form of the Law of the Excluded Middle (cf. *Top.* B 6, 112a24-31 and pp. 103f. below), the hypothetical premiss 'A is either B or not-B'. The exact workings of the topos-hypothesis will be given in this chapter, pp. 113ff.

arguments in the *Topics* are governed by what would nowadays be described as Modus ponens and tollens, not all of them are; the other kinds of hypothetical syllogisms will be discussed on the following pages.[19]

Sainati (1968), pp. 51-54, gives another interpretation of the argument above. He remarks, p. 53, that if this passage is taken in its own right, Modus ponens and tollens appear to be evident here, which would be the beginning of propositional logic, but that «in realtà, ad Aristotele manca il concetto di proposizione atomica come unità elementare e non analizzata di un più complesso costrutto proposizionale.» Sainati maintains that the argument-schema should be interpreted in terms of the logic of classes rather than propositional logic and finds his interpretation confirmed by the topos on the next Bekker-page in B 5, 112a16-23.

In the first instance, it is true to a large extent that Aristotle lacks the concept of an atomic proposition as an elementary unit. However, it is not missing completely. His very definition of the syllogism has a propositional character.[20] The very examples above show that Aristotle expressed arguments with respect to relations between propositions. The fact that "to follow/be consequent upon" (ἕπεσθαι/ἀκολουθεῖν), "to substitute" (μεταλαμβάνειν), and other words sometimes relate to terms, but sometimes to propositions show that Aristotle could think of propositions as elementary objects between which certain relations exist. I shall show that this is the case with respect to "to follow" shortly; as to "to substitute" this fact has been observed by many scholars and may thus be taken for granted.[21]

Secondly, Sainati seems to assume that because the topos in B 5, 112a16-21 comes after the topos in B 4, 111b17-23, it is also chronologically later and is thus a further interpretation of the latter one. Given the character of Aristotle's writings which are lecture notes not intended for publication and reworked again and again, Sainati's assumption cannot be sustained. In fact I am rather inclined to assume that the topos in B 4, 111b17-23 has been inserted later, for reasons which I shall shortly describe as 'reductionism' (see pp. 111-113) in the *Topics*.

Thirdly, the interpretation Sainati gives of the topos in B 5, 112a16-21, which he maintains also applies to the one in B 4, seems to me to be mistaken. The text reads:

> Further, anyone who has asserted something (πᾶς ὁ εἰρηκὼς ὁτιοῦν) has in a way asserted many things (πολλὰ εἴρηκεν), because everything is necessarily followed by many things (πλείω ἑκάστῳ ἐξ ἀνάγκης ἀκόλουθά ἐστιν): e.g. he who has said that something is a man (οἷον ὁ

---

[19] Also, it is striking that Brunschwig, p. 51n.3 and 52n.2 stresses that «consequence» (ἀκολούθησις) denotes «la relation entre l'attribut et le sujet d'une même proposition, non la relation qui peut s'établir entre deux propositions.» Here and in a few other passages this is obviously not the case. Correspondingly, he takes μετάληψις in 112a22 to be «le terme remplaçant», (p. 46n.6) whereas it clearly designates a proposition, not a term.

[20] Συλλογισμός is in fact now usually understood as deduction; cf. Smiley (1973) and Barnes (1981), p. 23ff. Cf. also Enskat (1986), p. 132: „[Aristoteles'] undifferenzierte Syllogismusdefinition [hat] ganz genau das syntaktische Abstraktionsniveau der Aussagenlogik" (although I do not agree with Enskat that this character of the definition of the syllogism precludes arguments of propositional logic—it obviously covers hypothetical syllogisms).

[21] Cf. e.g. Striker (1979), p. 43n 18.

εἰρηκὼς ἄνθρωπον εἶναι) has also said that it is an animal and that it is animate and that it is receptive of reason and knowledge (καὶ ὅτι ζῷον ἐστιν εἴρηκε καὶ ὅτι ἔμψυχον καὶ ὅτι δίπουν καὶ ὅτι νοῦ καὶ ἐπιστήμης δεκτικόν); so that if any one of these consequents is demolished (ὥστε ὁποιουοῦν ἑνὸς τῶν ἀκολούθων ἀναιρεθέντος), the original assertion is demolished as well (ἀναιρεῖται καὶ τὸ ἐν ἀρχῇ).
But we must beware here of substituting the thesis (τὴν μετάληψιν ποιεῖσθαι) by a more difficult one;[22] for sometimes the consequents (τὸ ἀκόλουθον), but sometimes the original thesis (τὸ προκείμενον), is the easier to destroy.

I have translated the Greek words ὁτιοῦν, πολλά and ἑκάστῳ in a16f. carefully by "thing" but the examples Aristotle gives make it quite clear that not just predicates, but *predicated* predicates are meant, and they clearly have to be predicated of a subject, which in English I have denoted by "it". Not untypically, Aristotle vacillates between talking of predicated predicates as in the examples and assertions or statements, as he does when using familiar expressions such as "that which has been laid down in the beginning" (τὸ ἐν ἀρχῇ (sc. κείμενον)) which always designates the thesis, i.e. a proposition. Thus, even in this passage (just as in B 4, 111b17-23) "consequents" (ἀκόλουθα) are best interpreted as the protaseis which follow the thesis (τὸ ἐν ἀρχῇ or τὸ προκείμενον);[23] the destruction of "the consequent" (ἀκόλουθον) only makes sense as referring to the predication of the subject by the predicate, not just to the predicate alone.

Sainati maintains that this argument should be understood in terms of the logic of classes and does not coincide with the rules of Modus ponens; he gives the following schemata:

$A \subset B$ $\quad\quad\quad\quad\quad\quad\quad\quad$ $A \subset B$
$x \in A$ $\quad\quad\quad\quad\quad\quad\quad\quad$ not $(x \in B)$
------- $\quad\quad\quad\quad\quad\quad\quad\quad$ -------
$x \in B$ $\quad\quad\quad\quad\quad\quad\quad\quad$ not $(x \in A)$

Sainati differentiates between inclusion of one class in another and class-membership. This is a distinction Aristotle does not make. Aristotle takes the difference between singular and general propositions to differ only in the nature of the subject term—Callias versus man—while the predicate and the copula have the same function (cf. *De Int.* 7, 17a38-b3). Thus, he seems to regard propositions like "Callias is an animal" and "man is an animal" as being of the same kind, obviously relying on their grammatical similarity with regard to the subject-predicate form.[24]

---

[22] Omitting τὰ τοιαῦτα with Ross (1958).

[23] Τὸ ἐν ἀρχῇ is a familiar expression from book Θ which designates the thesis and is thus a proposition; cf. e.g. Θ 3, 159a8; 4, 160a5; 13, 162b31; et al. As for Aristotle's vascillation cf. also Ackrill (1963), p. 150 who writes (with respect to a passage in *De Int.*): "It must, however, be allowed that Aristotle may not always clearly distinguish talk of a statement's being true and a talk of a predicate's being true of something."

[24] It is only at a much later stage that Aristotle realized that general propositions are more complex and he seems in fact to have analysed them in a similar way to ours, i.e. as an

102   CHAPTER FOUR

In any case I see no reason why the subject of "is an animal" etc. should be restricted to individuals. We could very well have say 'Greek' or 'geometrician' as the subject; in the *Topics* in fact we usually have general terms as subjects. Sainati's schematisation could then be reformulated as:

$$
\begin{array}{ll}
A \subset B & A \subset B \\
C \subset A & \text{not } (C \subset B) \\
\hline
C \subset B & \text{not } (C \subset A)
\end{array}
$$

Thus we have categorical syllogisms. Sainati's reading obviously has the effect of reducing hypothetical syllogisms to categorical syllogisms. Some later Peripatetics might have been happy with this, but certainly not Aristotle himself who clearly distinguished between the essentially different kinds of reasoning—cf. *APr.* A 44, 50a16ff. which I discuss on pp. 113ff. above. The first premiss in Sanati's schema above ($A \subset B$) stands for one proposition (e.g. 'man is an animal'), whereas it is absolutely clear that the two terms in the text above are meant to be predicates in two different propositions and that their relation has to be stated in an if-then-sentence, for the reasons given above. In set theory $A \subset B$ is equivalent to $\forall x$ (if $x \in A$, then $x \in B$), but clearly we cannot assume that Aristotle was aware of this, let alone that he had a reduction of this kind in view. The topos in B 4, 111b17-23 in fact shows that Aristotle obviously did not want to restrict hypothetical premisses to cases where only the predicates change.

Thus, with respect to the topos in B 5, 112a16-21 it could be argued that strictly speaking it should be formalized in the following way:

If something is A, then it is B.
Something is A.
Hence, something is B.

or, as is also common, as:

If Ax, then Bx.
Ax.
Hence, Bx.[25]

I have deliberately left out the quantifiers, since in B 5, 112a16-21 they are certainly presupposed, but not explicitly stated.

Although a formalization of this kind would be correct with respect to the topos in B 5, 112a16-21, it would be not with respect to the one in B 4, 111b17-23 which has a more general character and allows not only different predicates but also different subjects in the hypothesis. As far as the *Topics* generally is concerned, many hypotheses can be found in the *Topics* which could not be described by 'If Ax, then Bx'. Thus, in the topos from the

---

implication (cf. *APr.* A 41, 49b14-31 and Bocheński (1970²), pp. 42, 80 [14.24], 83f. [15.13]. In the *Topics* his view certainly appears to be closer to the less sophisticated analysis of *De Int.*

[25] Ebert (1991), p. 17 fn. 16 in fact criticises Barnes (1985a) for illustrating Modus ponens in his article on Theophrastus' hypothetical syllogisms as 'If P, then Q; P; hence, Q', rather than 'If a is F, then a is G; a is F; hence, a is G'.

similar degree (ἐπὶ τῶν ὁμοίων) in B 10, 114b25-27, to which I shall come shortly in another context (cf. p. 111), the first example is "if one branch of knowledge deals with several objects, so also will opinion" (εἰ ἐπιστήμη μία πλειόνων, καὶ δόξα), which clearly is of the form 'If Ax, then Bx', but the second example is "if to have sight is to see, then also to have hearing is to hear" (εἰ τὸ ὄψιν ἔχειν ὁρᾶν, καὶ τὸ ἀκοὴν ἔχειν ἀκούειν), which is not of the above mentioned form any more but would have to be formalized as 'If P, then Q' or as 'If A is B, then C is D', where A, B, C and D stand for terms. Obviously, when Aristotle can, he expresses hypotheses in the short form 'If Ax, then Bx', if he cannot, he does not.[26] This is especially obvious in cases where Aristotle explicitly speaks about two predicates being predicated of two subjects.[27] Now, it is true that there is always some connection between the propositions in the hypothesis and that Aristotle explains this connection by some relations which exist between the content of the propositions. However, this connection can have many various forms, including hypotheses of the form 'If Fa, then ∀xFx', as e.g. in B 3, 110a37-b4. The most accurate way to describe the hypothesis would perhaps be 'If P, then f(P)', where P is a proposition and f(P) a proposition which is in some way related to P. I shall adhere to the formalization 'If P, then Q', albeit with the reservations made above. This schematisation comes closest to the text in B 4, 111b17-23 cited above in which Aristotle clearly refers to propositions, not to terms. Whenever it seems appropriate I shall switch to the formalization containing terms. When giving examples Aristotle always gives concrete propositions which of course contain terms; thus I shall normally follow him in doing this using letter A, B, C, etc. standing for terms.[28].

2. *Hypothetical syllogisms proceeding by way of the diairetic proposition*

The origins of these hypothetical syllogisms seem to be found in *Top.* B 6, 112a24-31. The topos runs:

> In regard to subjects which necessarily have only one of two predicates, as a man must either have illness or health, supposing we are well supplied as regards the one for arguing its presence or absence, we shall be well equipped as regards the remaining one as well. This is convertible for both purposes; for when we have proved that the one attribute belongs, we shall have proved that the remaining one does not belong; while if we prove that

---

[26] Cf. also *De Int.* 8, 18a21-23 where Aristotle says that "a horse and a man is white" is no different from saying "a horse is white and a man is white".

[27] Cf. e.g. B 10, 115a11-14, 21-24 (cf. p. 147), B 2, 109b30-110a9 (cf. p. 155), H 3, 154a4-8; cf. also *APr.* B 4, 57b6f. ("if this, A, is white, it is necessary that that, B, is great"). There are also cases where the subject changes, but not the predicate, i.e. where the structure of the topos-principle has the form 'If Ax, then Ay', cf. e.g. B 10, 115a6, 16 and the topos-hypothesis of the topos discussed on p. 153f.

[28] The use of letters for propositions, incidentally, is not as un-Aristotelian as is widely believed. In *APr.* A 14, 34a5-24 'A' stands for a conjunction of premisses and 'B' for the conclusion, as Aristotle explicitly says (a22f.); the same is the case in B 2, 53b12-25 (explicitly stated in a23f.). Cf also B 16, 65a1-4, *APst.* A 3, 72b37-73a5, and *Met.* Θ 4, 1047b14-30, esp. 20-22 where Aristotle refers to the antecedent by "the first" (τὸ πρῶτον) and to the consequent by "the second" (τὸ δεύτερον), just as the Stoics did later.

the one does not belong, we shall have proved that the remaining one does belong. Clearly then, the topos is useful for both purposes.

I shall call this argument 'diairetic hypothetical syllogism' and abbreviate it as (Hd). It can be schematized in the following way:[29]

(Hd)c

A is either B or C
.
.
.
A is not B.
Hence A is C.

(Hd)d

A is either B or C.
.
.
.
A is B
Hence A is not C

3. *Hypothetical syllogisms proceeding by way of a negated conjunction*

As for this third kind of hypothetical syllogism, Alexander introduces it with considerable hesitation—"and maybe also", "if they are indeed different from the ones already mentioned". His hesitation clearly mirrors the dispute between the Peripatetics and the Stoics as to whether the third indemonstrable is an independent form of hypothetical syllogisms.[30] He uses the terminology which is familiar to us from the Stoics; however, the Peripatetic terminology is in this case the same. Possibly, Alexander failed to see any such argument in Theophrastus' work but wanted to leave open the possibility that Aristotle considered hypothetical syllogisms of this form as well; or, perhaps rather, Alexander did see an argument of this sort, but had reservations about admitting it fully, because of the dispute mentioned above.[31]

Whatever the speculations, there is a topos in *Top.* B 7, 113a20-23 which seems to correspond to the description:

> Moreover, if the sumbebekos of a thing has a contrary, see whether it belongs to that (subject) to which the sumbebekos has been said to belong. For if the former belongs, the latter could not belong; for it is impossible for two contraries to belong to the same thing at the same time (ἀδύνατον γὰρ τὰ ἐναντία ἅμα τῷ αὐτῷ ὑπάρχειν).

In the passage before the topos in B 7 Aristotle enumerates all possible combinations (συμπλοκαί) of contraries[32] and all the remaining topoi in B 7

---

[29] Aristotle can use the short form here and does so. We do not find a more reduced topos in the *Topics* which would express the hypothesis as 'Either P or Q', thus allowing for different subjects or both different subject and predicates; the destructive and constructive parts of such a diairetic hypothetical syllogism would correspond to the Modus ponendo tollens and Modus tollendo ponens of the traditional logic respectively. However, when using the Law of the Excluded Middle Aristotle sometimes refers to propositions rather than to terms, cf. e.g. *APr.* B 11, 61a30f. (cited on p. 118 below).

[30] Cf. e.g. Galen, *Inst. Log.* 3, 1.

[31] Peripatetics held the negation of a conjunction 'Not (both P and Q)' to be equivalent to a conditional of the form 'If P, then not Q' (cf. e.g. Alex. in *APr.* 264, 14-17).

[32] The contraries here (112b27-113a19) are nominalized elliptical sentences consisting of an infinitive with an object such as "to do good to friends", "to do good to enemies" etc. which if stated in full would have to be completed by expressions such as "is to be chosen/avoided" (αἱρετόν/φευκτόν), "is good/bad" or "one ought/ought not to" ((οὐ) δεῖ) (cf. A 10, 104a22-31). The contrariety of these expressions depends on their being worthy of choice or not (cf.

deal with contraries. Contraries cannot belong at the same time, but neither of them need belong.³³ Hence, they are only useful for destruction: when one contrary belongs, the other does not.³⁴ I shall call this argument 'conjunctive hypothetical syllogism' and abbreviate it as (Hc)d.³⁵ It can be schematised in the following way; let C (X) stand for 'contrary of X':³⁶

(Hc)d

A is not (B and C (B)).

.
.
.

A is B / A is C (B)
Hence, A is not C (B) / Hence, A is not B

4. *Hypothetical syllogisms on the basis of analogy*

The rule for the construction and the workings of the fourth hypothetical syllogism which Alexander mentions seems to me to be found in the *Topics* as the topos derived from things which are in a like relation (ἐκ τῶν ὁμοίως ἐχόντων). The most interesting occurrence is found at E 7, 136b33-137a7, since Aristotle explicitly says in E 8, 138b23-26 that this topos is derived from things which are in a like relation *by analogy* (κατ' ἀναλογίαν λαμβάνεται) (b24). The example of the constructive case is as follows (136b33;137a3-7):

> Next look from the point of view of things that are in a like relation [...]. For constructive purposes [...] see if what is in a like relation is a proprium of what is in a like relation; for then also what is in a relation like that of the first will be a proprium of what is in a relation like that of the second. E.g., since the relation of a doctor towards the possession of ability to produce health (ἰατρός τε πρὸς τὸ ποιητικὸς ὑγιείας) is like that (ὁμοίως ἔχει) of a trainer towards the possession of ability to produce good condition (γυμναστὴς πρὸς τὸ ποιητικὸς εὐεξίας), and it is a proprium of the trainer to be productive of good condition (ἔστι δ' ἴδιον γυμναστοῦ τὸ ποιητικὸν εἶναι εὐεξίας), it would be a proprium of the doctor to be productive of health (εἴη ἂν ἴδιον ἰατροῦ τὸ ποιητικὸν εἶναι ὑγιείας).

113a11). It is interesting to note that the word "contrary" (ἐναντίον) is used both to refer to the complex expressions (e.g. 113a3, 10) as well as their parts (e.g. 112b27, 31): "to do good to friends" is the contrary of "to do harm to friends" as well as "to do good" is a contrary to "to do harm".

³³ Alex. *in Top.* 187, 28-188, 3 brings this topos in connection with (Hd). He points out that in the case of (Hd) we have contradictories (ἄμεσα ἐναντία), whereas here, we have contraries (ἔμμεσα ἐναντία). Galen speaks of complete and incomplete incompatibility (τελεία and ἐλλιπὴς μάχη).

³⁴ Aristotle says it explicitly in the next but one topos in B 7 (113b6-14); the constructive argument merely shows a possible belonging of a predicate.

³⁵ 'Conjunctive' is short for 'based on negated conjunction'; 'd' stands for 'destructive'.

³⁶ Here again we do not find a more reduced topos which could be expressed by not (P and C (P)). However, it is interesting to note that in *Met.* Γ 6, 1011b20f. Aristotle derives the topos above from the Principle of Contradiction (cf. p. 116n.77) and he uses the latter in *APr.* B 2, 53b11-16 with respect to the conjunction of two premisses.

Aristotle just gives the hypothesis in the example as he usually does in E, but it is fairly clear how the argument works.[37] I shall call this type of argument 'analogical hypothetical syllogism' and abbreviate it as (Ha)c. The argument can be formalized in the following way; let A stand for 'doctor', B for 'productive of health', C for 'trainer', D for 'productive of good condition', P (X, Y) for 'X is proprium of Y':

(Ha)c

If (A is to B, as C is to D) and P (B, A), then P (D, C)
.
.
(A is to B, as C is to D) and P (B, A).
Hence P (D, C).

The destructive part works in the same way.[38]

5. *Qualitative hypothetical syllogisms*

The qualitative hypothetical syllogism (κατὰ ποιότητα) is mentioned by Aristotle himself.[39] Aristotle states four cases of topoi from the greater and lesser degree (ἐκ τοῦ μᾶλλον καὶ ἧττον) in B 10, 114b37-115a14 and three from the like degree (ἐκ τοῦ ὁμοίως) in 115a15-24. Examples of some of them can be found in Γ 6, 119b17-30. I shall deal with these topoi in some detail in the next chapter.[40]

6. *Other varieties of hypothetical syllogisms*

Alexander mentions other varieties of hypothetical arguments. Alexander might have thought here of wholly hypothetical syllogisms, as Barnes (1985a), p. 570 suggests.[41] We find one concrete example in the *Analytics*,[42]

---

[37] Reading the passage on its own, it is of course tempting to interpret it as an argument rather than a hypothesis. It is especially tempting since the antecedent consists of two parts so that taken as an argument it at least satisfies one requirement for an argument to be a syllogism, namely it having at least two premisses. It is clear from most other topoi in E in which the antecedent consists just of one part, that a hypothesis, not an argument is expressed. Similar problems occur in the case of the topos of the greater and lesser degree according to which the qualitative hypothetical syllogism is constructed; I shall deal with the problem more fully in Chapter Five, pp. 147-149.

[38] In *APr*. A 46, 51b10-25 Aristotle gives an argument which Alex. *in APr*. 397, 26 explicitly calls a hypothetical proof on the basis of analogy (ἡ δὲ δεῖξις δι' ἀναλογίας, ἥτις ἐστὶ δεῖξις ὑποθετικὴ καὶ αὐτή). Aristotle names here the hypothesis at the very end (b24f.) of the argument: "for if one pair of corresponding terms in an analogical group is different, so is the other" (τῶν γὰρ ἀνὰ λόγον ἐὰν θάτερα ἦ ἕτερα, καὶ θάτερα). Alex. *in APr*. 400, 7-17 puts the hypothesis, which he almost literally takes over from Aristotle, at the very beginning of the syllogism (ll. 9f.).

[39] I assume that the name κατὰ ποιότητα derives from the fact that Aristotle regards the predicate which belongs, to a greater or smaller degree, to a subject as a quality (μᾶλλον/ ἧττον *τοιοῦτο*), cf. Γ 5.

[40] Cf. pp. 146-150 below.

[41] On wholly hypothetical arguments cf. Barnes (1983).

[42] The argument in *APr*. A 32, 47a28-30 very much resembles a wholly hypothetical syllogism: "If it is necessary that if something is a man, it is an animal (εἰ ἀνθρώπου ὄντος ἀνάγκη ζῷον εἶναι), and that if it is an animal, it is a substance, then it is necessary that if

none however in the *Topics*. However, we also find other forms of hypothetical syllogisms in the *Topics* which Alexander might have had in mind: e.g. syllogisms constructed with the help of the topoi of "what is more worthy of choice" (αἱρετώτερον) and of "what is the same" (ταὐτό). I shall deal with them in the next chapter (pp. 156-160).

D. *Confirmation by Galen's Institutio Logica*

The fact that we find mixed hypothetical syllogisms in the early Peripatetics is confirmed by Galen's *Institutio Logica*. He mentions in several places[43] that the "modern philosophers" (οἱ νεώτεροι φιλοσόφοι, e.g. 9,3), i.e. the Stoics[44] called disjunctive propositions διεζευγμένα, and the conditional propositions συνημμένα, whereas the "older philosophers" (οἱ παλαιοὶ φιλόσοφοι, e.g. 8, 10), i.e. the Peripatetics,[45] called them "diairetic" (ὑποθετικαὶ κατὰ διαίρεσιν) and "by connection" (ὑποθετικαὶ κατὰ συνέχειαν) respectively. Not only is the terminology very similar to that found in Alexander, but also the nature of hypothetical propositions as expressed in *Inst. Log.* 7, 12-19 is very similar to the way Aristotle expresses investigation-instructions in the *Topics*. He uses the genetivus (sg.) absolutus of the verb "to be" (εἶναι) for the antecedent, the present of "to be" (εἶναι) for the consequent. In addition he does not bother to mention the word "necessarily" (ἐξ ἀνάγκης) in each case.[46]

---

something is a man, it is a substance" (εἶναι here is usually translated by "to exist", i.e. "if man exists, then animal exists", but it seems to me that it is better to interpret it as standing for a copula with an indefinite subject—cf. *Top.* B 5, 112a18 where ἄνθρωπον εἶναι stands for '*something is* a man'). Interestingly it has not been recognized by scholars as such. The syllogism is in fact the same as the example Alexander gives for a wholly hypothetical syllogism in *in APr.* 326, 24f., in a passage which is our main source for Theophrastus' treatment of wholly hypothetical syllogisms (325, 31-328, 7). Aristotle gives it as one example of arguments in which "something necessary results from what has been laid down" (διὰ τὸ ἀναγκαῖον τι συμβαίνειν ἐκ τῶν κειμένων). He does not mention hypothetical syllogisms in this context.

[43] *Inst. Log.* 8, 7-9; 32, 11-17.

[44] In *Inst. Log.* 32, 14 the "modern philosophers" are explicitly specified as the Stoics (οἱ Στωικοί).

[45] Ebert (1991), p. 19 doubts whether this is the meaning of the "older philosophers" (οἱ παλαίοι). His doubts rest on a critique of another scholar's slightly rhetorical argument confirming that Peripatetics are meant (Bocheński (1947), p. 108). It is enough to look at other occurrences of this term in Galen to see that as far as Galen is concerned, Peripatetics are meant by "the old ones". In 6, 1-5 Galen calls the parts propositions are composed of "terms" (ὅρους), "following the old custom" (τῇ παλαιᾷ συνηθείᾳ); in 4, 13-22 he makes a distinction between a premiss (πρότασις) and an axiom (ἀξίωμα) contra Stoics who called both axioms (ἀξιώματα); his justification for adhereing to the expression "premiss" is that "this was the usual term among the ancients" (οὕτω γὰρ καὶ τοῖς παλαιοῖς ἔθος ἦν καλεῖν;) and in 18, 23-19, 5 he offers a description of the three Aristotelian figures of the syllogism and tells us that "the old philosophers" (οἱ παλαίοι φιλόσοφοι) called them "first" (πρῶτον), "second" (δεύτερον) and "third figure" (τρίτον σχῆμα) respectively. All these are of course terms which Aristotle himself introduced and are thus a fortiori Peripatetic.

Alexander, incidentally, calls the Peripatetics "the old ones" (οἱ ἀρχαῖοι) as well; this is especially obvious in *in APr.* 3, 3; 262, 31; 263, 26.

[46] Cf. the similar way of expression e.g. in *Inst. Log.* 7, 14 (τίνος ὄντος τί ἐστι) with *Top.* B 4, 111b17f. (τίνος ὄντος τὸ προκείμενον ἔστιν). For other passages in which

E. *Origins of Galen's and Alexander's terminology*

Where does the terminology which Galen and Alexander mention for the conditional and disjunctive proposition originate from? It does not seem to stem from Aristotle directly. Aristotle did not speak of a "hypothetical protasis" (ὑποθετικὴ πρότασις) but of a "hypothesis" (ὑπόθεσις); he seems to have called the argument from the connected premiss simply "proceeding by substitution" (κατὰ μετάληψιν)—the argument from the disjunctive hypothesis is not mentioned by name in the *Analytics* at all. However, all the expressions which occur under these names do occur in Aristotle with the appropriate meaning. The similarity of "hypothesis" (ὑπόθεσις) to "hypothetical" (ὑποθετικός) does not need to be commented upon. "Division" (διαίρεσις) in the *Topics* usually refers to a division of a notion into two or more groups which exclude each other and which is usually indicated by an exclusive "or" (ἤ).[47] As far as the term "continuity" or "connection" (συνέχεια) is concerned we find an interesting occurrence of "connected" (συνεχές) in *APr.* B 17, 65b20ff. where Aristotle writes about the fallacy of the mistaken cause. This fallacy occurs in arguments per impossibile[48] when the proposition which has been proved to be impossible and false has no connection to the thesis which was supposed to be destroyed. The connection which should be present is described by the word "connected" (συνεχές). In a hypothesis which expresses a conditional statement we clearly have this connection. Thus, it seems that the terminology was introduced at the latest by Aristotle's pupils, "Theophrastus, Eudemus, or some other of Aristotle's associates", if not by Aristotle himself in his lectures.

F. *Alexander's explanation of the workings of the metaleptic and diairetic hypothetical syllogisms (Hm) and (Hd)*

Interestingly, both Alexander and Galen do not object to using the Stoic terminology to describe hypothetical syllogisms, as if the difference between the Stoic arguments and the Peripatetic hypothetical syllogisms was only terminological. Alexander in his commentary on the *Topics* explains the workings of the hypothetical syllogisms in B 4, 111b17-23 and B 6, 112a16-23, which I dealt with on pp. 98-104 above, simply by referring to the Stoic

---

Aristotle uses the genitivus (sg.) absolutus for the antecedent and "to be" (sometimes together with "necessarily") cf. all the passages in which letters stand for propositions cited in 103n.28, except *APr.* B 16, 65a1-4. Cf. also *APr.* A 32, 47a28-30 and B 4, 57a36-b17. Only very seldom does ὄντος refer not to a proposition's being the case, but to a predicate's being predicated of a subject, as it does in *APr.* A 32, 47a28-31 (cf. p. 106n.42 above).

[47] Cf. e.g. A 4, 101b23f.; 7, 103a6f.; Θ 1, 157a8-13. The last example is especially interesting since Aristotle names dividing (διαιρεῖσθαι) as a means of constructing protaseis (157a6 and 155b22f.); cf. p. 35 above. Cf. e.g. also *APst.* B 5, 92a2f.: "He will prove by the division (δείξει τῇ διαιρέσει) as he thinks, that everything is either (ἤ) mortal or (ἤ) immortal".

[48] Cf. *Soph. El.* 5, 167b21-37.

indemonstrables, not even mentioning hypothetical syllogisms; however he uses Peripatetic terms for the parts of the complex propositions.

The topos in B 4, 111b17-23, which Alexander calls "on the basis of consequence" (ἐξ ἀκολουθίας), is explained in the following way:

> For, according to the so-called first indemonstrable which is constructive on the basis of consequence (κατὰ τὸν πρῶτον λεγόμενον ἀναπόδεικτον ὄντα ἐξ ἀκολουθίας κατασκευαστικόν), if the antecedent, then also the consequent (εἰ γὰρ τὸ ἡγούμενον, καὶ τὸ ἑπόμενον[49]).[50]
>
> For, according to the so-called second indemonstrable which is destructive on the basis of consequence (κατὰ τὸν δεύτερον λεγόμενον ἀναπόδεικτον, ὅς ἐστιν ἐξ ἀκολουθίας ἀνασκευαστικός), if not the consequent, then neither the antecedent (εἰ γὰρ μὴ τὸ ἑπόμενον, οὐδὲ τὸ ἡγούμενον).[51]

The topos in B 6, 112a24-31 is simply called "the topos which is constructive and destructive on the basis of incompatibility" (τόπον ἐκ μάχης κατασκευαστικόν τε καὶ ἀνασκευαστικόν).[52] Alexander explains its working first, roughly, in the way Aristotle describes it in the *Topics*, specifying that the topos is true for contradictories (ἄμεσα ἐναντία), whereas in the case of contraries (ἐναντία) only the destructive part works.[53] He then explicitly refers to the Stoic indemonstrables:[54]

> The proof through the so-called fifth indemonstrable (ἡ δεῖξις ἡ διὰ τοῦ πέμπτου λεγομένου ἀναποδείκτου), which consists in concluding from the diairetic hypothesis and the negation of one of the predications contained in the diairetic hypothesis the remaining predication (ὅς ἐστιν ἐκ διαιρετικοῦ[55] καὶ τοῦ ἀντικειμένου ἑνὶ τῶν ἐν τῷ διαιρετικῷ τὸ λοιπὸν συνάγων), is more fitting for the contradictories (τοῖς μὲν ἀμέσοις ἐφαρμοζούσα μᾶλλον), whereas the proof through the so-called fourth indemonstrable (ἡ διὰ τοῦ τετάρτου), which consists in disproving from the diairetic hypothesis and the assertion of one of the predications in the diairetic hypothesis the remaining predication (ὅς ἐστιν ἐκ διαιρετικοῦ καὶ τοῦ ἑτέρου τῶν ἐν τῷ διαιρετικῷ ἀναιρῶν τὸ ἕτερον), fits more the contraries (τοῖς δὲ ἐμμέσοις).

In some places it is clear that Alexander was well aware of the fact that the Stoics considered their arguments to be in some way different from Peripatetic hypothetical syllogisms. He attributes this to their formalist way of looking at arguments: they merely considered the wording of the argument, not what

---

[49] The Stoic term would be λῆγον.
[50] *In Top.* 165, 12f.
[51] *In Top.* 166, 11-13.
[52] *In Top.* 174, 6f.
[53] It seems to me that Aristotle makes it perfectly clear that the topos is meant for contradictories by narrowing the scope for cases "where of necessity only one of two predicates must be true" (B 6, 112a24), which is true for contradictories only: e.g. a house of necessity has to be either white or non-white, but it does not have to be white or black (but could be for example pink). By proving that the house is black, we destroy the thesis that it is white, but by proving that it is not black we have not yet proved that it is white.
[54] *In Top.* 175, 21-26.
[55] The Stoic term would be διαζευγμένου.

was meant by it.[56] The same is true of Galen.[57] I hope that the following investigation of hypothetical syllogisms will show how they work in Aristotle. Once this is achieved the foundations for a more adequate comparison between Aristotle's hypothetical syllogisms and Stoic syllogisms will have been laid.

The fact that the origins of the above-mentioned hypothetical syllogisms can already be found in the *Topics* is of significant historical interest.[58] However, of even greater importance in the context of this work is that by recognizing the link between hypothetical syllogisms and certain topoi the functioning of these topoi can be better understood. Since it is not easy to tell how the topoi work on the basis of the *Topics* alone, such external information about how Aristotle and his followers later analysed these arguments is very helpful.

G. *Further evidence for topical arguments working as hypothetical syllogisms*

As evidence for the interpretation of the topical arguments as hypothetical syllogisms given above, I have pointed out the *similarity* of the arguments themselves to those which were later classified as hypothetical syllogisms and the terminology.[59] Are there any further points of evidence which show that the topical arguments work as hypothetical syllogisms, even if this is not explicitly stated? It would appear so.

Firstly, Aristotle expresses himself in a certain way when describing an argument which he explicitly calls hypothetical syllogism in *Top*. A 18, 108b7ff. He uses the aorist of "to show" (δεικνύναι) to demonstrate the minor premiss (δείξαντες) and future perfect of "to show" in order to

---

[56] Cf. e.g. *in APr*. 84, 12-19, where with respect to one syllogism Alexander says: "but those (sc. the moderns, i.e. the Stoics) deny that such arguments are syllogisms, because they look to the words and the expression (εἰς τὴν φωνὴν καὶ τὴν λέξιν βλεπόντες), whereas Aristotle looks to the meanings (πρὸς τὰ σημαινόμενα ὁρῶν)" (ll.15-17). On Stoic formalism and Peripatetic lack of it cf. Łukasiewicz (1957²), pp. 15-19.

[57] Cf. e.g. *Inst. Log.* 9, 8-13: " [...]'if it is not day, it is night,' which all those who attend to the words alone call a conditional (ὅσοι μὲν ταῖς φωναῖς μόνον προσέχουσι, συνημμένον ὀνομάζουσιν [clearly the Stoics]), because it is expressed in the conditional form of speech, but those who attend to the nature of the facts call it disjunctive (ὅσοι δὲ τῇ φύσει τῶν πραγμάτων, διεζευγμένον [clearly the Peripatetics])."

[58] The fact that the Peripatetics developed these hypothetical syllogisms at such an early stage makes it more understandable that some of them thought that the Stoics were not original merely developing further what Aristotle had already started; cf. e.g. Simpl. *in Cat.* 387, 17ff. The claim is certainly exaggerated, but on the other hand, given the many similarities, it is highly likely that Aristotle and especially his *Topics*, was of some influence on the Stoics—be it through the influence of his pupils Theophrastus and Eudemus on the dialecticians (on whom see Sedley (1977)) or in some other way (live disputes between schools, etc). Cf. also Long (1978), 111f.: "Chrysippus' logical works prove that he wrote at enormous length on techniques of argument and the handling of sophisms; in this respect he may be regarded as one of the heirs of Aristotle's *Topica*." Boethius' claim that he scarcely found anything on hypothetical syllogisms in his predecesors' writings (in *De hyp. syll*. I, I, 3f.) has to be taken with a pinch of salt, cf. Striker (1973).

[59] I shall demonstrate many more topoi which clearly show a similarity to what were to become classified later on as hypothetical syllogisms, in the next chapter.

demonstrate the conclusion (δεδειχότες ἐσόμεθα): "having demonstrated the former, we shall have also demonstrated, on the basis of the hypothesis, the thesis at hand" (108b16f.). We find exactly the same pair of tenses[60] in metaleptic ((Hm)) and diairetic ((Hd)) hypothetical syllogisms; in the next chapter I shall deal with many topoi in which this type of expression occurs.

Secondly, the hypothetical syllogism described in A 18, 108b7ff. rests on a hypothesis which expresses a relation of likeness (τὸ ὅμοιον): "whatever holds good of several like things (τῶν ὁμοίων), holds good also of the rest" (b13f.). Now, in B 10, 114b25-36 we find a topos based on the likeness of things which tells us how to construct a hypothetical syllogism which is specified in A 18 and explicitly called a hypothetical syllogism:

> Again, you must take the case of like things and see if the same is true of them (ἐπὶ τῶν ὁμοίων, εἰ ὁμοίως ἔχει); e.g. [...] if to have sight is to see, then also to have hearing is to hear, and so with the other examples of things which are like and of things which are generally considered to be like. This commonplace is useful for both purposes; for if it is as stated in the case of some one like thing (ἐπί τινος τῶν ὁμοίων ἔχει), it is so with the other like things as well (καὶ ἐπὶ τῶν ἄλλων τῶν ὁμοίων), but if it is not so in the case of some one of them, neither is it so in the case of the others.

Many topoi are expressed in a similar way as the topos above. Aristotle does not use the aorist-future perfect tenses here; but he explicitly calls the argument constructed according to this topos a hypothetical syllogism in A 18. From this we can infer that the way he expresses himself in the topos above, which is common to the topoi in the middle books, also indicates hypothetical syllogisms.

The mode of expression with the help of the aorist-future perfect tenses tells us something about the way Aristotle thought of the workings of a hypothetical syllogism—I shall investigate it further in this chapter, pp. 121-124.

H. *Reductionism*

I have argued above that the origins of the hypothetical syllogisms listed by Theophrastus are found in the *Topics* and that most of the arguments constructed by topoi work as metaleptic hypothetical syllogisms (Hm). Now, there is no such list in the *Topics*. When describing the topos in B 4, 111b17-23 Aristotle does not say that most topoi work according to it. When mentioning the syllogism about the sameness and difference in A 18, 108a38-b4 he does not say that all the topoi in H 1 work in the way described in A 18, even though this is clearly the case. However, we do find in the *Topics* a certain trend to classification of topoi that I shall call *reductionism*—less formal topoi are substituted by more formal topoi, which cover more arguments; Aristotle sometimes indicates the substitution explicitly, sometimes

---

[60] Not only of "to show" (δεικνύναι) of course, but also of "to destroy" (ἀναιρεῖσθαι), (less often) "to argue" (διαλέγεσθαι), and some other verbs.

not. In some places Aristotle speaks explicitly about the above-mentioned reductionism, e.g. in Γ 5, 119a12-16 we read:

> The topoi which deal with the more and the greater degree ought to be taken in the most general possible form; for when they are so taken they are most likely to be useful in a large number of instances. It is possible to render some of the topoi given above more universal by a slight alteration of the expression, e.g. [...] .

In 121b11-14 Aristotle summarizes the preceding topoi in b1-11 in the following way:

> The element (στοιχεῖον) in regard to all such cases is that the genus has a wider denotation than the species and its differentia; for the differentia too has a narrower denotation than the genus.

The topos in B 4, 111b12-16 does not seem to express anything more than the one in B 2, 109b30-110a9—both advise one to introduce definitions of the terms contained in the thesis—except that the latter seems to be expressed in a more explicit way.[61] The topos in B 5, 112a16-23 only mentions one form of the argument described in B 4, 111b17-23 ((Hm) c and (Hm)d), namely (Hm)d, the topos in B 4 being more formal, allowing for the antecedent and consequent not to have any terms in common. In B 9, 114b13-15 Aristotle himself explicitly equates the topos in B 9, 114b6-13 to the topos in B 8, 113b27-114a6 saying:

> This topos has been stated above in dealing with the sequence of contraries (ἐν ταῖς τῶν ἐναντίων ἀκολουθήσεσιν); for all we are claiming now is that the contrary follows the contrary (οὐδὲν γὰρ ἄλλο νῦν ἀξιοῦμεν ἢ τὸ ἐναντίον τῷ ἐναντίῳ ἀκολουθεῖν).

There are other examples. Interestingly, we find a work by Theophrastus entitled *On the Reduction of Topoi* (Ἀνηγμένων τόπων).[62] It is possible

---

[61] Cf. Alexander's commentary to B 4, 111b12ff., *in Top.* 163, 21ff. I assume that B 4, 111b12-16 is earlier than B 2, 109b30-110a9. The former topos is clearly nearer to the predecessor in *Top.* Θ 3, 158b24-159a2 (cf. p. 35n.135 above) in style (e.g. "easier to attack") and in the indefinite statement of what exactly to attack in the thesis (τὸ προκείμενον πρᾶγμα); for the phrase "real or apparent" cf. *Top.* Θ 8, 160b1-3. By contrast, in the latter topos subject and predicate are explicitly distinguished and the investigation-instruction is stated with reference to them.

[62] Most scholars assume that τόπων is corrupt for λόγων (cf. p. 62n.80 above); the reason for this is mainly that reduction of a topos did not mean anything to them. There are two exceptions: Solmsen (1929), p. 70 fn. 1 and Bocheński (1947), p. 29f. who offers the conciliatory solution that both books existed. For the sources cf. Fortenbaugh, Huby, Sharples, Gutas (1992), vol. 1, p. 118 (18a).

Also of interest in this respect is the Florentine logical papyrus (PSI 1095), cf. Fortenbaugh, Huby, Sharples, Gutas (1992), vol. 1 (appendix), pp. 460-463. The papyrus is clearly of Peripatetic origin and obviously deals with formalization of topical arguments, mainly with the topos ἐκ τῶν ὁμοίως ἐχόντων (sc. ἰδίων) (*Top.* E 7, 136b33-137a7). The author uses letters in the place of terms and distinguishes it from other topoi; see Fortenbaugh, Huby, Sharples, Gutas (1992) for the corresponding references. It is possible that this fragment stems from Theophrastus' Ἀνηγμένων τόπων. The author of the papyrus interprets the topos in the same way as I do.

that such reductions as indicated above were carried out and general forms of the hypothetical syllogisms were stated in this book.[63]

I. *How does a hypothetical syllogism work?*

The central problem of this chapter now has to be addressed: *How does a hypothetical syllogism work?* When this difficult question has been answered in a satisfactory way, it will also become clear how most topoi work. Much has been written on hypothetical syllogisms, but it seems to me that the correct account of what they are exactly, has still not been given. This is mainly due to the fact that the relevant passages in the *Topics* have scarcely been taken into account. I shall start with the investigation of the hypothetical syllogisms in the *Prior Analytics*. Aristotle does not say much about them here and it seems to me that they can be understood adequately only when the passages in the *Topics* are taken into account as well.

1. *Locus classicus on the hypothetical syllogism: APr. A 44, 50a16-28*

> Further we must not try to reduce (ἀνάγειν) hypothetical syllogisms; for with the given premisses (ἐκ τῶν κειμένων) it is not possible to reduce them. For they all [i.e. the conclusions of the hypothetical syllogisms] have not been proved by syllogism (οὐ γὰρ διὰ συλλογισμοῦ δεδειγμένοι εἰσίν), but assented by agreement (ἀλλὰ διὰ συνθήκης ὡμολογημένοι πάντες). E.g. if a man should suppose (εἰ ὑποθέμενος) that unless there is one faculty of contraries, there cannot be one science, and should then argue that not every faculty is of contraries, e. g. of what is healthy and what is sickly; for the same thing will then be at the same time healthy and sickly. Then it has been shown (ἐπιδέδεικται) that there is not one faculty of all contraries, but it has not been shown (οὐ δέδεικται) that there is not one science. And yet it is necessary to admit the latter (καίτοι ὁμολογεῖν ἀναγκαῖον), but on the basis of the hypothesis and not of the syllogism (ἀλλ' οὐκ ἐκ συλλογισμοῦ, ἀλλ' ἐξ ὑποθέσεως). This argument cannot be reduced (ἀναγαγεῖν); but the argument that there is not one single faculty can; for presumably (ἴσως) the latter argument actually was a syllogism, whereas the former was a hypothesis (ὑπόθεσις).

I take the subject of a17, as does Ross, to be the conclusion of the hypothetical syllogism,[64] as indicated in the square brackets above. Thus, the

---

[63] Hypothetical syllogims constructed according to most topoi in the central books work as metaleptic hypothetical syllogisms ((Hm)) does. This does not mean that all these topoi should be reduced to the topos in B 4, 111b17-23 in which (Hm) is expressly explained and which simply tells the questioner to construct a hypothesis in which a necessary relation between the thesis and the metaleptic proposition is expressed. Topoi are supposed to help to *find* such hypotheses (and corresponding arguments) and it is of course helpful to get some advice on what aspects of the thesis to look out for (contradictories, contraries, genus, etc.).

[64] The grammar would rather suggest "premisses" (κείμενα) as the subject of "they all" (πάντες). However, in the first instance it would simply not be true that *all* premisses are agreed (διὰ συνθήκης ὡμολογημένοι πάντες), since one is shown by the syllogism and secondly, when Aristotle says that "they have not been proved by syllogism" (syllogism here in the narrow sense of a categorical syllogism) he clearly refers to conclusions. The passage is

conclusions of the hypothetical syllogisms have not been proved by a syllogism (i.e. a categorical one), but have all been admitted by agreement (διὰ συνθήκης[65] ὡμολογημένοι πάντες) (a18f.); it is necessary to admit them because of the hypothesis (καίτοι ὁμολογεῖν ἀναγκαῖον [...] ἐξ ὑποθέσεως) (a24-26). The word "necessary" (ἀναγκαῖον) shows that the accepting the conclusion is not some friendly act—once the opponent has agreed to the hypothesis[66] and the substituted proposition has been proved, he *has* to accept the conclusion, as well as having to accept the syllogistically deduced conclusion. But the necessity here is not produced by a syllogism, but by a hypothesis[67].

The hypothetical syllogism seems to have, roughly, the following form:

(hypothesis)   If P, then also Q.
                                .
                                .
(substituted proposition)   P.
(conclusion)   Hence, Q.

P is the substituted proposition (μεταλαμβανόμενον) for the thesis to be proved, namely Q, and is "presumably" proved by a categorical syllogism (δέδεικται ἐκ συλλογισμοῦ), whereas "it is necessary to admit" Q on the basis of the hypothesis. In 50a32 Aristotle expresses himself slightly differently saying that Q "is concluded from the hypothesis" (ἐξ ὑποθέσεως περαίνεται[68]). Aristotle does not tell us here what is so special about the

---

clearly parallel to a23-25, where it is absolutely clear that the final conclusions have not been shown by a syllogism but have to be accepted because of the hypothesis; also in 50a34 the expression "to agree" (συμφάναι) refers to the conclusion of the hypothetical syllogism, as "to accept" (συγχωρεῖν) in a36 refers to the conclusion of the argument per impossibile, which is a kind of hypothetical syllogism as well.

[65] I take συνθήκη to have the same meaning as ὁμολογία (A 23, 41a40); Aristotle seems to use the former expression simply for reasons of style, avoiding the awkward δι' ὁμολογίας ὡμολογημένοι.

[66] In 50a33 it is stated explicitly that "a preliminary agreement must be reached" (δεῖ προδιομολογήσασθαι).

[67] Cf. A 32, 47a22-36 where Aristotle explains that not all arguments which conclude necessarily are categorical syllogisms: "In some arguments it is easy to see what is wanting, but some escape us, and appear to be syllogisms, because something necessary results from what has been laid down (δοκοῦσι συλλογίζεσθαι διὰ τὸ ἀναγκαῖόν τι συμβαίνειν ἐκ τῶν κειμένων)" (a22-24). Aristotle gives two examples of such arguments, the second one (a28-31) clearly having the form of a wholly hypothetical syllogism. He then says: "We are deceived in such cases because something necessary results from what is assumed (διὰ τὸ ἀναγκαῖόν τι συμβαίνειν ἐκ τῶν κειμένων), since a syllogism is also necessary. But that which is necessary is wider than a syllogism (ἐπὶ πλέον δὲ τὸ ἀναγκαῖον ἢ ὁ συλλογισμός); for every syllogism is necessary, but not everything which is necessary is a syllogism. Consequently, though something results when certain propositions are assumed, we must not try to reduce them directly (ὥστ' οὐκ εἴ τι συμβαίνει τεθέντων τινῶν, πειρατέον ἀνάγειν εὐθύς) [...]" (a31-36). Syllogism here clearly has the narrow meaning of a categorical syllogism.

[68] Περαίνεσθαι seems to have a wider meaning than συλλογίζεσθαι (including the latter) i.e. reaching the conclusion in whatever way. Similarly δεικνύναι which usually seems to have the same scope as συλλογίζεσθαι (e.g. 50a24), sometimes a larger one, as e.g. in 41a20-24: "the probative syllogismoi are effected by means of the aforesaid figures (περαίνονται διὰ τῶν προειρημένων σχημάτων) [...] all who effect an argument per

hypothesis, apart from that it has to be accepted by the opponent. The examples he gives in 50a19f. and 50a33-35 are of no immediate help:

> unless there is one faculty of contraries, there cannot be one science (ἂν δύναμις τις μία μὴ ᾖ τῶν ἐναντίων, μηδ' ἐπιστήμην μίαν εἶναι).
> if there is proved to be one faculty of contraries, the contraries fall under the same science (οἷον ἂν δειχθῇ μία δύναμις, καὶ ἐπιστήμην εἶναι τὴν αὐτήν).[69]

Given the context of the academic debate, which the second example makes especially clear, the opponent must be aware that the questioner makes the hypothesis because he thinks he has a proof for the substituted proposition (μεταλαμβανόμενον), although in a real debate the questioner would scarcely point this out as explicitly as Aristotle does here. But even if it is not stated explicitly, the opponent, simply by seeing the contradictory of his thesis in a hypothesis, should be on his guard and be rather unwilling to grant it. Why does the answerer grant the hypothesis? There must be some pressure behind the hypothesis. Certainly, the answerer will not grant just any hypothesis. If the questioner happened to know how to prove some mathematical theorem and asked the answerer to grant him the hypothesis that if this theorem holds, pleasure is a good, the answerer would not grant it; clearly there must be some connection between the thesis and the proposition substituted for the thesis (μεταλαμβανόμενον). If the hypothesis were a mere agreement,[70] we would have infinitely more possible types of hypo-

---

impossibile deduce what is false, and prove the original conclusion hypothetically (οἱ διὰ τοῦ ἀδυνάτου περαίνοντες τὸ μὲν συλλογίζονται, τὸ δ' ἐξ ἀρχῆς ἐξ ὑποθέσεως δεικνύουσιν.) [...]"

It is interesting to note that the Stoics divided concludent arguments (περαντικοί or συνακτικοί) into two groups, namely into συλλογιστικοί and περαντικοί (in its narrower meaning) (cf. Diog. Laert. VII 77-78). Thus, in Stoic logic too περαντικός (in the broad meaning) had a wider scope than συλλογιστικός.

[69] Strictly speaking, the hypothetical premiss here has the form 'if not Aa, then not Ba', as Bocheński (1951b), p. 65 points out, but as I have already argued, we should not infer from this that Aristotle only had propositions of the form 'if not Ax, then not Bx' in mind.

[70] This is the common interpretation of the hypothesis, cf. e.g. Patzig (1968), p. 149; Lear (1980), p. 35; Frede (1987a), p. 119f., Striker (1979), p. 43 (it should be acknowledged however that Striker, p. 50, rightly surmises that the arguments found in the *Topics* are arguably hypothetical syllogisms). According to all of them the hypothesis 'if P, then Q' is to be understood in such a way that the questioner asks the answerer to accept the proof of P instead of Q. Once, the proof of P has been delivered, Q is proved as well by that agreement; the move to Q would not be a logical step any more. Now, this interpretation works quite well in what we nowadays call Modus ponens, found in *APr.* A 44, 50a16-28. However, it does not work any more in the more complicated cases that we find in the *Topics*, like destructive metaleptic (Modus tollens) or diairetic hypothetical syllogisms. These cases show that hypothesis had a logical significance and that the conclusion logically follows from it. Expressions like "concluding from the hypothesis" (περαίνεσθαι ἐξ ὑποθέσεως) or the connection of "being consequent upon" (ἀκολουθεῖν) between the two parts of the hypothesis (which I shall discuss on pp. 129-131 below) would make little sense if the hypothesis were a mere agreement. It must be admitted that the way Aristotle expresses himself might easily mislead one into thinking that the hypothesis is a mere agreement; one might wonder how well Aristotle's practice of using hypothetical syllogisms squares with what he says about them in A 44. However, when one looks at places in the *Topics*, things certainly become much more clear. I shall discuss this problem further when dealing with the way Aristotle expresses hypothetical syllogisms (using the aorist and future perfect tenses).

theses and it would be hard to understand why Aristotle distinguished certain sorts of hypothetical arguments which seem to differ with respect to their hypotheses. The hypothesis has to be agreed—that is true; but there is more to it than that.

2. *The hypothesis has to be endoxical*

A clear answer to this question is given in the *Topics*: the hypothesis has to be endoxical. In several passages Aristotle explicitly specifies that the hypothesis has to be "plausible" (πιθανὸν)[71] or "endoxical" (ἔνδοξον).[72] The degree of the endoxical character of a proposition can vary. In the two examples given above the link between the antecedent and the consequent is created by likeness (ὁμοιότης)[73]—I shall deal with this kind of hypothetical syllogism in more detail below, pp. 120f. In the case of arguments per impossibile the hypothesis is the Law of the Excluded Middle which says that "of any subject we must either affirm or deny any one predicate."[74] This law is one of the two "common principles" (κοιναὶ ἀρχαί) Aristotle discusses in Met Γ, the other being the Law or Principle of Contradiction, which says that "the same attribute cannot at the same time belong and not belong to the same subject in the same respect".[75] The Law of the Excluded Middle seems to have similar, although not equal strength to that of the Law of Contradiction of which Aristotle says it is the most firm of all principles and beliefs.[76] A form of the Law of Contradiction seems to be used in the conjunctive hypothetical syllogism ((Hc)d, B 7, 113a20-23).[77] The hypotheses in the metaleptic and diairetic hypothetical syllogisms ((Hm) and (Hd)) express a necessary connection between the two parts of the hypothesis.[78] In the hypothesis in B 10, 115a6-14 (topoi 2-4 of the greater and lesser degree) a comparison of probabilities of two predications (μᾶλλον and ἧττον εἰκός) constitutes the endoxicality. There are other examples.

It has been shown that the hypothesis is endoxical. This creates pressure on the opponent to grant the same. If he does not accept the hypothesis he is expected to give an objection, i.e. an instance where the general protasis is

---

[71] "We ought to obtain a preliminary admission (προδιομολογητέον) [...], supposing the claim is a plausible one (ἂν πιθανὸν ᾖ τὸ ἀξίωμα)" (B 3, 110a37f.).

[72] A 18, 108b13; Γ 6, 119a38f.

[73] A 18, 108b7 and 17, 108a7.

[74] ἀνάγκη ἢ φάναι ἢ ἀποφάναι ἓν καθ' ἑνὸς ὁτιοῦν, *Met.* Γ 7, 1011b24. That the Law of the Excluded Middle is assumed in the arguments per impossibile is explicitly stated in *APst.* A 11, 77a22f. I shall explain later how this is to be understood (see pp. 118f.).

[75] Γ 3, 1005b19f.

[76] βεβαιότατη τῶν ἀρχῶν πασῶν, e.g. *Met.* Γ 6, 1006a4f.; βεβαιοτάτη δόξα πασῶν, *Met.* Γ 6, 1011b13.

[77] Cf. *Met.* Γ 6, 1011b20f. where the above mentioned form of the Law of Contradiction (for contraries) is deduced from a more general one (for contradictories).

[78] (Hd) seems in fact to be deduced from the Law of the Excluded Middle; cf. Z 6, 143b13-16 where the correctness of the proposition "length must always either lack breadth or possess it" is confirmed with reference to a form of the Law of the Excluded Middle: "since of everything either the affirmation or the negation is true" (ἐπεὶ κατὰ παντὸς ἢ ἡ κατάφασις ἢ ἡ ἀποφάσις ἀληθεύεται).

not true.⁷⁹ In the case of some of the hypotheses mentioned above this is virtually impossible, in others certainly not easy.⁸⁰

3. *Concluding on the basis of a hypothesis (Περαίνεσθαι ἐξ ὑποθέ-σεως)*

There remains another question which has to be resolved: How is the concluding on the basis of the hypothesis (περαίνεσθαι ἐξ ὑποθέσεως) of the conclusion of the hypothetical argument to be understood?

Nowadays we would simply say that we infer 'Q' from 'If P, then Q' and 'P' by using the inference rule of Modus (ponendo) ponens, i.e. referring to an inference schema. Alexander, when commenting on the metaleptic and diairetic hypothetical syllogisms, refers to the Stoic indemonstrables and says that the conclusion follows from the premisses (ἐκ συνάγειν). Aristotle however does not do this, i.e. he does not refer to a single inference schema. He says that he can reduce *one part*, namely the syllogistic part of the argument, to a schema, namely the categorical syllogism; the other part is, so to speak, reduced to the hypothesis: "for presumably⁸¹ the latter argument actually was a syllogism, whereas the former was a hypothesis" (50a27f.). Hypothesis seems to be on a par with the syllogism. In each hypothesis a more or less strong connection between the substituted proposition (μεταλαμβανόμενον) and the thesis is expressed. Once this connection has been granted and the substitute proved, the conclusion is generated by the hypothesis, or more exactly, by the connection in the hypothesis. The hypothesis is a protasis which as a result of the connection it expresses seems to have inferential power itself.⁸² Thus, the hypothetical syllogism seems to consist of two arguments: syllogism and hypothesis. This interpretation will

---

⁷⁹ Cf. e.g. Θ 8, 160b3-5; 10-13.

⁸⁰ Thus, the hypotheses fulfil the requirement for a dialectical protasis given in Θ 2, 157b32f. in the fullest degree: "dialectical protasis is one which rests on a number of instances and against which no objection is forthcoming."

⁸¹ Aristotle says "presumably" because of course in a dialectical debate another hypothetical syllogism or induction could be used.

⁸² Only then can the criticism be adequately understood which Aristotle makes in *APst.* B 6, 92a11-19 of the hypothetical syllogism containing the statement of what a definition (τὸ τί ἦν εἶναι) is used as the hypothesis, purporting to prove (in the strict sense that the word "proof" has in *APst.*, namely by employing the middle term) the definition. Aristotle argues that as we do not state what a syllogism is as a premiss in a (categorical) syllogism, so we should not state what a definition is as a premiss in a syllogism—this is exactly what happens in the hypothetical syllogism. We have to think here of the definition as having the form of an implication, i.e. roughly: 'If A is a complex phrase the parts of which are predicated in the essence of and convertibly with B (i.e. if A consists of the genus proximum and differentia specifica of B), then A is definition of B' (cf. H 3, 153a15-21); similarly in the second example in B 6 (92a20-24) where, however, *another* definition (ἕτερον, 92a25), namely of the contrary term, is assumed: 'if the contrary of A is definition of the contrary of B, then A is definition of B' (cf. p. 145 below). Aristotle seems to think that in an argument 'If P, then Q; P; hence Q' the rule of the argument is expressed in the hypothetical premiss 'If P, then Q'. Obviously, Aristotle considers the hypothesis here to be on a par with the syllogism: for just as a syllogism can be thought of as a scheme which generates a conclusion, so too can the hypothesis. Aristotle is of course content to use this hypothetical syllogism to prove the definition dialectically in *Top.* H 3 (cf. Cherniss (1944), pp. 34-36 contra Maier (1896-1900), II 2, p. 80n.3 and Solmsen (1929), p. 181). I shall deal with the hypothetical syllogism which establishes the definition assuming the definition of the contrary term in *APst.* B 6 in Chapter Five, p. 145.

be confirmed and further illuminated by other passages in the *Topics*. First, however, the argument per impossibile needs to be investigated.

4. *Argument per impossibile*

The argument per impossibile is notoriously difficult and scholars are not altogether of one mind as to how to interpret it. Here, I shall merely concentrate on some of the issues which are relevant to the discussion of the hypothetical syllogism and which seem to me to be fairly clear. Aristotle explicitly says that the argument per impossibile is one kind of hypothetical syllogism.[83] In an argument per impossibile one proves a thesis Q from a set of premises by assuming not-Q as one of the premises and inferring from it and the rest of the premises, something impossible. The arising impossibility shows that the assumption not-Q was wrong and, with the Law of the Excluded Middle (either Q or not-Q) one infers Q. Aristotle describes the reductio ad impossibile in the passage directly following the passage on hypothetical syllogisms:

> The same holds true of arguments which are brought to a conclusion per impossibile (διὰ τοῦ ἀδυνάτου περαινομένων). These cannot be analysed (ἀναλύειν) either. The reduction ad impossibile (εἰς τὸ ἀδύνατον ἀπαγωγήν) can be analysed, because it is proved by a syllogism; but the rest of the conclusion cannot, because the conclusion is drawn from a hypothesis (ἐξ ὑποθέσεως γὰρ περαίνεται).[84]

Thus, the reductio ad impossibile, i.e. the inference of an impossible proposition is the syllogistic part of the argument, and the rest is not syllogistic, but hypothetical. The hypothetical part of the argument is easily recognizable in concrete examples: it is the part after the statement that a proposition expresses something impossible (ἀδύνατον). To give one example:

> [...]. But this is impossible (τοῦτο δ' ἀδύνατον); consequently the supposition is false (ὥστε ψεῦδος τὸ ὑποτεθέν); hence, its opposite is true (ἀληθὲς ἄρα τὸ ἀντικείμενον).[85]

Now, what is the hypothesis here? Aristotle says explicitly that in the case of arguments per impossibile in contrast to other kinds of hypothetical syllogisms it is not necessary to make an agreement, i.e. to state the hypothesis explicitly, because the falsity of the assumption is obvious.[86] The hypothesis which is assumed in arguments per impossibile is according to *APst*. A 11, 77a22-25 the Principle of the Excluded Middle,[87] and it is fairly clear that the inference in the hypothetical part indicated by the particle hence (ἄρα) works

---

[83] τοῦ δ' ἐξ ὑποθέσεως μέρος τὸ διὰ τοῦ ἀδυνάτου (A 23, 40b25f.).

[84] A 44, 50a29-32.

[85] *APr*. B 11, 61a30f. Cf. also 61b13-15; 21f., and many others; also already in *Soph. El.* 5, 167b30f.

[86] ἐνθαῦτα δὲ καὶ μὴ προδιομολογησάμενοι συγχωροῦσι διὰ τὸ φανερὸν εἶναι τὸ ψεῦδος (*APr*. A 44, 50a35-37).

[87] Τὸ δ' ἅπαν φάναι ἢ ἀποφάναι ἡ εἰς ἀδύνατον ἀπόδειξις λαμβάνει (a22f.).

on the strength of this principle.[88] Having syllogized the impossibility, the assumption 'not-Q' is rejected, i.e. the premiss 'not not-Q' is established, and assuming the Law of the Excluded Middle in the specific form 'Q or not-Q' one infers 'Q'. This is very clearly expressed in *APr.* B 11, 62a12-17 which deals with the argument per impossibile:

> It is clear then that not the contrary but the opposite ought to be supposed in all the syllogisms. For thus we shall have the necessity (ἀναγκαῖον), and the claim we make will be reputable (τὸ ἀξίωμα ἔνδοξον). For if of everything either the affirmation or the negation holds good (εἰ γὰρ κατὰ παντὸς ἡ φάσις ἢ ἡ ἀπόφασις), then if it is proved that the negation does not hold, the affirmation must be true (δειχθέντος ὅτι οὐχ ἡ ἀπόφασις, ἀνάγκη τὴν κατάφασιν ἀληθεύεσθαι). Again if it is not admitted that the affirmation is true, the claim that the negation is true will be reputable (πάλιν εἰ μὴ τίθησιν ἀληθεύεσθαι τὴν κατάφασιν, ἔνδοξον τὸ ἀξιῶσαι τὴν ἀπόφασιν).

Aristotle states the Principle of the Excluded Middle ("of everything either the affirmation or the negation holds good") and on the basis of it ("for if") we can make an inference from the negative to the contradictory proposition, and vice versa.

There are many more examples of arguments based on the Principle of the Excluded Middle. An interesting example can be found in *De Int.* 13, 22b11-14 where Aristotle shows that "the necessary to be is possible to be":

> For the necessary to be is possible to be (τὸ μὲν ἀναγκαῖον εἶναι δυνατὸν εἶναι). Otherwise the negation will follow (εἰ γὰρ μή, ἡ ἀπόφασις ἀκολουθήσει), since it is necessary either to affirm or to deny it (ἀνάγκη γὰρ ἢ φάναι ἢ ἀποφάναι); and then, if it is not possible to be, it is impossible to be (ὥστ' εἰ μὴ δυνατὸν εἶναι, ἀδύνατον εἶναι); so the necessary to be is impossible to be (ἀδύνατον ἄρα εἶναι τὸ ἀναγκαῖον εἶναι)—which is absurd.

Cf. also the passage in 10, 20a23-30:

> It is clear too that, with regard to particulars, if it is true, when asked something, to deny it, it is true also to affirm something. For instance: Is Socrates wise? No. Then Socrates is not-wise (οἷον ἀρά γε Σωκράτης σοφός; οὔ· Σωκράτης ἄρα οὐ σοφός). With universals, on the other hand, the corresponding affirmation is not true, but the negation is true. For instance, is every man wise? No. Then every man is not-wise. This is false, but "then not every man is wise" is true (οἷον· ἀρά γε πᾶς ἄνθρωπος σοφός; οὔ· πᾶς ἄρα ἄνθρωπος οὐ σοφός· τοῦτο γὰρ ψεῦδος, ἀλλὰ τὸ οὐ πᾶς ἄρα ἄνθρωπος σοφός ἀληθές); this is the opposite statement, the other is the contrary.

---

[88] The step from ἀδύνατον (of the syllogistically proved conclusion) to the falsity of the assumed premiss, indicated by ὥστε, also belongs to the hypothetical part. The question is whether we have to assume another hypothesis here or not. Not only modern scholars, but also the Peripatetics had already seen this as a problem and tried to resolve it. In Ammonius *in APr.* XI, 6f. we read: σιωπάσθω γὰρ ὁ δι' ἀδυνάτου ὡς ἐκ δύο ὑποθετικῶν καὶ ἑνὸς κατηγορικοῦ συγκείμενος ἀλλ' οὐκ ἐξ ἑνὸς ὑποθετικοῦ καὶ ἑνὸς κατηγορικοῦ.

J. Hypothetical syllogisms in the Topics

Let us now turn to the *Topics*. The hypothetical syllogism is explicitly referred to as such (ἐξ ὑποθέσεως συλλογισμός) in A 18, 108b8 and b12 and explained in b12-19; it rests on likeness (ὁμοιότης):[89]

> It [i.e. the examination of likeness] is useful for hypothetical syllogisms because it is endoxical that whatever holds good of one of several similars, holds good also of the rest (ὥς ποτε ἐφ' ἑνὸς τῶν ὁμοίων, οὕτως καὶ ἐπὶ τῶν λοιπῶν). Therefore, if we are well supplied with material for discussing any one of them, we shall secure a preliminary admission (προδιομολογησόμεθα) that however it is in these cases, so it is also in the case before us (ὥς ποτε ἐπὶ τούτων ἔχει, οὕτω καὶ ἐπὶ τοῦ προκειμένου ἔχειν); then when we have proved the former (δείξαντες δὲ ἐκεῖνο) we shall have proved, on the strength of the hypothesis, the subject under discussion as well (καὶ τὸ προκείμενον ἐξ ὑποθέσεως δεδειχότες ἐσόμεθα); for we have first made the hypothesis (ὑποθέμενοι) that however it is in these cases, so it is also in the case before us, and have then produced the demonstration.

Thus the general form or the principle of a hypothesis based on likeness, of which the concrete hypotheses used in the argument are instances, is: "whatever holds good of one of several like things, holds good also of the rest" (108b13f.)—I shall formalize it as 'If P, then Q.' and refer to it as (Hh) ('h' standing for 'homoiotes'). The hypothetical syllogism allows us to prove proposition Q by proving another proposition, P. Such an indirect proof is useful when we have arguments for P (εὐπορῶμεν διαλέγεσθαι), rather than for Q.[90] In some cases we may not be able to prove Q directly at all, as seems to be the case in B 3, 110b4f. where Aristotle explains that a hypothetical syllogism should not be used except when we are able to argue for Q directly.[91] In some cases it may be that we can argue for Q directly, but it is easier to argue for P. This seems to be assumed in the warning Aristotle gives in B 5, 112a21-23 that we should be careful not to substitute the proposition to be proved by a more difficult one since sometimes the thesis itself is easier to refute.[92] This indirect proof is possible because having demonstrated (δείξαντες (aorist)) P, we shall have proved, on the strength of the hypothesis (ἐξ ὑποθέσεως δεδειχότες ἐσόμεθα (future perfect)), Q (108b16f.). As mentioned, the way Aristotle expresses himself is of great importance, since Aristotle uses this mode of expression (aorist-future perfect) without the explicit mention of "on the basis of the hypothesis" (ἐξ

---

[89] In B 10, 114b25-36 we find a topos according to which a syllogism based on likeness can be constructed (cf. p. 113 above); cf. also B 3, 110a32-b7 and Γ 6, 119b35-120a5. where similarity between the soul of man and that of other animals seems to be invoked.

[90] Cf. also B 6, 112a25-27; A 5, 102a11-14.

[91] Τοῦτο δ' οὐκ ἀεὶ ποιητέον, ἀλλ' ὅταν μὴ εὐπορῶμεν κοινὸν ἐπὶ πάντων ἕνα λόγον εἰπεῖν. Cf. also 110a32f.

[92] Εὐλαβεῖσθαι δὲ χρὴ εἰς τὸ χαλεπώτερον τὴν μετάληψιν ποιεῖσθαι· ἐνίοτε μὲν γὰρ ῥᾷον τὸ ἀκόλουθον ἀνελεῖν, ἐνίοτε δ' αὐτὸ τὸ προκείμενον.

ὑποθέσεως) in many other arguments in the *Topics*[93] and this serves to indicate that these arguments work like hypothetical syllogisms.

1. The mode of expression: aorist-future perfect

The way Aristotle expresses himself is somewhat puzzling. It seems that having proved P, we have already proved, at the same time, Q;[94] i.e. we prove P instead of Q and take this proof as the proof for Q. This seems to mean that the proof for Q ends with the proof of P. The argument would then have the schema: If P, then Q. P. To state the conclusion Q would appear to be redundant, since this would not represent a further logical step.

We have seen however that in the argument based on likeness and in the argument per impossibile the conclusion is clearly stated. In A 18, 108b1-4 Aristotle describes the workings of the hypothetical syllogism about sameness and difference (περὶ ταὐτοῦ καὶ ἑτέρου) using again the aorist-future perfect mode of expression: "when we have discovered (εὑρόντες) a difference of any kind whatever between the subjects under discussion, we shall already have shown (δεδειχότες ἐσόμεθα) that they are not the same." The examples of arguments of this kind are found in H 1 and they clearly do not end with the showing of differences but with the statement that the two things are not equal.[95] In all the other topoi I have named, the conclusion is clearly stated as well.[96]

1.1. The case of the Law of Subalternation

Let us investigate Aristotle's mode of expression in B 1, 109a1-6 where the interpretation that the proof of P is the proof of the thesis Q might appear particularly plausible. Understanding how these arguments function might help in the understanding of how hypotheses function:

> For when we have proved (δείξαντες) that a predicate belongs in every case, we shall also have proved (δεδειχότες ἐσόμεθα) that it belongs in some cases. Likewise, also, if we prove (δείξωμεν) that it does not belong in any case, we shall also have proved (δεδειχότες ἐσόμεθα) that it does not belong in every case.

---

[93] The same form of expression is found in (Hm) and (Hd) (B 4, 111b20f., b22f. & B 6, 112a27-30), in 108b2-4 (syllogisms about sameness and difference), Γ 1, 116a10-12 (arguments about what is more worthy of choice), B 2, 109b23f., B 9, 114a38-b1 (the last two belong to the topoi which Aristotle calls "the most opportune", e.g. in H 4, 154a12ff.), H 5, 154a34f., A 5, 102a13f., 102b29-33 (the last three are arguments for destruction of the definition), and many others.

[94] The perfect tense (more exact: aspect) in Greek expresses an attained state of affairs.

[95] Cf. Θ 1, 152a28 (ὥστε οὐκ ἀναγκαῖον τὸν αὐτὸν εἶναι), a 37 (δῆλον ὅτι οὐ ταὐτά), etc.

[96] Cf. e.g. B 8, 114a 4 (δῆλον ὅτι οὐδ'), a6 (καὶ ... ἀναγκαῖον); the most frequent particles are simply καὶ and οὐδὲ (e.g. Γ 6, 119b25, 26). Cf. also the hypothetical syllogism derived from contraries in *APst.* B 6, 92a20-24 which purports to prove the definition and in which the conclusion is clearly stated (a24, indicated by ἄρα); cf. the analysis given in Chapter Five, p. 145. Alexander uses the same mode of expression to describe the topical arguments and clearly takes it for granted that the conclusion is stated, cf. e.g. *in Top.* 166, 14f., 17f., et al.

The passage is often cited as the locus for a statement of Laws of Subalternation.⁹⁷ Due to these laws constructive and destructive topoi, i.e. topoi which establish universal positive and negative conclusions (τὰ καθόλου κατασκευαστικὰ καὶ ἀνασκευαστικά), are also useful for the establishing of the corresponding particular conclusions (109a1-3). That is to say that when we have shown that something belongs universally we will also have shown that it belongs particularly, i.e. a proof of a universal thesis is not only a proof of the universal thesis but at the same time also a proof of the particular thesis. Thus, a particular thesis can be proved in two ways, as in fact Aristotle explicitly says in Γ 6, 120a15-20: by proving the particular directly or by proving the universal conclusion.⁹⁸ In the *Prior Analytics* Aristotle mentions only four modes of the first and second figure (not six as in the third figure), probably taking it for granted that the two syllogisms with a universal conclusion in each of these figures (Barbara, Celarent, Cesare, Camestres) are *a fortiori* proofs of the particular conclusions.⁹⁹

This does not seem to mean however that when Aristotle stated the proof for the particular conclusion by proving the universal conclusion, he would not take a further step from the universal conclusion to the particular one, however trivial the step might be. In Γ 6, 119a34-36 Aristotle says the same as in B 1, 109a1-6, not using the aorist-future perfect mode of expression this time, but both times present tense.¹⁰⁰

> For, when we destroy or construct (ἀναιροῦντες ἢ κατασκευάζοντες) a thing universally, we also prove it in particular (καὶ ἐπὶ μέρους δείκνυμεν); for if it belongs to all (παντὶ), it also belongs to some (τινί), and if it belongs to none (μηδενί), neither does it belong to some (οὐδὲ τινι).

---

⁹⁷ Strictly speaking the formulas found here are not stated as laws, but rather as rules, i.e. Aristotle does not say that if a predicate belongs in every case, it also belongs in some cases, but that if we prove that it belongs in every case, we shall also have proved that it belongs in some cases.

⁹⁸ Also of interest is the following passage, 120a20-31, where Aristotle also uses the aorist-future perfect expression and where we learn that depending on the way in which the thesis is determined with respect to quantity it can be destroyed in two, three, or four ways. The "definite thesis" (διωρισμένη θέσις) in a21-24 can be expressed as 'At most and at least some A is B', the one in a24-27 as 'At most and at least one A is B', the one in 27-31 as 'At most and at least one A, namely A_1, is B' (not, as given by Brunschwig (1967), p. 77n.2 and p. 78n.1-3 or Brunschwig (1968), p. 17, who incorrectly leaves out the "at least" part).

⁹⁹ According to Apuleius, *De Int.*, 193, 16-20 "Ariston and some of the the more recent Peripatetics" added a further five syllogisms. They are the so-called subaltern moods, i.e. Barbari, Celaront, Celantos, Cesaro, and Camestrop. Cf. Sullivan (1967), p. 165f. and Patzig (1968), p. 2.

¹⁰⁰ There are other passages in which Aristotle's mode of expression is not consistent. Thus in the passage in B 3, 110a32-37 an argument is described which relies on the universal positive and particular negative proposition on the one side and the universal negative and particular positive proposition on the other being contradictory to each other. Aristotle vasicates in his mode of expression: in one case he uses future perfect (ἀνῃρηκότες ἐσόμεθα), in another he uses future simple (ἀναιρήσομεν). Cf. also the expression in B 5, 112a20 (ἀναιρεθέντος ... ἀναιρεῖται (present tense)).

In the second sentence the Law of Subalternation is expressed, given this time in the form of a law, not a rule; it gives the reason or warranty (εἰ γὰρ) why we can immediately infer the particular conclusion from the universal one.[101]

Aristotle uses the Laws of Subalternation in the *Prior Analytics* in the proofs "from the indefinite nature of the particular premiss" (ἐκ τοῦ ἀδιορίστου),[102] which is used as a proof of the non-conclusivity of certain premiss-pairs. In *APr.* A 5, 27b20-23 for example Aristotle proves that the premiss-pair "no N is M" & "some X is not M" does not yield a conclusion on the ground that we have proved that "no N is M" & "no X is M" yields no conclusion (shown in 27a20-23) and that "some X is not M" is true whenever "no X is M" is true:

> Our point must be proved from the indefinite nature of the particular statement (ἐκ τοῦ ἀδιορίστου). For since it is true that M does not belong to some X, if it in fact belongs to none, and we saw that if it belongs to no X a syllogism is not possible (οὐκ ἦν συλλογισμός), clearly it will not be possible in the present case either (οὐδὲ νῦν ἔσται).

In the context of this proof, we see that Aristotle uses the proof that the premiss-pair with the universal premiss does not yield a conclusion as a proof for a corresponding premiss-pair, with one identical premiss and one particular premiss, by explicitly using the Law of Subalternation. He does not take it for granted, but has a special proof for it ("from the indefinite nature of the particular statement"). I infer that in a dialectical debate he would also not take the inference from the universal conclusion to the particular described in *Top.* B 1 and Γ 6 for granted but would state it explicitly as a conclusion. Since the way of expression is the same as the one found in topical arguments, the conclusion of these arguments was obviously stated.

That the conclusion was explicitly stated is also confirmed by the fact that in several passages Aristotle says that the conclusion of the hypothetical syllogisms has to be granted (ὁμολογεῖν): "yet it is necessary to admit the latter [conclusion], but on the basis of the hypothesis and not of the syllogism" (*APr.* A 44, 50a25; cf. also a18f.). In H 3, 153b25-35 Aristotle says with respect to a hypothesis containing the so-called co-ordinates: "If anyone whatever of these is established (ληφθέντος), the rest must necessarily be granted (ὁμολογεῖται) as well." Clearly, only something which has been explicitly stated can be granted.

The expression which seems to me to be most illuminating is the one found in B 9, 114a38-b3 which again describes an argument constructed according to the topos on the basis of the co-ordinates:

---

[101] Cf. the similar passage in *APr.* B 11, 62a12-19 which I have already cited and in which the Law of the Excluded Middle justifies the move from the false assumed premiss to the contradictory of it; the latter is stated explicitly (with the particle ἄρα).

Cf. also Aristotle's usage of conversion in the *Prior Analytics*. He mentions that the premiss he wants to change converts (ἀντιστρέφει) and he immediately infers the converted premiss, e.g. in *APr.*, A 5, 27a6f.: "since (ἐπεί), then, the negative is convertible [referring to the premiss 'M belongs to no N'], N will belong to no M." Other examples: 27a13f.; 33f.; 6, 28a19f.; b9f., etc.

[102] *APr.* A 4, 26b14-20; 5, 27b20-23; 27f.; 6, 29a6; 15, 35b11.

> Clearly, then, when any one member, whatever its kind, of the same co-ordinate series is proved (δειχθέντος) to be good or praiseworthy, then all the rest as well *come to be proved* (δεδειγμένα γίνεται) to be so: e.g. if justice is something praiseworthy, then the just man and the just action and justly will be something praiseworthy.

When P is proved, Q *comes to be proved*. The proof of P so to speak entails the proof of Q; or, expressed differently, from the proof of P we can immediately infer the proof of Q.

From the arguments given above it is clear that the mode of expression (aorist-future perfect) Aristotle uses and which clearly indicates hypothetical syllogisms does not mean that the conclusion is not explicitly stated. However, is this statement of the conclusion a mere formality which, strictly speaking, would not have to be explicitly uttered? One might have this impression from Aristotle's mode of expression and his talking of the conclusion as being accepted on the basis of the hypothesis, the latter being specified as a mere agreement in *APr*. A 44; it has been agreed that instead of Q, P will be proved and with the proof of P the agreed task has been accomplished. But as I have already pointed out when dealing with hypothetical syllogisms in the *Prior Analytics*, the hypothesis is not a mere agreement, but has to be endoxical and usually the hypothesis expresses a certain more or less convincing relation between the two (or more) conjoined assertions. Thus, the statement of the conclusion does represent a further logical step. There are passages in which Aristotle expresses himself in a way which clearly suggest this interpretation, e.g. the expression "to conclude on the basis of the hypothesis" (περαίνεσθαι ἐξ ὑποθέσεως), the verb περαίνεσθαι being reminiscent of the later Stoic terminology. The example of the argument on the basis of the Law of Subalternation illustrated the sort of following which occurs in the hypothesis very well; nowadays we would say that, according to this law, the positive or negative universal proposition *implies* the corresponding positive or negative particular proposition. Aristotle says either that if the universal proposition holds, so does the particular or, if the universal proposition is proved, the particular has been proved as well. Aristotle seldom uses the word "to imply" (ἐπιφέρειν), but he often uses a word which describes the reverse relation, namely "to be consequent upon" (ἀκολουθεῖν) or "to follow upon" (ἕπεσθαι). He usually uses these words to describe a relation between terms, sometimes to describe a relation between propositions, and sometimes also to describe the following of the conclusion of a hypothetical syllogism on the strength of the following in the hypothesis: I shall discuss this in the next section.

The way Aristotle usually expresses himself (the aorist-future perfect pair) shows that in the *Topics* Aristotle had already thought of hypothetical syllogisms in a similar way to his later expositions in the *Analytics*: the proof actually consists of two proofs, of which the one is prior and the other follows from this proof in some way and is dependent on it.

2. Hypothesis

2.1. *Is it a protasis?*

Scholars often wonder whether the hypothesis is a protasis or not; the usual answer is negative. I have argued in Chapter Two that topoi are protaseis and have shown that Aristotle often calls fairly complicated compound propositions (conditional, disjunctive, etc.) protaseis. Since topoi have the rôle of hypotheses in hypothetical arguments, the answer is of course that hypotheses are protaseis; they are protaseis simply because they can be asked as questions in a debate. However, they are protaseis of a special kind.

Let us look briefly at concrete instances of hypotheses. The general form of the hypothesis expressing a likeness is: "whatever holds good of one of several similars also holds good of the rest"[103] (A 18, 108b13f.). One instance of it is "if (εἰ) to posses sight is to see, then (καὶ) also to posses hearing will be to hear" (B 10, 114b26f.). The general form of the hypothesis expressing an analogy, which is a special kind of likeness,[104] is: "As one thing is to one thing, so is another to another" (A 17, 108a8). Instances of it are e.g. "As (ὡς) knowledge is related to the object of knowledge, so (οὕτως) is sensation related to the object of sensation" (108a9f.) or "The relation of the healthy to health is like (ὁμοίως ἔχει) that of the vigorous to vigour" (105a30f.). The last example is explicitly called a protasis (A 13, 105a26f.; a31-33.) and is a product of the fourth organon.

In B 5, 112a17-19 Aristotle indicates instances of hypotheses of the metaleptic hypothetical syllogisms (Hm): "If something is a man, it is an animal" where the indefinite pronoun can be substituted by any subject which fits the two predications. In B 8, 113b17f. we find the topos-protasis "if man is an animal, not-animal is not-man".[105] In the wholly hypothetical syllogism in *APr.* A 32, 47a28-31 the premiss "if something is a man, it necessarily is an animal" (or "if man exists, animal necessarily exists") (ἀνθρώπου ὄντος ἀνάγκη ζῷον εἶναι) could clearly function as an instance of the hypothesis of (Hm)[106] and which is explicitly called a protasis (47a31).

One instance of the hypothesis of a diairetic hypothetical syllogism ((Hd)) is given in B 6, 112a24-31: "a man must have either illness or health."[107] Aristotle does not call the hypothesis here a protasis, but there are many other diairetic hypotheses which are explicitly specified as such. E.g. the disjunctive proposition "the desirable is either the honourable or the pleasant or the expedient" in A 13, 105a27f. is explicitly called a protasis (a26 and a32); in Θ 1, 157a9-11 the following disjunctive protaseis are cited: "One science is better than another, either (ἢ) because it is more exact or (ἢ) because it is

---

[103] ὥς ποτε ἐφ' ἑνὸς τῶν ὁμοίων ἔχει, οὕτως καὶ ἐπὶ τῶν λοιπῶν.

[104] In A 17 and 18 Aristotle does not differentiate between these two different kinds of likeness: in both cases he uses the same term (ὁμοιότης).

[105] For a discussion of this topos cf. pp. 141f. below.

[106] Cf. B 4, 111b17-19 where Aristotle also uses gen. (sg.) abs. of εἶναι and εἶναι with ἐξ ἀνάγκης.

[107] Other instances which satisfy the condition given in a24 for the subject of necessarily having only one predicate (ἀνάγκη θάτερον μόνον ὑπάρχειν) can be found in *Cat.* 10, 11b38-12a9.

concerned with better objects" and "some sciences are theoretical (αἱ μὲν), others practical (αἱ δὲ) and others (αἱ δὲ) productive." In *APr.* A 31, where Aristotle shows that division is "as it were, a weak syllogism" and that it commits a petitio principii, there are examples of syllogisms with disjunctive premisses such as "every length is either commensurate or incommensurate" (46b29-32).

It is striking that Aristotle clearly shows no concern about using set particles for each type of hypothesis. The instances of the hypothesis based on analogy for example do not necessarily have to contain the particles "as ... so" (ὡς ... οὕτως), but can also have the form "the relation between ... is like that between ..." (ὁμοίως ἔχει τὸ ... καὶ τὸ ....). The conditional can be expressed by "if ... then", but also by genetivus (sg.) absolutus of "to be" (ὄντος) together with "necessarily to be". The disjunctive proposition can be expressed by the particles "either ... or ..." but also by "some are ... others ..." etc. What matters is obviously what the hypotheses express (analogy etc.), not the wording.

It is clear from the above that hypotheses are in some passages explicitly called protaseis and thus are protaseis, at least in the way the word protasis is used in the *Topics*.[108]

2.2. *What kind of protaseis are the hypotheses?*

The hypotheses are however protaseis of a certain kind: they have what might be called inferential power. The inferential power can be especially well seen in book Θ where we find the origins of topoi, as I have indicated in Chapter One.[109] The form of the argument we find there is not, say in the case of (Hm) or (Hh), 'If P, then Q. P. Hence, Q', but 'P. Hence Q'. Thus, for example in the case of likeness, we do not establish a hypothetical protasis 'If P, then Q', then prove P and infer Q. We take (λαμβάνειν, 156b15f., 16) Q as a protasis by immediately inferring it from P (which has already been accepted by the opponent) on the grounds of its likeness to P. This procedure is called "securing of admissions by means of likeness" (διὰ τῆς ὁμοιότητος πυνθάνεσθαι) (b10)).[110] As I have fully described in Chapter One, the rôle of this procedure is to establish universal protaseis[111] and to conceal the conclusion of the main syllogism, whereas a hypothetical syllogism is supposed to establish the conclusion. In both cases similar particles are used: "as ... so" (ὡς ... οὕτως). The method of securing admission by means of

---

[108] In *De Int.* 5, 17a8-10; 15-17; 20-22; 8, 18a18-27 Aristotle deals with compound sentences. A statement-making sentence (λόγος ἀποφαντικός) is said to be one (εἷς) either through revealing a single thing (ἓν δηλῶν) or in virtue of a connective (ὁ συνδέσμῳ εἷς) (17a15f.); judging from the examples Aristotle seems to have primarily conjunctive sentences in mind. Aristotle is obviously aware of compound sentences (cf. e.g. *Met.* Γ 4, 1008a4-7, *APr.* A 37, 49a8f.), but the account he gives in *De Int.* is succinct and fairly problematic (cf. Ackrill (1963), pp. 125-127) and what he says elsewhere is at times somewhat surprising (e.g. the standard example for a λόγος which is one in virtue of a connective is the *Illias*: cf. *Poet.* 20, 1457a28-30, *Met.* Z 4, 1030b8-10, *APst.* B 10, 93b35-37).

[109] Cf. pp. 34f.

[110] This procedure is described in Θ 1, 156b10-17; cf. p . 35 above.

[111] Θ 1, 156b14-17; in 8, 160a37-39 Aristotle says explicitly that universal protaseis are mostly established by induction or likeness.

likeness is described as plausible (πιθανόν), similarly hypothesis is described as endoxical in A 18. What is plausible in both cases is the relation of likeness between the two propositions.

The relation between the two parts of the hypothesis is described by "to be consequent upon" or "to follow upon" (ἀκολουθεῖν and ἕπεσθαι). As I have already remarked in the previous section (p. 124), these words usually describe a relation between terms,[112] but sometimes also a relation between propositions.[113] There are some passages in which this word designates the following of a conclusion: either the following of a conclusion in an immediate inference or that of a hypothetical syllogism which follows on the strength of the hypothesis. We find the word "to follow" designating the following of a conclusion in an immediate inference in book Θ in a predecessor of the topos with the help of which the hypothetical syllogism (Hm) is constructed, which I have already cited on p. 34 above and which I shall cite again here (Θ 1, 156b27-30):

> Moreover, you should not put forward the very proposition which you need to secure as a premiss (ληφθῆναι), but rather something from which it necessarily *follows* (ᾧ τοῦτο ἕπεται ἐξ ἀνάγκης); for people are more willing to concede (συγχωροῦσι) the latter, because it is not so clear what the final conclusion will be (τὸ συμβησόμενον), and if the one has been secured, the other has also been secured (ληφθέντος τούτου εἴληπται κἀκεῖνο).

Thus, if the questioner wants to secure as a premiss Q, say the proposition 'geometers are animals', he is advised to ask a protasis P from which this proposition necessarily follows (ἕπεται ἐξ ἀνάγκης), say 'geometers are men'. Once the answerer has granted P, the questioner can immediately infer Q: it follows (ἕπεται) from P.

The occurrence of the word "to be consequent" (ἀκολουθεῖν) designating the following of the conclusion of a hypothetical syllogism is found in Γ 6, 119b38-120a1: the conclusion "will follow through the hypothesis" (ἀκολουθήσει διὰ τὴν ὑπόθεσιν). I cite the passage in full:

> Moreover, you should argue from a hypothesis: you should claim that the attribute, if it belongs or does not belong in one case, does so in a like degree in all, e.g. that if the soul of man is immortal, so are or other souls as well, while if this one is not so, neither are the others. If, then, it is maintained that in some instance the attribute belongs, you must prove that in some instance it does not belong; for then *it will follow on the strength of the hypothesis* (ἀκολουθήσει γὰρ διὰ τὴν ὑπόθεσιν), that it does not belong in any instance. If, on the other hand, it is maintained that it does not belong in some instance, you must prove that it does belong in some instance, for in this way it will follow (ἀκολουθήσει) that it belongs in all instances.

The fact that "to be consequent upon" (ἀκολουθεῖν) is used for the relation of implication within the hypothesis, for the following of the conclusion on

---

[112] E.g. "animal follows upon man"; cf. e.g. B 8, 113b20.
[113] In the sense that 'X is animal' is consequent upon 'X is a man'; cf. B 4, 111b22.

the strength of the hypothesis as well as the following of the conclusion in an immediate inference shows the 'inferential power' of the hypothesis.[114] The hypothesis is not a mere agreement but it expresses a certain formal relation (not necessarily a correct one); once the hypothesis and the additional premiss, which is a part of the hypothesis, has been agreed, the conclusion follows necessarily on the strength of the hypothesis: it is so to speak generated by the hypothesis.

It should be observed that the way the hypothetical syllogism works seems to satisfy the broad definition of the syllogism. The hypothetical and the additional premiss having been laid down, the conclusion necessarily follows through them. It would in fact be strange if it did not satisfy the conclusion, since it is called syllogism. Also, Aristotle would scarcely have put the definition of the syllogism at the beginning of the *Topics* if he did not regard hypothetical syllogisms, the main form of arguments in the *Topics*, as satisfying that definition.[115] In *APr.* A 44, 50a27f., a passage which I have already cited, Aristotle seems to put (categorical) syllogism on the same level as the hypothesis. This is confirmed by the passage in *APst.* B 6, 92a6-19. Aristotle denies here that it is possible to demonstrate definition with the help of a hypothetical syllogism, whereas he clearly affirms in the *Topics* H 3 that this is indeed possible. Obviously, in the *Posterior Analytics* Aristotle has more stringent criteria with respect to what a demonstration is and what is acceptable as a proof in a dialectical debate, is not good enough in a scientific context. "Proof must proceed through a middle term" (APst B 6, 92a10)—this clearly presupposes some of Aristotle's syllogistic, and only a categorical syllogism qualifies as an argument which can prove anything in this strict sense. However, what interests us is the difference Aristotle makes between a categorical and a hypothetical syllogism. The hypothesis Aristotle gives as an example is roughly as follows: 'A is definition of B, if and only if A is proper to B and all the parts of A, and only these parts, are predicated in the essence of B' (*APst.* B 6, 92a7-9). Once it has been shown that A is proper to B and all the parts of A, and only these parts, are predicated in the essence of B, it follows on the basis of the hypothesis that A is definition of B. One of the criticisms Aristotle makes is that just as in a categorical syllogism the definition of the syllogism is not used as premiss, so in a hypothetical syllogism the hypothesis—here definition of the definition—must not be asked

---

[114] Interestingly, Stoics also used the expression "to be consequent upon" both for the relation between propositions and for that of the following of the conclusion.

[115] Ancient Aristotelian commentators were divided on this issue: some thought that the definition of the syllogism covers hypothetical syllogisms (Ammonius *in APr.* 27, 6-14), some that it does not (Alex. *in APr.* 17, 5-10; 348, 29-32; *in Top.* 8, 8-14; Philop. *in APr.* 33, 6-10). The mere fact that Aristotle kept the term "hypothetical *syllogism*" (cf. e.g. *APr.* A 44, 50a16; *APst.* B 6, 92a20&29) seems to me to point in favour of Ammonius' stand. In A 32, 47a22-36, a passage I have already dealt with on p. 114n.67, Aristotle distinguishes between "syllogism" and the "necessary", which is wider and comprises wholly hypothetical syllogisms. But it is absolutely clear that by συλλογισμός here he means 'categorical syllogism' and that the "necessary" inferences he has in mind satisfy the broad definition of the syllogism (cf. especially a23f.: διὰ τὸ ἀναγκαῖόν τι συμβαίνειν ἐκ τῶν κειμένων). All that can be said is that in the *Prior Analytics* Aristotle sometimes used the term συλλογισμός to designate a categorical syllogism specifically, not that it is the only syllogism which satisfies the definition of the syllogism.

(a11-19). Here, Aristotle obviously sees the hypothesis as a rule, just as the syllogism, and finds it problematic that it is expressed as a premiss. Nowadays, we would say that a categorical syllogism is valid due to its form, just as we would say of a hypothetical syllogism, say 'If P, then Q; P; hence Q', that it is valid due to its form. Aristotle in contrast sees a difference between the two syllogisms. The hypothetical syllogism seems to satisfy the general definition of the syllogism, but it does not satisfy, according to Aristotle, an additional presupposition Aristotle stipulates here, namely that it should work according to an external rule only. Aristotle obviously thinks that the hypothetical syllogism works according to the rule specified in the hypothesis stated as a premiss, i.e. according to an internal rule. This is of course quite different from saying that the conclusion follows according to Modus ponens. In order to mark Aristotle's different explanation of the workings of this argument, I preferred to use the expressions 'metaleptic hypothetical syllo-gism' (Hm), etc., rather than Modus ponens, tollens, etc.[116]

3. Consequence (ἀκολουθεῖν) in the metaleptic hypothetical syllogism (Hm)

3.1. In the constructive case of (Hm)

In (Hm), the argument I located in B 4, 111b17-23 and 5, 112a16-23, Aristotle calls the following between the propositions P and Q in 'If P, then Q' "to be consequent upon" (ἀκολουθεῖν).[117] It is not at all surprising that he uses the same word for following of the conclusion, since he understands the proved protasis P as generated by the hypothesis. In the implication (hypothesis) we establish that if P is the case (ὄντος), then Q is the case (ἔστιν), i.e. Q follows. Next, we establish that P is indeed the case, and we can state Q as being the case, i.e. Q follows as proved from the proved P. The relation of following remains the same, only the status of the propositions changes: from assumed to proved.[118]

---

[116] There are of course other differences. For Aristotle 'If P, then Q. P; hence Q','If Aa, then Ba; Aa; hence Ba' and also 'If Ax, then Bx; Aa; hence Ba' (eminently in the case of the so-called "most opportune" topoi) would all qualify as metaleptic hypothetical syllogisms, but they would not all qualify as Modus ponens. In particular the last version would according to the formalist modern logic be unsatisfactory without the instantiation 'If Aa, then Ba'.
Interestingly, the terms "Modus ponens" and "Modus tollens" seem to be of Peripatetic origin, since ponere and tollere correspond to the Greek terms κατασκευάζειν and ἀνασκευάζειν.

[117] Strictly speaking, he calls the proposition which follows from P "ἀκόλουθον" (B 4, 111b22, B 5, 112a17, 20, 22), but this amounts to the same thing. In Θ 1, 156b28; 13, 163a11 we find occurrences of ἕπεσθαι (which is synonymous with ἀκολουθεῖν) which without any doubt designate a following between propositions.

[118] Cf. Hintikka (1973), p. 188f. who observes that Aristotle sometimes uses ἀκολουθεῖν for following of the conclusion, rather than the usual συμβαίνειν. For a later text in which ἀκολουθεῖν is used for following of the conclusion from an argument cf. Sextus Empiricus, A.M. 8.303: (...) καὶ συνακτικοὶ μὲν ἐφ' ὧν συγχωρηθέντων ὑπάρχειν τῶν λημμάτων παρὰ τὴν τούτων συγχώρησιν ἀκολουθεῖν φαίνεται καὶ ἡ ἐπιφορά (...).

3.2. *In the destructive case of (Hm)*

How does the consequence (ἀκολουθία) of the hypothesis in (Hm) function in the destructive case: 'If P, then Q; not Q (proved); hence, not P'? It might appear here as though Aristotle were drawing the conclusion from the two premisses according to a schema, not as if the conclusion 'not P' would follow as proved from the proved negation of the consequent, i.e. 'not Q', simply because they are not contained in the hypothesis.

The solution to this problem is fairly straightforward. Aristotle simply takes the contraposition of the hypothesis, 'If not Q, then not P' for granted, even though this admittedly is not trivial. Thus, in B 8, 113b15-26 Aristotle establishes by induction that "if animal follows upon man, then not-man follows upon not-animal" (113b17-19). He stresses that it is not the case that not-animal follows upon not-man (b20f.), but that "the consequence" (ἀκολούθησις) between the negated terms is "converse" (ἀνάπαλιν) with respect to the one between positive terms (b19).[119]

4. *Consequence (ἀκολούθησις) in the diairetic hypothetical syllogism (Hd)*

How is the conclusion supposed to follow from the diairetic hypothesis 'A is either B or C' in (Hd)? Prima facie, there does not seem to be any consequence (ἀκολούθησις) here. Let us briefly recall the workings of (Hd): 'A is either B or C. A is B (proved). Hence, A is not C' (destructive case); 'A is either B or C. A is not B (proved). Hence, A is C' (constructive case). These arguments correspond to the Stoic fourth and fifth indemonstrables,[120] and the Stoics did not interpret them as containing a consequence, as they did in the case of the first and second indemonstrables (which correspond to (Hm)), but as arguments that depend on incompatibility (μάχη).[121] Thus, it would not be necessary to reduce these arguments to those relying on consequence. Aristotle however seems to do that. He seems to take it for granted that 'A is either B or C' has as consequences the implications '(A is not B) implies (A is C)', '(A is not C) implies (A is B)' (needed for the constructive case); '(A is B) implies (A is not C)' and '(A is C) implies (A is not B)' (needed for the destructive case). This is not mere speculation: there are passages which strongly suggest such an interpretation.

Firstly, a passage in *De Int.* 22b10-14 that I have already cited (p. 119). Aristotle proves that "the necessary to be is possible to be" (τὸ μὲν ἀναγκαῖον εἶναι δυνατὸν εἶναι):

> Otherwise the negation will follow (εἰ γὰρ μή, ἡ ἀπόφασις ἀκολουθήσει), since it is necessary either to deny or to affirm it (ἀνάγκη γὰρ ἢ φάναι ἢ ἀποφάναι); and then, if it is not possible to be, it is impossible to be; so the necessary to be is impossible to be—which is absurd.

---

[119] In the *Topics* we often find topoi which are expressed as 'If P, then Q' and it is left open whether also 'If Q, then P', i.e. whether the equivalence 'P if and only if Q' holds, which is the case if the topos is said to be convertible for both destruction and construction, cf. p. 142 below. Now, if 'P if and only if Q', then also 'not P if and only if not Q', so that, in the case of equivalence, if 'If P then Q' then also 'If not P, then not Q' (Aristotle takes this for granted).

[120] 4. p or q; p; hence, not q. & 5. p or q; not p; hence, q.

[121] Cf. Galen, *Inst. Log.* 34, 14-23.

Let A stand for "necessary to be" and B for "possible to be". The hypothesis here is the Law of the Excluded Middle: 'A is either not B or B.' Aristotle shows that 'A is not B' is not the case and that hence 'A is B' (negation of 'A is not B') follows (ἀκολουθήσει).[122]

Another interesting occurrence is found in *APst*. A 4, 73b22: "even is what is not odd in numbers, insofar as even follows from not odd" (ἄρτιον τὸ μὴ περιττὸν ἐν ἀριθμοῖς ᾗ ἕπεται). I shall ignore the context here. What Aristotle is at any rate saying is that not odd in numbers implies even. We could certainly state more fully: a not odd number implies an even number (i.e. if the number is not odd, it is even). And this is exactly the following we need in "Number is either odd or even"[123] when we prove that a certain number is not odd; it follows from the hypothesis that the number is even.[124]

K. *Hypothetical syllogisms in APr. A 46*

Many hypothetical syllogisms seem to be found in *APr*. A 46. Familiar terms like "analogical" (ἀνάλογον), "to be consequent upon" (ἀκολουθεῖν), "to follow" (ἕπεσθαι), "to imply" (συνεπιφέρειν) and inferences which are certainly not syllogistic occur here; Pacius in his commentary discovers here many topical arguments. I shall merely analyse one of the arguments—*APr*. A 46, 52a39-b13. Three hypothetical syllogisms are found here mixed together: metaleptic, diairetic and conjunctive. In order to show this it will be helpful to formalize the entire argument. First, Aristotle names three hypotheses (52a39-b1), then he names three conclusions which follow from these hypotheses (b2-4), and then he proves the claim by deducing the conclusions from the hypotheses (b4-13). I shall cite the hypotheses first:

> In general whenever A and B are such (οὕτως ἔχῃ τὸ Α καὶ τὸ Β) that they cannot belong at the same time to the same thing (ὥστ᾽ ἅμα μὲν τῷ αὐτῷ μὴ ἐνδέχεσθαι), and one of the two necessarily belongs to everything (παντὶ δὲ ἐξ ἀνάγκης θάτερον), and again C and D are related in the same way (καὶ πάλιν τὸ Γ καὶ τὸ Δ ὡσαύτως), and A follows C but the relation cannot be converted (ἕπηται δὲ τῷ Γ τὸ Α καὶ μὴ ἀντιστρέφῃ),

Next, let us look at the conclusions:

---

[122] Similarly in 22b29f.: "for if it does not follow the contradictory will follow" (εἴ τε γὰρ μὴ ἕπεται, ἡ ἀντίφασις ἀκολουθήσει).

[123] In *Cat*. 10, 11b38-12a9 this proposition is cited alongside "animal is either ill or healthy", the example we have for (Hd); cf. also b38-a2 with *Top*. B 6, 112a24.

[124] Aristotle says the same again in *Met*. Γ 7, 1012a9-12: "the assertion of an attribute implies the assertion of its contrary" (ἡ ἀπόφασις τὸ ἐναντίον ἐπιφέρει) (a9f.). From the context it seems clear that, again, the implication between the negation of odd and even is meant; cf. Kirwan (1993²), ad loc.

This verb "to imply" (ἐπιφέρειν), which we also find in the form συνεπιφέρειν, has exactly the opposite meaning to "to be consequent upon" (ἀκολουθεῖν) or "to follow" (ἕπεσθαι), i.e. P "implies" (ἐπιφέρει) Q if and only if Q "is consequent upon" (ἀκολουθεῖ) P. However, it occurs much less frequently; cf. *Top*. Z 6, 144b16-18; 26-30, Θ 2, 157a31. The word ἐπιφορά was of course the Stoic term for 'conclusion'.

then D must follow B and the relation cannot be converted (καὶ τῷ Β τὸ Δ ἀκολουθήσει καὶ οὐκ ἀντιστρέφει). And A and D may belong to the same thing (καὶ τὸ μὲν Α καὶ Δ ἐνδέχεται τῷ αὐτω), but B and C cannot (τὸ δὲ Β καὶ Γ οὐκ ἐνδέχεται).

I shall concentrate on the proof of the first conclusion ("D follows B"), which is given in b4-8:

> First it is clear from the following consideration that D follows B (ὅτι τῷ Β τὸ Δ ἕπεται, ἐνθένδε φανερόν). [conclusion]
> For since either C or D necessarily belongs to everything (ἐπεὶ γὰρ παντὶ τῶν ΓΔ θάτερον ἐξ ἀνάγκης); [Hyp. 1]
> and since C cannot belong to that to which B belongs (ᾧ δὲ τὸ Β, οὐκ ἐνδέχεται τὸ Γ), [Hyp. 2]
> because it implies A (διὰ τὸ συνεπιφέρειν τὸ Α) [P₁]
> and A and B cannot belong to the same thing; (τὸ δὲ Α καὶ Β μὴ ἐνδεχεσθαι τῷ αὐτῷ) [P₂].
> it is clear that D must follow B (φανερὸν ὅτι τὸ Δ ἀκολουθήσει) [conclusion, again]

The final conclusion is deduced from Hyp. 1 and Hyp. 2. Hyp. 2 is deduced from the premisses P_1 and P_2. The letters seem to stand for terms. Let us first see how Hyp. 2 follows from the two premisses:

If Cx, then Ax   [P₁]
not (Ax and Bx)   [P₂]
Hence, (If Cx, then) not Bx
Hence, If Bx, then not Cx   (by contraposition) [Hyp. 2]

Let us now look at the deduction of the final conclusion:

If Bx, then either Cx or Dx   [Hyp. 1]
(If Bx, then) not Cx   [Hyp. 2]
Hence(, if Bx, then) Dx

The inferences are clearly correct. Take as examples 'animal' for A, 'not-animal' for B, 'man' for C, 'not-man' for D. Aristotle infers that if X is 'not-animal', then X is 'not-man'.

I have now shown how hypothetical syllogisms work, and hence how the majority of the arguments in the *Topics* work. I have shown that in the conditional and diairetic hypotheses an implication (ἀκολουθεῖν) is contained between the two parts of the hypotheses; we might thus assume that we have the same connection in all the other hypotheses (expressing "greater and lesser degree", an analogy, etc.). In the next chapter I shall investigate concrete examples of the arguments in the *Topics*, including those of "greater and lesser degree" and what I consider to be the "other varieties of hypothetical syllogisms".

CHAPTER FIVE

SELECTIVE INVESTIGATION OF CONCRETE TOPOI

In this chapter I shall investigate a number of topoi using and illustrating the results achieved through the previous chapters. In the main, I shall illustrate how topoi function as hypothetical protaseis in a hypothetical syllogism and how they can be extracted from the investigation-instructions. Many of the topoi are fairly complicated and Aristotle expresses himself very concisely. At times a reader of the *Topics* might wonder with good reason how the interpretation of the topoi given in the previous chapters squares with the concrete examples of topoi found in the central books. Aristotle very often merely states the hypothesis of the syllogism in the form 'If P, then Q' and takes it for granted that the hearer knows how to construct a corresponding argument; or he often states what appears to be an immediate inference, usually in the form 'P, hence Q', which clearly assumes that the corresponding hypothesis 'If P, then Q' has been stated. Thus one of the main tasks of this chapter is to show how the interpretation given in this book squares with the concrete topoi in the *Topics*.

There are around three hundred topoi[1] listed in the central books of the *Topics* and of course only a selective investigation can be provided in this chapter. I shall first investigate the so-called "most opportune" (ἐπικαιρότατοι) topoi. These topoi occur in every central book and can thus be used both for destruction and construction of theses containing any of the four predicables. They include the topos of the greater and lesser and the like degree with the help of which the qualitative (κατὰ ποιότητα) hypothetical syllogisms are constructed, which are mentioned as the fifth kind in Alexander's list. Aristotle explicitly says of some of these topoi that they have to be established by induction or that they can be objected to by counter-examples (ἐνστάσεις). These examples are important because one of the arguments in favour of interpreting topoi as universal protaseis was that they can be established by induction and objected to by objections, just as with the universal protaseis in book Θ.[2]

I shall also investigate several topoi of the sumbebekos in book B. These topoi have a special status, since they deal with pure predication and the destructive topoi of the sumbebekos can be used for the destruction of all the

---

[1] It is difficult to give an exact number, since it depends on the way one counts. Should one for example count the topos of the like degree as three or as one subdivided into three (cf. e.g. B 10, 115a15-24)? In Z 4 for example Aristotle seems to reduce all the topoi given there to just one: "Generally speaking, then, one topos concerns the failure to frame the account by means of prior and more intelligible terms, and of this the subdivisions are those specified above" (*Top.* Z 5, 142b20-22); cf. also Δ 1, 121b11-14. It is also clear from many passages that the list is not exhaustive. E.g. in Z 4, 141a23f. Aristotle says: "whether, then, the opponent has made a correct definition or not should be examined with the help of these and *similar* topoi (διὰ τούτων καὶ τῶν τοιούτων ἐπισκεπτέον)" or in Z 14, 151b24: "Let so much, therefore, suffice for our treatment of definition."

[2] I have already given some examples in Chapter Two, pp. 52 & 58-61.

other predicables as well.³ This investigation includes the very first topos in book B which is the only topos where συμβεβηκός clearly means "accident" and which works differently accordingly.

I shall also deal with topoi of "what is more worthy of choice" (αἱρετώτερον) and those of "what is the same" (ταὐτό), by which Alexander probably meant, among others, the "other varieties of hypothetical syllogisms" and which Galen considered to be a third kind of syllogisms, the so-called relational syllogisms.

Lastly, I shall deal with an interesting topos which apparently works not as a hypothetical but as a *categorical* syllogism—this is one of the few topoi which clearly point towards the *Analytics*. However, there are a few topoi where it is difficult to decide whether they work as a hypothetical or a categorical syllogism.

A. *Introductory chapter to B: B 1*

Before discussing the "most opportune" topoi—I shall concentrate on those found in B 8-10—and some other topoi in B, the introductory chapter B 1 should be discussed first. It consists of three passages: 108b34-109a10 (1), 109a10-26 (2), and 109a27-33 (3). The first and third passages are slightly confusing; there are some discrepancies between their contents and Aristotle's practice in B. The second passage is relevant to the entire *Topics* and helps solve a problem which was usually raised with respect to the *Analytics*. It shows the importance of the *Topics* in problems concerning the *Analytics*.

1. *Universal versus particular problemata: 108b34-109a10*

Firstly, Aristotle introduces the distinction between universal and particular problemata (108b34-109a1) and maintains that *universally* constructive and destructive topoi⁴ are useful not only for universal but also for particular problemata, giving the Laws of Subalternation, mentioned previously in Chapter Four (pp. 121-123), as the reason (109a1-6). He then concludes:

> First, then, we must speak of the universally destructive topoi, because such are common to both universal and particular problemata, and because people more usually introduce theses asserting a predicate than denying it, while those who argue with them destroy it.

Obviously Aristotle regards the topoi in B 2-Γ 5 as containing universal problemata, even though they are not universally quantified by the explicit mention of quantifiers. They are clearly universal in virtue of their containing general terms. It is only in Γ 6 that particular problemata are found which he

---

³ As for the construction, if a predicate is established as belonging as genus, proprium or definition it has implicitly also been established that it belongs simply, so that it is not necessary to establish it separately. However, in cases in which the belonging and the way of belonging are established separately, the topoi of the sumbebekos might also be useful for the construction of other predicables as well; cf. e.g. Δ 2, 122a10-30.

⁴ Aristotle actually says τὰ καθόλου κατασκευαστικὰ καὶ ἀνασκευαστικά, but it is quite clear that topoi are meant; cf. Γ 6, 119a33f., H 2, 152b36ff., 153a2.

explicitly states mentioning the Laws of Subalternation once again (119a32-36).[5]

Aristotle specifies the topoi of which we have to speak first as universally *destructive* ones. This does not fit the topoi listed in B and Γ 1-5 entirely. There are some topoi which are destructive only,[6] but there are many more which are both destructive and constructive[7] and which are found right at the beginning of B. Thus, we do not find first the destructive and then the constructive topoi as the passage would seem to imply. Interestingly, in the topos-entries the information about the constructive use of a topos always comes second and we sometimes have quite clear indications of a later addition.[8] It is also noteworthy that in book Θ, which I argued to be chronologically earlier than the central books of the *Topics*, only the expression "to destroy" (ἀναιρεῖν) is used. In the passage cited a certain notion of "to destroy" and "to construct" is suggested which represents only one of two possible options; I have discussed the different meanings of these two notions in Chapter One.[9]

2. *"To belong" versus "to be": 109a10-26*

This passage is of interest to the question of why Aristotle uses in the *Prior Analytics* the word "to belong" (ὑπάρχειν) instead of the everyday word "to be" (εἶναι) when describing the belonging of terms in a categorical syllogism—a question over which some ink has been spilled. But the question is ill-stated, since "to belong" is already much used in the *Topics* and thus not newly introduced in the *Analytics*; the question to ask is why *in the Topics* Aristotle uses "to belong" rather than "to be" to describe predication. This passage gives an example of how important the study of the *Topics* is for the *Analytics*. The passage runs:

> The conversion (ἀντιστρέφειν) of an appropriate appellation which is derived from an accident (τὴν ἀπὸ τοῦ συμβεβηκότος οἰκείαν ὀνομασίαν) is an extremely precarious thing; for only in the case of accidents can something be true in a certain respect (πῇ) and not universally (μὴ καθόλου). Appellations derived from definition, proprium and genus are bound to be convertible (ἀντιστρέφειν). For example, if being a two-footed terrestrial animal belongs to something (εἰ ὑπάρχει τινὶ ζώῳ πεζῷ δίποδι εἶναι), then it will be true by conversion to say that it is a two-footed terrestrial animal (ζῷον πεζὸν δίπουν ἐστίν). So too if the appellation is derived from genus; for, if being animal belongs to something (ζώῳ ὑπάρχει τινὶ εἶναι), then it is an animal (ζῷον ἐστιν). The same thing is true in the case of a proprium; for if being capable of learning grammar belongs to something (ὑπάρχει τινὶ

---

[5] "If the problema is put in a particular and not in a universal form, in the first place the universal constructive and destructive topoi mentioned above are all useful. For in destroying or constructing a thing universally we also prove it in particular; for if it belongs to all, it belongs also to some, and if to none, not to some."
[6] E.g. 109b30ff.; 110a10ff.; 111b12ff.; 112b1ff.; 112b21ff.
[7] E.g. 109b13ff.; 110a23ff.; 110b8ff.; 110b16ff.; 111a8ff.; 111a14ff.; etc.
[8] Cf. e.g. 111b8-11 where we have a doublet in b11 of b8.
[9] Cf. pp. 18f.

γραμματικῆς δεκτικῷ εἶναι), then it will be capable of learning grammar (γραμματικῆς δεκτικὸν ἔσται). For none of these attributes can possibly belong or not belong in part (κατά τι) only, but they must either belong or not belong absolutely (ἁπλῶς).

In the case of accidents, however, there is nothing to prevent an attribute (e.g. whiteness or justice) belonging in part only, and so it is not enough to show that whiteness or justice belongs to a man in order to show that he is white or just; for it is open of question whether he is only partly (κατά τι) white or just. In the case of accidents, therefore, conversion is not necessarily possible.

"Being convertible" (ἀντιστρέφειν) apparently has a unique meaning here which does not occur in any other place in Aristotle's works.[10] It is the passage from the phrase 'B belongs (ὑπάρχει) to A' to 'A is (ἐστὶν) B'. In the case of the predicables genus, proprium, and definition this conversion is necessary, in the case of the accident however it is not, for it might belong in a certain respect only and not universally. Thus "to be convertible" (ἀντιστρέφειν) here obviously refers to the change from "to belong" to "to be", not the changing of the position of subject and predicable, as is usually suggested.[11]

Now, what exactly does Aristotle mean here? Let us turn to *Soph. El.* 5, where I think the answer can be found. In this chapter seven kinds of paralogisms independent of language (ἔξω τῆς λέξεως)[12] are described, one of them being a paralogism "in which an expression is used absolutely (ἁπλῶς) or not absolutely but qualified as to a certain respect (πῆ) or place (ποῦ) or time (ποτέ) or relation (πρός τι)";[13] they are analysed in *Soph. El.* 5, 166b37-167a20. These paralogisms "occur when that which is predicated in part (ἐν μέρει) is taken as though it were stated absolutely (ἁπλῶς)".[14] Aristotle gives two nearly equivalent examples of paralogisms in which the predication is qualified in a certain respect (πῆ), which is relevant for us here;[15] in the first example he designates a black man by an "Indian", in the

---

[10] Brunschwig (1967), p. LXXXVII n.5 lists four meanings of ἀντιστρέφειν in the *Topics*, including the meaning here which he misinterprets (cf. next footnote). There is also a fifth meaning, namely that of "being convertibly predicated" (cf. *Top.* Δ 6, 128a38, b7; H 5, 154b2;6), for which Aristotle usually uses the expression ἀντικατηγορεῖσθαι; thus there are two meanings of ἀντιστρέφειν which also occur in the *Analytics* (cf. Ross (1949), p.293).

[11] Cf. Brunschwig (1967), p. LXXXVIII n.5: «(b) la conversion se dit aussi de la proposition, lorsque changement de copule permet d'y inverser les positions du sujet et du prédicat.» Cf. also Pacius (1597), p. 367, 4 and Alexander, *in Top.* 131, 30-32. Colli (1955), p. 927f. misinterprets the meaning of conversion here by wrongly assuming that it never occurs in the case of accidents, whereas all Aristotle says is that the conversion does not necessarily take place—but it might.

"Being convertible" here has of course nothing to do with the change of the position of the subject and the predicate. It is not true for the first three mentioned predicables, since in the first (a14-16) and the third example (a17f.) the position of the subject and predicate is the same in both propositions. As for the accident, the problem is not that one could not change the position of subject and predicate but that "to belong" cannot always be converted into an unqualified "to be", because it could be "to be in part.".

[12] There is also a second group of paradoxes which are dependent on language (παρὰ τὴν λέξιν) and which Aristotle describes in *Soph. El.* 4.

[13] *Soph. El.* 4, 166b20-27.

[14] *Soph. El.* 5, 166b38-167a1.

[15] *Soph. El.* 5, 167a7-9 & 11-14.

second by an "Ethiopian". The paralogism runs like this: Having secured (λαβών) the premisses that an Ethiopian is black and that he is white with respect to his teeth one concludes syllogistically that the Ethiopian is both black and not black (a12f.) or white and not white (a8f.). It is clear that something is awry here, and this is the passage from "the Ethiopian is white with respect to his teeth" to "the Ethiopian is white", i.e., in general terms, from "to be in a certain respect" (πῇ εἶναι) to "to be absolutely" (ἁπλῶς εἶναι) (a14f.). We would not say of an Ethiopian that he is white, although his teeth are white, because only a part of him—his teeth—is white (ἐν μέρει) and not his whole body (ὅλος), which is black.[16] The two premisses are true, the conclusion however is not, as two opposites (including contraries and contradictories) cannot both belong absolutely to a subject; it is possible however that both belong in a certain respect (πῇ) or that one of them belongs absolutely (ἁπλῶς) and the other in a certain respect (πῇ).[17] The conclusion does not really follow from the premisses which is why Aristotle says that the types of fallacies independent of the language fall under the ignorance of the definition of the syllogism.[18]

Transferred to the case in B 1, it means: "Whiteness belongs to the Ethiopian" cannot be converted to "The Ethiopian is white." The reason, or at least one of the reasons why Aristotle uses "to belong" instead of "to be" would appear to be that it encompasses both "to be absolutely" and "to be in a certain respect" and so catches more propositions and thus more reasonings than "to be" which only encompasses "to be absolutely".[19]

Aristotle seems to refer to this distinction in *APr.* A 37, 49a8 where he says that predicates can be predicated in a certain respect (πῇ) or absolutely (ἁπλῶς). *APr.* A 36 where Aristotle deals with the so-called syllogismi obliqui is also interesting, because it represents another passage where the broadness of the word "to belong" is stressed, albeit in a different respect. Aristotle points out that 'A belongs to B' (in contrast to the narrower 'A is predicated of B') cannot always be converted to 'B is A' with the terms in the nominative, these sometimes having to be in the genitive, dative or accusative, e.g. 'there being a single science belongs to things which are contrary to one another' does not convert to 'contraries are a single science', but to '*of* the contraries there is a single science' (48b4-9). Since in 'A belongs to B' the terms always remain in the same casus, the meaning due to the difference in casus has to be included in the relation "to belong"—in English we could say that it stands for "to be of", in Greek that it stands for εἶναι+subject in the genitive—and thus have a broader meaning than "to be"+subject in the nominative. Aristotle simply says that "to belong" has as

---

[16] *Soph. El.* 5, 166b38 and 167a8. Cf. also Δ 5, 126a26-29.: "the part is not in any way predicable of the whole" (l.27f.).

[17] *Soph. El.* 25, 180a26-29; 5, 167a9f., 17.

[18] *Soph. El.* 6, 169a20f. Cf. also 5, 167a13, where the person only believes that he has inferred the conclusion syllogistically; see also the definition of refutation (ἔλεγχος) in 167a22-28, esp. a26f. (κατὰ τοῦτο) and the examples in a31-34.

[19] Thus, from 'blackness belongs to the Ethiopian' and 'whiteness belongs to the Ethiopian' it indeed follows that 'blackness and whiteness belong to the Ethiopian', because "to belong" does not preclude that the contraries belong in different ways.

many meanings as "to be" (b2-4), obviously referring to the fact that "to be" can be constructed with terms in different casus, not just the nominative.

In any case, the explanations which have been given to date are wrong insofar as they presume that Aristotle introduced the term "to belong" in the *Analytics* whereas it already occurs in a technical sense in the *Topics*.[20]

3. *Definition of two errors (109a27-34)*

In this passage Aristotle distinguishes two errors in problemata:

> We must also define the errors (ἁμαρτίας) that occur in problemata. They are of two kinds, caused either by false statement (ψεύδεσθαι) or by transgression of the established use of language (παραβαίνειν τὴν κειμένην λέξιν). For those who make false statements, and say that something belongs to a thing which does not belong to it, commit error; and those who call objects by the names of other objects (e.g. calling a plane-tree a man) transgress the established terminology.

3.1. *The first error: false statement (ψεύδεσθαι)*

The opponent says of something that it belongs, whereas it does not belong, and thereby commits an error. Interestingly, Aristotle states here only the destructive case, i.e. the case in which the questioner refutes the opponent by proving that the predicate does not belong; the constructive case can easily be constructed. It might be queried how this ontological definition of error[21] is supposed to be compatible with the dialectical situation where the questioner has to prove the contradictory of the thesis taken by the answerer, whether he believes the thesis is true or not. What Aristotle might insinuate here is that, even though one can argue against a thesis and its opposite, there is only one which is true.[22] However, in Z 1, 139a36-b3, a passage I have already mentioned on p. 89, Aristotle defines the *assertion* of truth and falsehood in a way which suits the dialectical context more:

---

[20] Ebert (1977a) criticizes Łukasiewicz (1957²), p. 17 and Patzig (1968), pp. 8-12 who, both interpreting Alexander *in APr.* 54, 21-29, point out that Aristotle's usage of "to belong" instead of "to be" makes the predicate and subject better distinguishable, as the subject is put in the dative (in contrast to the nominative of the predicate)—the subject is clear enough in a normal sentence as Ebert rightly points out. Ebert himself argues that Aristotle introduced "to belong" in order to show the structure of the syllogisms (especially the middle term) more clearly. Now, what I have said above in the text, does not make Ebert's article useless. He is certainly wrong in assuming that the points he is making were the reason which made Aristotle introduce "to be"—he used this term already in the *Topics*. However, what Ebert says can still be relevant in order to see how Aristotle uses the possibilities of the verb "to belong" to describe syllogisms in an elegant (in the sense in which mathematicians use this word) way. There are many examples of topoi in the *Topics* which Aristotle can express more concisely with "to belong" than it would be with "to be".

Zadro (1974), p. 551 is the only modern commentator who observes the relevance of the passage and points out that "to belong" is not simply an alternative to "to be" as Łukasiewicz believed. However, his explanation (p. 358f. and appendix I on pp. 549-578) is highly obscure; cf. the review of Striker (1976).

[21] Cf. Aristotle's famous definition of truth and falsehood in *Met.* Γ 7, 1011b26f.: "to say of what is that it is not, or of what is not that it is, is false, while to say of what is that it is and of what is not that it is not, is true."

[22] In *Top.* A 2, 101a33-36 Aristotle maintains that the *Topics* is useful for philosophical sciences "because the ability to raise difficulties on both sides will make us discern more easily the truth and falsehood on (τἀληθές τε καὶ τὸ ψεῦδος) each point."

Whether, then, the account is not also true of that of which the name is true (ἀληθεύεται) you should examine according to the topoi of the sumbebekos. For there too the question is always "is so and so true or untrue?"; for whenever we argue (διαλεγώμεθα) that a sumbebekos belongs, we assert that it is true (ὅτι ἀληθές λέγομεν), while whenever we argue that it does not belong, we assert that it is untrue (ὅτι οὐκ ἀληθές).

3.2. *The second error: violation of the established terminology (παραβαίνειν τὴν κειμένην λέξιν)*

The opponent's error of violating the established terminology seems to be less familiar. Aristotle illustrates this error using a very striking example: "The plane-tree is a man". Interestingly, there are scarcely any topoi in the *Topics* which would deal with problemata in which the error of violating nomenclature is addressed.[23] As far as I can see, there are only three other topoi in the *Topics* where the answerer is charged with violating the established nomenclature, one of which can be found in Z 10, 148b16-22. However, the answerer here does not make the error in his thesis, but in the argument in defence of his thesis which expresses the definition of an ambiguous term. The questioner points out that the definition does not fit all the meanings of the ambiguous term. The answerer does not however admit that the term is homonymous,[24] but maintains that the term does not fit all meanings, just because the definition he has given does not, i.e. the term gets the meaning which is given to it by the definition, not by the sense it has in everyday-language. In this case Aristotle advises to retort to such a person that

> though sometimes one ought not to use the same language as the multitude, yet in a question of terminology (τῇ μὲν ὀνομασίᾳ) one ought to employ the received and traditional usage (τῇ παραδεδομένῃ καὶ παρεπομένῃ) and not to upset matters of that sort.

Clearly, the questioner does not prove that the answerer violates the established terminology, he simply states it. This also seems to be true of the other two examples.[25] Thus, the second kind of error might crop up in a debate, but is not the sort of error which would require a proof—the lack of appropriate topoi confirms such an interpretation strongly.

---

[23] The topoi in B 2, 109b1-12 and 110a14-22 might at first glance appear to deal with the second error, but actually deals with the first one (in the first mentioned topos this is in any case the more plausible option). I shall deal with these topoi in the third section of this chapter.

[24] Here, Aristotle obviously takes "ambiguous" to be synonymous with "homonymous".

[25] In Z 2, 140a3-5 the error of the poet is that he "uses terms of which the use is not well established (μὴ κειμένοις ὀνόμασι χρῆται)"; and his definition is thus obscure (μὴ σαφῶς)—this error is certainly simply pointed out to the opponent and not proved. In 140a6-17 Aristotle criticises those who define law as "the measure or image of things naturally just." In a13-17 he makes a distinction: if the opponent means it literally, then he is in error—this would have to be proved; if he does not mean it literally, then it is clear that he expressed himself obscurely (ἀσαφῶς)—this just needs pointing out.

B. *The most opportune topoi*

Having dealt with the introductory chapter the investigation of the concrete topoi in B can follow. This section deals with a special class of topoi which Aristotle describes as the "most opportune" (ἐπικαιρότατοι) and "most general" (μάλιστα κοινούς)[26] which are of course endoxical:[27]

> These therefore are those which it is most important to master and to have ready to hand; for they are the most useful on the greatest number of occasions.[28]

As already mentioned at the beginning of the chapter, "the most opportune topoi" occur in every central book[29] and can be used for destruction and construction of theses containing any of the four predicables. The topoi in B 8 are divided according to four oppositions of terms (ἀντιθέσεις τέτταρες) into the case of contradictories (ἐπὶ τῶν ἀντιφάσεων), contraries (τῶν ἐναντί-ων), privation and possession (τῶν στερήσεων καὶ ἕξεων), and rela-tives (τῶν πρός τι). In B 9 the topoi from co-ordinates and inflections (ἐπὶ τῶν συστοίχων καὶ ἐπὶ τῶν πτώσεων), from contraries (ἐπὶ τοῦ ἐναντίου), again, and from generation, corruption, and creative and corrup-tive agencies (ἐπὶ τῶν γενέσεων καὶ φθορῶν καὶ ποιητικῶν καὶ φθαρτικῶν) are found. In B 10 there are the topos from the case of like things (ἐπὶ τῶν ὁμοίων), from the greater and lesser degree (ἐκ τοῦ μᾶλλον καὶ ἧττον) and from the like degree (ἐκ τοῦ ὁμοίως).

The "most opportune" topoi all function in the same way as metaleptic hypothetical syllogisms (Hm).[30] I shall deal first with the topoi derived from the contradictories, the contraries and the relatives found in B 8. The first two are explicitly said to be established by induction; against the latter one Aristotle gives a possible objection. Thus, these topoi are further examples to those given in Chapter Two which confirm that topoi are protaseis, since according to Θ protaseis are established by induction and objected to by objections. I shall also deal with topoi from contraries found in other passages and used for construction and destruction of predicables other than sumbebekos. Next, I shall deal with the topoi from the greater, lesser and like degree in B 10. These topoi of the greater and lesser degree, apart from the first one, express a likelihood and that is probably why Theophrastus counted them as a separate sort of a hypothetical syllogism.

---

[26] H 4, 154a12-15, with respect to H 3, 153a26-154a11; Γ 6, 119a36-38, with respect to 119a38-120a5.

[27] Γ 6, 119a38; b16.

[28] H 4, 154a13-15.

[29] B 8-10, Γ 2, 117b3-9, Γ 5-6, Δ 3, 123b1-Δ 4, E 6-8, Z 7, 146a3-20, Z 9-10, 148a10-13, H 1, 151b28-152a4, H 3-4 and in a few other scattered passages.

[30] This is most obvious in the case of the topos from the contradictories and it is clear that the others function in the same way, since they all deal with different sorts of consequence. Aristotle indicates that the topos from privation and possession functions in the same way as the topos from contraries (114a7f.) and the topos from the relatives in the same way as the topos from privation and possession (b13f.), and hence as the topos from contraries.

1. *Topoi from the contradictories, contraries and relatives*

1.1. *Topos from the contradictories (ἐπὶ τῶν ἀντιφάσεων) (B 8, 113b15-26)*

> You should see if arguments can be derived from contradictories, reversing the order of their sequence, both when destroying and when constructing a thesis, and you should obtain them by induction. E.g. "If man is an animal, not-animal is not-man", and so with the other cases (ὁμοίως δὲ καὶ ἐπὶ τῶν ἄλλων). For here the following is reversed; for animal follows upon man, but not-animal does not follow upon not-man, but the reverse—not-man upon not-animal. In all cases a claim of the following kind should be made (τὸ τοιοῦτον ἀξιωτέον), e.g. that "if the honourable is pleasant, what is not pleasant is not honourable"; if the latter is not so, neither is the former (εἰ δὲ τοῦτο μὴ οὐδ' ἐκεῖνο). Likewise also, "if what is not pleasant is not honourable, what is honourable is pleasant". It is clear therefore that the reversed following in the case of the contradictories is a method convertible for both purposes.

The text put in quotation-marks I take to be the hypotheses to which the advice refers that "in all cases a claim of the following kind should be made". The rest of the sentence shows how the argument functions, namely as a destructive metaleptic hypothetical syllogism ((Hm)d) (i.e. roughly as Modus tollens). In the case of construction Aristotle *only mentions the hypothesis*, and takes it for granted that the constructive argument functions as a constructive metaleptic hypothetical syllogism ((Hm)c) (i.e. roughly as Modus ponens). Aristotle does not speak here about consequence (ἀκολουθεῖν) as a relation between propositions, but as one between terms of one proposition of the hypothesis with respect to another. However, the way he describes the destructive argument ("if the latter is not so, neither is the former") seems to me to indicate that the negation of a consequent in some way implies the negation of the antecedent, or, expressed differently, the negation of the antecedent (i.e. the conclusion) is "consequent upon" (in the sense that ἀκολουθεῖν has in B 4, 111b22) the negation of the consequent in the hypothesis. Let the thesis in the present topos be formalized as 'A is B'. The argument then has the following schema:

Destruction (b17f. 22f.):

If A is B, then not-B is not-A.

.

.

not (not-B is not-A)
Hence, not (A is B).

Construction (b23f.)

If not-B is not-A, then A is B.

.

.

Not-B is not-A.
Hence, A is B.

The hypothesis is supposed to be established by induction,[31] i.e. by giving several particular instances. Thus the hypothesis "if man is an animal, then not-animal is not-man" (113b17f.) is to be taken as an instantiation of a more general hypothesis with the form 'If A is B, then not-B is not-A'.[32] The general form is not stated here, but several instances *indicate* the general form of the hypothesis,[33] which expresses the so-called Law of Contraposition.

Aristotle emphasizes that "the reversed following in the case of contradictories is *convertible* (ἀντιστρέφει) for both purposes" (b24-26), i.e. for destruction and construction. More often Aristotle uses the turn of phrase with a topos as the subject, i.e. "this topos is convertible both for destruction and construction".[34] What it means is that if the topos-hypothesis has the form 'If P, then Q' for construction, as most topoi have, then it can have the form 'If Q, then P' or the equivalent 'If not P, then not Q' for destruction[35] as well. Thus if a topos is convertible for both destruction and construction, then it should, strictly speaking, represent an equivalence 'P if and only if Q', for which Aristotle does not have a particle. If a topos is useful for destruction only it has the form 'If P, then Q' only.

1.2. *Topos from the contraries (ἐπὶ τῶν ἐναντίων) (B 8, 113b27-114a3)*

> Then look also at the case of the contraries, and see if the contrary of the one follows upon the contrary of the other, either directly (ἐπὶ ταῦτα) or conversely (ἀνάπαλιν), both when you are destroying and when you are constructing a view; and obtain this too by means of induction. Now, the sequence (ἀκολούθησις) is direct in a case such as that of courage and cowardice; for upon the one of them virtue follows, and vice upon the other; and upon the one it follows that it is desirable, while upon the other it follows that it is objectionable. The sequence in the latter case is also direct; for the desirable is the contrary of the objectionable. Likewise also in other cases (ὁμοίως δὲ καὶ ἐπὶ τῶν ἄλλων). The sequence is converse in such a case as this: health follows upon vigour, but disease does not follow upon debility; rather debility follows upon disease. In this case, then, clearly the sequence is converse. Converse sequence is, however, rare in the case of contraries; usually the sequence is direct.

Here Aristotle distinguishes between a direct and a reverse following of the contrary terms, whereby the latter occurs much less often than the former

---

[31] B 8, 113b17; also b18f. and 22.

[32] As indicated by the expression "and so with the other cases" (113b18f.), which displays the inductive procedure.

[33] Aristotle could not represent the hypothesis with the help of letters as I did, since he starts representing terms by letters only in the chronologically later *Analytics*. But he could have used the general terms "affirmation" (φάσις) and "negation" or "contradictory" (ἀντιφάσις), cf. e.g. E 6, 136a5ff. In general though there is nothing wrong with merely indicating the universal hypothesis with the help of examples, as is explained in Θ 2, 157a21-24: "In induction, it is possible in some cases to ask the question in its universal form, but in others this is not easy, because there is no established general name that covers all the resemblances: in this case, when people need to secure the universal, they use the phrase 'in all cases of this sort' (οὕτως ἐπὶ πάντων τῶν τοιούτων)."

[34] Cf. e.g. B 2, 109b25; he also often uses the phrase "topos is useful (χρήσιμον) for both destruction and construction", cf. e.g. 113b8.

[35] Cf. e.g. B 4, 111b10f.

(114a1-3). Aristotle does not give concrete examples of the two possibilities but circumscribes them by specifying the relations of following between the terms. The corresponding concrete examples are obviously: "If courage is a virtue, then cowardice is a vice" and "If courage is an object of choice, then cowardice is an object of avoidance" (113b30-34). The latter example for the reverse following of the contrary terms is: "If health is vigour, then debility is disease" in (b35f.). Again, the hypotheses are established by induction (b34 & 39).

In the second paragraph (114a3-6) Aristotle describes the destruction and the construction of a thesis in the following way:

> If, therefore, the contrary of the one term is not consequent upon the contrary of the other either directly or conversely, clearly (δῆλον ὅτι) neither is the one term consequent upon the other in the statement made; whereas if the one is consequent upon the other in the case of contraries, it must of necessity (ἀναγκαῖον) be so as well in the original statement.

The argument is not stated in full but describes the working of the hypothetical syllogism, obviously assuming the hypothesis which has been established by induction as stated. I.e. what he says seems to describe an immediate inference: "if not P, neither Q" and "P, hence Q"; the hypothesis "if P, then Q" is taken for granted. Once the full form has been stated in the topos of the opposition of contradictories, Aristotle does not make the effort of stating the argument in full any more. This is true of all the following topoi in B 8.[36] Let C(X) stand for the contrary of the term X. The full form of the argument in the case of the direct following is then as follows:

Destruction:

If A is B, then C(A) is C(B).
.
.
not C(A) is C(B).
Hence, not (A is B).

Construction:

If C(A) is C(B), then A is B.
.
.
C(A) is C(B).
Hence, A is B.

The arguments clearly have the form of (Hm)d and (Hm)c.

Let us also look at the use of the topos of contraries with respect to other predicables. There are various topoi from contraries in Δ 3, 123b1-124a10, depending on what kind of term the genus given in the opponent's thesis is (whether the genus has a contrary or not, etc.). Let us turn briefly to the case

---

[36] Cf. 114a9-11; a15f.

in which the genus does have a contrary, which most resembles the topos from contraries above (123b1; 4-8):

> Further, examine any contrary that there may be of the species. This examination may take several forms [...]. If, however, there is a contrary to the genus, see if the contrary of the species is in the contrary genus; for the contrary species must necessarily be in the contrary genus, if the genus has a contrary. Each of these points is made clear by induction.

Only the investigation-instruction ("examine", "see if ...") and the reason for it is given here, in which the hypothesis is expressed. No example is given, but it is not difficult to find an appropriate example in other passages of the *Topics*. Thus, the thesis could be "Virtue is the genus of justice";[37] "virtue" has a contrary, namely "vice". The topos tells us that if virtue is genus of justice, then vice should be the genus of injustice—this is an instance of the universal hypothesis that "the contrary species must necessarily be in the contrary genus", which has to be established by induction. If vice is not the genus of injustice, neither is virtue genus of justice; if the former is the case, so too is the latter.[38]

Another interesting example of the topos from the contraries used with respect to theses containing a proprium-predication is found in E 6, 135b7-16; I cite the destructive part only:

> Next, examine from the point of view [...] of the contraries, and, for destructive purposes, see whether the contrary of the term rendered fails to be a proprium of the contrary subject; for then neither will the contrary of the former be a proprium of the latter. For example, since injustice is contrary to justice, and the greatest evil is contrary to the greatest good, but to be the greatest good is not a proprium of justice, then the greatest evil would not be a proprium of injustice.

In the explicit example Aristotle seems to leave out the hypothesis which can easily be extracted from the investigation-instruction: 'If B is a proprium of A, then C(B) is a proprium of C(A)'; an instance of this is: "If the greatest evil is the proprium of injustice, then the greatest good is the proprium of justice." However, the particular instance here does not seem to be made explicit in this form; what seems to be made explicit is the fact that "injustice is contrary to justice and the greatest evil is contrary to the greatest good", i.e. the fact that the two terms satisfy the specified term in the hypothesis. Then it is shown that the consequent is not true, and that, hence, the antecedent is not true either; the argument clearly works as a destructive metaleptic hypothetical syllogism ((Hm)d).

The constructive part of the topos from opposites, which also include contraries, for the construction of definition is given in H 3, 153a26-29:

---

[37] Cf. 123b32f.
[38] Aristotle does not say so explicitly in the destructive case, but he does in the constructive case which is found one Bekker-page later in 124a7-9.

For we have to examine into the contraries and other opposites of the thing [...]; for if the opposite definition defines the opposite term, the definition given must define the term before us.

The destructive part of the topos is given in *Top.* Z 9, 147a29-b25, giving the explicit example of the hypothesis: "if beneficial is productive of good, harmful is productive of evil or destructive of good." An interesting example of a hypothetical syllogism based on the constructive topos from contraries is found in *APst.* B 6, 92a20-24:

> Suppose you do prove something on the basis of a hypothesis, e.g. if being bad is being divisible, and if, for items which have a contrary, *being something is being contrary to what its contrary is*, and if the good is contrary to the bad, and the indivisible to the divisible, then being good is being indivisible.

The context makes it clear—Aristotle discusses definitions here—that the verb "to be" has to be understood here in the meaning "to be defined as"; i.e. the thesis to be proved is that "being indivisible" is the definition of "being good". The proposition in italics is clearly the hypothesis. Abbreviating 'X is definition of Y' by D (X, Y) 'the contrary term of X' as C (X), the hypothetical syllogism can be written in the following way:

D (C (X), C (Y)) if and only if D (X,Y)   [hypothesis]
.
.
[D (being divisible, being bad)] & [(being divisible) = C (being indivisible)] & [(being bad) = C (being good)], i.e.
D (C (being indivisible), C (being good))

Hence, D (being indivisible, being good).

The hypothesis in the universal form contains implicitly the instantiation 'D (C (being indivisible), C (being good)) if and only if D (being indivisible, being good)'; thus, this hypothetical syllogism works as constructive hypothetical syllogism ((Hm)c).

1.3. *Topos from the relatives (B 8, 114a 13-25)*

> You must also deal with relative terms (ἐπὶ τῶν πρός τι) in the same manner as with privation or presence of states; for here too the sequence (ἀκολουθέσις) is direct. For example, if three times is a multiple, then a third is a fraction; for three times is relative to a third, and a multiple is relative to a fraction. Again, if knowledge is a belief, then the object of knowledge is an object of belief; and if sight is a perception, then the object of sight is an object of perception.
> An objection (ἐνστάσις) may be made that in the case of relative terms the sequence does not necessarily take place in the manner just described; for an object of perception is an object of knowledge, but perception is not knowledge. [...]

> The principle stated (τὸ ῥηθέν) is just as useful for the contrary purpose, e.g. to show that the object of perception is not an object of knowledge, on the ground that neither is perception knowledge.

Let A and B stand for terms and Rel (A) and Rel (B) stand for the terms which are relative to A and B respectively and let 'A is B' be the thesis. The general form of the topos here is 'A is B if and only if Rel (A) is Rel (B)': 'If A is B, then Rel (A) is Rel (B)' for destruction and 'If Rel (A) is Rel (B), then A is B' for construction. Now, the objection is clearly against the topos-hypothesis: "an object of perception is an object of knowledge, but perception is not knowledge" (a20-23) is an instance in which the sequence expressed in 'A is B if and only if Rel (A) is Rel (B)' is not true.[39]

2. *Topoi from the greater, lesser and the like degree*

2.1. *The first topos from greater and lesser degree (B 10, 114b37-115a14)*
This is the topos that I used to illustrate the workings of topoi in general in Chapter Two, pp. 50-54; it runs (114b37-115a6):

> Moreover, argue from the greater and the lesser degree (ἐκ τοῦ μᾶλλον καὶ ἧττον). There are four topoi. One is to see whether the greater degree (of the predicate) is consequent upon (ἀκολουθεῖ) the greater degree (of the subject); e.g. if pleasure is good, see whether also a greater pleasure is a greater good; and if to do a wrong is evil, see whether also to do a greater wrong is a greater evil. This topos is useful for both purposes; for if an increase (ἐπίδοσις) of the sumbebekos is consequent upon an increase of the subject, as described above, clearly sumbebekos belongs; while if it is not consequent, the sumbebekos does not belong. This should be obtained (ληπτέον) by induction.

The corresponding syllogism clearly functions as (Hm):

Destruction (115a5):

> If A is B, then more A is more B.
> More A is not more B.
> Hence, A is not B.

Construction (115a3-5):

> If more A is more B, then A is B.
> More A is more B.
> Hence, A is B.

Aristotle does not specify the hypothesis of the destructive hypothetical syllogism in the way shown above, but as 'if more A is not more B, then A is not B', which however amounts to the same. Thus, Aristotle seems to

---

[39] The objection, Aristotle says, does not seem to be true, for many people deny that there is a knowledge of objects of perception (a22f.), i.e. they argue that an object of perception is not an object of knowledge either.

assume the equivalence 'More A is more B if and only if A is B'. It is clearly the hypothesis which is supposed to be obtained as a premiss by induction.[40]

Aristotle lists this topos as one of four derived from the greater and lesser degree, obviously assuming that they all have something in common. However, the first topos is different from the other three in that the term "greater degree" (μᾶλλον) indicates here a qualitative or quantitative "increase" (ἐπίδοσις),[41] while in the other three topoi it indicates greater "likelihood" (εἰκός)[42] or "greater repute" (μᾶλλον δοκοῦν).[43] Since Aristotle indicates the different meaning by the words just cited he seems to be aware of the differences in the meanings of "greater" and "lesser".[44]

2.2. *The three remaining topoi from the greater and lesser degree (ἐκ τοῦ μᾶλλον καὶ ἧττον) (115a6-14)*
The three cases are:

1) one predicate applied to two subjects;
2) two predicates applied to one subject;
3) two predicates applied to two subjects.[45]

Let us select the first case (115a6-8):

> Another topos is: when one predicate is applied to two subjects (ἑνὸς περὶ δύο λεγομένου), then, if it does not belong to the subject to which it is more likely to belong (εἰ ᾧ μᾶλλον εἰκὸς ὑπάρχειν μὴ ὑπάρχει), neither does it belong to the one to which it is less likely to belong (οὐδ' ᾧ ἧττον); and if it belongs to that to which it is less likely to belong (εἰ ᾧ ἧττον εἰκὸς ὑπάρχειν ὑπάρχει), then it belongs also to that to which it is more likely to belong (καὶ ᾧ μᾶλλον).

Aristotle does not give any concrete examples here, but fortunately there is one in Γ 6, 119b19-21 for the destructive part of the topos, except that the thesis here expresses particular belonging (τις):

> For example, if some kind of knowledge (ἐπιστήμη τις) were good in a greater degree than pleasure, while no knowledge is good, then neither would pleasure be good.

This topos of the greater and lesser degree is an excellent example for a topos which one might very much be inclined to interpret as a rule rather than the statement of a hypothetical protasis. The reason is that in contrast to most other examples of topoi, the topos here does not consist of two, but of three propositions and one might interpret the first two as the two premisses and the last as the conclusion of the hypothetical syllogism. Leaving aside the

---

[40] Cf. Brunschwig (1967), p. 153n.2.
[41] 115a3f.
[42] 115a6f., 8.
[43] 115a9-13.
[44] The constructive part of the topos seems to equal the topos in B 11, 115b3ff.
[45] This first and third cases are especially interesting, since they show that the hypothetical propositions do not necessarily have the form 'If Ax, then Bx', but also simply 'If P, then Q' and that obviously Aristotle uses the former way of expression only as an abbreviation of the latter, if he can do so (cf. Chapter Four, p. 102f.); for other examples see pp. 154 & 155.

particular belonging, the example for the topos given above could be understood as an argument of the following kind. Let A stand for "knowledge", B for "pleasure", and C for "good". "In a greater degree than" (μᾶλλον ἤ), which is to be understood in the sense of "more likely than", is abbreviated as M. The thesis is obviously 'B is C' ("Pleasure is a good"):

Destruction:

(A is C) M (B is C). (hypothesis)
A is not C.
Hence, B is not C.

Aristotle does not give an example for the construction of the thesis 'B is C', but the procedure is obvious from topoi investigated earlier. Let us assume that there is a proposition 'D is C' of which the truth of the predication is less likely than 'B is C' and let "in a lesser degree than" (ἧττον εἰκὸς) be abbreviated as L. The corresponding hypothetical syllogism would then be:

Construction:

(D is C) L (B is C).
D is C.
Hence, B is C.

In what way should the hypothesis, say in the destructive case, '(A is C) M (B is C)' imply the conclusion 'B is not C', once the negation of 'A is not C' in the additional premiss has been shown? One could think of this hypothesis, analogously to the diairetic hypothesis, as containing implications. Whereas there are four implications in a diairetic proposition, there are two in the hypothesis above: 'not (A is C)' implies 'not (B is C)' and '(B is C)' implies '(A is C)'. I.e. the negation of the more likely predication implies the negation of the less likely proposition and the assertion of the less likely proposition implies the assertion of the more likely predication. The former can be used for destruction of the thesis. The latter could theoretically be used for construction of the proposition 'A is C'; but the thesis 'B is C' is supposed to be constructed. Thus, here the hypothesis '(D is C) L (B is C)' is needed, which contains two implications: '(D is C) implies (B is C)' and 'not (B is C) implies not (D is C)'. The former is used for the construction of 'B is C'; the latter could theoretically be used for the destruction of 'D is C', which however is not the thesis.[46] The two relevant implications contained in the hypotheses for destruction and construction are explicitly stated in the passage 115a6-8 cited on the previous page.

However, the implication of the conclusion here is not necessary, but only probable. If knowledge is more likely good than pleasure and it is shown that knowledge is actually not good, then it makes the thesis that pleasure is good unlikely but not impossible; the opponent might very well not acknowledge his thesis to be refuted and contend that the questioner has only shown it to be

---

[46] Aristotle says explicitly that "the topos from the lesser degree can be used for construction only" (Γ 6, 119b23); of course, correspondingly, the topos from the greater degree is useful for destruction only.

unlikely. Also, such an argument would not classify as a syllogism, since the conclusion does not follow necessarily. There is one way to make the conclusion follow necessarily—one adds the whole implication to the reasoning and once the opponent has agreed to it, it will follow by necessity. The argument would then be, in the destructive case:

If ((A is C) M (B is C)) and (A is not C), then (B is not C).
(A is C) M (B is C). &
A is not C.
Hence, B is not C.

This hypothetical syllogism represents the fifth one enumerated by Theophrastus and obviously works as a metaleptic hypothetical syllogism (Hm); it is distinguished from the other hypothetical syllogisms by its use of the notion of probability. Alexander, *in APr.* 324, 26-29, gives the following example for a qualitative syllogism:

> If what would seem to be more self-sufficient with regard to happiness is not self-sufficient, then what is less so than it is not self-sufficient; but health, which would seem to be more self-sufficient than wealth with regard to happiness, is not self-sufficient; nor therefore is wealth.

This syllogism clearly satisfies the form given above, being in fact slightly more precise in that it states the hypothesis in general terms and not the needed instantiation which Aristotle clearly takes for granted.

Also in his commentary on the *Topics* Alexander clearly interprets the working of this topos in the same way as I do. In *in Top.* 206, 21-24 he only gives an example of the topos and thus it is unclear, in the same way as it is unclear in the *Topics*, as to whether he sees it as an argument or a hypothesis. However, he is unmistakably clear in *in Top.* 126, 31-127, 16 where he explains the working of the topos in general and illustrates it with an example of the topos of the greater and lesser degree, using as the hypothesis the same example as the one given in *in Top.* 206, 21-24. Thus he says that if someone wants to prove that wealth is not good he can find the protasis he needs with the help of the mentioned topos and syllogize the conclusion (127, 8-11):

> For if health is good in a higher degree than wealth and it is not good, then neither would wealth be good; if he takes this as a protasis (ἧς ληφθείσης προτάσεως) and adds some additional premiss (προσληφθείη) which says that health is not good because [...], then it would be shown (εἴη δεδειγμένον) according to the topos in hand (κατὰ τὸν προκείμενον τόπον) that wealth is not good.[47]

The example is obviously very similar to the one given in his commentary on the *Prior Analytics*, the only difference being that the predicate there is "self-sufficient" and not "good".[48]

---

[47] Alex. *in Top.* 127, 11-16.
[48] Even if the syllogism is interpreted as not having the form that I have argued, but rather the form of my first option, and one were to argue that the necessarily following of the conclusion is taken here in the more relaxed sense of high probability, this would not

2.3. The three topoi from the like degree (ἐκ τοῦ ὁμοίως)

Here, there are exactly the same three combinations of subjects and predicates as in the three last topoi from the greater and lesser degree. Again, I shall cite the first topos (115a17-19):

> For supposing that one predicate belongs or is generally regarded (δοκεῖ) to belong to two subjects in a like degree, then if it does not belong to the one neither does it belong to the other; while if it belongs to the one, it belongs to the remaining one as well.

This hypothetical syllogism functions analogously to the one constructed according to the topos from the greater and lesser degree. The main difference is that the like degree can be used both for destruction and construction, whereas the greater degree can be used for destruction and the lesser degree for construction only; for a concrete example of the hypothesis, see Γ 6, 119b24-27.

C. Selection of some topoi from book B

1. The first topos in B: 2, 109a34-b12

> Now one topos is to investigate whether the opponent has assigned (ἀποδέδωκεν) as an accident (ὡς συμβεβηκὸς) something which belongs in some other way (τὸ κατ' ἄλλον τινὰ τρόπον ὑπάρχον). This mistake is commonly made with respect to the genera of things, e.g. if someone were to say that being a colour is an accident (συμβεβηκέναι) of white—for being a colour is not an accident of white, but colour is its genus.

This is a very important topos since it is the only one in book B in which συμβεβηκός clearly has the meaning of "accident" and not sumbebekos or attribute. It is most probably a later addition[49] and constitutes a group with the topoi of the genus at the very beginning of Δ which are all in some way concerned with the relationship between genus and accident (120b15-121a11).[50] The expression "to assign" (ἀποδιδόναι τί (ὡς) τι) occurs very often in Δ[51] but scarcely in B, which again suggests a later addition.

The topos above is a clear example of what Theophrastus calls a parangelmatic topos, i.e. only the investigation-instruction is given and the topos has to be derived from it. Before deriving the topos however, first the investigation-instruction has to be made slightly more explicit. "In some other way" obviously refers to the three predicables other than the accident. Thus, the full and explicit instruction could be stated in the following way: '*investigate*

---

necessitate a rejection of my interpretation of the topos as a hypothetical protasis. As I have already said, the hypothesis containing the expression "in a greater/lesser degree than" contains two implications and it might be argued that the topoi in *Top.* B 10, 115a6-8 spell out these implications.

[49] Scholars are agreed on this; cf. Brunschwig (1967), p. LXXXf. and Sainati (1968), p. 72.

[50] The first one (1, 120b21-29) in fact deals with exactly the reverse error in which what belongs as an accident has been assigned as a genus.

[51] Δ 2, 122a22, b12; 3, 123a34; 5, 126b14, et al.; also (usually in the form ἀποδιδόναι τινός τι) in E 1, 128b28, 2, 130a37; 9, 139a14 and Z 6, 144b29, 145a3, 10, 14, et al.

whether the opponent has assigned something as an accident which in fact belongs as a genus or proprium or definition'.[52]

Now it is fairly clear which topos-hypothesis can be derived from that. Let A (X, Y) stand for 'X is an accident of Y', G (X, Y) stand for 'X is a genus of Y', P (X, Y) for 'X is a proprium of Y' and D (X, Y) for 'X is a definition of Y'. The topos-hypothesis can then be written in the following way: 'If G (X, Y) or P (X, Y) or D (X, Y), then not A (X, Y)'. This hypothesis can of course still be split further into parts: 'If G (X, Y), then not A (X, Y)', 'If P (X, Y), then not A (X, Y)', and 'If D (X, Y), then not A (X, Y)'.

This topos obviously derives from the first definition of the accident given in A 5, 102b4f.: 'A (X, Y) if and only if neither D (X, Y) nor P (X, Y) nor G (X, Y) and S (X, Y)'; S (X, Y) stands for 'X is a sumbebekos, i.e. an attribute, of Y'.[53]

The mistake of assigning the incorrect predicable "is most commonly made with respect to genera" (109a35f.) and Aristotle gives a corresponding example, which can be abbreviated as 'A (colour, white)'. But "being a colour is not an accident of white, but colour is its genus", i.e. to show that 'not A (colour, white)' it is enough to show that 'G (colour, white)'. The hypothetical argument runs in the following way:

If G (X, Y), then not A (X, Y).[54]

.

.

G (colour, white).
Hence, not A (colour, white).

The argument clearly functions as a destructive metaleptic hypothtical syllogism ((Hm)d).[55]

Aristotle goes on to make a very interesting specification as to the form of the thesis, which again points in the direction of a later addition:

> The opponent may of course expressly specify the appellation (κατὰ τὴν ὀνομασίαν διορίσαι) in his thesis (τιθέμενον), saying for example that to be a virtue is an accident (συμβέβηκε) of justice; but often even without such explicitness (μὴ διορίσαντι) it is obvious that he has assigned the genus as an accident (ὡς συμβεβηκὸς ἀποδέδωκεν); e.g. if someone were to say that whiteness is coloured (κέχρωται) or that walking is in motion (κινεῖσθαι). For a predicate (κατηγορία) derived from the genus is never said of a species in a derived form (παρωνύμως), but always the genera are predicated of their species synonymously (συνωνύμως); for the species

---

[52] The "or" is of course exclusive here.
[53] This definition in turn relies on the exclusive statement of the predicables given in Top. A 5: 'For all X and Y, either D (X, Y) or P (X, Y) or G (X, Y) or A (X, Y)'. From this even more implications can be derived: 'If G (X, Y), then not D (X, Y)', 'If (G (X, Y), then not P (X, Y)', etc.
[54] The hypothesis could also have the diairetic form 'Either G (X,Y) or A (X, Y)'.
[55] Aristotle does not explain here how to prove that colour is the genus of white. Of course, it would have to be shown that colour "is predicated in the essence of several things which differ in kind" (A 6, 102a31f.), one of which would have to be "white". This could be achieved with some of the topoi given in book Δ.

take on both the name and the definition of their genera. A man therefore who says that white is coloured has not assigned colour as its genus, since he has used a derived form (παρωνύμως), nor as a property, nor as a definition; for the definition and property of a thing belong to that thing and to nothing else, whereas many things besides white are coloured, e.g. a log, a stone, a man, a horse. Clearly then he assigns colour as an accident.[56]

I have shown in Chapter Three that in the case of definition, proprium and genus the predicate is explicitly stated as such whereas in the case of sumbebekos we have a simple predication of an attribute, without the attribute being specified in any way. Now, this topos deals with a thesis in which sumbebekos has the specific meaning of "accident" (συμβεβηκέναι[57]) and is explicitly stated as such (κατὰ τὴν ὀνομασίαν διορίσαι). However, Aristotle maintains that an accidental predication even if it is not explicitly specified as such (μὴ διορίσαντι) can be recognised by the derivative form (παρωνύμως)[58] that the accidental predicate has. The assertion of a genus, in contrast, is always synonymous.[59] The difference between the accident on the one hand and proprium and definition on the other is stated as follows: the latter can be predicated of exactly one thing, whereas the former of many things.

The purpose of the entire procedure is to assist the questioner in recognising that a predicate has been assigned as an accident. Having found out that the predicate has not been assigned either as a genus or as a proprium or as a definition, it is clear that it is assigned as an accident. Once the questioner has found out that the predicate has been assigned as an accident he can proceed as in the case described in the first part of the topos-entry in which the predicable was assigned explicitly; he might reassure himself by asking the opponent whether by saying "whiteness is coloured" he really means to say that colour is an accident of white.

There is also another way of interpreting the purpose of this procedure, which, however, seems to me to be less likely. It could be that the opponent himself agrees that colour is not an accident of white but its genus; however, he contests that the way he expresses himself indicates that he takes it to be an accident. In this case he would commit the error of violating the established terminology and this topos would be one of the few where this error is

---

[56] 109a39-b12. "Clearly" because Aristotle takes the definition of the accident (or the exclusive division of the predicables) for granted, as in the first part of the topos.

[57] ὑπάρχειν ὡς συμβεβηκός would be possible as well.

[58] Paronymity is defined in Cat. 1, 1a12-15 in the following way: "things are called paronymous which derive their name from something, being given a different inflection (διαφέροντα τῇ πτώσει). Thus, for example, the grammarian gets his name from grammar, the brave get theirs from bravery." "Inflection" (πτῶσις) can refer to different cases of a noun (Top. E 7, 136b18-22, De Int. 2, 16a32-b1, APr. A 36, 48b37-49a5 (including the nominative)), adjectives derived from nouns (Top. E 7, 136b15-18, b27f., Cat. 1a12-15), adverbs derived from nouns (Top. B 9, 114a33f., E 7, 136b15-18), superlatives of adjectives (Top. E 7, 136b28-32), genders (Top. Δ 4, 133b36-134a4, Soph. El. 14, 173b26f.), participles (Top. Z 10, 148a12f.), and various other inflections including those derived from verbs; cf. Steinthal (1890), 259ff.

[59] Aristotle specifies synonymous predication here in the following way: 'X is synonymously predicated of Y if and only if X and X's definition can be predicated of Y' (109b6f.). The same account is found in Cat. 1, 1a6-12.

proved. The procedure given above would tell the questioner how to prove that the way the answerer expresses himself commits him to the assertion of the predicate as an accident, i.e. he commits a linguistic error.[60] The reason why I think this interpretation is less likely is that Aristotle seems to refer in both cases, whether the belonging as an accident is explicitly stated or not, to the error of genuinely mixing up genus and accident.

2. *The second topos in B: 2, 109b13-29*

This topos is an important one which Aristotle counts among those "most universal" (μάλιστα κοινούς) and whose efficiency is only next to the "most opportune" topoi.[61] It can also be found in other books of the *Topics*.[62] The topos runs:

> Another topos is to examine all cases where a predicate has been said to belong to all or none of something. Look at them species by species (κατ' εἴδη) and not in their infinite number; for then the inquiry will proceed more methodically and in fewer steps. You should look and begin with the primary classes (ἀπὸ τῶν πρώτων), and then proceed step by step to those that are not further divisible: e.g. if a man has said that the knowledge of opposites is the same, you should look and see whether it be so of relatives and of contraries and of terms opposed as privation and possession, and of contradictory terms. [...]
> For if in any case it is proved that the knowledge of them is not the same (ἐὰν γὰρ ἐπὶ τινὸς δειχθῇ ὅτι οὐχ ἡ αὐτή), we shall have destroyed the problem (ἀνῃρηκότες ἐσόμεθα τὸ πρόβλημα). Likewise, also, if the predicate belongs in no case. This topos is convertible for both destructive and constructive purposes. [...][63]

This again is a parangelmatic topos from which a topos-hypothesis can be derived. The questioner is told to investigate the universal positive or negative thesis according to species. The example of the thesis—"the knowledge of opposites is the same"—makes it clear that the universality of the thesis consists in the thesis containing the general term "opposites". The questioner is told to divide (διαιρεῖν) it into its species (contradictories, contraries, relatives, etc.) and see whether the predicate "the knowledge is the same" is still true of them: "for if in any case it is proved that the knowledge of them is not the same we shall have destroyed the problem." The mode of expression (aorist-future perfect) clarifies that this argument is a hypothetical syllogism; it clearly works as a destructive metaleptic hypothetical syllogism ((Hm)d). One instance of the hypothesis could be for example "If the knowledge of opposites is the same, then the knowledge of contraries is the same." The argument could be written in the following way; let A and B stand for terms and S (A) for 'a species of A' and let the thesis be 'A is B'.

---

[60] Cf. Alex. *in Top.* 136, 8-11.
[61] H 4, 154a15-18
[62] Cf. Γ 6, 120a32-b6; Δ 1, 120b15-20.
[63] B 2, 109b13-20; 23-26.

Destruction:

> If B belongs to A, then B belongs to S(A).
> .
> .
> B does not belong to S(A)..
> Hence, B does not belong to A.

"To belong" stands here for "to be of" (εἶναι + subject in the genitive) (cf. p. 137f. above). The constructive argument described in b25-29 clearly works as a constructive metaleptic hypothetical syllogism ((Hm)c).

3. *The fourth topos in B: 2, 110a10-13*

> Moreover, one ought to turn the problema into a protasis for oneself (ἑαυτῷ ποιούμενον) and then raise an objection to it; for an objection (ἔνστασις) will be a ground of attack upon the thesis. This topos is very nearly the same as the topos to examine all cases where a predicate has been said to belong to all or none of something; but it differs in method (διαφέρει δὲ τῷ τρόπῳ).

I shall deal first with this fourth topos, since Aristotle says that this topos "is nearly the same" as the second one above. It is again a parangelmatic topos. It is not at all easy to see at first glance how a hypothetical syllogism could result from this topos. The crucial point is to understand the meaning of "problema" correctly. A problema is described in A 4 as a question of the form 'Is P the case, or not?' asked by the questioner and "it differs in the turn of phrase" (διαφέρει [...] τῷ τρόπῳ) (A 4, 101b28f.) from a protasis which has the form 'Is P the case?' "Out of every protasis you will make (ποιήσεις) a problema if you change the turn of phrase (μεταβάλλων τῷ τρόπῳ)" (A 4, 101b35). The similarity in expression might suggest that Aristotle has the same change in the turn of phrase in mind here, i.e. that the questioner is supposed to turn the problema which he asks into a protasis and then find an objection. However, such an interpretation would not make any sense, since the questioner cannot know the opponent's thesis before he has picked out an alternative from the problema, and thus he could not possibly find an objection.

Problema has obviously to be interpreted as having the meaning it in fact always has in books B-Θ, namely as the thesis—here clearly the opponent's thesis. Thus, the questioner is advised to turn the thesis into a protasis, i.e. a question, and find an objection to it. Why is it necessary to turn the thesis into a question? Simply because objections are made by the answerer to *protaseis* asked by the questioner: the questioner is told to put himself into the rôle of the answerer who tries to find an objection to a protasis, i.e. a contradictory instance to a general protasis.

Thus the topos functions as the above one, but "differs in method" (διαφέρει δὲ τῷ τρόπῳ).[64] The former topos is more methodical since an exact procedure is given for finding instances which are implied by the thesis through the dividing of a general term into species. Once a negative instance is found, we have actually thereby found an objection. This is exactly what the present topos instructs the questioner to do, however, without specifying how such an objection is found exactly. Aristotle does not give an example but it is not difficult to think of one. Let the thesis be for example "All pleasure is good." The questioner is supposed to turn it into a protasis for himself, i.e. "Is all pleasure good?", and find an objection, e.g. "Gluttony is not good." Having made the implication specific and proved that it is not the case that gluttony is good the thesis will be destroyed by the hypothetical syllogism of the form (Hm)d, just as in the topos above.

Thus one can see that even such an odd topos as this one can be understood as functioning as a hypothetical syllogism.

4. *The third topos in B: 2, 109b30-110a9*

> Another topos is to make definitions both of the sumbebekos and of that to which it belongs as a sumbebekos (i.e. its subject), either of both separately or of one of them, and then see if anything untrue has been assumed as true in the definitions. [...] Again, to see if the indignant man is envious, ask what each of these terms means; for thus it will be obvious whether the statement is true of false; e.g. if he is envious who grieves at the successes of the good, and he is indignant who grieves at the successes of the evil, then clearly the indignant man would not be jealous.

It is fairly clear how this topos (109b30-32; 38-110a4) works. The questioner is advised to make a definition of both predicate and subject or of one of them.[65] Let the thesis be 'A is B' and let Def(X) stand for 'the definition of X'. The three possible topos-hypotheses derived from the investigation-instruction are then: 'If A is B, then A is Def (B)', 'If A is B, then Def(A) is B' and 'If A is B, then Def(A) is Def(B)'. Let us formalize the third example that Aristotle gives (109b38-110a4). Let A stand for the "indignant man", B for "envious", Def(A) for "being pained at the prosperity of the wicked", Def (B) for "being pained at the prosperity of the good". The thesis is 'A is B'.

If A is B, then Def (A) is Def (B).
Def (A) is not Def (B)
Hence, A is not B.

---

[64] The Greek word τρόπος is sometimes used synonymously with the word μέθοδος, cf. *Top.* A 4, 102a10 and a12; *De An.* A 1, 402a19; *APr.* A 31, 46b36 (ὁ τρόπος τῆς ζητήσεως); *De Part. Anim.* A 5, 646a2 (ὁ τρόπος τῆς μεθοδοῦ), et al.

[65] He then goes on to say (110a4-9) that one should even define the terms used in the definitions: "One ought also to substitute definitions for the terms used in the definitions, and not stop until one arrives at something familiar; for often although the whole definition has been given, the point at issue is not yet clear, but it becomes clear when a definition has been given for one of the terms in the definition."

CHAPTER FIVE

The argument is of course a destructive one and it works as a destructive metaleptic hypothetical syllogism ((Hm)d).

D. *Topoi of "what is more worthy of choice" and of "what is the same"*

In the previous chapter I mentioned these topoi as among those which Alexander could have had in mind when writing of "other varieties of hypothetical syllogisms" (cf. p. 107). I shall deal with them now.

1. *Topoi of "what is more worthy of choice"*

In book Γ 1-4 we find theses asserting that something is "more worthy of choice" (αἱρετώτερον) or "better" (βέλτιον)[66] than some other thing. This class of predications is subordinated to those containing a sumbebekos-predication. Thus in A 5, 102b14-20 Aristotle writes:

> To sumbebekos are to be attached also all comparisons of things together, when expressed in language that is derived in any kind of way from sumbebekos; such as for example, the question "Is the honourable or the expedient more worthy of choice (αἱρετώτερον)?" and "Is the life of virtue or the life of self-indulgence the pleasanter (ἡδίων)?", and any other problem which may happen to be phrased in terms like this. For in all such cases the question is to which of the two does the predicate belong as a sumbebekos in a greater degree (μᾶλλον).

Aristotle also specifies the subject matter of problemata which deal with what of two things is more worthy of choice (Γ 1, 116a4-9)—it has to be problematic:

> But first it must be clearly laid down that the enquiry we are making concerns not things that are widely divergent and that exhibit great differences from one another (for nobody raises any doubt whether happiness or wealth is more desirable), but things that are nearly related and about which we discuss for which of the two we ought rather to vote, for we do not see any advantage (ὑπεροχήν) on either side as compared with the other.

In book Γ Aristotle gives a list of topoi which can be used as hypotheses in hypothetical syllogisms. The examples that Aristotle gives serve to illustrate the hypothesis, not the entire argument. One example is (116a29-33):

> Also, that which is worthy of choice (αἱρετόν) for its own sake is more worthy of choice than that which is so for some other reason; e.g. health is more worthy of choice than exercise; for the former is worthy of choice for its own sake, the latter for something else.

Clearly the proposition "what is worthy of choice for its own sake is more worthy of choice than that which is worthy of choice for some other reason" is being propounded here and made clear by an example. In a debate the questioner would of course have to deliver several examples to establish the

---

[66] Cf. 116a30 (sc. αἱρετώτερον), b8f. (sc. αἱρετώτερον), b18 (sc. βέλτιων), b30f. (sc. βέλτιων).

hypothesis inductively. Aristotle does not give a concrete example of a whole argument, but it is clear that, as in previous cases, the argument would work analogously to the establishing of the hypothesis. Let us then assume that the questioner's thesis is that "health is more worthy of choice than exercise". Let A stand for "that which is worthy of choice for its own sake", B for "that which is worthy of choice for some other reason", C for "health", D for "exercise". Let "more worthy of choice" (αἱρετώτερον) be abbreviated as A. The thesis to be constructed is 'C A D.'

A A B.
C is A; D is B.
Hence, C A D

How do we know that the argument functions as a hypothetical syllogism? At the very beginning of Γ Aristotle describes the workings of the arguments found in Γ 1 and his mode of expression—aorist-future perfect—makes clear that he thinks of them as of hypothetical syllogisms (116a10-12):

> If one or more points of superiority can be shown (δειχθείσης ὑπεροχῆς ἢ μιᾶς ἢ πλειόνων), the mind will agree (συγκαταθήσεται ἡ διάνοια) that whichever of the two alternatives is actually superior is the more worthy of choice (τοῦτ' ἐστιν αἱρετώτωρεον, ὁπότερον τυγχάνει αὐτῶν ὑπερέχον).

The working of the hypothetical syllogism is described here in psychological terms but it is clear that in the context of the debate the hypothesis in which the standard of superiority is set, has been agreed upon—the entire book Γ is mainly a list of these hypotheses.

The terms on the both sides of "... is more worthy of choice than ..." in the hypothesis can have different forms. Thus, at the beginning of Γ 2 another frequent form of the terms is specified (117a5-10):

> Whenever two things are very much like one another, and we cannot see any superiority (ὑπεροχήν) in the one over the other of them, we should look at them from the standpoint of their consequences. For the one which is followed by the greater good is the more desirable; or, if the consequences be evil, that is more desirable which is followed by the lesser evil. For though both may be desirable, yet there may still be some unpleasant consequence.

The hypothesis here is not just 'A A B', but '(A which has superior consequences) A (B which has inferior consequences)'; but the relation A and thus the main form of the argument remains the same.

2. Topoi of "what is the same"

Top. H 1 deals with theses which express the sameness or difference of something with or between something else (ταὐτό-predication): 'A is the same as (ταὐτό) B' or 'A is not the same as (οὐ ταὐτό) B'. At the beginning of H 1 the "most opportune" topoi are listed with the help of which the thesis expressing sameness can be constructed (151b30-152a4) whereas the rest of the chapter lists topoi on how to destroy theses expressing sameness. The theses containing "the same"-predication constitute a subclass of theses in which a definition-predication is expressed. In A 5, 102a5-9 Aristotle says:

> One may, however, call definitory such a remark as that the beautiful is the becoming, and likewise also the question, "Are perception and knowledge the same or different?"—for argument about definitions is mostly concerned with questions of sameness and difference.

Let us take as an example the topos in 152a31-33:

> Again, look and see if, supposing the one to be the same as something, the other also is the same as it; for if they are not both the same as the same thing, clearly neither are they the same as one another.

The first sentence contains the investigation-instruction, from which the hypothesis can be derived, whereas the second (after the semicolon) explains how the argument works. The argument can be formalized in the following way; let the thesis to be destroyed be 'A is the same as B':

> If X is the same as Y and X is the same as Z, then Y is the same as Z.
> A is the same as C, but B is not the same as C.
> Hence, A is not the same as B.

It is striking that Aristotle describes this argument with such brevity and that he takes so many steps for granted, which one would not take for granted in modern logic. In order to make it work logically in the modern sense the hypothesis has to be instantiated in a certain way and several steps have to be made explicit. Let us instantiate the hypothesis in the following way, substituting X, Y, Z by A, B, C respectively and writing 'A=B' for 'A is the same as B' and accordingly in the other two cases:

> If (A=B and A=C), then B=C.

To make the structure more clear, let us transform the above formula into propositional logic, substituting 'A=B' by 'P', 'A=C' by 'Q' and 'B=C' by 'R':

> $(P \land Q) \to R$
> $P \to (Q \to R)$ (by Exportation)
> $P \to \text{not } (Q \land \text{not } R)$ (by a Law of Implication)

Now the second premiss can be added:

> $(Q \land \text{not } R)$

The conclusion can now by deduced by Modus tollens, or rather with the help of the destructive metaleptic hypothetical syllogism ((Hm)d):

> Hence, not P

How can we know that the above arguments are syllogisms? They are mentioned explicitly in A 18, 108a38-b6 as the syllogisms about sameness and difference (συλλογισμοὶ περὶ ταὐτοῦ καὶ ἑτέρου). Aristotle describes the destructive workings of these arguments using the mode of expression common to hypothetical syllogisms, i.e. aorist-future perfect:

> For when we have discovered (εὑρόντες) a difference of any kind whatever between the subject under discussion, we shall have shown (δεδειχότες ἐσόμεθα) that they are not the same (ὅτι οὐ ταὐτόν).[67]

Since Aristotle distinguished between categorical and hypothetical syllogisms and the above syllogisms of "what is more worthy of choice" and of "what is the same" are not categorical syllogisms, I have inferred that they are hypothetical syllogisms. It is interesting to note that Galen in the sixteenth chapter of his *Institutio logica* speaks in cases in which the predicates "is more worthy of choice" and "is the same" occur, of a third kind of a syllogism: the *relational* syllogisms (συλλογισμὸς κατὰ τὸ πρός τι γενέσθαι).[68]

At least as far as the syllogisms of what is worthy of choice[69] are concerned it is to be said that they do not have the common characteristic of hypothetical syllogisms. In a hypothetical syllogism the thesis to be proved or refuted is "substituted" (μεταλαμβάνειν) by another one on which the proof concentrates and which is linked to the thesis through some kind of implication expressed in the hypothesis; there are at least two predications in a hypothesis. In the proposition 'A is more worthy of choice than B' this is of course not the case.[70] Neither is the syllogism with this hypothesis a categorical syllogism. Thus, one could indeed speak of a third sort of syllogism.

As for the syllogisms of "what is the same", the syllogism formalized above is certainly a hypothetical syllogism, since it satisfies all the conditions. The argument without the hypothesis, i.e. A=C, B≠C, hence A≠B, might still be considered to be a valid argument and it is this sort of argument which Galen seems to have classified as relational syllogisms. However, Galen himself suggests adding the hypothesis as a premiss,[71] but then that would not be another kind of syllogism any more. It would certainly be interesting to compare Galen's relational syllogisms with the arguments

---

[67] A 18, 108b2-4. Cf. also A 5, 102a6-17 where Aristotle explains that the topoi of "what is the same" are useful for the destruction, though not the construction of definitions: "for when we have shown (δείξαντες) that a thing is not the same as another, we shall have destroyed (ἀνῃρηκότες ἐσόμεθα) the definition" (a13f.).

[68] *Inst. Log.* 38, 13f.

[69] Galen obviously has a similar sort of syllogism in mind to the one found in *Top.* Γ. One example he gives, *Inst. Log.* 42, 1-3, is: "The virtue of the better is more worthy of choice (sc. than the virtue of the worse); soul is better than body; hence, the virtue of the soul is more worthy of choice than the virtue of the body."

[70] However, the "most opportune" topoi in Γ do represent hypotheses of the 'normal' sort, since they do not have the form 'X A Y', but 'If X A Y, then f(X) A f(Y)'; cf. e.g. Γ 3, 118a34-39: "Furthermore, we can judge things from their inflected forms, uses, actions and effects, and also vice versa; for they all follow one another (ἀκολουθεῖ γὰρ ἀλλήλοις). For example, if 'justly' is more worthy of choice than 'courageously', then also justice is more worthy of choice than courage; and if justice is more worthy of choice than courage, then also 'justly' is more worthy of choice than 'courageously'. Similarly also in the other cases."

[71] Cf. *Inst. Log.* 39, 17-19.

found in *Top.* Γ and H, but such an investigation would lead us too far astray from the *Topics*.[72] In any case it can be said that it was neither in Galen nor in the authors whom he cites as his predecessors[73] where the very origins of relational arguments are found but in Aristotle's *Topics*.

E. *Origins of categorical syllogisms in the Topics*

I have mentioned in the Introduction that we not only find the origins of hypothetical syllogisms in the *Topics* but also, to a much lesser extent, those of categorical syllogisms. In fact the topos in B 4, 111a14-32 seems to be the only clear case. Aristotle seems to run into problems here, principally because he does not seem to take into account the quantification but rather relies on the intensions of the terms. I shall also discuss a topos in which it is not obvious whether it works as a categorical or a hypothetical syllogism.

1. *The topos in B 4, 111a14-32*

This section will deal with the first topos described in 111a14-20 and the two passages in which Aristotle refers to the first topos (a23-27 and a29-31), reflecting on the value of the first topos for construction and destruction; I shall leave the second topos (a20-23) aside. The relevant passage is as follows:

> In order to prove that contrary attributes belong to the same thing (τὰ ἐναντία τῷ αὐτῷ ὑπάρχοντα), look at its genus; e.g. if we want to show that there is correctness and error in perception (ἔστι περὶ αἴσθησιν ὀρθότης καὶ ἁμαρτία): since to perceive is to distinguish (ἐπεὶ τὸ αἰσθάνεσθαι κρίνειν ἐστί), and there is distinguishing in a correct and an incorrect way (κρίνειν δ' ἔστιν ὀρθῶς καὶ μὴ ὀρθῶς), thus with regard to perception there is correctness and error as well (καὶ περὶ αἴσθησιν ἂν εἴη ὀρθότης καὶ ἁμαρτία). In the present instance the proof starts from the genus and relates to the species, for 'distinguishing' is the genus of 'perceiving', since he who perceives is distinguishing in a certain way [...]. Now, the former topos is false (ψευδής) for the purposes of construction [...]. For it is not necessary that all the attributes that belong to the genus should also belong to the species; for an animal is winged or (καὶ)[74] quadruped, but man is not. [...] On the other hand, for the purposes of destruction, the former argument is true [...]: for all the attributes which do not belong to the genus do not belong to the species either.

---

[72] On the relational syllogism in Galen cf. Barnes (1993), (1990b) and (1990a). The last mentioned work is very illuminating as to how the ancients, including Stoics and mathematicians, dealt with arguments of this sort and as to how one can deal with such arguments in general.

[73] Posidonius is cited by name in *Inst. Log.* 47, 16.

[74] The Greek καί is usually a conjunction and translated as 'and'. However, there is of course no animal which is winged *and* quadruped at the same time, but some are winged and some quadruped. Thus, this a clear instance in which καὶ has the meaning of a disjunction 'or', which is not unusual in Aristotle (cf. Bonitz (1870), 367b20-24).

The theses which can be dealt with through the help of this topos express a belonging of contraries to a term (a14). In the second part of the passage however (a23-32) Aristotle no longer confines the predicates to contraries, as the examples "animal is winged or quadruped, but man is not" (a26f.) and "if man is good, then animal is also good" (a28) clearly show.

The questioner is supposed to investigate whether the contraries belong to the genus of the term. He constructs the thesis by showing that they belong and destroys the thesis by showing that they do not belong, assuming the topos that 'that which belongs to the genus also belongs to the species'.[75]

In a15-18 Aristotle seems to give us an example of an argument which in a debate had to be formulated in the form of two protaseis and a conclusion; the thesis to be constructed is: "there is (ἔστιν) correctness and error in perception."

There is (ἔστιν) distinguishing (genus) in a correct and an incorrect way.
To perceive (species) is to distinguish (genus).

Hence, there is correctness and error in perception (species).

First of all, scholars are agreed that the predicate "is" (ἔστιν) in "there is (ἔστιν) correctness and error in perception" (a15f.&17f.) and also in "there is (ἔστιν) good and bad knowledge" (a21) is existential,[76] and that is why I have translated it as "there is". There is some dispute as to whether "is" in "an animal is winged or quadruped" (a26) and "if man is good, then animal is also good" (a28) is existential or copulative. However, whereas this is a problem for editors it is[77] not a problem in the context of analysing arguments, since Aristotle does not seem to see any important difference between the existential and copulative meaning of "to be" and he obviously takes "to belong" to encompass the meaning of the existential "to be" as well—the present topos is supposed to be useful for proving that "contrary attributes belong to the same thing" (a14) and an example for such a thesis is "there is correctness and error in perception" (a15f.).

Let us then formalize the first argument slightly and see why the protaseis necessitate the conclusion. Let A stand for 'in a correct and incorrect way'

---

[75] This is of course a false assumption, as Aristotle himself is aware, stating that "it is not necessary that all the attributes that belong to the genus should also belong to the species" (a25f.). That is the reason why the topos is false for construction.

[76] In both cases we have the typical position of ἔστι as a full and not an auxiliary verb before the subject. In the former case "perception" is not even the grammatical subject so that "is" could not be copulative here, and in the latter case "knowledge" cannot be both good and bad at the same time.

[77] The existential "is" in Greek is accentuated (ἔστι), the copulative "is" is not (ἐστι). In a26 and a28 Wallies and Ross choose the first option, Bekker, Waitz and Brunschwig the second.
From the standpoint of modern logic the existential 'is' would certainly make more sense—only *some* animals are winged—but cf. my remarks on p. 162. In any case, the explanation of Brunschwig (1967), p. 42n.2 for not accentuating ἐστιν in a26 and a 28 is not sound. He explains this by pointing out that according to B 1 ὑπάρχειν corresponds to the copulative εἶναι. In the same footnote he then correctly observes that the first part of our passage shows that ὑπάρχειν can also be transformed into an existential εἶναι. But then his argument for not accentuating εἶναι in a26 and 28 falls down and his decision is not backed by any reason at all.

(ὀρθῶς καὶ μὴ ὀρθῶς), B for 'distinguishing' (κρίνειν), C for 'perceiving' (αἰσθάνεσθαι). The constructive argument then has the form:

Construction:

B is A
C (species) is B (genus)

C (species) is A

The fact that ἔστιν is existential does not mean that we have to interpret the thesis as expressing a particular belonging, as modern logic tells us to do—in Aristotle's logic both universal and particular propositions have an existential import (a is clear from his Law of Subalternation). When Aristotle asserts the existence of correctness and incorrectness in perception, he obviously wants to assert it of every perception, i.e. every perception is either correct or incorrect (correspondingly in the case of distinguishing); for reasons of clarity I have taken the liberty of representing the disjunctive predicate here by a single term since the disjunctivity does not play a rôle here (although in *APr.* A 31, 46b3-19 where it does not play any rôle either Aristotle represents it by two terms). Thus we can write, substituting "is" by "belongs to all":

A belongs to all B
B belongs to all C

A belongs to all C.

The argument is clearly valid. It has the form of Barbara. Of course, Aristotle was certainly not aware of the argument having the exact structure given above. In fact, it will be shown that he saw its functioning differently. However, it can be seen that the argument has a formal structure which makes it valid and that Aristotle is progressing here towards his syllogistic in the *Prior Analytics*.

Aristotle says that this topos is wrong in the constructive case, because it is not necessarily the case that that which belongs to the genus also belongs to the species. He gives a counterexample: an animal is winged or quadruped, but not a man (a23-27). Does this mean that the above argument is invalid? This would be most unusual since it has the form of Barbara and is therefore always valid. What then is different about the counter-example? Let us have a closer look at it. Extensionally, the quantification of "an animal is winged or quadruped" seems to be different to that of "there is correctness and error in perception". The latter is a universal protasis—error or correctness is in all kinds of perception, the former a particular protasis—some animals are winged, some quadruped.

Let A be quadruped, B animal and C man. 'A belongs to some B and B belongs to all C' does not necessitate that A belongs to some, let alone to all C. Thus we see that the first argument is correct, the second false. Aristotle clearly says that the topos is false because, in the constructive case, we *do not always* necessitate a true conclusion. Admittedly, Aristotle does not argue here with quantification, but explains the point with the help of the concepts of genus and species. Some of the properties of a genus belong to all its species (in the case of animal, e.g. "having a soul"), some do not (in the case of animal, e.g. 'two-footed'), i.e.: 'X belongs to genus' does not necessitate 'X belongs to species' (cf. a25f.). The way I have formalized the two arguments is obviously not the way Aristotle thought of them here, as there are two syllogisms of different forms for the argument in a16-18 and the counterexample in a26f. He considers them both to have the same form or structure.[78]

It is interesting to compare the above topos with the one which immediately follows it in the text (111a33-b11). This topos actually consists of three topoi listed in the first three lines which differ only with respect to the exact way of their belonging (a 33-36). Let us look at the very first topos (a33f.):

> Of all those things of which the genus is predicated, some of its species (τῶν εἰδῶν τι) must necessarily (ἀναγκαῖον) also be predicated.

The difference between the present topos and the preceding topos which runs "all the attributes that belong to the genus should also belong to the species" is that in the former genus and species are *predicates* which are predicated of some subject whereas in the latter some predicate is predicated of the *subject* genus and species.

In contrast to the preceding topos the present topos is always true since Aristotle takes extensionality into consideration—he specifies here "species" by the quantifier "some". The preceding topos could always be made true by simply replacing "to the species" by "to *some* species". It is fairly clear that the present topos works as a hypothetical syllogism.[79] It seems as though in the *Topics* Aristotle was more clear about arguments which were later classified as hypothetical syllogisms than about those known later as categorical syllogisms.

Let us now turn to the destructive argument which Aristotle says is always correct (a29-31). Aristotle does not give any concrete argument, but it can easily be derived from the constructive argument by simply transforming the conclusion and the major premiss into a *negative* universal proposition.[80] The destructive argument then has the following form:

Destruction:

> A belongs to no B.
> B belongs to all C.
> _____
> A belongs to no C.

The argument is valid; it has the form of Celarent. Aristotle says that the topos is true in this destructive argument because the produced protaseis

---

[78] On this topos cf also Kneale and Kneale (1962), pp. 36f.
[79] Cf. especially 111b8-11.
[80] Aristotle does not use quantifiers explicitly here and thus I assume that "to destroy" is meant in the sense of proving a negative statement, as specified in Chapter One, p. 18f.

always necessitate the conclusion (a29-31). The reason is that that which does not belong to the genus does not belong to any of its species either: 'X does not belong to the genus' necessitates 'X does not belong to the species' (cf. a30f.).

So, why does the topos always deliver valid arguments for destruction and not always for construction? It would seem that, expressed in terms of quantification, 'X belongs to the genus' (the case of construction) can mean, with respect to its species: 'X belongs to all species of the genus' or 'X belongs to some species of the genus'. In contrast, 'X does not belong to the genus' (the case of destruction) can only mean: 'X does not belong to any species.'

So, if X belongs only to some of the species of the genus, it cannot be guaranteed that the species which has to be proved as having the property X happens to be among those ("some") species which share with the genus the property X. Of course, Aristotle does not operate here with quantification but with the concepts of genus and species. The quantifications are however implicitly contained in these concepts. Aristotle is content to state simply that that which belongs to the genus does not necessarily belong to the species, and as proof he gives a counterexample.

Finally it can be queried what the topos for the construction of a categorical syllogism actually provides us with here. The topos tells us to find the genus of the subject, which I have designated with the letter B; in concreto, it tells us to look at the genus of "perception" which is "distinguishing". Thus, what is found with the help of the topos is clearly the middle term or, stated more fully, the proposition containing the middle term. As in all topoi, a proposition is found which is in some way or another related to the thesis—here the subject is substituted by its genus. However, the relation between the thesis (=conclusion) and the substituting proposition is not expressed as an implication in a protasis, but is expressed in the minor premiss by making explicit the connection between the substituted and substituting terms of the two propositions. The substituting premiss together with the minor premiss then yield the conclusion.

2. *The topos in B 2, 110a14-22*

> Furthermore, you must determine what kind of things (ποῖα) should be called as the majority call them, and what should not; for this is useful both for constructive and destructive purposes. For instance, you should determine that things (πράγματα) ought to be described in the language used by the majority, but when it is asked what kinds of things (ποῖα πράγματα) are or are not of such and such a kind (τοιαῦτα ἢ οὐ τοιαῦτα), you must no longer pay attention to the majority. For example, it is right to call healthy whatever is productive of health, as does the majority; but when it is asked whether the subject under discussion is productive of health or not, you must no longer use the language of the majority, but that of the doctor.

This is a topical argument where it is not easy to decide whether it works as a hypothetical or a categorical syllogism, simply because no explanation is given as to how the argument constructed according to the topos works formally. Thus it is possible to interpret it as a hypothetical or a categorical syllogism. I shall demonstrate these two possible of interpretations.

In the investigation-instruction the advice is given to determine what kind of things should be called as most men call them, and what should not: words (ὀνομασίαι) that mean the same things (πράγματα) to most people should be normally used, but when the question is what kinds of things (ποῖα πράγματα) are or are not of such and such a kind, one should use the language of the specialist. The concrete example (a19-22) makes the procedure perfectly clear. We should use the word (ὀνομασία) "healthy" to call those things (πράγματα) which are productive of health; but the kind of things (ποῖα πράγματα) which are productive of health should be determined by the doctor and not the multitude. One should define names like "healthy" according to everyman's belief, but when specifying what things are actually healthy for men, one should follow the opinion of the doctors.[81]

Let us take as an example the thesis 'Boxing is healthy' and show how to destroy it, in the first instance with the help of a hypothetical syllogism, and afterwards with the help of a categorical syllogism.

2.1. *The topical argument interpreted as a hypothetical syllogism*
One could think of a simplified dialectical debate taking the following course: "You mean by healthy 'that which is productive of health', as in fact the majority does?"[82]; "Yes." "Thus, 'if boxing is healthy, then it is also productive of health?'"; "Yes." "Now, what is productive of health is the subject-matter of medicine,[83] is it not, and so we should call those things productive of health which the doctor calls so". "Yes". "But the doctors say that boxing is not productive of health, that in fact it may cause serious damage to our health, do they not?"[84] "Yes." The questioner concludes thus, that according to the linguistic usage of the majority which was agreed upon in the hypothesis, boxing is not healthy.

In order to see the structure of the destructive argument more clearly, I shall use letters instead of terms. Let B stand for 'boxing', H for 'healthy', P for 'productive of health'. The thesis is then 'B is H.'

    If B is H, then B is P.
    B is not P
    Hence, B is not H

---

[81] In A 10, 104a33-37 Aristotle explicitly states that the technical opinions belong to the dialectical protaseis as well: "It is also obvious that all opinions which accord with the arts are dialectical protaseis; for people are likely to assent to the opinions of those who have examined the subjects in question, e.g. on questions of medicine people would assent to the opinion of the doctor and in matters of geometry to the opinion of the geometrician, and so too with the other arts."

[82] Cf. Θ 1, 156b20-23: "It is also useful to add that such and such a view is that generally held and expressed; for people shrink from trying to upset the received opinions unless they have some objection to bring, and they are wary of upsetting them at the same time as they are themselves also making use of such things."

[83] Cf. e.g. 110b18f.: "Medicine is the science both of producing health and of dieting." Cf. also 107a6f.

[84] This would have to be confirmed in some way, e.g. by citing some famous school of medicine.

The syllogism clearly works as a destructive metaleptic hypothetical syllogism ((Hm)d). The formal procedure is similar to the one in 109b30-110a9. The topos there tells us to define the subject or the predicate or both and see if the thesis turns out to be false. Here, Aristotle gives us a clue as to how to define a term of the thesis—according to common usage—and how to refute the proposition implied by the thesis—by referring to the opinion of an expert.

2.2. *The topical argument interpreted as a categorical syllogism*

A debate could follow a very similar course to the one described above but with a slight difference. In the debate above the positively answered proposition "You mean by healthy 'that which is productive of health', as in fact the majority does?" was used as an argument for the establishing of the hypothesis 'if boxing is healthy, then it is also productive of health?' However, we could take this proposition itself as a premiss and do without the hypothesis. The argument would then have to be formalized in a different way; let the letters stand for the same terms as before:

P is H.   (common usage of the majority)
B is not P. (that is what the doctor says)
Hence, B is not H.

This is clearly a categorical syllogism. When we add the universal quantifiers we have the syllogism of the form Celarent.

It seems to me to be impossible, having the investigation-instruction only, to decide whether this topical argument works as a hypothetical or a categorical syllogism. With the example above I hope to have illustrated this difficulty. However, since the great majority of the topoi work as hypotheses in hypothetical syllogisms I would rather opt for the first interpretation.

3. *Categorical syllogisms in dialectical debates*

It is not surprising that some predecessors of categorical syllogisms are found in the *Topics*. Categorical syllogisms were clearly used in dialectical debates as well and some predecessors seem to be found in book Θ.[85] The entire terminology in the *Prior Analytics* is dialectical—problema, protasis, syllogism, prosyllogism, constructing and destroying of a thesis, all the various ways of describing predication as "to belong", etc.—and it is clear that categorical syllogisms as well as hypothetical ones originate in dialectical debates; both kinds of syllogism can be used in a debate using endoxical protaseis and thus both can be dialectical syllogisms. There are many parallel passages in the *Topics* and the *Prior Analytics*. In *APr.* A 26 for example Aristotle speaks about the relative difficulty of constructing and destroying theses, just as he does in *Top.* H 5. The difference is that in *Top.* H 5 the relative difficulty is discussed with respect to each predicable whereas in *APr.* A 26 it is discussed with respect to positive or negative universal and

---

[85] Cf. Chapter One, p. 26f.

particular conclusions; the common ground is thus that of sumbebekos. Aristotle first gives reasons peculiar to syllogistic for a thesis being hard to attack (42b27-43a2)—"that which is concluded in more figures and by more moods is easier, while that which is concluded in fewer figures and by fewer moods is harder to refute" (42b29-32). He then says that universal theses are easier to destroy than particular ones, because the former we can destroy both by another universal or by a particular conclusion, whereas the latter can only be destroyed by a universal one (43a2-15). This is exactly what Aristotle says in H 5, 154b33-155a2.

An even more striking similarity is found in *APr.* A 27-28 where it is explained how to find a categorical syllogism to a given thesis or conclusion,[86] just as it is explained in the *Topics*, for the most part, how to find hypothetical syllogisms. The passage here is analogous to the passage in *Top.* B 4, 111b17-23 where Aristotle advises us to select propositions consequent or antecedent to the thesis, depending on whether we want to destroy or construct a thesis. In *APr.* A 27-28 Aristotle advises to select antecedents and consequents as well, but here these expressions refer to terms and not propositions. What is being sought is the middle term,[87] and this is exactly what the topos in B 4, 111a14-32 discussed above (pp. 160-164) provides us with. But Aristotle does not speak in *APr.* A 27-28 of topoi. The term seems to have been reserved for means of finding a hypothetical syllogism. The topos in B 4 just mentioned is one of a few exceptions; the topoi in books Δ, E and Z on principle could not tell us how to construct a categorical syllogism, since conclusions of the sort 'A is a genus/proprium/definition of B' cannot be established by them—we have three and not only two terms here. Categorical syllogisms establish or destroy propositions which are implied or which imply such theses. For example 'Animal is a genus of man' implies that 'All men are animals' and the latter proposition could of course be destroyed by a categorical syllogism; the thesis that 'Animal is a genus of man' however would only be destroyed on the basis of a hypothesis. Thus, apart from the few exceptions found in book B, the vast majority of topoi in the *Topics* tell us how to construct hypothetical syllogisms.

In this chapter I have shown a considerable number of topoi which clearly work, with the exception of a few, as hypotheses in hypothetical syllogisms. I have also demonstrated passages where Aristotle explicitly speaks about hypothetical syllogisms with respect to topoi. In the case of a few topoi it has sometimes been difficult to see how they work exactly, but the mode of expression often proves helpful in showing that they work as hypotheses of hypothetical syllogisms. All this makes it very likely that other topoi where Aristotle expresses himself very concisely also work as hypotheses. I have shown how such concisely expressed topoi, which are often just investigation-instructions, can be understood as working as hypotheses. Aristotle

---

[86] In *APr.* A 4-22 Aristotle merely lists various moods and figures of categorical syllogisms; he does not explain how to find them.

[87] Cf. A 28, 44b40: "The object of our invetigation is to discover the middle term" (τοῦ μέσου χάριν ἡ ἐπίβλεψις).

clearly realized, to a considerable extent by the time the *Topics* was written, that the vast majority of topical arguments work as hypothetical arguments. Theophrastus undertook the task of finishing a project begun by Aristotle, which the latter, for whatever reason, had not done himself.

SUMMARY

In this book I set out to answer the question of what a topos is and how the arguments constructed with the help of the topoi work.

In Chapter One I described the dialectical debates as they are delineated by Aristotle in book Θ, with a few characterizations from book A and the central books B-H. It is very important to understand this procedure, because it represents the context of the topoi in the central books which is taken for granted. I first provided a note on chronology maintaining that, in contrast to the common opinion, the core of Θ was actually written earlier than the rest of the *Topics*. This is especially important with respect to the fact that we do not find topoi in Θ, but instead a certain kind of universal protaseis which have a similar function in Θ to that of topoi in the central books. Firstly, I specified the principal purpose behind the *Topics*, namely training in disputation (γυμνασία), where there are two opponents, the questioner and the answerer. The former asks the latter a question of the form 'Is it the case that P, or not?' and whichever alternative ('P' or 'not P') the answerer chooses, the questioner takes over the other. The questioner poses questions and tries to deduce from the answers the contradictory of the answerer's thesis. I then went on to describe these exercises thoroughly, first the rôle of the questioner, then that of the answerer.

With respect to the rôle of the questioner I discussed the notions of the problema and protasis. I discussed the distinction between these two notions with regard to form, the problema having the form 'Is it the case that P, or not?', the protasis having the form 'Is it the case that P?' I then specified the notion of problema with respect to content that has to be in some way puzzling. I also specified the notions of "constructing" and "destroying" a thesis, both of which are tasks of the questioner, and which have two slightly different meanings. To destroy means either to refute a *positive* thesis (by concluding the negative thesis) or to refute an explicitly quantified universal *positive or negative* statement by proving a particular negative or positive thesis. To construct means, accordingly, to prove a *positive* thesis or a universal *positive or negative* thesis.

I then went on to describe the different sorts of protaseis described in Θ. There are necessary and auxiliary protaseis, and these can be divided into universal and singular protaseis. In order to understand the former distinction it is necessary in the first instance to make a distinction between two different sorts of syllogisms. There is a necessary syllogism with the help of which the thesis of the answerer is refuted; it is deduced from necessary protaseis. There are also syllogisms of the necessary premisses of the main syllogism (the so-called prosyllogisms), and these are deduced from auxiliary protaseis. The necessary protaseis are established, in the main, by induction or syllogism or can be advanced in their original form. Accordingly, the auxiliary protaseis are those with the help of which induction or syllogism of the necessary protaseis proceeds. Apart from that there are also auxiliary protaseis to add weight to the argument, to conceal the conclusion, or to render the argument more clear. Those used for concealing the conclusion are especially important, since induction and syllogisms serve to a large extent this purpose as well. The answerer of course does not want to be refuted and thus the questioner tries to hide the fact that the protaseis he propounds bring him nearer to the intended conclusion. Aristotle mentions various tactics for doing this.

Lastly, I stressed that universal and particular protaseis in Θ are not distinguished by quantifiers but by general and particular terms.

I then investigated the rôle of the answerer, which coincided with the investigation of "solution" and "objection". When the answerer objects to the whole reasoning he has to expose the error in the reasoning, i.e. solve it. The answerer is supposed to accept singular protaseis if they are endoxical. If he does not accept a universal protasis, he is supposed to give an objection, i.e. an instance of the contradictory of the universal protasis. If he does not do this he behaves peevishly.

In Chapter Two I turned to passages where Aristotle says something *about* the topoi. Aristotle does not give a definition of a topos anywhere in the *Topics*—he simply lists the topoi in the central books—but a quasi-definition can be found in the *Rhetoric*. The result of my investigation was that a topos turned out to be 'that under which many syllogisms fall'. I also looked at several other passages in the *Rhetoric* and the *Topics*. The context of these passages made it clear that Aristotle takes a topos to be a certain sort of general protasis and principle.

Next, other interpretations of the topos were examined, the most prominent one being the interpretation of topoi as rules. I have shown that this interpretation is very implausible in the context of a debate and that an argument constructed with the help of a rule does not fulfil the requirements of the definition of a syllogism. I suggested that the argument becomes cogent only if the topos is explicitly uttered. I then turned to a concrete example of a topos, namely the topos of the greater and lesser degree. The interpretation of this topos confirmed the earlier result: the topos is established by induction and stated as a protasis; the argument works as a hypothetical syllogism. However, as eventually became clear in Chapter Four, Aristotle seems to think of the working of a topos as a hypothesis, as a sort of rule and often expresses topoi correspondingly. Thus, it is not surprising that this interpretation is the prevalent one.

I then discussed the interpretation of topoi as laws and found that this does not conflict with my interpretation of topoi as protaseis and principles since the topoi expressed in the hypotheses can certainly be seen as certain logical laws; Aristotle in fact often says 'principle' where we would more commonly say 'law'.

This was also true of the interpretation of topoi as investigation-instructions, since topoi as principles and hypotheses of arguments can be derived from them. An especially impressive confirmation of this is provided by the investigation of organa. Organa are very similar to topoi, most strikingly as being investigation-instructions. In one passage Aristotle explicitly says of them that they are "in a way protaseis, since it is possible to make a protasis in accordance with each of them". It can be inferred that to topoi, corresponding protaseis can be produced as well, which of course confirms my interpretation.

Next, I turned to the topoi in central books and cited one topos of which Aristotle explicitly says that it is uttered as a protasis. I demonstrated several topoi which are objected to by objections; in the previous section on the interpretation of topoi as rules I also demonstrated topoi which are established by induction. Thus, just as the universal protaseis in Θ are established by induction and objected to by objections, so too are the topoi in the central books. This confirms my interpretation of topoi as protaseis uttered explicitly in the debate.

Finally, I mentioned authors who interpret topoi as principles and protaseis, above all Theophrastus, Aristotle's immediate successor. I investigated his definition of the topos which confirms my own interpretation. It is especially interesting that Theophrastus uses a specific name for the investigation-instruction, namely "parangelma", and that he specifies the topos not only formally as a principle and protasis but also so to speak, materially as a principle "determined in its compass, but indeterminate with respect to particulars".

In Chapter Three I dealt with predicables. Predicables are of great importance in the *Topics* because all topoi are divided according to them. One part of a topos expresses one of the predicables just as every thesis does. I concentrated on the notion of sumbebekos because Aristotle seems to use a different notion of it in the central books to that found in the two definitions in A 5, i.e. it seems to have a different meaning to the usual definition of an accident. I first offered a critique of Brunschwig's interpretation given in the introduction to his edition of the *Topics*. Brunschwig assumes two interpretations of predicables in the *Topics*. I have shown that, apart from sumbebekos, this is incorrect. Next, I gave a critique of Sainati's interpretation of sumbebekos as "predicate". Then I offered my own interpretation. I mainly concentrated on a passage in H 5. As it turns out, a sumbebekos designates an attribute which is stated in the problema and is not specified as to whether it is a definition, a proprium, or a genus. In contrast, the three remaining predicables are always explicitly stated in problemata as such. This is a very important insight, since if we understand sumbebekos as defined in A 5, most of the topoi in B and Γ appear incomprehensible. The topoi of sumbebekos in general are particularly important, since they deal with the level of belonging (ὑπάρχειν) only and can thus be used for the destruction of all the other predicables as well.

In Chapter Four I turned to the main form of arguments in the *Topics*, namely hypothetical syllogisms. Aristotle mentions some of them in the *Analytics*, but defers treatment of the same until later. However, there is no known book by Aristotle on hypothetical syllogisms. We know from Alexander that Theophrastus worked on hypothetical syllogisms and specified several kinds, of which Alexander provides a list. I have shown that these hypothetical syllogisms can be found in the *Topics*. The fact that Aristotle thought of these arguments as hypothetical syllogisms is especially clear from the mode of expression he uses in the case of the hypothetical syllogism: aorist-future perfect and genetivus absolutus in the singular + "necessary to be". The workings of the hypothetical syllogism are explained in the *Prior Analytics* and in the arguments in the *Topics*. Further evidence for Aristotle being the originator of hypothetical syllogisms is founded in the fact that the Peripatetic terminology for the names of hypothetical syllogisms clearly stems from him. The *reductionism* of less formal to more formal topoi, which can be found in the *Topics*, and the fact that Aristotle mentions several hypothetical syllogisms by specific names in the *Analytics*, shows that he was working on the abstraction of hypothetical syllogisms from the arguments which he wrote in the *Topics*.

Before turning to the *Topics* and further verifying my thesis that the arguments found here are hypothetical syllogisms, I first had to answer the difficult question of what a hypothetical syllogism is and how it works. Much has been written on it, but no interpretation seemed to me to be satisfactory, mainly because relevant passages in the *Topics* have not been taken into account. I have shown that the hypothesis is not only an agreement, but also contains an implication (ἀκολούθησις) and is regarded by Aristotle, at least in the *Topics*, as a protasis. Furthermore, it has to be endoxical. It is a protasis of a certain kind, namely one which possesses what could be called inferential power. The conclusion is concluded on the basis of a hypothesis (περαίνεσθαι ἐξ ὑποθέσεως) despite the misleading mode of expression which suggests that the proof ends with the proof of the substituted proposition. This result was confirmed by the investigation of the argument per impossibile and the Law of Subalternation. I explained how the implication works in the case of continuous and diairetic hypotheses. Finally, I pointed out that hypothetical syllogisms are found in *APr.* A 46 which further confirms that Aristotle worked on hypothetical syllogisms.

In Chapter Five I was able at last to come to the investigation of concrete topoi. I concentrated on the "most opportune" topoi and a selection of topoi from book B. I first dealt with the introductory chapter to B, which has three sections. The first and the third are directly relevant to the *Topics*, but slightly confusing. In the first Aristotle makes the distinction between universal and particular problemata (the former are found in B 2-Γ 5, the latter in Γ 6). In the third section he specifies two errors which can occur in problemata: false statement and transgression of the established use of language. The latter error scarcely seems to occur in the *Topics* and is not meant to be proved, but only pointed out. In the second section we find an interesting explanation as to why in the case of belonging of sumbebekota we can always use the word "to belong", but not always the word "to be". The passage is a case in point which shows the relevance of the *Topics* for questions in the *Analytics*, where many scholars have tried to establish *why* Aristotle "introduced" the expression "to belong" in the description of categorical syllogisms—this expression is in fact already found in the *Topics*.

I then turned to the so-called "most opportune" topoi which work as metaleptic hypothetical syllogisms ((Hm)), i.e. roughly as Modus ponens and tollens. I highlighted passages where Aristotle describes the arguments in full and other passages in which he just names the hypotheses and takes it for granted that the reader (or hearer) of the *Topics* knows how to construct an argument according to them. In the selection of the topoi from book B I showed how while some topical arguments clearly work as hypothetical syllogisms, in other topoi only an investigation-instruction is given. I showed how easily and most naturally hypotheses of hypothetical syllogisms can be derived from these investigation-instructions. I then turned to the topoi of "what is more worthy of choice" and of "what is the same", the hypotheses of which work in a specific way; Galen later categorized them as relational syllogisms as opposed to categorical and hypothetical syllogisms. Lastly, I discussed a topos which apparently explains how to construct a categorical syllogism, and a topos according to which both a hypothetical and a categorical syllogism could theoretically be constructed. I regard the former topical argument as an exception and assume that the latter works rather as a hypothetical syllogism, simply because the vast majority of topical arguments work in this way. In identifying the occurrence of three kinds of syllogisms—hypothetical, categorical and relational—I have shown the *Topics* to be the place of origin of the three branches of logic: logic of propositions, logic of predicates and logic of relations.

The investigation of specific topoi in Chapter Five confirms my contention that the vast majority of topoi are principles according to which hypothetical syllogisms can be constructed in which they work as hypotheses.

BIBLIOGRAPHY

This bibliography is primarily intended as a guide to the secondary literature relevant to any aspect of Aristotle's *Topics*, and secondarily as a list of texts cited in my work (those marked by an asterisk). Items are listed alphabetically by author except sections A-C. I have relied in the main on Marouzeau's *L'Anée philologique* (1st ed. 1896) and the *Philosopher's Index*. In the case of publications of which there are more than one edition, the date of the first edition is usually indicated by the second date in the brackets, e.g. Jäger (1955^2, 1923). To assist the aim of the bibliography as a guide to various aspects of the *Topics*, I have also provided a classified bibliography (pp. 195-198) divided into several subheadings where the vast majority of the items cited below are listed under their relevant headings. Items in the classified bibliography are referred to only by name and date; for full information, the reader should consult this bibliography.

A. Editions

Bekker, I. (ed.) (1831), *Aristotelis opera*, vol. 1, Berlin.
*Waitz, Th. (ed.) (1844-6), *Aristotelis Organon graece*, 2 vols., Leipzig.
*Wallies, M. (ed.) (1923), (e schedis I. Strache), *Aristotelis Topica cum libro de Sophisticis Elenchis*, Leipzig.
*Ross, W. D. (ed.) (1958), *Aristotelis Topica et Sophistici Elenchi*, Oxford.
*Brunschwig, J. (ed. and tr.) (1967), *Aristote: Topiques I-IV*, with an introduction and notes, Paris.

Editions of other Aristotelian texts:
*Minio-Palluelo, L. (ed.) (1949), *Aristotelis Categoriae et Liber De Interpreta-tione*, Oxford.
*Ross, W. D. (ed.) (1964), *Aristotelis Analytica Priora et Posteriora*, Oxford.
*Drossaart Lulofs, K. J. (ed.) (1965), *Aristotelis De Generatione Animalium*, Oxford.
*Ross, W. D. (ed.) (1955), *Aristotelis Fragmenta Selecta*, Oxford.
*Jaeger, W. (ed.) (1957), *Aristotelis Metaphysica*, Oxford.
*Kassel, R. (ed.) (1976), *Aristotelis Ars Rhetorica*, Berlin.

For Plato's texts I have used:
*Burnet, I. (ed.) (1900-7), *Platonis Opera*, 5 vols., Oxford.

B. Commentaries

*Alexander Aphrodisiensis, *In Aristotelis Topicorum Libros Octo Commentaria*, (Commentaria in Aristotelem Graeca II 2), ed. M. Wallies, Berlin 1891.
Averroes, *Paraphrasis Topicorum. In Aristotelis omnia quae extant opera*. Vol. 1, pt. 3. Topicorum atque Elenchorum libri cum Averrois Cordubensis in eos media expositione Abramo de Balmes et Mantino interpretibus. Venice 1562 (repr. Frankfurt 1962).
*Pacius, J., *In Porphyrii Isagogen et Aristotelis Organum Commentarius*, Frankfurt 1597 (repr. Hildesheim 1966).
Mang, A. (1854), *Das erste Buch der aristotelischen Topik erläutert*, Neuburg.
Von Kirchmann, J. H. (1883), *Erläuterungen zu dem Organon*, Leipzig.
Maurus, S. (1885), *Aristotelis Opera Omnia*, vol 1, Paris (originally Rome 1668).
Grote, G. (1880^2, 1872), Aristotle, ed. A. Bain and G. C. Robertson, 2 vols., London.
*Brunschwig,J. (ed. and tr.) (1967), op. cit.
*Colli, G. (tr.) (1955), *Aristotele: Organon*, with an introduction and notes, Torino.
*Waitz, Th. (ed.) (1844-6), op. cit.
*Zadro, A. (tr.) (1974), *I Topici*, with an introduction and notes, Napoli.

C. Translations

in Latin:
Pacius, J., *Aristotelis Organum*, Frankfurt 1597 (editio secunda, with marginal notes) (repr. Hildesheim 1966).
Boethius, *Aristoteles Latinus V, 1-3. Topica. Translatio Boethii*, ed. L. Minio-Paluello, Bruxelles and Paris 1969.

in English:
*Forster, E. S. (tr.) (1960), *Aristotle: Topica*, Loeb Translation, Cambridge (Mass.) and London.
*Pickard-Cambridge, W. D. (tr.) (1984), *Topica and De Sophisticis Elenchis*, revised version in Barnes (1984).

in French:
Tricot, J. (1950^2), *Les Topiques*, Paris.
Brunschwig, J. (ed. and tr.) (1967), op. cit.

in German:
Von Kirchmann, J. H. (1882), *Die Topik des Aristoteles*, Heidelberg.
Rolfes, E. (1919), *Aristoteles: Topik*, Leipzig.
Gohlke, P. (1952), *Topik*, Paderborn.

in Italian:
Colli, G. (tr.) (1955), op. cit.
Zadro, A. (tr.) (1974), op. cit.

As for tranlstions of other Aristotelian texts, I have used the following:

*Barnes, J. (ed.) (1984), *Complete Works of Aristotle: the Revised Oxford Translation*, 2 vols., Princeton.
Forster, E. S. (tr.) (1955), *Aristotle: On Sophistical Refutations*, Loeb Classical Library, Cambridge (Mass.) and London.
*Freese, J. H. (tr.) (1926), *Aristotle: "Art" of Rhetoric*, Loeb Classical Library, Cambridge (Mass.) and London.
*Rhys Roberts, W. (tr.) (1984), *Aristotle: Rhetoric*, in Barnes (1984).

D. Other ancient texts

1. The fragments of Theophrastus

*Fortenbaugh, W. W., Huby, P. M., Sharples, R. W. and Gutas, D. (eds. and trs.) (1992), *Theophrastus of Eresus*, 2 vols., Philosophia antiqua 54, 1 and 2, Leiden, New York, Köln.
*Gräser, A. (1973) (ed.), *Die logischen Fragmente des Theophrast*, Berlin.
*Repici, L. (1977) (ed. and tr.), *La logica di Teofrasto*, Bologna.

2. Other texts

*Alexander Aphrodisiensis, *In Aristotelis analyticorum priorum librum I*, ed. M. Wallies, Commentaria in Aristotelem Graeca II, 1, Berlin 1883.
*Ammonius, *In Aristotelis analyticorum priorum librum I*, ed. M. Wallies, Commentaria in Aristotelem Graeca IV, 6, Berlin 1899 (Praefatio, pp. XI-XII, by Pseudo-Ammonius).
*Apuleius, *De Interpretatione*, in *Apulei Opera* vol. 3, ed. P. Thomas, Stuttgart 1970.
*Boethius, *De hypotheticis syllogismis*, ed. L. Obertello, Brescia 1969.
*——, *De topicis differentiis*, ed. J.-P. Migne. *Patrologiae latinae*, vol. LXIV, Paris 1860. (repr. Turnhout 1969)
Boethius of Dacia, *Questiones super librum Topicorum*, Corpus philosophicorum Danicorum medii aevi 6, 1, ed. Green-Pedersen, N. J. and Pinborg, J., Copenhagen 1976.
Butterworth, C. E. (ed.) (1976), *Averroës' three short commentaries on Aristotle's Topics, Rhetoric, and Poetics*, Albany.
Cicero, *Topica*, tr. by H.M. Hubbell, Loeb Classical Library, London 1960.
*Diogenes Laertius, *Vitae philosophorum*, ed. H. S. Long, Oxford 1964.
*Galen, *Institutio logica*, ed. K. Kalbfleisch, Leipzig 1896.

Kieffer, J. S. (1964), *Galen's Institutio Logica*, English translation, introduction and commentary, Baltimore.
*Sextus Empiricus, *Opera*, 3 vols., ed. H. Mutschmann and J. Mau, Leipzig 1912-1958
*Proclus, *Commentarium in Parmenidem*, ed. R. Klibansky and C. Labowsky, *Plato Latinus* vol. 3, London 1953.
Simon of Faversham, *Quaestiones super librum Elenchorum*, ed. by Ebbesen S. et al., Toronto 1984.
*Simplicius, *In Aristotelis categorias*, ed. C. Kalbfleisch, Commentaria in Aristotelem Graeca VIII, Berlin 1907.
*Sollenberger, M. G. (1984), *Diogenes Laertius' Life of Theophrastus*, Diss. Rutgers University, New Brunswick,
*—— (1985), *Diogenes Laertius 5.36-57: The Vita Theophratsi*, in Fortenbaugh (1985), 1-62. (revised form of Sollenberger (1984))

E. Secondary literature

*Ackrill, J. L. (ed. and tr.) (1963), *Aristotle's Categories and De Interpretatione*, Oxford.
Alberti, A. (ed.) (1990), *Logica mente e persona*, Firenze.
Angelleli, I. (1970), "The techniques of disputation in the history of logic", *Journal of Philosophy* 67, 800-815.
Anton, H.S. (1859), "Über die Rhetorik des Aristoteles in ihrem Verhältnis zu Platon's Gorgias", *Rheinisches Museum* 14, 570-598.
Anton, J.P. (1957), *Aristotle's theory of contrariety*, London.
—— (1968), "The Aristotelian doctrine of homonyma in the *Categories* and its Platonic antecedents", *Journal of the History of Philosophy* 6, 315-326
—— (1969), "Ancient interpretations of Aristotle's doctrine of homonyma", *Journal of the History of Philosophy* 7, 1-18; repr. in Anton and Kustas (1972), 569-592.
—— (1975), "Some observations on Aristotle's theory of categories", *Diotima* 3, 67-81.
—— and Kustas, G. L. (eds.) (1972), *Essays in Ancient Greek Philosophy*, Albany.
—— and Preus, A. (eds.) (1992), *Aristotle's Ontology: Essays in Ancient Philosophy*, vol. 5, Albany, NY.
Arens, A. (ed.) (1987), *Text-Etymologie. Untersuchungen zu Textkörper und Textinhalt: Festschrift für H. Lausberg*, Stuttgart.
Arentz, D.W. (1975), *Aristotle's dialectical ethics*, Diss. Syracuse University.
Arpe, C. (1938), *Das τί ἦν εἶναι bei Aristoteles*, Hamburg.
Aubenque, P. (1960), "Science, culture et dialectique chez Aristote", *Association G. Budé. Actes du Congrès de Lyon*, Paris, 144-149.
—— (1961), "Sur la notion aristotélicienne d'aporie", in Mansion (1961), 3-19.
—— (1966[2], 1962), *Le problème de l'être chez Aristote*, Paris.
—— (1970), "La dialectique chez Aristote", in *L'attualità della problematica aristotelica*. Atti del Convegno franco-italiano su Aristotele, Padova 6-8 apr. 1967. Studia Aristotelica III, Padova, 9-31.
—— (1989), "Dialectique et métaphysique aristotéliciennes selon Éric Weil", in *É. Weil et la pensée antique. Cahiers Éric Weil* 2, Lille, 197-213.
Babin, A. E. (1940), *The theory of opposition in Aristotle*, Diss. University of Notre-Dame.
Baeumer, M. L. (ed.) (1973), *Toposforschung*, Wege der Forschung 395, Darmstadt.
Baldassarri, M. (1986), *Alessandro di Afrodisia, Dal Commento agli Analitici primi. Dal commento ai Topici*, in *La logica stoica. Testimonianze e framenti. Testi originali con introduzione e traduzione commentata*, vol. V A, Como.
Balme, D. M. (1961), "Aristotle's use of differentiae in Zoology", in Mansion (1961), 195-212; repr. in Barnes, Schofield, Sorabji (1975-79), vol. 1, 183-193.
—— (1987), "Aristotle's use of division and differentiae", in Gotthelf and Lennox (1987), 69-89.
Baltussen, H. (1992), "Peripatetic dialectic in the De sensibus", in Fortenbaugh and Gustas (1992), 1-19.
Barnes, J. (1969a), "Aristotle's theory of demonstration", *Phronesis* 14, 123-152; repr. in a revised form in Barnes, Schofield and Sorabji (1975-1979), vol. 1, 65-87.
—— (1969b),"The Law of Contradiction", *Philosophical Quarterly* 19, 302-309.
*—— (1970), "Property in Aristotle's *Topics*", *Archiv für Gechichte der Philosophie* 52, 136-155.
—— (1971), "Homonymy in Aristotle and Speusippus", *Classical Quarterly* 21, 65-80.
*—— (1980), "Aristotle and the methods of ethics", *Revue internationale de Philosophie* 34, 490-511.

*—— (1981), "Proof and the syllogism", in Berti (1981), 17-59.
*—— (1983), "Terms and sentences. Theophrastus on hypothetical syllogisms", *Proceedings of the British Academy* 69, 279-326.
*—— (1985a), "Theophrastus and hypothetical syllogistic", in Wiesner (1985), 557-576 and Fortenbaugh (1985), 125-141.
—— (1985b), "Uma terceira espécie de silogismo: Galeno e a lógica das relações", *Análise* 2, 35-61.
—— (1986), "Is rhetoric an art?", *Darg Newsletter* 2.
*—— (1990a), "Logical form and logical matter", in Alberti (1990).
*—— (1990b), "Galen and the utility of logic", in Kollesch (1993), 33-52
*——, Brunschwig J., and Frede M. (1990c), "Le propre de la prudence", in Brague and Courtino (1990), 79-96.
——, Bobzien, S., Flannery, K., S. J. and Ierodiakonou, K. (1991a), Alexander of Aphrodisias, *On Aristotle Prior Analytics 1.1-7*, London.
—— (1991b), "Philosophie et dialectique", in Sinaceur (1991), 107-116.
*—— (1993), "'A third sort of syllogism': Galen and the logic of relations", in Sharples (1993), 172-194. (a revised, English version of Barnes (1985b))
*—— (1994^2, 1975), *Aristotle's Posterior Analytics*, Oxford.
——, Schofield, M., Sorabji, R. (eds.), (1975-1979), *Articles on Aristotle*, 4 vols., London.
——, Brunschwig, J., Burnyeat, M. F., Schofield, M. (eds.) (1982), *Science and Speculation*, Cambridge
Barnes, K. T. (1977), "Aristotle on identity and its problems", *Phronesis* 22, 48-62.
Barth, T. (1942), "Das Problem der Vieldeutigkeit bei Aristoteles", *Sophia* 10, 11-30.
Basakos, P. (1981), "La place de la sophistique dans la dialectique d'Aristote. Remarques sur les *Topiques* et les *Réfutations sophistiques*", *Deucalion* 9, 389-403.
Bassenge, F. (1963), "Der Fall τὸ τί ἦν εἶναι", *Helikon* 3, 505-518.
Baynes, K. (1990), "Dialectic and deliberation in Aristotle's practical philosophy", *Southwest Philosophy Review* 6, 19-42.
Belnap, N. P. (1976), *The Logic of Questions and Answers*, New Haven.
Benoit, W.L. (1948), "Aristotle's example. The rhetorical induction", *Quarterly Journal of Speech* 66, 182-192.
Beriger, A. (1989), *Die aristotelische Dialektik. Ihre Darstellung in der Topik und in den Sophistichen Widerlegungen und ihre Anwendung in der Metaphysik M 1-3*, Heidelberg.
Berka, K. (1964, 1), "L'évolution de la dialectique depuis Socrate et Platon jusqu'à Aristote" [in Czech], *Acta Universitatis Carolinae: Philosophica et Historica*, 79-105.
—— (1968), "Aristotle and modern methodology", in Burian and Vidman (1968), 193-201.
Berti, E. (1970), "La dialettica in Aristotele", in *L'attualità della problematica aristotelica*, Padova 1970, 33-80 and in Berti (1975), 109-133.
—— (1975), *Studi aristotelici*, L'Aquila.
—— (1977), *Aristotele, dalla dialettica alla filosofia prima*, Padova.
*—— (1980), "Aristote et la méthode dialectique du *Parménide* de Platon", *Revue internationale de philosophie* 34, 341-358.
—— (ed.) (1981), *Aristotle on Science: The Posterior Analytics*. Proceedings of the 8th Symposium Aristotelicum, Padua.
—— (1983), *Logica aristotelica e dialettica*, Bologna.
—— (1986), "Sul carattere dialettico della storiografia filosofica di Aristotele", in Cambiano (1986), 101-125.
—— (1986), "Differenze tra la dialettica socratica e quella platonica secondo Aristotle, Metaph. M 4", in *Energeia* (1986), 50-65.
—— (1988), "Zenone di Elea, inventore della dialettica?", *La Parola del Passato* 43, 19-41.
—— (1991), "Les méthodes d'argumentation et de démonstration dans la Physique (apories, phénomènes, principes)", in de Gandt and Souffrin (1991), 53-72.
Bird, O. (1955), "Dialectic in philosophical inquiry", *Proceedings of the American Catholic Philosophical Association* 29, 234-246.
—— (1959), "The logical interest in the topics as seen in Abelard", *Modern Schoolman* 37, 53-57.
—— (1960a), "The formalizing of the topics in medieval logic", *Notre Dame Journal of Formal Logic* 1, 138-149.
—— (1960b), "The re-discovery of the 'Topics': Professor Toulmin's inference-warrants", *Proceedings of the American Catholic Philosophical Association* 34, 200-205.
—— (1961), "Topic and consequence in Ockham's logic", *Notre Dame Journal of Formal Logic* 2, 65-78.
—— (1962), "The tradition of the logical topics: Aristotle to Ockham", *Journal of the History of Ideas* 23, 307-323.

—— (1978), "The *Topics* and the art of teaching by discussion", in *Paideia* (1978), 196-201.
Blank, D.L. (1984), "Dialectical method in Aristotle's *Athenaion Politeia*", *Greek, Roman and Byzantine Studies* 25, 275-284.
Blom, S. (1955), "Concerning a controversy on the meaning of 'probability'", *Theoria* 21, 65-98.
*Bocheński, J. M. (1947), *La logique de Théophraste*, Fribourg.
*—— (1951a), "Non-analytical laws and rules in Aristotle", *Methodos* 3,70-80.
*—— (1951b), *Ancient Formal Logic*, Amsterdam.
—— (1978[4], 1956), *Formale Logik*, Freiburg, München.
*—— (1970[2], 1961), *A History of Formal Logic*, translated and edited by I. Thomas, New York. (English transaltion of Bocheński (1978[4], 1956))
Boeder, H. (1968), "Der Ursprung der Dialektik in der Theorie des Seienden. Parmenides und Zenon", *Studium Generale* 21, 84-202.
Boger, R. (1993), "The logical sense of παράδοξον in Aristotle's *Sophistical Refutations*", *Ancient Philosophy* 13, 55-78.
Bolton, R. (1987), "Definition and scientific method in Aristotle's *Posterior Analytics* and *Generation of Animals*", in Gotthelf and Lennox (1987), 120-166.
—— (1990), "The epistemological basis of Aristotelian dialectic", in Devereux and Pellegrin (1990), 185-236.
—— (1991), "Aristotle's method in natural science: Physics 1", in Judson (1991), 1-29.
—— (1994), "The problem of dialectical reasoning in Aristotle", *Ancient Philosophy* 14, 99-132.
Bonitz, H. (1853), *Über die Kategorienlehre des Aristoteles*, Sitzungsberichte der Kaiserlichen Akademie der Wissenschaften, Phil.-hist. Klasse, vol. 10, Vienna (repr. Darmstadt 1967).
*—— (1870), *Index Aristotelicus*, vol. 5 of the Akademieausgabe by I. Bekker, Berlin (repr. Berlin 1961).
Bornscheuer, L. (1976), *Topik. Zur Struktur der gesellschaftlichen Einbildungskraft*, Frankfurt.
Bouchard, G. and Valois, R. (1983), "(Nouvelle) rhétorique et syllogisme", *Laval Théologique et Philosophique* 39, 127-150.
Boylan, M. (1983), *Method and practice in Aristotle's biology*, Washington, D.C.
Brague, R. and Courtino, J. F. (eds.) (1990), *Herméneutique et ontologie: mélanges en hommage à Pierre Aubenque*, Paris.
Brake, R. (1965), "A reconsideration of Aristotle's conception of topics", *Central States Speech Journal* 11, 106-112.
Brandis, Ch. A. (1827), "Über die Schicksale der aristotelischen Bücher und einige Kriterien ihrer Echtheit", *Rheinisches Museum* I 4.
—— (1833), "Über die Reihenfolge der Bücher des aristotelischen Organon und ihre griechischen Ausleger", *Abhandlungen der königlichen Akademie der Wissenschaften*, Berlin, 249-299.
Brandon, E.P. (1978), "Hintikka on ἀκολουθεῖν", *Phronesis* 23, 173-178.
Braswell, B. (1964), "Godfrey of Fontaine's Abridgement of Boetius of Dacia's *Quaestiones supra librum Topicorum Aristotelis*", *Mediaeval Studies* 26, 302-314.
*Braun, E. (1959) *Zur Einheit der aristotelischen Topik*, Diss. Köln.
Brennan, R.E. (1955), "Dialectic in philosophical inquiry", *Proceedings of the American Catholic Philosophical Association* 29, 246-258.
Breuer, D. and Schanze, H. (eds.) (1981), *Topik. Beiträge zur interdisziplinären Diskussion*, Stuttgart.
Brunschwig, J. (1964), "Dialectique et ontolgie chez Aristote.", *Revue Philosophique de la France et de l'étranger* 154, 179-200.
—— (1968), "Observations sur les manuscrits parisiens des *Topiques*", in Owen (1968), 3-21.
*—— (1986), "Sur le système des prédicables dans les *Topiques* d'Aristote", in *Energeia* (1986), 145-157.
—— (1990), "Remarques sur la communication de R. Bolton", in Devereux and Pellegrin, 237-261.
—— (1994), "Rhétorique et dialectique, *Rhétorique* et *Topiques*", in Furley and Nehamas (1994), 57-96.
Bueno, A. A. (1988), "Aristotle, the fallacy of accident and the nature of predication. A historical enquiry", *Journal of the History of Philosophy* 26, 5-24.
Buhl, G. (1979) ,"Zur Funktion der Topoi in der aristotelischen Topik", in Lorenz (1979), 169-175.
Burian, J. and Vidman, L. (eds.) (1968), *Antiquitas Graeco-Romana ac tempora nostra. Acta congressus internationalis habiti Brunae diebus 12-16 mensis Aprilis 1966*, Prague 1968.
Burnyeat, M. F. (1981), "Aristotle on understanding knowledge", in Berti (1981), 97-139.

―― (1982), "The origins of non-deductive inference", in Barnes, Brunschwig, Burnyeat, Schofield (1982), 193-238.
*―― (1994), "Enthymeme: Aristotle on the logic of persuasion", in Furley and Nehamas (1994), 3-55.
Butterworth, C. E. (ed.) (1976), *Averroës' three short commentaries on Aristotle's Topics, Rhetoric, and Poetics*, Albany.
Cadion, R. (1956), "Le problème de méthode dans le traité aristotélicien *Des Idées*", *Revue philosophique de la France et de l'étranger* 146, 94-100.
Cambiano, G. (ed.) (1986), *Storiografia e dossografia nella filosofia antica*, Torino.
Casari, E. (1984), "Note sulla logica aristotelica della comparazione", *Sileno* 10, 131-146.
Cassin, B. (ed.) (1986), *La Sophistique. Colloque de Cérisy*, Paris.
Cassini, A. (1986), "Naturaleza y función de los axiomas en la epistemología aristotélica", *Revista de Filosofía* (Argentina) 1, 75-97.
―― (1991), "La justificación aristotélica de los axiomas: una evaluación global", *Revista latinoamericana de Filosofía* 17, 291-306.
Cavini, W. (1979), "Categorie e predicazione in Aristotele", *Annali dell' Istituto de filosofia di Firenze* 1, 1-16.
―― (1985), "La negazione Aristotelica", in Cavini, Donnini Macciò, Funghi, Manetti (1985), 11-45.
―― (1989), "Modalità dialettiche nei Topici di Aristotele", in Corsi, Mangione, Mugnai (1989), 15-46.
――, Donnini Macciò, M. C., Funghi, M. S., Manetti (eds.) (1985), *Studi su Papiri Greci di Logica e Medicina*, Firenze.
Cazzola Gastaldi, S. (1976), "Lo statuto concettuale della retorica aristotelica", *Rivista critica di storia della Filosofia* 31, 41-72.
*Cherniss, H. (1944), *Aristotle's Criticism of Plato and the Academy*, vol. 1, Baltimore.
Chichi, G. M. (1989), "El status lógico de los topos aristotélicos", *Revista latinoamericana de Filosofía* 15, 131-145.
Christensen, J. (1988), "The formal character of koinoi topoi in Aristotle's rhetoric and dialectic. Illustrated by the list in Rhetorica II, 23", *Cahiers de l'institut du moyen âge grec et latin* 57, 3-10.
*Chroust, A.H. (1963), "The first thirty years of modern Aristotelian scholarship", *Classica et Mediaevalia* 24, 27-57.
Classen, C.J. (1981), "Aristotle's picture of the sophists", in Kerferd (1981), 7-24.
―― and Müllenbrock, H.-J. (eds.) (1992), *Die Macht des Wortes: Aspekte gegenwärtiger Rhetorikforschung*, Marburg.
Claussen, R. and Daube-Schackat, R. (eds.) (1988), *Gedankenzeichen: Festschrift für K. Oehler*, Tübingen.
Cleary, J. J. (1994), "Phainomena in Aristotle's methodology", *International Journal of Philosophical Studies* 2, 61-97.
―― (1995), *Aristotle and Mathematics*, Philosophia antiqua 67, Leiden, New York, Köln.
Cobet, J., Leimbach R. and Neschke-Hentschke, A. B. (eds.) (1975), *Dialogos: Festschrift für H. Patzer*, Wiesbaden 1975.
Code, A. (1986), "Aristotle's investigation of a basic logical principle. Which science investigates the principle of non-contradiction?", *Canadian Journal of Philosophy* 16, 341-357.
Coenen, H.G. (1987), "Der aristotelische Topos aus dem Mehr und Weniger (Rhetorik 2, 23, 4f.)", in Arens (1987), 74-89.
Cohen, S.M. (1973), "<Predicable of> in Aristotle's *Categories*", *Phronesis* 18, 69-70.
―― (1986), "Aristotle on the Principle of Non-Contradiction", *Canadian Journal of Philosophy* 16, 359-370.
Consigny, S. (1989), "Dialectical, rhetorical, and Aristotelian rhetoric", *Philosophy and Rhetoric* 22, 281-287.
Cooper, N. (1989), "Aristotle's crowning virtue", *Apeiron*, 22, 191-205.
Cope, E. M. and Sandys, J. E. (1877), *The Rhetoric of Aristotle*, vol. I-III, Cambridge (repr. 1973).
Corcoran, J. (1994), "The Founding of Logic", *Ancient Philosophy* 14, 9-24.
Corsi, G., Mangione, C., Mugnai, M. (eds.) (1989), *Atti del Convegno internazionale di storia della logica. Le teorie delle modalità* (San Gimignano, 5-8 decembre 1987), Bologna.
Côté, A. (1964), "Le nombre des catégories aristotéliciennes", *Laval théologique et philosophique* 20, 165-175.
Couloubaritsis, L. (1980), "Y a-t-il intuition des principes chez Aristote?", *Revue internationale de Philosophie* 34, 440-471.
―― (1986a), "Legomenon et katégoroumenon chez Aristote", in *Philosophie du langage et grammaire dans l'Antiquité*, Cahiers de philosophie ancienne 5, Bruxelles, 219-238.

—— (1986b), "Dialectique, rhétorique et critique chez Aristote", in Meyer (1986), 103-118 and in Meyer (1989), 95-110.
Crem, T. M. (1956), "The definition of rhetoric according to Aristotle", *Laval Théologique et Philosophique* 12, 233-250.
Crisp, R. (1991), "Aristotle on dialectic", *Philosophy* 66, 522-524.
Croissant, J. (1986), "La dialectique chez Aristote", in her *Études de philosophie ancienne*, Cahiers de philosophie ancienne 4, Bruxelles, 161-183.
Dancy, R. M. (1975), *Sense and Contradiction: A study in Aristotle*, Dordrecht and Boston.
Davies, J. C. (1975-76), "Aristotle's theory of definition", *Euphrosyne* 7, 129-135.
De Blic, J. (1930), "Un aspect remarquable de la dialectique aristotélicienne", *Gregorianum* 11, 567-577.
De Domenico, N., Di Stefano, A. E., Puglisi, G. (eds.) (1990), Ermeneutica e filosofia pratica, Atti del Convegno internazionale di Catania (8-10 ottobre 1987), Venice.
De Gandt, F. and Souffrin, P. (eds.) (1991), *La Physique d'Aristote et les conditions d'une science de la nature*, Paris.
*De Pater, W. A. (1965), *Les Topiques d'Aristote et la dialectique platonicienne*, Fribourg (repr. Paris 1987).
—— (1968), "La fonction du lieu et de l'instrument dans les *Topiques*", in Owen (1968a), 164-188.
De Strycker, E., (1968a), "Prédicats univoques et prédicats analogiques dans le Protreptique d'Aristote", *Revue philosophique de Louvain* 66, 597-618.
—— (1968b), "Concept-clés et terminologie dans les livres ii à vii des *Topiques*", in Owen (1968a), 141-163.
—— (1969), "Sur un emploi technique de μᾶλλον chez Aristote", *Mnemosyne* 22, 303-304.
Devereux, D. (1990), "Comments on Robert Bolton's 'The epistemological basis of Aristotelian dialectic'", in Devereux and Pellegrin (1990), 263-286.
—— and Pellegrin, P. (eds.) (1990), *Biologie, logique et métaphysique chez Aristote*, Paris.
De Vogel, C. J. (1968), "Aristotle's attitude to Plato and the Theory of Ideas, according to the *Topics*", in Owen (1968a), 91-102.
Donaldson, J. (1972), "Aristotle's *Categories* and the *Organon*", *Proceedings of the American Catholic Philosophical Association* 46, 149-156.
Dorion, L.-A. (1990), "Le statut de l'argument dialectique d'après Réf. soph. 11, 172a9-15", *Dialogue* (Canada) 29, 95-110.
Duerlinger, J. (1969), "Συλλογισμός und συλλογίζεσθαι in Aristotle's Organon", *American Journal of Philology* 90, 320-323.
Duhem, P. (1908), *Sozein ta Phainomena*, Paris.
—— (1969), *To Save the Phenomena*, Chicago. (translation of Duhem (1908))
Dumont, J.-P. (1986), *Introduction à la méthode d'Aristote*, Paris.
Düring, I. (1966), *Aristoteles*, Heidelberg.
—— (1968), "Aristotle's use of examples in the *Topics*", in Owen (1968a), 202-229.
—— and Owen, G. E. L. (eds.) (1960), *Aristotle and Plato in the Mid-Fourth Century*, 1st Symposium Aristotelicum, Göteborg.
Ebbesen, S. (1981), *Commentaries and Commentators on Aristotle's Sophistici Elenchi*, 3 vols., Leiden.
*Ebert, T. (1977a), "Zur Formulierung prädikativer Aussagen in den logischen Schriften des Aristoteles", *Phronesis* 22, 123-145.
—— (1977b), "Aristotelischer und traditioneller Akzidenzbegriff", in Patzig, Scheibe, Wieland (1977), 338-349.
—— (1985), "Gattungen der Prädikate und Gattungen des Seienden bei Aristotles. Zum Verhältnis von Kat. 4 und Top. A 9", *Archiv für Geschichte der Philosopie* 67, 113-138.
*—— (1991), *Dialektiker und frühe Stoiker bei Sextus Empiricus,* Hypomnemata 95, Göttingen 1991.
Edel, A. (1975), "Aristotle's categories and the nature of categorical theory", *Review of Metaphysics* 29, 45-65.
Einarson, B. (1936), "On certain mathematical terms in Aristotle's Logic", *American Journal of Philology* 57, 33-54 and 151-172.
Elders, L. (1968), "The *Topics* and the Platonic Theory of Principles of Being", in Owen (1968a), 126-137.
Emrich, B. (1972), "Topik und Topoi", in Jehn (1972), 90-120.
Energeia (1986), *Études aristotéliciennes offertes à A. Jannone*, Paris.
Engberg-Pedersen, T. (1979), "More on Aristotelian epagoge", *Phronesis* 24, 301-319.
Enskat, R. (1986), "Ein aussagenlogischer Aspekt der aristotelischen Syllogistik", *Archiv für Geschichte der Philosophie* 68, 126-135.
Eucken, R. (1872), *Die Methode der aristotelischen Forschung*, Berlin.

Evans, J. D. G. (1975), "The codification of false refutations in Aristotle's De sophisticis elenchis", *Proceedings of the Cambridge Philological Society* 21, 42-51.
*—— (1977), *Aristotle's Concept of Dialectic*, Cambridge.
—— (1978), "Aristotle *Topics* E 5, 135a20-36; the ontology of ὁμοιομερῆ", *Archiv für Geschichte der Philosophie* 60, 234-292.
Flashar, H. and Gaiser, K. (eds.) (1965), *Synusia: Festgabe für W. Schadewaldt*, Pfullingen.
Forster, E. S. (1955), *Aristotle, On Sophistical Refutations*, Loeb Translation, Cambridge (Mass.) and London.
Fortenbaugh, W. W. (1965), "Τὰ πρὸς τὸ τέλος and syllogistic vocabulary in Aristotle's Ethics", *Phronesis* 10, 191-201.
—— (ed.) (1985), *Theophrastus of Eresus*, Rutgers University Studies in Classical Humanities 2, New Brunswick and London
—— and Gutas, D. (eds.) (1992), *Theophratus. His Psychological, Doxographical and Scientific Writings*, Rutgers University studies in Classics and Humanities 5, New Brunswick and London.
—— and Mirhady, D. C. (ed.) (1994), *Peripatetic Rhetoric after Aristotle*, New Brunswick and London.
Frappier, G. (1974), *L'art dialectique dans le traité De l'âme d'Aristote*, Ouébec 1974.
—— (1977), "L'art dialectique dans la philosophie d'Aristote", *Laval théologique et philosophique* 33, 115-134.
*Frede, M. (1974), *Die stoische Logik*, Abhandlungen der Akademie der Wissenschaften in Göttingen, Phil.-Hist. Klasse, Folge 3, Nr. 88, Göttingen.
—— (1987a), *Essays in Ancient Philosophy*, Oxford.
*—— (1987b), "Stoic vs. Aristotelian syllogistic", *Archiv für Geschichte der Philosophie*, 56 (1974), 1-32; repr. in Frede (1987a), 99-124.
—— (1987c), "Categories in Aristotle", in O'Meara (1981), 1-24; repr. in Frede (1987a), 29-48.
Freeland, C. A. (1990), "Scientific explanation and empirical data in Aristotle's Meteorology", in Devereux and Pellegrin (1990), 287-320.
Fritsche, J. (1986), *Methode und Beweisziel im ersten Buch der 'Physikvorlesung' des Aristoteles*, Frankfurt.
Furley, D. J. and Nehamas, A. (eds.) (1994), *Aristotle's Rhetoric. Philosophical essays*, Proceedings of the 12th Symposium Aristotelicum, Princeton.
Furth, M. (1986), "A note on Aristotle's Principle of Non-Contradiction", *Canadian Journal of Philosophy* 16, 371-381.
Gallavotti, G. (1968), "Paralogismi di Ulisse nella Poetica di Aristotele", *La parola del passato* 23, 241-261.
Galston, M. (1982), "Aristotle's dialectic, refutation and inquiry", *Dialogue* 21, 79-83.
Gambra, J. M. (1988), "La lógica aristotélica de los predicables", *Annario Filosofico* 21, 89-118.
Gardies, L. (1989), "La définition de l'identité d'Aristote à Zermelo", *Theoria* (Spain) 4, 55-79.
Garver, E. (1986), "Aristotle's *Rhetoric* as a work of philosophy", *Philosophy and Rhetoric* 19, 1-23.
—— (1988), "Aristotle's *Rhetoric* on unintentionally hitting the principles of the sciences", *Rhetorica* 6, 381-393.
—— (1994), *Aristotle's Rhetoric*, Chicago and London.
Gastaldi, S. (1993), "Aristotele e la retorica: il discorso tra persuasione e dimostrazione", *Lexis* 11, 119-134.
Geach, P. T. (1963), "Aristotle on conjunctive propositions", *Ratio* 5, 33-45.
Gercke, A. (1891), "Ursprung der aristotelischen Kategorien", *Archiv für Geschichte der Philosophie* 4, 424-441.
Gigon, O. "Cicero und Aristoteles", *Hermes* 87, 143-162.
—— (1968), "Aristoteles, *Topik* iii. 1-3", in Owen (1968a), 233-256.
Giguère, J. (1966), *Du lieu commun*, Québec 1966.
Gillespie, G. M. (1925), "The Aristotelian categories", *Classical Quarterly* 19, 75-85; repr. in Barnes, Schofield, Sorabji (1975-79), vol. 3, 1-12.
Giuliani, A. (1972), "The Aristotelian theory of the dialectical definition", *Philosophy and Rhetoric* 5, 129-142.
Goebel, G. H. (1989), "Probability in the earliest rhetorical theory", *Mnemosyne* 42, 41-53.
Gohlke, P. (1928), "Untersuchungen zur Topik des Aristoteles", *Hermes* 63, 457-480.
—— (1936), *Die Entstehung der aristotelischen Logik*, Berlin.
—— (1954), *Die Entstehung der aristotelischen Prinzipienlehre*, Tübingen.
Gómez-Lobo, A. (1966), *Συμβεβηκός in der Metaphysik des Aristoteles. Eine Untersuchung zu Voraussetzungen und Grenzen des aristotelischen Denkens*, Dissertation München.

―― (1977), "Aristotle's hypotheses and the Euclidean postulates", *Review of Metaphysics* 30, 430-439.
―― (1979), "Aristotle's First Philosophy and the principles of particular disciplines. An interpretation of Met. E, 1, 10256 10-13", *Zeitschift für philosophische Forschung* 32, 183-194.
Goodwin, D. (1992), "The dialectic of second-order Distinctions: The structure of arguments about fallacies", *Informal Logic* 14, 11-22.
Gotthelf A. and Lennox, J. G. (eds.) (1987), *Philosophical issues in Aristotle's biology*, Cambridge.
Gotthelf, A., "First principles in Aristotle's parts of animals", in Gotthelf and Lennox (1987), 165-198.
Grabmann, M. (1937), "Bearbeitungen und Auslegungen der aristotelischen Logik aus der Zeit von Peter Abaelard bis Petrus Hispanus", *Abhandlungen der preussischen Akademie der Wissenschaften*, phil.-hist. Kl., Nr. 5, 1-58, Berlin.
*Graham, W. (1975), "Counterpredicability and per se accidents", *Archiv für Geschichte der Philosophie* 67, 182-187.
Granger, H. (1981), "The differentia and the per se accident in Aristotle", *Archiv für Geschichte der Philosophie* 63, 118-129.
―― (1984), "Aristotle on genus and differentia", *Journal of the History of Philosophy* 22, 1-23.
Green-Pedersen, N. J. (1973), "On the interpretation of Aristotle's *'Topics'* in the 13th Century", *Cahiers de l'Institut du moyen âge grec et latin* 9, 1-46.
―― (1977a), "The doctrine of 'maxima propositio' and 'locus differentia' in commentaries from the 12th century on Boethius' 'Topics'", *Studia Mediewistyczne* 18, 125-163.
―― (1977b), "Discussions about the status of the loci dialectici in works from the middle of the 13th Century", *Cahiers de l'Institut du moyen âge grec et latin* 20, 38-78.
*―― (1984), *The Tradition of the Topics in the Middle Ages*, Munich and Vienna.
Grimaldi, W. M. A. (1955), *The enthymeme in Aristotle*, Diss. Princeton University.
―― (1957), "A note on πίστεις in Aristotle's *Rhetoric* 1354-56", *American Journal of Philology* 78, 188-192.
―― (1958), "Rhetoric and the philosophy of Aristotle", *The Classical Journal* 53, 371-375.
*―― (1958), "The Aristotelian topics", *Traditio* 14, 1-16.
―― (1961), "Aristotle *Rhetoric* 1391b29 and 1396b29", *Classical Philology* 56, 38-43.
―― (1972), *Studies in the Philosophy of Aristotle's Rhetoric*, Hermes Einzelschriften 25, Wiesbaden.
―― (1978), "Rhetoric and truth. A note on Rhet. 1355a21-24," *Philosophy and Rhetoric* 11, 173-177.
―― (1980), "Semeion, tekmerion, eikos in Aristotle's *Rhetoric*", *American Journal of Philology* 101, 383-398.
―― (1980-1988), *Aristotle Rhetoric I-II. A commentary*, 2 vols., New York.
Guariglia, O. N. (1977), "Las categorías en los Tópicos de Aristóteles", *Cuadernos de Filosofía* (Buones Aires) 17, 43-68.
―― (1978), *Quellenkritische und logische Untersuchungen zur Gegensatzlehre des Aristoteles*, Hildesheim.
―― (1982), "Paideia y dialéctica en la ética de Aristóteles", *Dianoia*, 23-49.
Gueroult, M. (1963), "Logique, argumentation, et histoire de la philosophie chez Aristote", in *Logique et Analyse* 6 (la théorie de l'argumentation, perspectives et applications), 431-449.
Guthrie, W. K. C. (1981), *A History of Greek Philosophy*, vol. VI, *Aristotle: an Encounter*, Cambridge.
Hadgopoulos, D. J. (1974), "A note on Aristotle's theory of identity", *Philosophy and Phenomenological Research* 35, 113-114.
*―― (1976), "The definition of the predicable", *Phronesis* 21, 59-63
*―― (1976), "*Protasis* and *problêma* in the *Topics*", *Phronesis* 21, 266-276.
Hadot, P. (1980), "Philosophie, dialectique, rhétorique dans l'antiquité", *Studia Philosophica. Jahrbuch der Schweizerischen Philosophischen Gesellschaft* 39, 139-166.
Halper, E. (1987), "Aristotle on the possibility of metaphysics", *Revue de philosophie ancienne* 5, 99-131.
Hamblin, C. L. (1970), *Fallacies*, London.
*Hambruch, E. (1904), *Logische Regeln der platonischen Schule in der aristotelischen Topik*, Wissenschaftliche Beilage zum Jahresbericht des Askanischen Gymnasiums zu Berlin, Programm, Nr. 56, Berlin.
*Hamelin, O. (1920), *Le système d'Aristote*, Paris.
Hamlyn, D. W. (1961), "Aristotle on predication", *Phronesis* 5, 110-126.

—— (1976), "Aristotelian epagoge", *Phronesis* 21, 167-184.
—— (1990), "Aristotle on dialectic", *Philosophy* 65, 465-476.
Hauser, G. A. (1968), "The example in Aristotle's *Rhetoric*. Bifurcation or contradiction?", *Philosophy and Rhetoric* 1, 78-90.
Hayden, D. (1957), "Notes on Aristotelian dialectic in theological method", *Thomist* 20, 383-418.
Heath, T. (1949), *Mathematics in Aristotle*, Oxford.
Hellwig, A. (1973), *Untersuchungen zur Theorie der Rhetorik bei Platon und Aristoteles*, Hypomnemata 38, Göttingen.
Heß, W. (1970), "Erfahrung und Intuition bei Aristoteles", *Phronesis* 15, 48-82.
Hesse, M. (1965), "Aristotle's logic of analogy", *Philosophical Quarterly* 15, 328-340.
Hill, F. (1981), "The amorality of Aristotle's rhetoric", *Greek, Roman and Byzantine Studies* 22, 133-147.
*Hintikka, J. (1973), *Time and Necessity*, Oxford.
—— (1980), "Aristotelian induction", *Revue internationale de philosophie* 34, 422-439.
—— (1993), "Socratic questioning, logic and rhetoric", *Revue International de Philosophie* 47, 5-30.
Hirschberger, J. (1960), "Paronymie und Analogie bei Aristoteles", *Philosophisches Jahrbuch* 68, 191-203.
Hiż, H. (1978) (ed.), *Questions*, Dordrecht.
Hoffman, F., Scheffczyk, L., Feiernis, K. (eds.) (1969), *Sapienter Ordinare: Festgabe für E. Kleineidam*, Erfurter Theologische Studien 24, Leipzig.
Hogan, J. (1955), "The dialectic of Aristotle", *Philosophical Studies* (Ireland) 5, 3-21.
*Huby, P. M. (1962), "The date of Aristotle's Topics and its treatment of the theory of ideas", *Classical Quarterly* 12, 72-80.
Hutchinson, D. S. (1989), "L'épistémologie des principes de contradiction chez Aristote", *Revue de philosophie ancienne* 6, 213-227.
Imelmann, J. (1870), "Zur Aristoteles' Topik", Wissenschaftliche Beilage zum Programm des Joachimsthaler Gymnasiums.
Infante, D. A. (1971a), *The function of 'eide topoi' in rhetorical invention, cognitive structure, and attitude change*, Diss. Kent State University.
—— (1971b), "The influence of a topical system on the discovery of arguments", *Speech Monographs* 38, 125-128.
Irmscher, J. and Steffen, W (eds.) (1959), *Philologische Vorträge*, Wrocław.
Irwin, T. H. (1977), "Aristotle's discovery of metaphysics", *Review of Metaphysics* 31, 210-229.
—— (1978), "First principles in Aristotle's ethics", *Midwest Studies in Philosophy* 3, 252-272.
—— (1981), "Homonymy in Aristotle", *Review of Metaphysics* 34, 523-544.
—— (1981), "Aristotle and the methods of ethics", in O'Meara (1981), 193-223.
—— (1987), "Ways to first principles: Aristotle's methods of discovery", *Philosophical Topics* 15, 109-134.
*—— (1988), *Aristotle's First Principles*, Oxford.
Isnardi Parente, M. (1966), "Per l'interpretazione dei Topici VI 6, 145a 19 sgg.", *Rivista di Filologia et di Istruzione Classica* 94, 149-161.
Jacob, B. (1993-94), "Aristotle's dialectical purposes", *Interpretation* 21, 135-167.
Jaeger, W. (1955[2], 1923), *Aristoteles*, Berlin (repr. Zürich and Hildesheim 1985).
—— (1948[2]), *Aristotle: Fundamentals of the History of his Development*, Oxford. (English translation of Jaeger (1955[2], 1923))
Janssens, E. (1968), "The concept of dialectic in the Ancient world", *Philosophy and Rhetoric* 1, 174-181.
Jehn, P. (ed.) (1972), *Toposforschung. Eine Dokumentation.* Republica Literaria 10, Frankfurt.
Judson, L. (ed.) (1991), *Aristotle's Physics*, Oxford.
Kahn, C. (1973), *The Vern Be in Ancient Greek*, Dordrecht.
—— (1976), "Why existence does not emerge as a distinct concept in Greek philosophy", *Archiv für Geschichte der Philosophie* 58, 323-34.
—— (1978), "Questions and categories", in Hiż (1978), 227-278.
—— (1981), "The role of νοῦς in the cognition of first principles in Post. An. II 19" in Berti (1981), 385-414.
Kal, V. (1988), *On Intuition and Discursive Reasoning in Aristotle*, Philosophia antiqua 46, Leiden, New York, Kopenhagen, Köln.
Kapp, E. (1920), *Die Kategorienlehre in der aristotelischen Topik*. (Habilitationsschrift), in Kapp (1968), 215-253.

*—— (1931), "Syllogistik", in Wissowa (1893-1972), 2 Reihe, IV A 1, cols. 1046-67; repr. in Kapp (1968), 254-277 and as "Syllogistic" in Barnes, Schofield, Sorabji (1975-79), vol. 1, 35-49.
*—— (1942), *Greek foundations of traditional logic*, New York.
—— (1968), *Ausgewählte Schriften*, Berlin.
Kennedy, G. A. (tr.) (1991), *Aristotle: On Rhetoric. A Theory of Civic Discourse*. Newly translated with introduction, notes and appendixes, Oxford.
Kerferd, G. B. (ed.) (1981), *The Sophists and their Legacy*, Hermes Einzelschriften 44, Wiesbaden 1981.
Kessler, M. (1976), *Aristoteles' Lehre von der Einheit der Definition*, Epimeleia 26, München.
Kinneavy, J. G. W. (1987), "Reinterpreting Aristotle", *Philosophy and Rhetoric* 20, 183-200.
*Kirwan, C. A. (1993^2, 1976), *Aristotle's Metaphysics, Books Gamma, Delta, Epsilon*, Oxford 1993.
—— (1979), "Aristotle and the so-called fallacy of equivocation", *Philosophical Quarterly* 29, 35-46.
Kleger, H. (1990), "Common sense als Argument", *Archiv für Begriffsgeschichte* 33, 22-59.
Klein, J. (1989), "Der Syllogismus als Bindeglied zwischen Philosophie und Rhetorik bei Aristoteles. Anmerkungen aus sprachhandlungstheoretischer Perspektive", in Schanze and Kopperschmidt (1989), 35-54.
Klein, S. (1988), "An analysis and defense of Aristotle's method in *Nicomachean Ethics* I & X", *Ancient Philosophy* 8, 63-72.
—— (1992), "The value of endoxa in ethical argument", *History of Philosophy Quarterly* 9, 141-157.
*Kneale, W. and M. (1989^{10}, 1962), *The Development of Logic*, Oxford.
Knuuttila, S. (1989), "Modalities in obligational disputations", in Corsi, Mangione, Mugnai (1989), 79-92.
—— (1993), "Remarks on induction in Aristotle's Dialectic and Rhetoric", *Revue International de Philosophie* 47, 78-88.
Koeningshausen, J. H. (1989), *Ursprung und Thema von erster Wissenschaft. Die aristotelische Entwicklung des Problems*, Amsterdam.
Koller, H. (1955), "Stoicheion", *Glotta* 34, 161-174.
Kollesch, J. and Nickel, D. (eds.) (1993), *Galen und das hellenistische Erbe*, Verhandlungen des IV Internationalen Galen-Symposiums, Stuttgart.
Krämer, H. J. (1968), "Grundbegriffe akademischer Dialektik in den biologischen Schriften von Aristoteles und Theophrast", *Rheinisches Museum* 111, 293-333.
Kretzmann, N., Kenny, A., Pinborg, J. (eds.) (1982), *The Cambridge History of Later Medieval Philosophy*, Cambridge.
Kullmann, W. (1965), "Zur Wissenschaft und Methode des Aristoteles", in Flashar and Gaiser (1965), 247-274.
Kwiatkowski, T. (1963), "La dialectique d'Aristote", *Roczniki filozoficzne* 11, 81-101.
La Croce, E. (1978-1979), "Alexandri Aphrodisiensis, Commentario al tratado de los Tópicos de Aristóteles. Proemio al libro I, traducción e notas", *Ethos* 6-7, 227-244.
—— (1990), "La dialéctica aristotélica y los principios de la ciencia", *Elenchos* 11, 187-202
—— (1991), "La dialéctica y la fundamentación de los principios de la ética aristotélica", Méthexis 4, 59-80.
*Lear, J. (1980), *Aristotle and Logical Theory*, Cambridge.
Le Blond, J. M. (1938), *Eulogos et l'argument de convenance*, Paris.
*—— (1939a), *Logique et méthode chez Aristote, Études sur la recherche des principes dans la physique aristotélicienne*, Paris (repr. 1970).
—— (1939b), "La définition chez Aristote", *Gregorianum* 20, 351-380; repr. as "Aristotle on definition" in Barnes, Schofield, Sorabji (1975-1979), vol. 3, 63-79.
Lee, H. D. P. (1935), "Geometrical method and Aristotle's account of first principles", *Classical Quarterly* 29, 113-124.
Lee, T.-S. (1984), *Die griechische Tradition der aristotelischen Syllogistik in der Spätantike*, Hypomnemata 79, Göttingen.
Lejewski, C. (1961), "On prosleptic syllogisms", *Notre Dame Journal of Formal Logic* 1, 158-167.
Lennox, J. G. (1980), "Aristotle on genera, species and 'the more and the less'", *Journal of the History of Biology* 13, 321-346.
—— (1987), "Kinds, forms of kinds, and the more and the less in Aristotle's biology", in Gotthelf and Lennox (1987), 339-359.
*—— (1994), "Aristotelian problems", *Ancient Philosophy* 14, 53-77.
Lesher, J. H. (1973), "The meaning of νοῦς in the *Posterior Analytics*", *Phronesis* 18, 44-68.
Leszl, W. (1975), *Aristotle's Conception of Ontology*, Padova.

Lewis, F. A. (1982), "Accidental sameness in Aristotle", *Philosophical Studies* 42, 1-36.
*Liddell, H. G., Scott, R., Jones, H. S. (1968[9]), A Greek-English Lexicon, Oxford. (abbrev. LSJ)
Lienhard, J. T. (1966), "A note on the meaning of πίστις in Aristotle's *Rhetoric*"" *Archiv für Geschichte der Philosophie* 87, 446-454.
Lloyd, A. C. (1955-1956), "Neoplatonic logic and Aristotelian logic", *Phronesis* 1, 58-72 & 146-160.
—— (1962), "Genus, species and ordered series in Aristotle", *Phronesis* 7, 67-90.
Lloyd, G. E. R. (1961), "The development of Aristotle's theory of the classification of animals", *Phronesis* 6, 59-81.
—— (1978), "Saving the appearances", *Classical Quarterly* 28, 202-222.
Long, A.A. (1978), "Dialectic and the Stoic sage", in Rist (1978), 101-124.
Lorenz, K. (ed.) (1979), *Konstruktionen versus Positionen, vol. 1, Spezielle Wissenschaftstheorie*, Berlin and New York.
Lossau, M. (1974), "Der aristotelische Gryllos antilogisch", *Philologus* 118, 12-21.
—— (1981), Πρὸς κρίσιν τινα πολιτικήν. *Untersuchungen zur aristotelischen Rhetorik*,Wiesbaden.
Lugarini, L. (1959), "Dialettica e filosofia in Aristotele", *Pensiero* 4, 48-69.
Łukasiewicz, J. (1935), "Zur Geschichte der Aussagenlogik", *Erkenntnis* 5, 111-131.
*—— (1957[2], 1951), *Aristotle's Syllogistic*, Oxford.
—— (1971), "The principle of contradiction in Aristotle", *Review of Metaphysics* 95, 485-509; repr. in Barnes, Schofield, Sorabji (1975-79), vol. 3, 50-62 and as "Über den Satz des Widerspruchs bei Aristoteles" in Menne and Öffenberger (1982), vol. 1, 5-28.
Lumpe, A. (1955), "Der Terminus Prinzip (ἀρχή) von den Vorsokratikern bis auf Aristoteles", *Archiv für Begriffsgeschichte* 1, 104-116.
Madden, E. H. (1952), "The enthymeme. Crossroads of logic, rhetoric, and metaphysics", *Philosophical Review* 61, 368-376.
Maguiness, W. S. (1946), "Aristotle, *Topica* 107a 8-10", *Classical Review* 60, 19.
—— (1947), "Notes on the *Topics* of Aristotle", *Classical Review* 61, 11-12.
*Maier, H. (1896-1900), *Die Syllogistik des Aristoteles*, 3 vols., Tübingen.
Mainberger, G. (1955), *Die Seinsstufung als Methode und Metaphysik. Untersuchungen über Mehr und Weniger als Grundlage zu einem möglichen Gottesbeweis bei Platon und Aristoteles*, Studia Friburgensia N.F. 24, Freiburg (Schweiz).
Mansion, A. (1961), "L'origine du syllogisme et la théorie de la science chez Aristote", in Mansion (1961), 57-81.
Mansion, S. (1955a),*Autour d'Aristote*, Louvain
—— (1955b), "Les apories de la métaphysique aristotélicienne", in Mansion (1955a), 141-179.
—— (1968), "Notes sur la doctrine des Catégories dans les *Topiques*", in Owen (1968a), 189-201; repr. in Mansion (1984).
—— (1984), *Études aristotéliciennes*, Louvain.
—— (ed.) (1961), *Aristote et les problèmes de méthode*, 2nd Symposium Aristotelicum, Louvain and Paris.
Markowski, M. (1968), "Les Questions de Jean Buridan sur les *Topiques* d'Aristote", *Mediaevalia Philosophica Polonorum* 13, 3-7.
Maróth, M. (1979), "Die hypothetischen Syllogismen", *Acta antiqua Academiae Scientiarum Hungaricae* 27, 407-436.
—— (1981), "Die Topik Avicennas und ihre Rolle in den arabischen Wissenschaften", *Acta antiqua Academiae Scientiarum Hungaricae* 29, 33-41.
Martano, G. (1986), "Aristotle e Perelman, argomentazione scientifica e argomentazione dialettica", in *Energeia*. (1986), 373-386.
Masi, M. (ed.) (1981), *Boethius and the Liberal Arts*, Bern.
Mates, B. (1961[2], 1953), *Stoic Logic*, Berkeley and Los Angeles.
Mattew, G. B. and Cohen, S. M. (1968), "The one and the many", *Review of Metaphysics* 21, 630-655.
Mau, J. (1959), "Zum Begriff des Syllogismus bei Aristoteles und den Stoikern", in Irmscher and Steffen (1959), 65-69.
McCabe, M. M. (1994), "Arguments in context: Aristotle's defense of Rhetoric", in Furley and Nehemas (1994), 129-165.
McKeon, R. (1954), "Dialectic and political thought and action", *Ethics* 65, 1-33.
McKirahan, R. D. (1983), "Aristotelian epagoge in Prior Analytics 2. 21 and Posterior Analytics 1.1", *Journal of the History of Philosophy* 21, 1-13.
McMahon, G. J. (1956), "The proemium to the *Physics* of Aristotle", *Laval théologique et philosophique* 12, 9-57.

Menn, S. (1995), "Metaphysic, Dialectic and the *Categories*", Revue de Métaphysique et de Morale, 311-337.
Menne, A. and Öffenberger, N. (edd.) (1982-1990), *Zur modernen Deutung der aristotelischen Logik*, 4 vols., Hildesheim, Zürich, New York.
Meyer, M. (ed.) (1986), *De la métaphysique á la rhétorique*, Bruxelles 1986
—— (ed.) (1989), *From Metaphysics to Rhetoric*, Norwell and Kluwer. (English translation of Meyer (1986))
Mignucci, M. (1985), "Puzzles about identity. Aristotle and his Greek commentators", in Wiesner (1985), 57-97.
Miner, D. H. (1978), *Aristotle's theory of predication*, Diss. Southern Illinois University at Carbondale.
Minio-Paluello, L. (1955), "The text of Aristotle's *Topics* and *Sophistici Elenchi*: The Latin tradition", *Classical Quarterly* 49, 108-118; repr. in Minio-Paluello (1972), 299-327.
—— (1958), "Note sull'Aristotele latino medievale.X.I 'Topici' nel X-XI secolo ...", *Rivista di filosofia neo-scolastica* 50, 97-116.
—— (1972), *Opuscula: The Latin Aristotle*, Amsterdam.
Morales, F. (1991), *Antikeimena: Untersuchungen zur aristotelischen Auffassung der Gegensätze*, Europäische Hochschulschriften Reihe 20, Nr. 337, Frankfurt.
Moreau, J. (1968), "Aristote et la dialectique platonicienne", in Owen (1968a), 80-90.
*Moreau, P. (1968), "La joute d'après le huitième livre des Topiques", in Owen (1968a), 277-311.
Morel, G. (1960), "De la notion de principe chez Aristote", *Archives de Philosophie* 23, 487-511.
Morpurgo-Tagliabue, G. (1971), "Asserzione ed esistenza nella logica di Aristotele", *Filosofia* 22, 29-60.
Morrison, D. (1987), "The evidence for degrees of being in Aristotle", *Classical Quarterly* 37, 382-401.
Morsink, J. (1975), *Science and Dialectic in Aristotle. A Philosophical Study of the Generation of Animals*, Diss. University of Wisconsin - Madison.
—— (1982), "The mandate of *Topics* A 2", *Apeiron* 16, 102-128.
Moser, S. (1935), *Zur Lehre von der Definition bei Aristoteles*, Part 1 (Organon und Metaphysik), Innsbruck.
Most, G. W. (1994), "The uses of endoxa: philosophy and rhetoric in the Rhetoric", in Furley and Nehamas (1994), 167-190.
Mráz, M. (1976), "Zum Ausdruck ἀκολούθησις in der aristotelischen Logik", *Graecolatina Pragensia* 7, 141-158.
—— (1986-87), "Die Ausdrücke für das Folgern in der Sprache der Logik des Aristoteles", *Zprávy Jednoty Klasických Filologů*, 28-29 & 53-67.
Mueller, I. (1969), "Stoic Logic and Peripatetic Logic", *Archiv für Geschichte der Philosophie* 51, 173-187.
Müri, W. (1944), "Das Wort Dialektik bei Platon", *Museum Helveticum* 1, 152-168.
Mulhern, M. M. (1970), *Aristotle's theory of predication. The 'Categoriae' account*, Diss State University of New York at Buffalo.
Muskens, G.L. (1943), *De vocis ΑΝΑΛΟΓΙΑΣ significatione ac usu apud Aristotelem*, Groningen.
Natali, C. (1984), "Virtù o scienza. Aspetti della frovnhsi" nei Topici e nelle Etiche di Aristotele", *Phronesis* 29, 50-72.
—— (1986), "Aristote et les méthodes d'enseignement de Gorgias", in Cassin (1986), 105-116.
—— (1990a), "Due modi di trattare le opinioni notevoli. La nozione di felicità in Aristotele, Retorica I 5", Méthexis 3, 51-63.
—— (1990b), "Fino a che punto rispettare le opinioni in etica: Aristotele e gli endoxa", in De Domenico, Di Stefano, G. Puglisi (1990), 191-201.
Nelson, J. O. (1954), "In defense of the traditional interpretation of the square", *Philosophical Review* 63, 401-413.
Nguemning, A. (1990), *Untersuchungen zur "Topik" des Aristoteles mit besonderer Berücksichtigung der Regeln, Verfahren und Ratschläge zur Bildung von Definitionen*, Europäische Hochschulschriften Reihe 20, Nr. 308, Frankfurt.
Nussbaum, M. C. (1982), "Saving Aristotle's Appearances", in Schofield and Nussbaum (1982), 267-293.
—— (1986), *The Fragility of Goodness*, Cambridge.
Obbink, D. (1992), "'What all men believe must be true': Common conceptions and consensus omnium in Aristotle and Hellenistic philosophy", *Oxford Studies in Ancient Philosophy* 10, 193-231.

Ochs, D. J. (1969), "Aristotle's concept of formal topics", *Speech Monographs* 36, 419-425.
Oehler, K. (1961), "Der Consensus omnium als Kriterium der Wahrheit in der antiken Philosophie und der Patristik", *Antike und Abendland* 10, 103-129.
—— (1966), "Der geschichtliche Ort der formalen Logik", *Studium Generale* 19, 453-461.
—— (1982), "Die Anfänge der Relationenlogik und der Zeichenschlusses bei Aristoteles", *Zeitschrift für Semiotik*, 259-266.
Olivieri, L. (1983), "Probabilità e suggetività dell'apparire nella dialettica aristotelica dei Topici", *Verifiche* 12, 333-347.
Olshewsky, T. M. (1968), "Aristotle's use of analogia", *Apeiron* 2, 1-10.
O'Meara, D. J. (ed.) (1981), *Studies in Aristotle*, Washington.
*Owen, G. E. L. (1959), "The place of the *Timaeus* in Plato's Dialogues", *Classical Quarterly* NS 3, 79-95.
—— (1961), "Tithenai ta Phainomena", in Mansion (1961), 83-103; repr. in Barnes, Schofield, Sorabji, vol. 1, 113-126.
—— (1965), "The Platonism of Aristotle", Proceedings of the British Academy 50, 125-150; repr. in Barnes, Schofield, Sorabji, vol 1, 14-34.
*—— (ed.) (1968a), *Aristotle on Dialectic. The Topics* Proceedings of the Third Symposium Aristotelicum, Oxford.
—— (1968b), "Dialectic and eristic in the treatment of the Forms", in Owen (1968), 103-125.
—— (1969), "Logic and metaphysics in some earlier works of Aristotle", in Düring and Owen (1960), 163-190., repr. in Barnes, Schofield, Sorabji, vol. 3, 13-32.
—— (1986), *Logic, Science and Dialectic*. Collected Papers in Greek philosophy, ed. by M. Nussbaum, London and Ithaca.
Owens, J. (1978³, 1951), *The Doctrine of Being in the Aristotelian Metaphysics*, Toronto.
—— (1987), "Aristotle's notion of wisdom", *Apeiron* 20, 1-16.
Paideia (1978), Special Aristotle Issue, Second Special Issue, State University College at Buffalo and State University College at Brockport.
Palmer, G.P. (1934), *The τόποι of Aristotle's Rhetoric as exemplified in the Oratores*, Diss. Univ of Chicago.
*Patzig, G. (1969³, 1959), *Die aristotelische Syllogistik*, Göttingen.
*—— (1968), *Aristotle's Theory of the Syllogism*, Dordrecht. (translation of Patzig (1969³, 1959))
——, Scheibe, E., Wieland, W. (eds.) (1977), *Logik, Ethik, Theorie der Geisteswissenschaften*, Hamburg.
Pellegrin, P. (1981), "Division et syllogisme chez Aristote", *Revue Philosophique de la France et de l'étranger* 172, 169-187.
Pelletier, Y. (1979), "Espèces et arguments oratoires", *Laval théologique et philosophique* 35, 3-20.
—— (1980), "Espèces communes et arguments oratoires", *Laval théologique et philosophique* 36, 29-46.
—— (1981), "Lieux et arguments oratoires", *Laval théologique et philosophique* 37, 45-67.
*—— (1985), "Pour une définition claire et nette du lieu dialectique", *Laval théologique et philosophique* 41, 403-445.
—— (1989), "L'articulation de la dialectique aristotélicienne", *Angelicum* 66 (1989), 603-620.
*—— (1991), *La dialectique aristotélicienne: les principes clés des Topiques*, Montreal
Perelman, Ch. (1955), "La méthode dialectique et le rôle de l'interlocuteur dans le dialogue", *Revue de métaphysique et de morale* 60, 26-31.
—— and Olbrechts-Tyteca, L. (1958), *La nouvalle rhétorique. Traité de l'argumentation*, 2 vols., Paris.
—— and Olbrechts-Tyteca, L. (1969), *The New Rhetoric. A Treatise on Argumentation*, London. (translation of Perelman and Olbrechts-Tyteca (1958))
—— (1979), "Philosophie et rhétorique", *Tijdschrift voor Philosophie* 41, 33-77.
*Pflug, J. (1908), *De Topicorum libro V*, Leipzig.
Pflugmacher, E. (1909), *Locorum Communium Specimen*, Gryphiae.
Pickard, J. (1936), "Syllogismes catégoriques et hypothétiques", *Revue de métaphysique et de morale*, 231-267 and 403-430.
Pietsch, Ch. (1992), *Prinzipienfindung bei Aristoteles. Methode und erkenntnistheoretische Grundlagen*, Stuttgart.
Pinborg, J. (1969), "Topik und Syllogistik im Mittelalter", in Hoffman (1969), 157-178.
Platzeck, E. W. (1954), *Von der Analogie zum Syllogismus. Ein systematisch-historischer Darstellungsversuch der Entfaltung des methodischen Logos bei Socrates, Platon, Aristoteles*, Paderborn.
Plebe, A. (1959), "Retorica aristotelica e logica stoica", *Filosofia* 10, 391-424.

—— (1993), "La possibilità di una formalizzazione della logica Aristotelica degli entimemi", *Revue International de Philosophie* 47, 70-77.
Plöbst, W. (1911), *Die Auxesis (Amplificatio). Studien zu ihrer Entwicklung und Anwendung*, Diss. phil. München.
Pöggeler, O. (1974), "Dialektik und Topik", in Riedel M. (1974), 291-331.
Poste, E. (1866), *Aristotle On Fallacies or The Sophistici Elenchi*, London.
Prantl, C. (1853), "Über die Entwicklung der aristotelischen Logik aus der platonischen Philosophie", *Abhandlungen der Bayerischen Akademie der Wissenschaften* 7, 1.
—— (1855-67), *Geschichte der Logik im Abendlande*, Leipzig.
Price, R. (1968), "Some antistrophes to the Rhetoric", *Philosophy and Rhetoric* 2, 145-164.
Primavesi, O. (1992), "Dionysios der Dialektiker und Aristoteles über die Definition des Lebens", *Rheinisches Museum für Philologie* 135, 246-261.
Pritzl, K. (1993), "Aristotle: ways of truth and ways of opinion", *Proceedings of the American Catholic Philosophical Association* 67, 241-252.
—— (1994), "Opinions as appearances: endoxa in Aristotle", *Ancient Philosophy* 14, 41-50.
Raphael, S. (1974), "Rhetoric, dialectic and syllogistic argument. Aristotle's position in Rhetoric I-II", *Phronesis* 19, 153-167.
Rapp, C. (1992), "Ähnlichkeit, Analogie und Homonymie bei Aristoteles", *Zeitschrift für Philosophische Forschung* 46, 526-544.
—— (1993), "Aristoteles über die Rechtfertigung des Satzes vom Widerspruch", *Zeitschrift für Philosophische Forschung* 47, 521-541.
Régis, L. M. (1935), *L'opinion selon Aristote*, Paris and Ottawa.
Rehbock, K. (1988), *Topik und Recht. Eine Standortanalyse unter besonderer Berücksichtigung der aristotelischen Topik*, München.
Richards, H. (1915-1918), "Aristotelica", *Journal of Philology* 34, 247-254.
Riedel, M. (ed.) (1974), *Rehabilitierung der praktischen Philosophie*, vol. 2, Freiburg.
Rigamonti, G. (1980), *L'origine del sillogismo in Aristotele*, Palermo.
Riondato, E. (1985), "La pragmateia di Gorgia secondo Aristotele (El.soph. 34, 183b36-39)", *Siculorum Gymnasium* 38, 81-95.
Riposati, B. (1944), "Quid Cicero de thesi et hypothesi in «Topicis» senserit", *Aevum* 18, 61-71.
Rist, J.M. (ed.) (1978), *The Stoics*, Berkeley and Los Angeles.
Ritoók, Z. (1975), "Zur Geschichte des Topos-Begriffes", in *Eirene. Actes de la XIIe Conférence internationale d'Études Classiques*, Bucuresti and Amsterdam 1975, 111-114.
Robert, S. (1957), "Rhetoric and dialectic according to the first Latin commentary on the *Rhetoric* of Aristotle", *The New Scholasticism* 31, 484-498.
*Robinson, R. (1931), "The historical background of Aristotle's *Topics* VIII", in: *Proceedings of the 7th International Congress of Philosophy*, Oxford and London, 437-442.
—— (1950), *Definition*, Oxford.
—— (1958), "La pétition de principe", *Communication présentée au Congrès de l'Association G. Budé*, Lyon, 75-80.
Roelants, H. (1966), "De methodologie van de Topika", *Tijdschrift voor Philosophie* 28, 495-517.
Rohr, M. D. (1975), *Aspects of Aristotle's earlier theory of predication*, Diss. Stanford University Palo Alto, California.
—— (1978), "Aristotle on the transitivity of being said of", *Journal of the History of Philosophy* 16, 379-385.
Rose, L. E. (1968), *Aristotle's Syllogistic*, Springfield, IL.
*Ross, W. D. (ed. and tr.) (1924), *Aristotle's Metaphysics*, 2 vols., Oxford.
—— (1939), "The discovery of the syllogism", *Philosophical Review* 48, 251-272.
*—— (ed. and tr.) (1949), *Aristotle's Prior and Posterior Analytics*, Oxford.
—— (1956), "The text of Aristotle's *Topics* and *Sophistici Elenchi*", in *Mélanges de philosophie grecque offerts à Mgr. Diès*, Paris, 215-219.
*—— (1995[6], 1923), *Aristotle*, London and New York.
Rossitto, C. (1977-8), "La dialettica platonica in Aristotele, Met. A 6 and M 4", *Atti e Memorie dell'Academia Patavina di Scienze*, 90, parte III, 75-87.
—— (1984), "La dimostrazione dialettica in Aristotele", *La Nottola* 3, 5-40.
—— (1987), "Problemi e ricerche sulla dialettica aristotelica", *Cultura e Scuola* 26, 102-113.
—— (1993), "La dialettica e il suo ruolo nella Metafisica di Aristotele", *Rivista di Filosofia Neo-Scolastica* 85, 370-424.
Ruiz, Y. E. (1987-88), "La interrogación en Aristóteles", *Habis* 18-19, 29-37.
Russo, A. (1962), *La filosofia della retorica in Aristotle*, Napoli.
Rutten, C. (1964), "Note sur le syllogisme de l'essence chez Aristote", *Phronesis* 9, 72-81.
Ryan, E. E. (1979), "Plato's Gorgias and Phaedrus and Aristotle's theory of rhetoric, a speculative account", *Athenaeum* 57, 452-461.

―― (1984), *Aristotle's theory of rhetorical argumentation*, Montréal.
*Ryle, G. (1966), *Plato's Progress*, Cambridge.
*―― (1968), "Dialectic in the Academy", in Owen (1968a), 69-79.
*Sainati, V. (1968), *Storia dell'Organon aristotelico, I. Dai Topici al De interpretatione*, Firenze.
―― (1973), *Storia dell' Organon aristotelico, II. L'analitica. Parte 1. La crisi epistemologica della Topica*, Firenze.
―― (1985), "Die 'Kategorien' und die Theorie der Prädikation", in Menne and Öffenberger (1985), vol. 2, 26-79 (German translation of Sainati (1968), 146-198).
*―― (1993), "Aristotele. Dalla Topica all'Analitica", *Teoria* 13, 1-117. (reprint of Sainati (1973))
Sandbach, F.H. (1985), *Aristotle and the Stoics*, Cambridge.
Sorio, G. (1982), "*Topici*, libro II. Regolae dialetiche e valore di verità", *Verifiche* 11, 199-226.
Scarpat, G. (1950), *Il discorso et le sue parti in Aristotele*, Arona.
Schanze, H. and Kopperschmidt, J. (eds.) (1989), *Rhetorik und Philosophie*, München.
Schickert, K. (1977), *Die Form der Widerlegung beim frühen Aristoteles*, Zetemata 65, München.
Schlueter, H. (1954), *Untersuchungen zur Lehre von den Kategorien vor und bei Aristoteles*, Diss. Göttingen.
Schmidt, W. (1974), *Theorie der Induktion. Die prinzipielle Bedeutung der Epagoge bei Aristoteles*, München.
Schöpsdau, K. (1981), "Topik und Rhetorik. Zur aristotelischen Rhet. B 22", *Würzburger Jahrbücher für die Altertumswissenschaft* N.F. 7, 63-84.
Schofield, M. and Nussbaum, M. (eds.) (1982), *Language and Logos*, Cambridge.
Scholz, H. (1930), "Die Axiomatik der Alten", *Blätter für deutsche Philosophie* 4, 259-278; repr. as "The Ancient Axiomati Theory" in Barnes, Schofield, Sorabji, vol 1, 50-64.
Scholz, H. (1931), *Geschichte der Logik*, Berlin.
Schröder (1985), "῞Ωστε ἑκάτερον αὐτῶν ἑκατέρῳ τούτων τὸ αὐτὸ εἶναι (Rhet. A 2, 1356a 35-110, 1337a 22-61)", *Hermes* 113, 172-183.
Schüssler, I. (1974), "Semantik und Logik. Der elenktische Beweis des Satzes vom Widerspuch", in Schüssler and Janke (1974), 53-66.
Schüssler, I. and Janke, W. (eds.) (1974), *Festschrift für K. H. Volkmann-Schluck*, Frankfurt.
Seaton, R. C. (1914), "The Aristotelian enthymeme", *Classical Review* 28, 113-119.
Sedley, D.N. (1977), "Diodorus Cronus and Hellenistic philosophy", *Proceedings of the Cambridge Philological Society* 23, 74-120.
Self, L. S. (1979), "Rhetoric and phronesis. The Aristotelian ideal", *Philosophy and Rhetoric* 12, 130-145.
Sharples, R. W. (ed.) (1993), *Modern thinkersand ancient thinkers*. The Stanley Victor Keeling Memorial lectures at University college London, 1981-1991, London.
Shellens, M. S. (1963), "Giustificationi della dialettica in Aristotele (ontologia, storia, politica)", *Studia Urbani* 37, 65-114, 279-313.
Shorey, P. (1889), "Συλλογισμὸς ἐξ ὑποθέσεως in Aristotle", *American Journal of Philology* 10, 430-462.
Sichirollo, L. (1957), *Logica e dialettica*, Milan.
―― (1961a), *Aristotelica*, Urbino.
―― (1961b), "Recenti ricerche sulla dialettica aristotelica", in Sichirollo (1961a), 109-119.
―― (1963), *Giustificazioni della dialectica in Aristotele (ontologia, storia, politica)*, Studia Urbani 37, 65-114 and 279-313.
―― (1965), *Storicità della dialettica antica. Platone, Aristotle, Hegel*, Padova.
―― (1966), Διαλέγεσθαι―*Dialektik von Homer bis Aristoteles*, Hildesheim.
Sillitti, G. (1968), "Il non ente fra Platone e Aristotele", *Cultura* 6, 474-488.
Silnizki, M. (1988), *Die Entstehung und Entwicklung der Syllogistik bei Aristotles*, Diss. Köln.
Silvestre, M. L. (1984), "L'ambiguo attegiamento aristotelico nei confronti della sofistica", *Discorsi* 4, 63-82.
Simonson, S. (1944), "The Aristotelian forms of disputation", *New Scholasticism* 18, 385-390.
Simonson, S. (1945), "A definitive note on the enthymeme", *American Journal of Philology*, 303-306.
Sinaceur, M. A. (ed.) (1991), *Penser avec Aristote*, Tolouse.
Slater, B. H. (1979), "Aristotle's propositional logic", *Philosophical Studies* 36, 35-49.
Slattery, M. (1958), "Genus and differentiae", *Thomist* 21, 343-364.
*Smiley, T. (1973), "What is a syllogism?", *Journal of Philosophical Logic* 2, 136-154.
Smith, R. A. (1974), *Plato's Dialectic from the Standpoint of Aristotle's First Logic*, Diss. Claremont Graduate School, Claremont, California.
―― (1989), *Aristotle: Prior Analytics*, Indianapolis.

—— (1991), "Predication and deduction in Aristotle: Aspirations to completeness", *Topoi* 10, 43-52.
*—— (1993), "Aristotle on the uses of dialectic", *Synthese* 96, 335-358.
—— (1994), "Dialectic and the syllogism", *Ancient Philosophy* 14, 133-151.
*Solmsen, F. (1929), *Die Entwicklung der aristotelischen Logik und Rhetorik*, Berlin.
—— (1941), "The discovery of the syllogism", *Philosophical Review* 50, 410-421.
—— (1944), "Boethius and the history of the *Organon*", *American Journal of Philology* 65, 69-74.
—— (1951), "Aristotle's syllogism and its Platonic background", *Philosophical Review* 60, 563-571.
—— (1968), "Dialectic without the Forms", in Owen (1968a), 49-68.
Soreth, M. (1968), "Zur Topik E 7, 137a8-20 und b3-13", in Owen (1968a), 43-45.
Spanu, H. (1983), "Homonymität und Synonymität bei Plato und Aristoteles", in *Mélanges Vourveris*, Athens, 113-120.
Sprague, R. K. (1977), "Plato's sophistry, II", *Proceedings of the Aristotelian Society* 51, 45-61.
—— (1986), "Apories sophistiques et description du processus", in Cassin (1986), 91-104.
Sprute, J. (1975), "Topos und Enthymeme in der aristotelishen Rhetorik", *Hermes* 103, 68-90.
—— (1977), "Der Zweck der aristotelischen Rhetorik", in Patzig, Scheibe and Wieland (1977), 469-476.
—— (1981), "Aristoteles' Theorie rhetorischer Argumentation", *Gymnasium* 88, 254-273.
—— (1982), *Die Enthymemtheorie der aristotelischen Rhetorik*, Abhandlungen der Akademie der Wissenschaften in Göttingen, Phil.-Hist. Klasse, Folge 3, Nr. 124, Göttingen.
—— (1992), "Philosophie und Rhetorik bei Platon und Aristoteles", in Classen and Müllenbrock (1992), 29-45.
Stakelum, J. W. (1940), *Galen and the logic of propositions*, Diss. Angelicum, Rome.
Stark, R., (ed.) (1968), *Rhetorika. Schriften zur aristotelischen und hellenistischen Rhetorik*, Hildesheim.
*Steinthal, H. (1890), *Geschichte der Sprachwissenschaft bei den Griechen und Römern*, Berlin.
Stenzel, J. (1929), "Zur Theorie des Logos bei Aristoteles", *Quellen und Studien zur Geschichte der Mathematik* B I 1, 34-66, Berlin; repr. in Stenzel (1957^2), 188-219.
—— (1931^2, 1917), *Studien zur Entwicklung der Platonischen Dialektik von Sokrates zu Aristoteles*, Leipzig und Berlin.
Stenzel, J. (1957^2), *Kleine Schriften*, Darmstadt .
Stocks, J. L. (1933), "The composition of Aristotle's logical works", *Classical Quarterly* 27, 115-124.
*Striker, G. (1973), "Zur Frage nach den Quellen von Boethius' 'De hypotheticis syllogismis'", *Archiv für Geschichte der Philosophie* 55, 70-75.
*—— (1976), Review of Zadro (1974), *Archiv für Geschichte der Philosophie* 58, 278-281.
*—— (1979), "Aristoteles über Syllogismus 'aufgrund einer Hypothese'", *Hermes* 108, 33-50.
Stump, E. (1974), "Boethius's works on the Topics", *Vivarium* 12, 77-93.
*—— (1978), *Boethius' De Topicis Differentiis*, Ithaca.
—— (1981), "Boethius and Peter of Spain on the 'Topics'", in Masi (1981), 35-50.
—— (1982), "Topics: Their development and absorption into the consequences", in Kretzmann, Kenny, Pinborg (1982), 273-299.
—— (1988), *Boethius' In Ciceronis Topica*, Ithaca and London.
*—— (1989), *Dialectic and its place in the development of medieval logic*, Ithaca.
*Sullivan, M. W. (1967), *Apuleian Logic*, Amsterdam.
Szabó, A. (1951-1952), "Beiträge zur Geschichte der griechischen Dialektik", *Acta antiqua* (Budapest) 1, 377-410.
—— (1964), "Ein Beleg für die voreudoxische Proportionenlehre? Aristoteles Topik Θ 3, 158 b29-35", *Archiv für Begriffsgeschichte* 9, 151-171.
Tanner, R. G. (1983), "Form and substance in Aristotle", *Prudentia* 15, 87-108.
Tarán, L. (1978), "Speusippus and Aristotle on homonymy and synonymy", *Hermes* 106, 73-99.
Tegge, A. (1877), *De vi ac notione dialecticae aristoteleae*, Programm Treptow.
Tessmer, R. (1957), *Untersuchungen zur aristotelischen Rhetorik*, Diss. Humboldt-Universität Berlin.
Thiel, N.M. (1920), *Die Bedeutung des Wortes ὑπόθεσις bei Aristoteles*, Diss. Freiburg, Fulda.
—— (1930), "Die hypothetischen Schlüsse des Aristoteles", *Philosophisches Jahrbuch der Görresgesellschaft* 33, 1-17.
Thielscher, P. (1908), "Cicero's Topik und Aristoteles", *Philologus* 67, 52-67.
—— (1948), "Die relative Chronologie der erhaltenen Schriften des Aristoteles nach den bestimmten Selbstzitaten", *Philologus* 97 (1948), 229-265.

*Thionville, E. (1855), *De la théorie des lieux communs*, Paris (repr. Osnabrück 1965).
Thompson, W. N. (1975), *Aristotle's deduction and induction*, Amsterdam.
Thornton, A. M. (1986), "Logos-phrase et logos-texte chez Platon et Aristote", in *Philosophie du langage et grammaire dans l'Antiquité*, Cahiers de philosophie ancienne 5, Bruxelles, 165-179.
Throm, H. (1932), *Die Thesis*, Paderborn.
Thurot, C. (1860), *Études sur Aristote. Politique, dialectique, rhétorique*, Paris.
Tiles, J. E. (1983), "Why the triangle has two right angles καθ' αὐτός, *Phronesis* 28, 1-16.
*Toulmin, S. (1964), *The Uses of Argument*, Cambridge.
Trendelenburg, F. A. (1846), *Geschichte der Kategorienlehre*, Berlin (repr. Hildesheim 1963).
Trépanier, E. (1943), "La connaisance des premiers principes", *Laval Théologique et Philosophique* 4, 289-310.
Tsouyopoulos, N. (1970), "Die Entdeckung der Struktur komparativer Begriffe in der Antike. Zur Begriffsbildung bei Aristoteles und Proklos", *Archiv für Begriffsgeschichte* 14, 152-171
Tugendhat, E. (1958), *TI KATA TINOS. Eine Untersuchung zur Struktur und Ursprung aristotelischer Grundbegriffe*, Freiburg und München.
Upton, T. V. (1981), "Infinity and perfect induction in Aristotle", *Proceedings of the American Catholic Philosophical Association* 55, 149-157.
—— (1983), "Psychological and metaphysical dimensions of non-contradiction in Aristotle", *Review of Metaphysics* 36, 591-606.
—— (1985), "Aristotle on hypothesis and the unhypothesized first principle", *Review of Metaphysics* 39, 283-301.
Urbanas, A. (1988), *La notion d'accident chez Aristote. Logique et métaphysique*, Montréal and Paris.
Vahlen, J. (1867), "Rhetorik und Topik. Ein Beitrag zu Aristoteles' Rhetorik", *Rheinisches Museum* 22, 101-110; repr. in Vahlen (1911-1923), 106-116
—— (1911-1923), *Gesammelte philologische Schriften*, Leipzig and Berlin.
Van Aubel, M. (1963), "Accident, catégories et prédicables dans l'oeuvre d'Aristote", *Revue philosophique de Louvain* 61, 361-401.
Van Brennekom, R. (1986), "Aristotle and the copula", *Journal of the History of Philosphy* 24, 1-18.
Van der Weel, R. L. (1969), "The *Posterior Analytics* and the *Topics*", *Laval Théologique et Philosophique* 25, 130-141.
Van Eemeren, F. H., Grootendorst, R., Blair, J. A., Willard C. A. (eds.) (1987), *Argumentation: Perspectives and Approaches*. Proceedings of the Conference on Argumentation 1986, 3 vols. (3, 3A, 3B), Dordrecht and Providence.
Van Noorden, S. (1979), "Rhetorical arguments in Aristotle and Perelman", *Revue internationale de philosophie* 33, 178-187.
Van Ophuijsen, J. (1994), "Where have the *Topics* gone?", in Fortenbaugh and Mirhady (1994), 131-173.
Verbeke, G. (1968), "La notion de propriété dans les Topiques", in Owen (1968a), 257-276.
Verdenius, W. J. (1968), "Notes on the *Topics*", in Owen (1968a), 22-42.
Viano, C. A. (1958), "La dialettica in Aristotele", *Rivista di Filosofia* 49, 154-178; repr. in Viano (1969a), 38-62.
—— (1969a), *Studi sulla dialettica*, Turin.
—— (1969b), "La dialettica stoica", in Viano (1969a), 63-111.
Viehweg, T. (1953), *Topik und Jurisprudenz*, München.
*Von Arnim, H. (1927), "Das Ethische in Aristoteles' Topik", *Sitzungsberichte der Akademie der Wissenschaften in Wien* 205, 4.
Von Fragstein, A. (1967), *Die Diairesis bei Aristoteles*, Amsterdam.
Von Fritz, K. (1931), "Der Ursprung der aristotelischen Kategorienlehre", *Archiv für Geschichte der Philosophie* 44, 449-496.
—— (1955), "Die ARXAI in der griechischen Mathematik", *Archiv für Begriffsgeschichte* 1, 13-103.
*—— (1964), "Die ἐπαγωγή bei Aristoteles", *Sitzungsberichte der Bayerischen Akademie der Wissenschaften* 1964,3, München.
—— (1975), "Versuch einer Richtigstellung neuerer Thesen über Ursprung und Entwicklung von Aristoteles' Logik", in Cobet (1975), 93-102.
Waitz, T. (1857), "Varianten zu Aristoteles' Organon", *Philologus* 12, 726-734.
Wallies, M. (1878), *De fontibus Topicorum Ciceronis*, Berlin.
—— (1891), *Die griechischen Ausleger der aristotelischen Topik*, Wissenschaftliche Beilage zum Programm, Sophien-Gymnasium zu Berlin, Berlin.

—— (1922), "Textkritisches zu der aristotelischen Topik und den sophistischen Widerlegungen", *Philologus* 78, 301-330.
Wardy, R. (1991), "Transcendental dialectic", *Phronesis* 26, 86-106.
Watson, G. (1989), "Plato's Gorgias and Aristotle", *Maynooth Review* 14, 51-66.
*Wedin, V. E. (1973), "A remark on per se accidens and properties", *Archiv für Geschichte der Philosophie* 55, 30-35.
Weidemann, H. (1988), "Aristoteles über Schlüsse aus Zeichen (Rhetorik I 2,1357b1-25)", in Claussen and Daube-Schakat (1988), 27-34.
*Weil, E. (1951), "La place de la logique dans la pensée aristotelicienne", *Revue de métaphysique et morale* 56, 283-315; repr. as "The Place of Logic in Aristotle's Thought", in Barnes, Schofield, Sorabji (1975-79), vol 1, 88-112.
White, N. P. (1971), "Aristotle on sameness and oneness", *Philosophical Review* 80, 177-197.
Wians, W. (1992), "Saving Aristotle from Nussbaum's phainomena", in Anton and Preus (1992), 133-149.
Wieland, W. (1958), "Aristoteles als Rhetoriker und das Problem der exoterischen Schriften", *Hermes* 86, 323-346.
—— (1960/61), "Das Problem der Prinzipienforschung und die aristotelische Physik", *Kant-Studien* 52, 206-219; repr. as "Aristotle's Physics and the Problem of Inquiry into Principles" in Barnes, Schofield, Sorabji (1975-79), vol. 1, 127-140.
*—— (1970^2, 1962), *Die aristotelische Physik*, Göttingen.
Wiesner, J. (ed.) (1985), *Aristoteles: Werk und Wirkung*, vol. 1, Berlin, New York.
Wiggins, D. (1980), *Sameness and Substance*, Oxford.
*Wilpert, P. (1956/57), "Aristotles und die Dialektik", *Kant-Studien* 48, 247-257.
Wirkramanayake, G. H. (1961), "A note on the πίστεις in Aristotle's Rhetoric", *American Journal of Philology* 82, 193-196.
—— (1965), *Das Verhältnis von Philosophie und Rhetorik bei Platon und Aristoteles*, Diss. Göttingen.
Wissowa, G. (ed.) (1893-1972), Paulys Realencyclopädie der klassischen Altertumswissenschaften, Stuttgart.
Wolfson, H. A. (1938), "The amphibolous terms in Aristotle, Arabic philosophy and Maimonides", *Harvard Theological Review* 31, 151-173.
Woods, M. (1993), "Form, species, and predication in Aristotle", *Synthèse* 96, 399-415.
Yrjönsuuri, M. (1993), "Aristotle's *Topics* and Medieval obligational disputations", *Synthèse* 96, 59-82.
Zahlfleisch, J. (1878), *Über die Aristotelischen Begriffe* ὑπάρχει, ἐνδέχεσθαι ὑπάρχειν *und ἐξ ἀνάγκης ὑπάρχειν*, Programm der Gymnasien, Ried.
—— (1890), "Zu Aristoteles' Topik 137a8-20, 133b5", *Zeitschrift für die österreichischen Gymnasien* 41, 301-304.
Zaslawsky, D. (1982), "Sur la solution aristotélicienne de deux paradoxes logiques", *Études de littérature ancienne, II: Questions de sens*, Paris, 93-110.
—— (1986), "Le sophisme comme anomalie. Le plaisir de parler" in Cassin (1986), 172-199.
Ziegelmeyer, E. H. (1945), "The discovery of first principles according to Aristotle", *Modern Schoolman* 22, 133-143.
Zimmermann, F. W. (1994), "*Topics* and the misnamed Book of Poetic Gleanings", in Fortenbaugh (1994), 314-319.
Zumsteg, G. (1989), *Wahrheit und Volksmeinung: zur Entstehung und Bedeutung der aristotelischen Topik, Grundmodell des Denkens und Handelns in der Demokratie*, Bern und Stuttgart.

CLASSIFIED BIBLIOGRAPHY

A. Editions

    see Bibliography

B. Commentaries

    see Bibliography

C. Translations

    see Bibliography

D. Other ancient texts

    see Bibliography

E. History of Logic

    Bocheński (1947), (1951a), (1978^4, 1956), (1970^2); Corcoran (1994); Frede (1974), (1987b); Kapp (1942); Kneale and Kneale (1989^{10}, 1962); Lear (1980); Lee (1984); Łukasiewicz, (1935), (1957^2, 1951); Maier (1896-1900); Mates (1961^2, 1953); Mueller (1969); Patzig (1969^3, 1959), (1968); Prantl (1855-67); Rose (1968); Scholz (1931); Stakelum (1940); Sullivan (1967); von Fritz (1975)

F. Textual criticism

    Brunschwig (1968); Imelmann (1870); Maguiness (1946), (1947); Minio-Paluello (1955); Richards (1915-1918); Ross (1956); Waitz (1857); Wallies (1922)

G Chronological questions

    Brandis (1827), (1833); Huby (1962); Owen (1959); Thielscher (1948)

H. Books on the *Topics*

    Thionville (1855); Hambruch (1904); Pflug (1908); von Arnim (1927); Braun (1959); De Pater (1965); Brunschwig (1967); Sainati (1968), (1993), Pelletier (1991)

I. Books to some extent dealing with the *Topics*

    Le Blond (1939a); Leszl (1975); Solmsen (1929); Wieland (1970^2, 1962)

J. Notion and working of topoi

1. In the *Topics*
    Bocheński (1951b); Brake (1965); Buhl (1979); Casari (1984); Chichi (1989); De Pater (1968); Emrich (1972); Giguère (1966); Mainberger (1955); Morrison (1987); Nguemning (1990); Ochs (1969); Pelletier (1985); Pflugmacher (1909); Ritoók (1975); Sorio (1982)

2. In *Rhetoric* (mainly II 23-24)
   Christensen (1988); Coenen (1987); Grimaldi (1958); (1961); Infante (1971); Palmer (1934); Pelletier (1979), (1980), (1981); Plöbst (1911); Schöpsdau (1981); Sprute (1975), (1981)

K. Syllogism

1. Notion of the syllogism
   Barnes (1969a), (1981); Cavini (1989); Duerlinger (1969); Enskat (1986); Kapp (1931); Mansion (1961); Mau (1959); Pellegrin (1981); Platzeck (1954); Rigamonti (1980); Ross (1939); Rutten (1964); Silnizki (1988); Smiley (1973); Solmsen (1941), (1951); Thompson (1975)

2. Hypothetical syllogism
   Barnes (1983), (1985a); Maróth (1979); Pickard (1936); Shorey (1889); Striker (1979), (1973); Thiel (1920)

3. Enthymeme
   Burnyeat (1994); Grimaldi (1955), (1957); Lienhard (1966); Madden (1952); Plebe (1959), (1993); Ryan (1984); Seaton (1914); Simonson (1945); Sprute (1981), (1982); Wirkramanayake (1961)

4. Relational syllogism
   Barnes (1985b), (1990a), (1990b), (1993)

L. Induction

Benoit (1948); Caujolle-Zaslawsky (1990); Engberg-Pedersen (1979); Hamlyn (1976); Heß, (1970); Hintikka (1980); Knuuttila (1993); McKirahan (1983); Schmidt (1974); Upton (1981); von Fritz (1964)

M. Predication

Cohen (1973); Couloubaritsis (1986); De Strycker (1968a); Ebert (1977a); Hamlyn (1961); Kahn (1973), (1976); Mattew and Cohen (1968); Miner (1978); Mulhern (1970); Rohr (1975), (1978); Smith (1991); Thornton (1986); van Brennekom (1986); Zahlfleisch (1878)

N. Predicables

Barnes (1970), Barnes, Brunschwig, Frede (1990); Brunschwig (1986); Davies (1975-76); Ebert (1977b); Gambra (1988); Giuliani (1972); Graham (1975); Granger (1981), (1984); Hadgopoulos (1976); Le Blond (1939b); Lloyd (1962); Moser (1935); Robinson (1950); Slattery (1958); Urbanas (1988); van Aubel (1963); Verbeke (1968); Wedin (1973)

O. Categories

Bonitz (1853); Cavini (1979); Donaldson (1972); Ebert (1985); Edel (1975); Frede (1987c); Gercke (1891); Gillespie (1925); Guariglia (1977); Kahn (1978); Kapp (1920); Mansion (1968); Menn (1995); Sainati (1985); Schlueter (1954); Trendelenburg (1846); von Fritz (1931)

P. Homonymy and Synonymy, Analogy, Diairesis, Contrariety, Identity, Sameness, Problema and Protasis, some other dialectical notions

Anton (1957), (1968), (1969); Arpe (1938); Babin (1940); Barnes (1971); Barnes (1977); Barth (1942); Bassenge (1963); Blom (1955); Cavini (1985); Einarson (1936); Gardies (1989); Geach (1963); Goebel (1989); Grimaldi (1980); Guariglia (1978); Hadgopoulos (1974), (1976); Hesse (1965); Hirschberger (1960); Irwin (1981); Koller (1955); Lennox

(1994); Lewis (1982); Mignucci (1985); Morales (1991); Muskens (1943); Rapp (1992); Ruiz (1987-88); Spanu (1983); Tarán (1978); Thiel (1920); von Fragstein (1967); White (1971); Wiggins (1980)

Q. Dialectic

1. General
Aubenque (1960), (1966[2], 1962), (1970), (1989); Baltussen (1992); Barnes (1991); Berka (1964, 1); Berti (1970), (1977), (1978), (1983), (1986), (1988); Bird (1955); Boeder (1968); Bolton (1990), (1994); Brennan (1955); Brunschwig (1964), (1990); Cleary (1995); Crisp (1991); Croissant (1986); Devereux (1990); Duhem (1908), (1969); Evans (1977); Frappier (1977); Freeland (1990); Galston (1982); Hadot (1980); Hamlyn (1990); Hogan (1955); Irwin (1977), (1988); Jacob (1993-94); Janssens (1968); Kleger (1990); Kwiatkowski (1963); Lloyd (1978); Lugarini (1959); Müri (1944); Natali (1986), (1990); Nussbaum (1982), (1986); Obbink (1992); Oehler (1961); Olivieri (1983); Owen (1961); Pelletier (1989); Pöggeler (1974); Primavesi (1992); Pritzl (1993), (1994); Régis (1935); Roelants (1966); Rossitto (1977-8), (1984), (1987), (1993); Sichirollo (1957), (1961), (1965), (1966); Smith (1993), (1994); Stenzel (1931[2], 1917); Szabó (1951-1952); Tegge (1877); Thurot (1860); Véraquin (1980); Viano (1958), (1969a), (1969b); Wardy (1991); Wians (1992); Wilpert (1956-57); Zumsteg (1989)

2. Dialectical gymnastic (mainly Top. Θ)
De Blic (1930); Moreau (1968); Robinson (1931); Ryle (1968); Weil (1951)

3. Status of dialectic and rhetoric (the counterpart of dialectic) & relation between dialectic on the one hand and rhetoric/ syllogistic/ontology on the other
Anton (1859); Barnes (1986); Brunschwig (1994); Cazzola Gastaldi (1976); Couloubaritsis (1978/79), (1986); Crem (1956); Dorion (1990); Garver (1986), (1994); Gastaldi (1993); Goebel (1989); Grimaldi (1958), (1972), (1978); Hellwig (1973); Hill (1981); Hintikka (1993); Hunt (1925), Kinneavy (1987), Klein (1989); Lossau (1974), (1981); McCabe (1994); Mesch (1994); Most (1994); Natali (1990a), (1990b); Price (1968); Raphael (1974); Robert (1957); Russo (1962); Ryan (1979); Silvestre (1984); Sprute (1977), (1992); Stark (1968); Stocks (1933); Tessmer (1957); Vahlen (1867); van der Weel (1969); Watson (1989); Wieland (1958); Wikramanayake (1965)

4. Dialectic and the principles
Barnes (1969b); Cassini (1986), (1991); Code (1986); Cohen (1986); Couloubaritsis (1980); Dancy (1975); Furth (1986); Garver (1988); Gómez-Lobo (1977), (1979); Hutchinson (1989); Irwin (1978), (1987); Kahn (1981); Kal (1988); La Croce (1990), (1991); Lee (1935); Lesher (1973); Łukasiewicz (1971); Lumpe (1955); Morel (1960); Morsink (1982); Pietsch (1992); Rapp (1993); Robinson (1958); Schüssler (1974); Trépanier (1943); Upton (1983), (1985); von Fritz (1955); Wieland (1960/61); Ziegelmeyer (1945)

5. Dialectical method in other writings
Arentz (1975); Balme (1961), (1987), Barnes (1980), Baynes (1990); Beriger (1989); Berti (1986), (1991); Blank (1984); Bolton (1987), (1991); Boylan (1983); Cadion (1956); Cleary (1994); Cooper (1989); Dumont (1986); Eucken (1872); Fortenbaugh (1965); Frappier (1974); Fritsche (1986); Guariglia (1982); Gueroult (1963); Irwin (1981); Klein (1988), (1992); Krämer (1968); Kullmann (1965); Lennox (1980), (1987); Lloyd (1961); McMahon (1956); Morsink (1975); Olshewsky (1968); Schickert (1977); Sichirollo (1963)

R. Aristotle and Plato

Berti (1980); De Vogel (1968); Elders (1968); Moreau (1968); Owen (1965), (1968b); Prantl (1853); Smith (1974); Solmsen (1968)

S. Texts on various other aspects of the *Topics*

Bird (1978); De Strycker (1968b); Düring (1968); Evans (1978); Gigon (1968); Gohlke

(1928); Isnardi Parente (1966); Mráz (1976), (1986-87); Natali (1984); Oehler (1966); Soreth (1968); Szabó (1964); Verdenius (1968); Wallies (1891); Zahlfleisch (1890)

T. *Sophistici Elenchi*

Basakos (1981); Boger (1993); Bueno (1988); Classen (1981); Dorion (1995); Ebbesen (1981); Evans (1975); Goodwin (1992); Hamblin (1970); Kirwan (1979); Poste (1866); Riondato (1985); Simonson (1944); Sprague (1977), (1986); Zaslawsky (1982), (1986)

U. Tradition and influence of the *Topics* in Late Antiquity and the Middle Ages

Angelleli (1970); Bird (1959), (1960a), (1961), (1962); Braswell (1964); Grabmann (1937); Green-Pedersen (1973), (1977a), (1977b), (1984); Hayden (1957); Knuuttila (1989); Lloyd (1955-1956); Long (1978); Markowski (1968); Maróth (1981); Minio-Paluello (1958); Pinborg (1969); Riposati (1944); Solmsen (1944); Stump (1974), (1978), (1981), (1982), (1988), (1989); Thielscher (1908); van Ophuijsen (1994); Wolfson (1938); Yrjönsuuri (1993); Zimmermann (1994)

V. Topics in modern methodology and theory of argumentation

Baeumer (1973); Berka (1968); Bird (1955), (1960b); Bornscheuer (1976); Bouchard and Valois (1983); Brennan (1955); Breuer and Schanze (1981); Infante (1971); Martano (1986); Perelman (1955), Perelman and Olbrechts-Tyteca (1958), (1969); Rehbock (1988); Toulmin (1964); van Noorden (1979); Viehweg (1953)

GREEK-ENGLISH GLOSSARY

This glossary is designed in the main to help the reader interested in a Greek term find it through the index under the English equivalent.

ἄδοξος	adoxical
αἱρετώτερον	more worthy of choice
ἀκολουθεῖν	follow
ἀληθεύεσθαι	be truly predicated of
ἄμεσα ἐναντία	contradictories
ἀναιρεῖν	destroy
ἀναπόδεικτα	indemonstrables
ἀνασκευάζειν	argue destructively
ἀντικατηγορεῖσθαι	be convertibly predicated of
ἀντικείμενα	opposites
ἀντιστροφή	conversion
ἀντιφάσεις	contradictories
ἀπόδειξις	proof
ἀρχή	principle, law, rule
γένος	genus
γυμναστική	training in disputation
δεικνύναι	show, prove
διαιρετικόν	diairetic
διαίρησις	division
διαφορά	differentia
διεζευγμένον	disjunctive
δυσκολαίνειν	behave peevishly
εἶδος	species
εἰκός	probable
ἔμμεσα ἐνατία	contraries
ἐμπίπτειν εἰς	fall under
ἐναντία	contraries
ἔνδοξον	endoxical
ἔνστασις	objection
ἐπαγωγή	induction
ἕπεσθαι	follow
ἐπιφέρειν	imply
ἐπιχειρεῖν	attack
θέσις	thesis
ἴδιον	proprium
καθ' ἕκαστον	particular
κατὰ διαίρεσιν	diairetic
κατασκευάζειν	argue constructively
κατὰ συνέχειαν	continuous
κατηγορεῖσθαί τινός	be predicated of
κατηγορία	predicate
κρύψις τοῦ συμπεράσματος	concealment of the conclusion
λαμβάνειν	take (as a premiss)
λύσις	solution
μᾶλλον	in a greater degree
μεταλαμβάνειν	substitute
μετάληψις	substitution
οἱ νεώτεροι φιλόσοφοι	"modern philosophers"
ὁμοιότης	likeness
ὁμώνυμος	homonymous

GLOSSARY

ὅπερ	that which
ὅρος	definition
οὐσία	the very essence
οἱ παλαίοι	"old philosophers"
παραβολή	illustration
παράγγελμα	investigation-instruction
παράδειγμα	example
παράδοξος	paradoxical
περαίνεσθαι	conclude
περαντικοί	concludent arguments
πιθανόν	plausible
ποιότης	quality
πρόβλημα	problema
πρόσληψις	additional premiss
προσσημαίνειν	indicate additionally
προσυλλογισμός	prosyllogism
πρότασις	protasis
πτῶσις	inflexion
στοιχεῖον	element
συλλογισμός	syllogism
συλλογισμός ἐξ ὑποθέσεως	syllogism, hypothetical
κατὰ μετάληψιν	proceeding by substitution (metaleptic)
διὰ συνεχοῦς/συνημμένου καὶ τῆς προσλήψεως	proceeding by way of a continuous/connected protasis together with an additional premiss
διὰ τοῦ διαιρετικοῦ τε καὶ διεζευγμένου	proceeding by way of a diairetic/disjunctive protasis
διὰ ἀποφατικῆς συμπλοκῆς	proceeding by way of a negated conjunction
κατὰ ποιότητα/ἀπὸ τοῦ μᾶλλον καὶ ἧττον καὶ ὁμοίως	qualitative/from the greater and lesser and like degree
οἱ ἐξ ἀναλογίας	on the basis of an analogy
δι' ὁμολογίας	on the basis of a concession
συμβαίνειν	follow
συμβεβηκός	sumbebekos, attribute; accident
συνεχές	continuous
συνημμένον	connected
συνώνυμος	synonymous
συστοίχα	co-ordinates
τὸ ἐν ἀρχῇ/ἐξ ἀρχῆς (κείμενον)	thesis
τὸ τί ἐστι	essence
τὸ τί ἦν εἶναι	the very essence
τόπος	topos
ἐκ μάχης	on the basis of incompatibility
ἐκ τοῦ μᾶλλον καὶ ἧττον	from the greater and lesser degree
ἐκ τοῦ ὁμοίως	from the like degree
ἐκ τῶν ἐναντίων	from the contraries
ἐκ τῶν ὁμοίως ἐχόντων	from things which are in a like relation by analogy
ἐξ ἀκολουθίας	on the basis of consequence
ἐπὶ τῶν ἀντιφάσεων	from the contradictories
ἐπὶ τῶν γενέσεων καὶ φθορῶν καὶ ποιητικῶν καὶ φθαρτικῶν	from generation and corruption and creative and corruptive agencies
ἐπὶ τῶν στερήσεων καὶ ἕξεων	from privation and possession
ἐπὶ τῶν συστοίχων καὶ τῶν πτώσεων	from co-ordinates and inflexions
ἐπικαιρότατοι	the most opportune
κατασκευαστικά-ἀνασκευαστικά	constructive-destructive topoi

τρόπος	mode (topos; method; turn of phrase)
ὑπάρχειν	belong

INDEX OF PASSAGES

A. ARISTOTLE

Cat.
1	1a6-12	152n.59
	1a12-15	152n.58
5	2b7-14	63n.91
7	7a22-25	92n.109
	7a34-37	92n.109
10	11b38-a2	131n.123
	11b38-12a9	125n.107, 131n.123

De Int.
2	16a32-b1	152n.58
3	16b6-10	81n.48
5	17a8-10	126n.108
	17a15-17	126n.108
	17a20-22	126n.108
7	17a38-b3	101
8	18a18-27	126n.108
	18a21-23	103n.26
10	20a23-30	119
11	20b23-30	22n.64
13	22b10-14	130
	22b11-14	117
	22b29f.	131n.122

APr.
A		
1	24a16	14n.31
	24a16-19	24
	24b18-20	15n.31, 25
	24b20-22	25
4	26b14-20	123n.102
	26b31	16n.41
5	27a6f.	123n.101
	27a13f.	123n.101
	27a20-23	123
	27a33f.	123n.101
	27b20-23	123, n.102
6	28a19f.	123n.101
	28b9f.	123n.101
	29a6	123n.102
15	34a5-24	103n.28
	35b11	123n.102
23	40b25f.	95, 118n.83
	41a20-24	114n.68
	41a34	95
	41a38-b1	95n.1, n.2, 98
	41a40	114n.65
	41a40f.	96n.5
26	42b27-43a2	167
	42b29	16n.41
	42b29-32	167
	42a33f.	31n.119
	43a2-15	167
	43a18	16n.41
27	43b34	16n.41
28	44b40	167n.87
29	45a36	16n.41
	45b15-20	95, 98

APr.
	45b17f.	95n.2
	45b17-19	95n.1
	45b19f.	96, n.10
	45b21	16n.41
30	46a18	64n.97
31	46a33	71n.13
	46b29-32	61n.76, 126
	46b36	155n.64
32	47a22-36	114n.67, 128n.115
	47a28-30	106n.42, 108n.46
	47a28-31	108n.46, 114n.67, 125
	47a31	125
33	47b15ff.	27n.90
36	48a40-49a5	137f.
	48b2-9	135
	48b37-49a5	152n.58
37	49a8	137
	49a8f.	126n.108
39	49b6-8	85n.64
41	49b14-31	101n.24
44	50a16	128n.115
	50a16-28	102, 113, 115n.70
	50a17	113
	50a18f.	114, 123
	50a19f.	96n.6, 115
	50a19-25	95
	50a23-25	114n.64
	50a24	114n.68
	50a24-26	114
	50a25	123
	50a27f.	117, 128
	50a29-32	118n.84
	50a32	114
	50a33	114n.66
	50a33-35	115
	50a34	114n.64
	50a34f.	96n.6
	50a35-37	118n.86
	50a36	113n.64
	50a39-b2	96
46	51b10-25	106n.38
	52a39-b1	131
	52a39-b13	131f.
B		
2	53b11-16	105n.36
	53b12-25	103n.28
	53b26ff.	11n.13
4	57a36-b17	108n.46
11	61a30f.	104n.29, 118n.85
	61b13-15	118n.85
	61b21f.	118n.85
	62a12-17	119
	62a12-19	123n.101
16	64b28ff.	11n.13
	65a1-4	103n.28, 108n.46
17	65b20ff.	108

INDEX OF PASSAGES

	APr.			*Top.*	
26	69a37	39n.165		101b32f.	15, 88
27	70a10	43n.4		101b35	154
	70a16ff.	27n.90	5	101b38	69n.2
				102a1	74n.19
	APst.			102a3f.	85n.64
A				102a5-9	69n.4, 158
1	71a20f.	41n.169		102a6f.	69n.3
2	71b23	65		102a6-17	159n.67
3	72b37-73a5	103n.28		102a10	155n.64
4	73b11-13	92n.109		102a11-14	120n.90
	73b22	131		102a12	155n.64
	73b32f.	41n.169		102a13f.	121n.93, 159n.57
10	76a37-b2	53		102a18f.	77
	76a41	49n.32, 50n.36		102a18-22	70n.6
	76b14	50n.36		102a19	80n.44
11	77a22	49n.31		102a27f.	75n.24
	77a22f.	116n.74, 118n.87		102a31	92n.108
	77a22-25	118		102a31f.	81, 151n.55
	77a27	50n.36		102a31-35	70n.7
30	88b27-29	48n.24		102a34f.	90n.96
B				102b4f.	151
5	92a2f.	108n.47		102b4-14	70n.8
6	92a7-9	128		102b6-9	93
	92a6-19	128		102b7	27n.91
	92a10	128		102b10-14	93
	92a11-19	54n.49, 117n.82, 128		102b14-20	70n.10, 156
				102b20	92n.108
	92a20	128n.115		102b29f.	78
	92a20-25	117n.82, 121n.96, 145	6	102b29-33	74, 121n.93
				102b29-34	74n.19
	92a29	128n.115		102b35-38	94n.115
10	93b35-37	126n.108		103a6f.	108n.47
			7	103a30f.	27n.91
	Top.			103b3-6	71n.12
A				103b6-19	71n.13
1	100a18-20	16n.35	8	103b8	92n.108
	100a18-21	9		103b29-35	27n.91
	100a19f.	48n.24	9	104a4-8	17n.46
2	100a25-27	15, 25, 51n.41, 52n.42	10	104a5-8	20
	100a26f.	52n.43		104a8-15	19
	100b21-23	20, 48n.27		104a16	22n.61
	100a30	48n.27		104a22-31	104n.32
	101a14	25n.80, 52n.45		104a33-37	165n.81
	101a26-30	11		104b1-5	17
	101a28-30	12	11	104b4f.	22n.62
	101a30	16n.35		104b5-12	21n.57, 22n.63
	101a33-36	138n.22		104b7	16n.39
	101a34-b4	14n.27		104b8	16n.39, 22n.62
	101a37	64n.97	.	104b16	16n.39, 22n.62
4	101b14-16	48n.26		104b18-28	17
	101b15f:	15		104b19-22	19n.54
	101b16	16n.35, 75		104b29-34	17f.
	101b17	69n.1		104b34-36	12n.18
	101b17-25	77		104b34-105a2	18
	101b18f.	86		105a3-7	17n.47, 93
	101b19-23	95n.2		105a7	93
	101b21-23	74n.22		105a7-9	17n.48
	101b23f.	108n.47		105a10-12	29
	101b25	69n.1, 75	12	105a13f.	15
	101b28f.	154		105a13-16	30n.108
	101b29-36	16n.35		105a16-19	30n.112
	101b30f.	69n.5		105a21f.	55n.55
	101b31	90n.96	13	105a21-24	55
				105a23	52n.45

INDEX OF PASSAGES

	Top.			*Top.*	
	105a25f.	55	2	109a28	16n.42
	105a26,	125		109a34	46n.15, 50n.34
	105a26f.	125		109a34f.	54, 62n.82
	105a27f.	56, 125		109a34-36	94
	105a28-30	50, 56		109a34-38	57
	105a29	56		109a34-b12	73n.18, 79n.36, 93, 150
	105a30f.	56, 125			
	105a31-33	125		109a35f.	151
	105a32	125		109a37f.	72n.15
	105a34	52n.45		109a39-b1	85n.60
14	105b5f.	56		109a39-b12	152n.56
	105b19-29	20, n.56, 21		109b1-12	139n.23
	105b22f.	50f.		109b6f.	159n.59
	105b36	31n.116		109b13	50n.34
	106a1-8	56		109b13ff.	135n.7
15	106a10f.	55n.54		109b13-18	55
	106a10ff.	57n.61		109b13-26	151n.63
	106a10-17	57n.63		109b13-29	18, 85n.61, 153
	106a23ff.	57n.61		109b17	90n.99
	106a36ff.	57n.61		109b23f.	121n.93
	106b13	55n.54		109b24	16n.40
	106b21	58n.66		109b25	46n.15, 142n.34
	106b22	55n.54		109b25-29	152
	106b29	58n.66		109b30ff.	135n.6
	107a6f.	165n.83		109b30-32	55, 79n.38, 90
	107a35	58n.66		109b30-110a9	35n.135, 112, n.61, 155, 166
	107b38	57n.59			
	108a4	56		109a33	84n.59
17	108a7	116n.73		109b34	90n.95
	108a8	125		109b37f.	90n.95
	108a9f.	125		109b39-110a1	90
18	108a20-22	58		110a4	90n.95
	108a38-b4	111		110a4-9	155n.65
	108a38-b6	58		110a10	16n.40
	108b1-4	121		110a10ff.	133n.6
	108b2-4	121n.93, 159n.67		110a10-13	55, 154
	108b7	116n.73		110a11	16n.43
	108b7ff.	110f.		110a14-22	139n.23, 164
	108b7-19	35n.134, 96, n.7	3	110a23-b7	18
	108b7-31	58, 158		110a23ff.	135n.7
	108b8	120		110a23-111a7	35n.135
	108b9-12	30n.109		110a30-b1	90n.94
	108b12	120		110a32f.	120n.91
	108b12-19	120		110a32-b7	120n.89
	108b13	116n.72		110a32-37	122n.100
	108b13f.	111, 120, 125		110a37f.	116n.71
	108b16f.	111, 120		110a37-b4	96n.7, 103
	108b24-27	56		110b4f.	120
	108b32	55n.55		110b5-7	41n.169
B				110b8ff.	135n.7
1	108b34	16n.42		110b11f.	90n.95
	108b34ff.	24n.77		110b13f.	82n.53
	108b34-109a1	24, 89n.89, 90n.97, 134		110b16ff.	135n.7
				110b18f.	165n.83
	108b34-109a10	18, 134		111a8	135n.7
	109a1-3	71n.14, 122	4	111a11	16n.43
	109a1-6	121, 122, 134		111a14	90n.94, 161
	109a2	16n.42		111a14ff.	135n.7
	109a8-10	18		111a14-32	18n.50, 160, 167
	109a10-26	135f.		111a14-b16	79n.36
	109a16f.	90n.96		111a15f.	90n.95, 90n.100, 161
	109a27-30	89		111a15-18	161
	109a27-34	138		111a17f.	161

INDEX OF PASSAGES

Top.
111a20-23	160	
111a21	161	8
111a23-27	160, 162	
111a24	46n.15	
111a25f.	163	
111a26	161, n.77	
111a28	161, n.77	
111a29-31	160, 164	
111a30f.	164	
111a33f.	163	
111a33-36	163	
111a33-b11	163	
111a33-b16	18n.50	
111b5	90n.101	
111b8-11	135n.8, 163n.79	
111b10f.	90n.95, 142n.35	
111b12	16n.43	
111b12ff.	112n.61, 135n.6	
111b12-16	35n.135, 112	
111b13ff.	58n.66	
111b17f.	107n.46	
111b17-19	125n.106	
111b17-23	18n.50, 34n.132, 96, 98-103, 108, 109, 111, 113n.63, 125n.106, 129, 167	
111b20f.	121n.93	
111b22	127n.113, 129n.117, 141	
111b22f.	121n.93	
111b25	84n.59	
5	111b32	46n.16
	111b36	16n.43
	112a10	46n.16
	112a16-21	100f.
	112a16-23	18n.50, 34n.132, 96, 98, 100f., 102, 108, 112, 129
	112a17	129n.117
	112a17-19	125
	112a20	122n.100, 129n.117
	112a21-23	120
	112a22	99n.18, 129n.117
6	112a24	49, 109n.53, 131n.123
	112a24-31	99n.18, 103, 109, 125
	112a25-27	120n.90
	112a27-30	90n.94, 121n.93
	112b1ff.	135n.6
	112b1-20	84n.59
	112b21ff.	135n.6
	112b21-26	79n.38, 91
7	112b27-	
	113a19	104n32
	113a17	46n.16
	113a20-23	79n.38, 90, 104, 116
	113a22f.	49
	113a23	90n.94
	113a33ff.	79n.38
	113b6-14	105n.34
	113b8	142n.34
	113b9-14	90n.94

Top.
113b13	84n.59	
113b15ff.	57n.61	
113b15-26	18n.50, 90n.96, 99n.18, 130, 141	
113b17	52, n.46, 142n.31	
113b17f.	90, 125, 142	
113b17-19	130	
113b18	53n.46	
113b18f.	142n.31, n.32	
113b19	130	
113b20	127n.112	
113b20f.	130	
113b22	52, 142n.31	
113b24-26	142	
113b27ff.	57n.61	
113b27-114a3	142	
113b27-114a6	112	
113b29	52, n.46	
113b30-34	143	
113b31-33	91n.104	
113b34	53n.46, 143	
113b35f.	143	
113b39	143	
114a1-3	143	
114a3-6	143	
114a4	121n.96	
114a7f.	140n.30	
114a7ff.	57n.61	
114a9-11	143n.36	
114a13ff.	58n.66	
114a13-25	145	
114a15f.	143n.36	
114a20-23	146	
114a22f.	146n.39	
9	114a26ff.	58n.66
	114a26-b5	35n.133
	114a33f.	152n.58
	114a38-b1	121n.93
	114a38-b3	123
	114b6-13	112
	114b13	46n.15
	114b13f.	140n.30
	114b13-15	112
10	114b25f.	96n.6
	114b25-27	102
	114b25-36	35n.134, 111, 120n.89
	114b26f.	125
	114b27	53n.46
	114b37-115a14	18n.50, 50n.35, 96, 106, 146
	114b39	16n.37
	114b39f.	52
	114b39-115a5	90n.97
	115a3f.	147n.41
	115a5	52n.46
	115a5f.	52
	115a6	103n.27
	115a6f.	147n.42
	115a6-14	147
	115a9-13	147n.43
	115a11-14	103n.27
	115a15-24	133n.1

INDEX OF PASSAGES

Top.

	115a16	103n.27		120b15-20	153n.62
	115a17-19	150		120b15-29	93
	115a21-24	103n.27		120b15-121a9	93n.112
11	115a27-29	90n.102		120b15-121a11	150
	115a31	53n.46		120b17-19	85, 90n.98
	115a33	46n.15		120b21f.	93
	115a33ff.	79n.38		120b21-23	79n.37
	115b3ff.	147n.44		120b21-24	85n.64
	115b7	46n.15		120b21-29	150n.50
	115b11	46n.16		120b21-35	73n.18
	115b19	46n.16		120b23	94n.114
	115b22	46n.16		120b24	94n.114
Γ				120b28	94n.114
1	116a4-9	21n.58, 156		120b29f.	85n.64
	116a10-12	121n.93, 157		120b30-35	72n.16, 93
	116a23-27	85n.64		120b33	85n.63
	116a27	53n.46		120b38f.	93n.112
	116a29-33	156		120b39	85n.63
	116a30	156n.66		121a2f.	85n.63
	116b8f.	156n.66		121a9	53n.46
	116b18	156n.66		121a30-39	86n.66
	116b30f.	156n.66		121b3	85n.63
2	117a5-10	157		121b1-11	110
	117a16-24	60		121b11-14	112, 133n.1
	117b3-9	140n.29		121b19	85n.63
	117b12-17	60n.73	2	121b26-28	85n.63
	117b13-25	27n.91		122a2	85n.63
	117b19-25	60n.73		122a4	29n.103
3	118a34-39	159n.70		122a9	29n.103
4	119a6	53n.46		122a10-12	85n.62
5	119a12-16	112		122a10-30	134
6	119a32-36	135		122a13f.	92n.108
	119a33f.	71n.14, 134n.4		122a18-24	86n.64
	119a34-36	122		122a19	53n.46
	119a36-38	140n.26		122a19f.	85n.62
	119a37	71n.14		122a22	150n.51
	119a38	140n.27		122b12	150n.51
	119a38f.	60n.69, 116n72		122b26-36	86n.71
	119a38-120a5	140n.26		122b30	53n.46
	119a39f.	90n.96		123a3-5	86n.67
	119b16	140n.27		123a4	16n.43
	119b17-30	106		123a23-26	86n.65
	119b19-21	147	3	123a27	45n.14
	119b23	148n.46		123a34	86n.69, 150n.51
	119b24-27	150		123b1	144
	119b25	121n.96		123b1-124a10	143
	119b26	121n.96		123b1-Δ4	140n.29
	119b35-120a5	96n.5, 120n.89		123b4-8	144
	119b38-120a1	127		123b7	53n.46
	120a6-27	90n.97		123b17	60n.70
	120a15-20	122		123b27	60n.70
	120a20-31	122n.98		123b31-33	91n.104
	120a21	16n.43		123b32f.	144n.37
	120a21-24	122n.98		123b33	53n.46
	120a24-27	122n.98		123b34	60n.70
	120a27-31	122n.98		124a7-9	144n.38
	120a27	16n.43		124a12f.	86n.69
	120a32-b6	85n.61, 153n.62		124a17f.	85n.63
	120a38-39	79n.38	4	124a17-20	90n.98
	120b7	79n.38		124b7f.	90n.96
	120b7f.	71n.14		124b8-14	90n.98
Δ				124b32	60n.70
1	120b11f.	71n.14		124b35-125a4	60
	120b13	45n.14			

208 INDEX OF PASSAGES

Top.

	Passage	Reference
	125a26	85n.63
	125a28	86n.64
	125a33-b10	84
	125a33-37	84n.57
	125a37-b1	84n.57
	125b1-4	84n.57
	125b6-14	86n.71
	125b10-14	84, 86n.73
	125b11	71n.14, 79n.37
5	125b15-19	86n.71
	125b20-27	86n.71
	125b28-30	85n.63
	126a6	86n.69, 86n.70
	126a10	86n.70
	126a14-16	79n.37
	126a20	53n.46
	126a26-29	86n.71, n.72, 137n.16
	126a30-36	86n.71
	126b13-19	86n.71
	126b14	150n.51
	126b34-127a2	86n.71
	127a3-19	86n.71
	127a4	86n.71
	127a8	53n.46
	127a13f.	86n.71
	127a14f.	86n.71
	127a18f.	86n.71
6	127a26	85n.63, 86n.67
	127a34	86n.67
	127b2	94n.114
	127b29	92n.108
	128a9-12	86n.65
	128a26	85n.63
	128a35	46n.16
	128a37:	46n.16
	128a38	136n.10
	128a38-b9	59
E 1	128b7	136n.10
	128b14	57n.59
	128b20	27n.91
	128b22-24	87n.74
	128b23	16n.42
	128b24	16n.42
	128b24f.	87n.75
	128b28	150n.51
	128b28f.	87n.74
	128b29	16n.42
	128b29f.	87n.75
	128b34-36	76
	128b35f.	87n.75
	128b39	77
	129a2	87n.75
	129a4	87n.75
	129a5	27n.91
	129a6-10	75n.24
	129a11	87n.75
	129a19	16n.42, 87n.74
	129a20	16n.42
	129a30	16n.42, 87n.74
2	129a34f.	76
	129b7	87n.76
	129b9-11	87n.79

Top.

	Passage	Reference
	129b18f.	87n.79
	129b23	87n.76
	129b26	87n.80
	130a7	11
	130a29-b10	91n.105
	130a32-34	91n.106
	130a36f.	87n.81
	130a37	150n.51
	130a39-b1	87n.81
	130a39-b5	91n.105
	130b8	87n.80
3	131a8f.	87n.79
	131a12	46n.16
	131b12	27n.91
	131b37-132a9	73n.18, 76n.28
	132a4	92n.108
	132a7	92n.108
4	132a30f.	87n.77
	132a36	87n.77
	132b21f.	87n.81
	132b23	92n.108
	132b31f.	87n.80
	132b8-18	76n.29
	132b19-34	76n.29
	132b35ff.	73n.18
	132b35-133a3	75
	132b35-133a5	75n.24
	132b35-133a11	76n.28
	133a8f.	87n.79
	133a12-23	76n.28
	133a18ff.	73n.18
	133b8	75n.24
	133b15-134a4	93n.113
	133b17-19	79n.37
	133b31-36	79n.37
	133b36-134a4	152n.58
	134a8f.	87n.80
	134a14f.	87n.81
	134a18f.	87n.79
	134a18-25	76n.29
	134a26-135a8	83
	134a28-b4	83
	134b5-135a5	83
	134b5-7	83n.54
	134b6f.	87n.79
	134b18	83n.55
	135a9-19	73n.18, 76n.28
6	135a11-19	91
	135b7-16	144
	135b12	87n.82
	135b14-16	91n.104
	135b16	87n.82
	135b21f.	87n.82
	136a5ff.	142n.33
	136a6	92n.108
7	136a15	92n.108
	136b15-22	152n.58
	136b20-22	75n.24
	136b28-32	152n.58
	136b33	105
	136b33-137a7	105, 112n.62
	137a3-7	105
	137a21-b2	76n.29

INDEX OF PASSAGES

	Top.			Top.	
	137a27	46n.16		151b30-152a4	157
	137a37	46n.16		152a10	53n.46
8	138a2	46n.16		152a28	121n.95
	138b23-26	105		152a31-33	158
9	138b30f.	87n.80		152a37	121n.95
Z				152b5	53n.46
1	139a4f.	87n.81		152b13-15	49, n.33
	139a14	150n.51		152b25f.	92n.108
	139a25-27	89	2	152b36ff.	134n.4
	139a27-31	74n.20		152b37f.	71n.14
	139a29-31	74		153a1f.	71n.14
	139a36-b3	89, 138		153a2	134n.4
	139a38-b1	89	3	153a9	52n.45
2	139b19	46n.15		153a15-21	117n.82
	139b20f.	87n.83		153a16	92n.108
	139b30	11n.9		153a18	80n.40
	132b32f.	87n.83		153a21f.	74n.21
	140a3-5	139n.25		153a26-29	144
	140a6-17	139n.25		153a26-	
	140a7f.	87n.83		154a11	140n.26
	146a13-17	137n.25		153b13	80n.40
	140a19f.	82		153b14f.	80n.40
3	140a34	74n.22		153b14-24	82n.51
	140b27-			153b25-35	123
	141a14	91n.105		153b33f.	53n.46
	141a4-14	91n.105		154a4-8	103n.27
4	141a23f.	133n.1	4	154a12ff.	121n.93
	141a26ff.	46n.16		154a12-15	140n.26
	142a17	46n.16		154a13-15	140n.28
	142a22	46n.16		154a15-18	153n.61
5	142b20	46n.15		154a16	71n.14
	142b20-22	133n.1	5	154a23-b12	78
	142b35-143a8	93n.113		154a26f.	80n.40
	143a13	45n.14		154a26-29	74n.19
6	143b13-16	116n.78		154a32-361	74n.19
	144a23-27	72n.16, 79n.37, 93		154a34f.	121n.93
	144b16-18	131n.123		154a35f.	80n.40
	144b26-30	131n.123		154a36-b1	80n.41
	144b29	150n.51		154a37-b3	78n.34
	145a3	150n.51		154b1-3	80n.42
	145a10	150n.51		154b2	80n.44, 136n.10
	145a14	150n.51		154b6	136n.10
	145a15f.	21n.59		154b11	80n.44
7	146a3-20	140n.29		154b13-23	76, n.26
8	146b30	53n.46		154b15f.	74
9	147a13	53n.46		154b18-23	78
	147a15-22	82n.51		154b19-21	80n.43
	147a22	45n.14		154b22	80n.45
	147a29-b25	145		154b23-28	80n.46
	147a31ff.	91n.104		154b33-155a2	88, 167
10	148a10-13	140n.29		155a3-18	71f.
	148a12f.	152n.58		155a3-36	79
	148b8	11n.9, 25n.81		155a7	16n.40
	148b16-22	139		155a8	71n.14
12	149a30f.	88n.84		155a8-10	74, 78
	149a34f.	88n.84		155a11	16n.40
	149a37:	11n.9		155a11-13	81n.47
	149b4-23	93n.113		155a13	80n.45
	149b6f.	88n.85		155a17	16n.40
	149b11	53n.46		155a18	75
14	151b18	45n.14		155a18-22	75, 80
	151b24	133n.1		155a23-27	76, n.26
H				155a25-27	80n.45
1	151b28-152a4	140n.29		155a28-31	71f., 79, 81

210 INDEX OF PASSAGES

Top.

155a28-36		79
155a32f.		81
155a37		16n.40, 71n.14
155a37f.		16n.40
Θ 1		
155b3-16		9
155b4-7		10
155b4-17		9
155b10		28n.99
155b10-16		28n.100
155b13		16n.45
155b18-28		32
155b19		25n.80
155b20		25n.79
155b20-24		32
155b22f.		108n.47
155b24f.		32
155b26-28		28n.97
155b29:		25n.79
155b29-156a3		27-31, 32n.124
155b29-156a7		32, n.124
155b30		28n.95, 29n.103
155b30-34		29
155b32-34		26n.86
155b34f.		31n.115
155b35		24n.77
155b35-38		27n.92
155b37f.		31n.120
155b38f.		28n.95
155b38-156a1		30n.111
156a3		25n.80
156a3-7		32n.124
156a3-157a17		33-36
156a5-7		30n.113
156a7-11		25n.82
156a7-157a5		33
156a8		16n.45, 25n.79, 25n.81
156a10		25n.80
156a11-13		33n.127
156a11-14		29n.105
156a12f.		28n.95
156a13		16n. 44, n.45
156a13-15		28n.96
156a21		52n.45
156a21f.		25n.80
156a23-26		33n.126
156a27-b3		35n.133
156a28		23n.66, 23n.67
156a29f.		28n.96
156a30		23n.67
156a31		23n.67
156a31f.		39n.164
156a36-38		39n.164
156a37		23n.68
156b5		16n.44
156b6-9		29n.102
156b10-17		27n.94, 32n.123, 35n.134, 96n.6, 126n.110
156b11-13		23n.73
156b14-17		126
156b15		23n.73
156b15f.		126

Top.

156b16		126
156b16f.		30n.109
156b17		29n.103
156b18-20		34n.130
156b20		82n.53
156b20-23		34n.131, 165n.82
156b23-25		33n.128
156b25-27		36n.144
156b27-30		34n.132, 99, 127
156b28		129n.117
156b30-157a1		33n.129
157a1-3		36n.143
157a5		33
157a6		33, 108n.47
157a6-13		35
157a8-13		108n.47
157a9-11		125
157a10		21n.59
157a12f.		35n.136
157a14-17		35
2 157a18-21		30n.112
157a18-33		30n.106, 39
157a21-24		30n.110, 142n.33
157a27ff.		30n.109
157a31		131n.124
157a34		40n.169
157a34f.		31n.118
157a34-b33		39
157a35f.		31n.114, 40n.167
157a37-b2		40n.168, n.169
157b2-8		35n.135, 41n.170
157b5f.		23n.74
157b8-16		41n.172
157b12f.		23n.69
157b13f.		23n.70
157b15f.		23n.73, 27n.88
157b17		23n.71
157b17-22		41n.172
157b18-20		23n.72
157b28-31		41n.171
157b31		128n.123
157b32f.		20, 117n.80
157b34f.		39n.162
157b34-158a2		96n.8
158a7-13		29n.104
158a14-22		19n.53
158a16f.		15n.32
158a22-24		19n.53
158a28f.		31n.119
3 158a31f.		9n.1, 16n.40
158b5		16n.40
158b13		16n.40
158b16		16n.40
158b24-159a2		35n.135, 112n.61
158b35		46n.17
159a8		16n.45, 101n.23
4 159a18-24		12n.16
159a20		16n.43
159a23		9n.1
5 159a25		12n.15
159a25f.		12n.17
159a30-34		12n.16
159a33-36		12n.17
159a32-34		12n.15

INDEX OF PASSAGES

	Top.				*Top.*	
	159a36	9n.1, 16n.43			163a5f.	24n.77
	159a38	9n.1			163a8f.	16n.41
	159a38ff.	36			163a11	129n.117
	159b8f.	37n.145	14		163a29	12n.15
	159b9-16	37n.146			163b1	16n.40
	159b16-20	37n.147			163b13	10
	159b20-23	37n.148			163b17f.	47n.22
6	160a1-6	37n.149			163b22	47
	160a3	82			163b22ff.	47n.22
	160a3-6	28n.98			163b22-33	46f., 61n.79
	160a5	101n.23			163b27f.	47
	160a6-11	37n.149			163b32	23n.66, 47
	160a10	82n.53			163b35f.	28n.95
	160a11	16n.45			164a8	24n.77
	160a11-14	37n.150			164a9	24n.77
7	160a17-23	37n.151			164a12f.	30n.112
	160a23-29	38n.152			164a16-b7	12n.14
	160a29-33	38n.153			164b1	12n.14
	160a34	19n.53			164b1f.	12n.14
8	160a35f.	24				
	160a36-39	30n.109			*Soph. El.*	
	160a37	27n.94	1		165a1f.	52n.42
	160a37-39	32n.123, 126n.111			165a2	52n.43
	160a39f.	31n.117	4		166b20-27	136n.13
	160a39-b1	23	5		166b28-36	92n.109
	160a39-b2	30n.113			166b32	27n.91
	160b1-3	39n.161, 112n.61			166b33f.	27n.91
	160b3	13n.19			166b37-	
	160b3-5	31n.118, 117n.79			167a20	136
	169b4f.	39n.163			166b38	137n.16
	160b6	13n.19			166b38-167a1	136n.14
	160b10-13	117n79			167a7-9	136n.15
9	160b14	16n.43			167a8	137n.16
	160b14f.	9n.1			167a9	137n.17
10	160b23-39	38			167a10ff.	83n.55
	160b26f.:	23n.73			167a11-14	136n.15
	160b26-28	27n.87			167a13	137n.18
	160b27	23n.74			167a17	137n.17
	160b28	23n.74			167b21-37	108n.48
	160b32f.	27n.89			167a22-28	137n.18
	160b33f.	38			167a26f.	137n.18
	161a1-12	38			167b30f.	118n.85
	161a14	38			167a31-34	137n.18
	161a15	39n.158	6		168b24	52n.44
11	161a16-b10	13n.20			169a7f.	50
	161a24f.	12n.15			169a18	46n.15
	161b19-33	13n.20			169a20f.	137n.18
	161b29f.	26n.85	7		169b9-12	83n.55
	161b32f.	16n41	8		169b31	13n.19
	161b34f.	16n.41	9		170a34-36	48n.24
	161b34-	13n.20			170b4f.	38n.154
	162a11		10		171a19-21	19n.52
	161b36	10	11		172a17-21	52
	162a6	16n.41	12		172b25	46n.15
	162a11	11n.13			173a7-18	22
	162a16	63n.89	14		173b30	27n.91
	162a24ff.	31n.119	15		174a37	13n.19
	162a26	10	16		175a17-30	13
12	162b5-7	96n.8	17		175a31-35	38n.155
13	162b31	101n.23			176a19-23	38n.155
	162b31ff.	11n.13			176a27-33	28n.98
	162b34-	28n.98	25		180a26-29	137n.17
	163a13		33		183a15	25n.80
	163a1	24n.77			183a21-23	38n.154

INDEX OF PASSAGES

	Soph. El.			Rhet.	
34	183b38-184a2	47n.22		1357a32f.	43n.4
				1357b25-36:	36n.141
	De An.			1358a10-20	47f.
A				1358a10f.	48n.24
1	402a19	155n.64		1358a10ff.	61
				1358a12-17	47n.21
	De Part. Anim.			1358a12	48n.24
A				1358a15	48n.25, n.28, 51n.39
5	646a2	155n.64		1358a18	48n.25
	De Gen. Anim.			1358a19	48n.28
B				1358a20	48n.28
6	743b20-22	66n.106		1358a27	48n.25, n.28
8	747b30	64n.97		1358a28	48n.25, n.28
	748a8	64n.97		1358a30	48n.25
				1358a17	64n.97
	Met.			1358a17ff.	48n.24
B				1358a19	48n.24
2	997a25-34	92n.109		1358a22	48
3	996b29-31	50n.36		1358a27f.	48n.24
Γ				1358a28	48n.24
3	1005b2-5	21n.59		1358a29-33	47f.
	1005b19f.	49n.30, 116n.75		1358a31	48n.24
	1005b26-28	50n.36		1358a32	48n.24
4	1006a4f.	116n.76	9	1366b32	52n.45
	1006a5-8	21n.59	13	1374a12f.	81n.49
	1008a4-7	126n.108	20	1393a22f.	48n.24
6	1011b13	20n.55, 116n.76		1393a24	43
	1011b20f.	105n.36, 116n.77		1393a26	36n.140
7	1011b24	116n.74		1393a27-30	36n.142
	1011b26f.	138n.21		1393b4-8	36n.142
	1012a9-12	131n.124	22	1396b15ff.	92n.109
Δ				1396b22	46
7	1017a31-35	89n.91		1396b30	48n.24
29	1025a6-13	52n.45		1396b32	48n.24
E			23	1397a7-9	44n.7
1	1025b25ff.	21n.59		1397a10f.	44n.6
Z				1397a20-23	44n.8
4	1030b8-10	126n.108		1397a21f.	21n.58
Θ				1397b12-15:	44n.9
4	1047b14-30	103n.28		1397b12-27	44
K				1397b15f.	44n.10
7	1064b1-3	21n.59		1399a19	46n.15
N			25	1402a32	51n.39
2	1089a24f.	14n.31		1402a32-34	49, 61n.79
				1402b1-4	40n.166
	Rhet.		26	1403a18f.	43, 46, 47
A			Γ		
1	1354a14f.	16n.35	1 ·	1403b14f.	48n.24
	1355a6	43n.2	15	1416a6	46n.15
	1355a6ff.	16n.35		1416a13	46n.15
	1355a8	43n.3	19	1419b18	48n.24
	1356a4[1]	36n.139		1419b23	48n.24
	1356a35-b5	43n.5, 47n.20		1419b27	48n.24
	1356b15-17	52n.42			
	1356b16	52n.44		Poet.	
2	1357a16-19	45n.13	20	1457a28-30	126n.108

B. OTHER ANCIENT AUTHORS

ALEXANDER OF APHRODISIAS

in APr.

1, 7-2, 33	21n.59
3, 3	107n.45
17, 5-10	128n.115
54, 21-29	138n.20
84, 12-19	110n.56
262, 31	107n.45
263, 26	107n.45
264, 5f.	98n.15
264, 14-17	104n.31
324, 17	98
324, 19-325, 24	95
324, 26-29	149
325, 31-328, 7	107n.42
325, 37-326, 1	96n.5
326, 24f.	107n.42
348, 29-32	128n.115
389, 31-390, 9	96n.9
390, 2f.	63n.95, 97
390, 3-9	97
397, 26	106n.38
400, 7-17	106n.38
587, 4f.	63n.94

in Top.

5, 20f.	16n.35
5, 21-23	61n.75
5, 21-27	64
5, 22	64
5, 23	65
5, 25f.	66
5, 26f.	61n.76, 66f.
6, 1-5	63n.94, 67n.108
6, 1-11	63n.93, 67n.102
6, 2-5	67n.110
6, 13f.	65n.102
7, 1	16n.35
8, 8-14	128n.115
28, 6	67n.109
55, 24-27	62n.80
55, 25f.	94n.115
55, 26f.	94n.115
100, 17	57n.60
101, 18	57n.60
122, 16f.	96n.5
126, 11-127, 16	64
126, 12	63n.89
126, 14-16	61n.75, 64
126, 16f.	65n.100
126, 16ff.	61n.77
126, 16-20	65
126, 20	67n.109
126, 21-23	64
126, 22	67n.109
126, 22f.	67n.108, n110
126, 25-30	63n.93
126, 27f.	65n.101
126, 30	65n.101

in Top.

126, 31-127, 16	149
127, 6-8	64n.96, 67n.108, n.110
127, 6-16	63n.93
127, 7	67n.109
127, 8	65n.99
127, 8-11	149
127, 10	67n.109
127, 11-16	149n.47
127, 21	65n.102
131, 30-32	136n.11
135, 2-23	62
135, 3-6	63n.89
135, 4	63n.91
135, 6f.	62n.84
135, 7-10	62n.85
135, 10	61n.77
135, 10f.	61n.76
135, 13	62n.83
135, 13-15	62n.82
136, 8-11	153n.60
163, 21ff.	112n.61
165, 12f.	109n.50
166, 11-13	109n.51
166, 14f.	121n.96
166, 17f.	121n.96
174, 6f.	109n.52
175, 21-26	109n.54
181, 16	67n.109
187, 28-188, 3	105n.33
206, 21-24	149
276, 7	63n.91
300, 29	67n.109
517, 16	67n.109
527, 18-22	25n.80
541, 11	63n.89
585, 24	47n.19
586, 3f.	46n.18
586, 23f.	61n.77
587, 4f.	63n.94

AMMONIUS

in APr.

XI, 6f.	98n.13, 119n.88
27, 6-14	128n.115

APULEIUS

De Int.

193, 16-20	122n.99

BOETHIUS

De top. diff.

II, 1185	61

De hyp. syll.

1, 1, 3f.	110n.58

DIOGENES LAERTIUS

V 45	62n.80
V 50	62n.80
VII 77-78	115n.68

GALEN

Inst. Log.

3, 1	104n.30
4, 13-22	107n.45
6, 1-5	107n.45
7, 12-19	107
7, 14	107n.46
8, 7-9	107n.43
8, 10	107
9, 3	107
9, 8-13	110n.57
18, 23-19, 5	107n.45
32, 11-17	107n.43
32, 14	107n.44
34, 14-23	130n.121
38, 13f.	159n.68
39, 17-19	159n.71
42, 1-3	159n.69
47, 16	160n.73

PHILOPONUS

in APr.

33, 6-10	128n.115
242, 18-21	63n.95
301, 11-20	95n.3

PLATO

Euthyd.

276a3f.	19n.52
295b2f.	19n.52

Gorg.

479c6	11n.12
498e10	11n.12

Hip. Min.

373-375	52n.45
375d1f.	52n.45

Parm.

127d2f.	13n.25
128d4-6	13n.24
135c8-136c5	13
135e9-136a1	13n.23
137b2-4	13

Phileb.

41c9	11n.12

Resp.

365a8	11n.12
516b9	11n.12
517c1	11n.12
530b6	22
531c2-5	22n.65
531d2	11n.12

Soph.

261a6f.	22n.65

Theaet.

159bff.	38n.157
165c9f.	11n.12
180c5ff.	22

PROCLUS

in Parm.

635, 2-12	94n.115

SEXTUS EMPIRICUS

Adversus Mathematicos (A.M.)

8. 303	129n.118

SIMPLICIUS

in Cat.

387, 17ff.	110n.58

GENERAL INDEX

accident (συμβεβηκός) 5, 7, 70 (def. 1 and 2), 134, 135, 150-153; Sainati's interpretation (συμβεβηκός=predicate) 71, 72, 78f.; my interpretation (συμβεβηκός= attribute or sumbebekos) 79-94 (esp. 92), 155
Ackrill, J. 101n.23, 126n.108
adoxical (ἄδοξος) 19n.54, 36f.
answerer 9, 14, 15, 36-41
Antisthenes 17
argue constructively (κατασκευάζειν) 11, 18f., 135
argue destructively (ἀνασκευάζειν) 11, 18f.; (ἀναιρεῖν) 135
argument per impossibile 95, 96, 107, 118f., 199
attack (ἐπιχειρεῖν) 12, 16n.40

babble 91
Barnes, J. 2, 20n.55, 24n.77, 27n.91, 41n.169, 74n.21, 76n.27, 77n.31, 96n.9, 97, n.12, 100n.20, 102n.25, 106, n.41, 160n.72
behave peevishly (δυσκολαίνειν) 31
Bekker, I. 161n.77
belong (ὑπάρχειν) 10, 88f., 98n.16; absolutely-partly (ἁπλῶς-κατά τι) 135-138; standing for predicative and existential 'to be' 161f.; cf. be predicated of (κατηγορεῖσθαι)
Berti, E. 2, 13n.26
Bocheński, J. 2, 3, n.9, 4, 54, n.48, 65n.103, 101n.24, 107n.45, 112n.62, 115n.69
Bolton, R. 2
Bonitz, H. 47n.19, 49n.29, 160n.74
Braun, E. 2, 6n.14
Brunschwig, J. 2, 3, 4, 5, 7, 14n.27, 16n.35, 30n.107, 46n.15, 72-78, 73n.17, n.18, 75n.23, n.25, 77n.32, 78n.35, 79, 81, 93, 99, n.18, 100n.19, 122n.98, 136n.10, n.11, 147n.40, 150n.49, 161n.77
Burnyeat, M. 45n.13

Cherniss 117n.82
Choirilos 36
chronology 6, 9
Chroust A.-H. 1n.2
Chrysippus 110n.58
Colli, G. 62, 136n.11
concealment of the conclusion 28f., 31, 33-35
conclude (περαίνεσθαι) 16n.41, 114n.68, 117f., 124
concludent arguments (περαντικοί) 115n.68
connected (συνημμένον) 97, 107; cf. the Peripatetic term continuous
be consequent upon (ἀκολουθεῖν) 98,
100, n.19, 124, 127f., 128n.114, 129f., 131n.124, 131f., 141, 143, 145, 146; cf. follow (ἕπεσθαι) & imply (ἐπιφέρειν) & to conclude (περαίνεσθαι)
continuous (συνεχές) 97, 98, 107 (κατὰ συνέχειαν), 108
contradictories (ἄμεσα ἐναντία) 105n.33, 108, (ἀντιφάσεις) 153; cf. topos from contradictories
contraries (ἐναντία) 60, 82; (ἔμεσα ἐναντία) 105n.33, 109; combinations (συμπλοκαί) of contraries 104, n.32, 153, 161; cf. also topos from contraries
conversion (ἀντιστροφή), = being convertibly predicated of (ἀντικατηγορεῖσθαι) 78, 80n.42, n.44; 123n.101 (in APr.); of to be 135-138, 136n.10; of topos 142, 153
co-ordinates (συστοίχα) 34, 123f.; cf. also topos from co-ordinates

definition 69 (definition of), 73-78, 80, 81, 87f., 91, 92, 117n.82, 145, 151, 155, 158
demonstration (ἀπόδειξις) 128, rhetorical 43
De Pater, W. A. 2, 3, 48n.24, 54n.48, 54, n.50, 63n.92, 65n.103
De Strycker, E. 85n.64
diairetic (διαιρετικόν) 97, 107 (κατὰ διαίρεσιν)
dialecticians 110n.58
disjunctive (διεζευγμένον) 97, 107; cf. the Peripatetic term diairetic
division (διαίρησις) 35, 108, n.47, 153; weak syllogism, petitio principii 125f.
dialectic 1; versus philosophy 28f.
dialectical method 7
differentia 75, n.24, 86

Ebert, T. 2, 102n.25, 107n.45, 138n.20
element (στοιχεῖον) 43, 45f., 49
endoxical (ἔνδοξον) 19, n.54, 20, n.55, 36f., 48, 49, 60n.69, 116f., 126f.
Enskat, R. 100n.20
enthymeme 43-45, 47, 48
epicheireme 62
essence (τὸ τί ἐστι) 70; essence versus the very essence (τὸ τί ἦν εἶναι) 74f., 74n.22 (=οὐσία), 75
Eudemus 97, 108, 110n.58
Evans, J. D. G. 6, 7
example (παράδειγμα) 35f.

fall under (ἐμπίπτειν εἰς) 43, 45, 46, 47
false statement 136
follow (ἕπεσθαι) 34, 100, 124, 127f., 129f., 131f., n.124; cf. to be consequent upon

(ἀκολουθεῖν) and to imply (ἐπιφέρ-ειν); follow (συμβαίνειν) 92n.109; to conclude (περαίνεσθαι)
Forster, E. S. 10n.4, 29n.103, 32n.124, 50n.34
Fortenbaugh, W. W., 62n.80, 64n.96, 65n.103, 112n.62
Frede, M. 97n.11, 115n.70
Freese, J. H. 49, 92n.109

general term 101f., 151
genus 59, 60, 70 (definition of), 73, 74f., 80, 81, 85f., 88-92 (passim), 136, 143f., 150-153, 160-164
Gohlke, P. 6, 10n.7
in a greater degree (μᾶλλον) 116, 147, 156; cf. qualitative hypothetical syllogism and topos from the greater and lesser degree
Graeser, A. 64n.96
Graham, W. 77n.31
Green-Pedersen, N. J. 2, 62n.81
Grimaldi, W. M. A. 51n.38, 61
Gutas, D. 62n.80, 64n.96, 65n.103, 112n.62

Hadgopoulos, D. J. 2, 21f., 77n.31
Hambruch, E. 1, 54n.52
Hamelin, O. 1n.4
Heraclitus 19n.54
Hintikka, J. 129n.118
Homer 36
homonymous (ὁμώνυμος) 57
Huby, P. M. 10n.7, 62n.80, 64n.96, 65n.103, 112n.62
hypothesis 16n.43, 47, 108, 116-119; as a protasis 125-131, inferential power of 127f.

Illias 126n.108
illustration (παραβολή) 35f.
to imply ((συν)ἐπιφέρειν) 124, 130; versus to be consequent upon (ἀκολυ-θεῖν) and to follow (ἕπεσθαι) 131n.124
incompatibility (μάχη) 105n.33, 130
indemonstrables (ἀναπόδεικτα), Stoic 108f., 117, 130
indicate additionally (προσσημαίνειν) 81-83
induction (ἐπαγωγή) 5, 15, 27, 29-32 35, 40n.169, 42, 52, n.45, 53n.46, 58f., 70f., 133, 140, 142, 143, 144, 146; versus syllogism 30, n.112,; rhetorical 36
inflexion (πτῶσις) 140, 152n.58; cf. topos from inflexions
investigation-instruction (παράγγελμα) 62f., 150f., 153, 154, 155, 158, 165
Irwin, T. 7, 14n.27

Kapp, E. 3n.13, 14n.30, 30n.107
Kirwan, C. 131n.124
Kneale, W. & M. 14n.28, 21n.60, 163n.78

Law of Contraposition 52, 99n.18, 141f.

Law of Subalternation 121-123, 124, 134f.
law, see principle, rule
Lear, J. 115n.70
Le Blond, J. M. 1, 7, 20n.55
Lee, T.-S. 21n.59
Lennox, J. G. 22n.65
likeness (ὁμοιότης) (inclusive analogy) 27n.94, 32n.123, 35, 110, 120f., 125n.104, 126f.
logic, instrument versus part of philosophy 21n.59
Long, A.A. 110n.58
Łukasiewicz, J. 110n.56, 138n.20

Maier, H. 1n.2, 1n.4, 10, n.8, 11n.12, 47n.23, 117n.82
middle term 164, 167, n.87
mode (τρόπος) =topos 46, n.16; =method 155, n.64; =turn of phrase 154
"modern philosophers" (οἱ νεώτεροι φιλόσοφοι), i.e. the Stoics, 107, n.45
Modus ponens and tollens 3, 4, 5, 99, 129n.116
Modus tollendo ponens and ponendo tollens 104n.29
Moreau, J. 14n.30, 18n.49
more worthy of choice (αἱρετώτερον) 60, 70, n.9; cf. topoi from what is more worthy of choice
Mueller 21n.59

objection (ἔνστασις) 5, 15, 20, 23, 31, 34, 38-42, 58-60, 133, 140, 145f., 154f.; apparent 41
"older philosophers" (οἱ παλαίοι), i.e. the Peripatetics 107, n.45
opposites (ἀντικείμενα) (contradictories, contraries, relatives, privation and possession) 151
organa 54-58
Owen, G. E. L. 6n.15

Pacius, J. 24n.80, 47n.19, 136n.11
paradoxical (παράδοξος) 19n.54
Parmenides 13
paronymous 152n.58
particular (καθ' ἕκαστον) 66f., 88f., 101
Patzig, G. 27n.90, 115n.70, 122n.99, 138n.20
Pelletier, Y. 2, 99n.18
Pflug, J. 76n.30
Pickard-Cambridge, W. A. 10n.4, 50n.34, 52n.45
plausible (πιθανόν) 126; cf. endoxical
Posidonius 160n.73
predicables 4, 5, 10, 57, ch. 3, 150f.; exclusive versus inclusive interpretation (Brunschwig) 72; cf. accident, genus, species, differentia, proprium, definition
predicate (κατηγορία) 151; cf. accident
be predicated of (κατηγορεῖσθαι τινός) 10, 80n.41, 92, n.107
be predicated convertibly of (ἀντικατηγ-

ὀρεῖσθαι) 69, 76, 77, 92n.108; see also conversion
be truly predicated of (ἀληθεύεσθαι) 89f., 92n.107
predication, double 91
premiss 5, 9, 14n.31; additional (πρόσληψις) 97, 98, n.15, 149; cf. protasis & to take (as a premiss)
principle (ἀρχή) 45-47 (passim), 62; common 48n.24, 50, 53; specific 48n.24; appropriate 64, n.97, n.99, 65, 67
Principle/Law of Contradiction 49, n.30, 50n.36, 105n.36, 116
Principle/Law of the Excluded Middle 49, n.31, 50n.36, 99n.18, 104n.29, 116, 118f., 123n.101, 130
Principle "if equals are taken from equals equals remain" 49, n.32, 50n.36
probable (εἰκός) 147
problema (πρόβλημα) 15, n.31, 16n.35, 17, 18, 20, 21, 154; universal versus particular 134f.
Prodicus 91
proof from the indefinite nature of the particular premiss (ἐκ τοῦ ἀδιορίστου) 123
proposition 5, 9, 10, 14n.31; cf. protasis
proprium 69 (definition of), 76-78, 80, 81, 87-89 (passim), 91, 92, 105f., 135f., 144, 151; proprium versus peculiar 77
prosyllogism (προσυλλογισμός) 25, 27, 27n.93
protasis (πρότασις) 5, 15, 16, 19, 20, 21, 22, 45, 46; = proposition & premiss 14n.31; syllogistic 24; compound 50, 124-127, 126n.108 (De int.); universal 46, 47; universal-particular, 23f.; particular, ambiguity of 24, n.77; necessary 24f., 27-32, 33n.125; auxiliary 24, 32-36, 33n125; to conceal the conclusion 32-35; ornamental/adding weight 32, 35; to render the argument more clear 32, 35f.
prove see: show
Pythagoras 22

quality (ποιότης) 95n.2; cf. hypothetical syllogism, qualitative
quantification, universal and particular 24n.75, 27, 88f., 157, 159, 160, 161
questions, ambiguous 37

reductionism 111-113, 112n.62
relevance of the argument 37
Repici, L. 64n.96
Rhys Roberts, W. 49, 92n.109
Robinson, R. 14n.30
Ross, W. D. 1n.3, 13n.22, 30n.107, 41n.169, 46n.15, 49n.32, 82n.52, 101n.22, 113, 136n.10, 161n.77
rule 126, 145; rule versus law 45, 122n.97; cf. principle, law
Ryle, G. 13n.21, 13n.25,

Sainati, V. 2, 5, 6n.16, 7, 50n.34, 51n.40, 78, n.35, 79n.39, 81, 84n.59, 92, 93, 100, 150n.49
Sedley, D. 110n.58
Sharples, R. 62n.80, 64n.96, 65n.103, 112n.62
show (or prove) (δεικνύναι) 16n.41, 110, n.60, 114n.68
Smiley, T. 100n.20
Smith, R. 2, 14n.29
Socrates 13, 22, 36n.142, 38n.157
Sollenberger, M. G. 62n.80
Solmsen, F. 1, 4, 11n.8, 11n.11, 47n.22, 48n.24, 51, 61, n.79, 66n.107, 112n.62, 117n.82
solution (λύσις) 15, 38
species (εἶδος) 86, 153, 160-164
Steinthal, H. 152n.58
Stoics ch. 4 passim; their formalism 104, 109, 110n.56, n.57, versus Peripatetic lack of formalism 102f., 104, 125f.; Peripatetic influence 103n.28, 110n.58
Striker, G. 100n.21, 110n.58, 115n.70, 138n.20
Stump, E. 2, 54n.50, 61n.78
Sullivan, M. W. 122n.99
subaltern moods of the syllogism 122n.99
substitute (μεταλαμβάνειν) 100, 157
substitution (μετάληψις) 95n.2, 96, n.5, 100n.19
sumbebekos, cf. accident
syllogism (συλλογισμός) 3n.10, 11, 14n.31; definition of 25f., 51f.; versus induction 30, n.112; 70f. (≈diairetic division), 70n.13; as deductive argument 15n.31, 100n.20, counter-syllogism 49; categorical 3, 6, 26f., 134, 160-167; derived from topos (Solmsen) 51f.; number of premisses 31n.119; dialectical 48f.; main 24; for concealment 28f.; of what is the same 107, 121, 157-160; of what is more worthy of choice 107, 156f.; relational 134, 159f.
syllogism, hypothetical (ἐξ ὑποθέσεως) 4, 5, 26f., 45, 53, ch. 4 passim, satisfying the definition of the syllogism 128f., 128n.115; 163f. (or categorical); typical way of expression (aorist-future perfect) 110, 121-124, 153, 157, 158f.; (genetivus (sing.) absolutus of εἶναι) 107, n.46, 125n.106, 126, 129
proceeding by substitution (κατὰ μετάληψιν)/ by way of a continuous/ connected protasis together with the additional assumption (διὰ συνεχοῦς, ὃ καὶ συνημμένον λέγεται, καὶ τῆς προσλήψεως ὑποθετικούς), 95, n.2, 96, 97, 98-103, 108, 116, 125, 128n.116, 129, 131, 153, 155, 158, 166; abbreviated as metaleptic hypothetical syllogism or (Hm)c/d 99, n.17;
proceeding by way of a diairetic/ disjunctive protasis (διὰ τοῦ διαιρετικοῦ τε καὶ διεζευγμένου) 97, 103f., 109f., 116, 131f.; rests on the Principle of the Excluded Middle 49; abbreviated as diairetic hypothetical syllogism or (Hd)c/d 103;
by way of a negated conjunction (διὰ ἀποφατικῆς συμπλοκῆς) 97, 104f., 116, 130, 131; rests on the Principle of Contradiction 49; abbreviated as conjunctive hypothetical syllogism or (Hc)c/d 104f., 105n.35;
qualitative, i.e. arguments from the greater, lesser or like degree (κατὰ ποιότητα/ἀπὸ τοῦ μᾶλλον καὶ

ἧττον καὶ ὁμοίως) 95, n.2, 96, 97,,106, 116, 133;
on the basis of an analogy (οἱ ἐξ ἀναλογίας), 97, 105f., 106n.38 (in APr.); abbreviated as analogical hypothetical syllogism or (Ha) 104;
on the basis of a concession (δι' ὁμολογίας) resting on likeness (ὁμοιότης), 96, 111, 120, 121, 125, 126; abbreviated as (Hh) 120
wholly hypothetical 106, n.41, n.42 (an example in APr.), 125
synonymous (συνώνυμος) 149, 150, n.59

take (as a premiss) (λαμβάνειν) 52n.45, 126
that which (ὅπερ) 85, n.64
Theodorus 22
Theophrastus 4, 5, 7, 61, 94n.114, 96f., 108, 110n.58, 140
thesis (θέσις) 16, n.43, 17, 18, 20; original (τὸ ἐν ἀρχῇ/ἐξ ἀρχῆς (κείμενον)) 16, 101, n.23; in hand (τὸ προκείμενον) 101; =ὑπόθεσις 9n.1
Thionville, E. 61
Throm, H. 47n.23
Topics versus *Analytics* 1, 2, 163f.
topos (τόπος) passim; common-specific 48, n.24, 49; definition of 43, 45; destructive-constructive (κατασκευαστικά-ἀνασκευαστικά) 134n.4; =element, 45f., 49f.; implicit use 71n.14; as investigation-instructions 54-58; as points of view 54n.52; as laws 54; instantiation of 53, 99n.18; most opportune (ἐπικαιρότατοι) 60n.69, 61, 94, n.115, 133, 137-148, 157n.70 (in book Γ); number of 131; origin of (mnemotechnic), 46, 47, n.22; parangelmatic 150, 153, 154, 155; predecessors of 34f., 126f.; as a protasis 46-49, 58f. (explicitly stated as such), 99n.18; as a 'machine to produce premisses' 99n.18, textual structure 57;
from the contradictories (ἐπὶ τῶν ἀντιφάσεων) 140, 141f.;
from the contraries (ἐκ τῶν ἐναντίων) 43, 44, 62, 65f., 140, 142-145;
from generation, corruption and creative and corruptive agencies (ἐπὶ τῶν γενέσεων καὶ φθορῶν καὶ ποιητικῶν καὶ φθαρτικῶν) 140;

from the greater and lesser degree (ἐκ τοῦ μᾶλλον καὶ ἧττον) 43, 48, 50, 96, 106, 140, 146-149;
from the like degree (ἐκ τοῦ ὁμοίως) 96, 101, 106, 140, 150;
from co-ordinates and inflexions (ἐπὶ τῶν συστοίχων καὶ τῶν πτώσεων) 43, 44, 62, 65f., 123, 140;
from privation and possession (ἐπὶ τῶν στερήσεων καὶ ἕξεων) 140;
from relatives (ἐκ τῶν πρός τι) 140, 145f.;
from things which are in like relation by analogy (ἐκ τῶν ὁμοίως ἐχόντων) 105;
based on likeness (ὁμοιότης) 111, 125
of "what is more worthy of choice/better" 107, 134, 156f., 159f.;
of "what is the same" 107, 134, 156-159, 160;
on the basis of consequence (ἐξ ἀκολουθίας) 108; cf. hypothetical syllogism proceeding by way of substitution is constructed;
on the basis of incompatibility (ἐκ μάχης) 109; cf. hypothetical syllogism proceeding by way of a diairetic protasis
Toulmin, S. 54
training in disputation (γυμναστική) 12, 13, 17

van der Weel, R.L. 3n.12
violation of the established terminology 139, 152f.
von Arnim, H. 1
von Fritz, K. 40n.169

Waitz, T. 24n.80, 47n.19, 82n.52, 161n.77
Wallies, M. 64n.96, 82n.52, 161n.77
Wedin, V. E. 77n.31
Weil, E. 14n.30
Wieland, W. 41n.169, 47n.23, 54n.52
Wilpert, P. 7

Xenocrates 21

Zeno 7, 13, n.22
Zadro, A. 2, 24n.80, 138n.20

PHILOSOPHIA ANTIQUA

A SERIES OF STUDIES ON ANCIENT PHILOSOPHY

EDITED BY

J. MANSFELD, D.T. RUNIA
AND J.C.M. VAN WINDEN

1. VERDENIUS, W.J. and WASZINK, J.H. *Aristotle on Coming-to-Be and Passing-Away.* Some Comments. Reprint of the 2nd (1966) ed. 1968. ISBN 90 04 01718 6
7. SAFFREY, H.D. *Le περὶ φιλοσοφίας d'Aristote et la théorie platonicienne des idées nombres.* 2ème éd. revue et accompagnée du compte-rendu critique par H. Cherniss. 1971. ISBN 90 04 01720 8
13. NICOLAUS DAMASCENUS. *On the Philosophy of Aristotle.* Fragments of the First Five Books, Translated from the Syriac with an Introduction and Commentary by H.J. Drossaart Lulofs. Reprint of the 1st (1965) ed. 1969. ISBN 90 04 01725 9
14. EDELSTEIN, L. *Plato's Seventh Letter.* 1966. ISBN 90 04 01726 7
15. PORPHYRIUS. Πρὸς Μαρκέλλαν. Griechischer Text, herausgegeben, übersetzt, eingeleitet und erklärt von W. Pötscher. 1969. ISBN 90 04 01727 5
17. GOULD, J.B. *The Philosophy of Chrysippus.* Reprint 1971. ISBN 90 04 01729 1
18. BOEFT, J. DEN. *Calcidius on Fate.* His Doctrine and Sources. 1970. ISBN 90 04 01730 5
19. PÖTSCHER, W. *Strukturprobleme der aristotelischen und theophrastischen Gottesvorstellung.* 1970. ISBN 90 04 01731 3
20. BERTIER, J. *Mnésithée et Dieuchès.* 1972. ISBN 90 04 03468 4
21. TIMAIOS LOKROS. *Über die Natur des Kosmos und der Seele.* Kommentiert von M. Baltes. 1972. ISBN 90 04 03344 0
22. GRAESER, A. *Plotinus and the Stoics.* A Preliminary Study. 1972. ISBN 90 04 03345 9
23. IAMBLICHUS CHALCIDENSIS. *In Platonis dialogos commentariorum fragmenta.* Edited with Translation and Commentary by J.M. Dillon. 1973. ISBN 90 04 03578 8
24. TIMAEUS LOCRUS. *De natura mundi et animae.* Überlieferung, Testimonia, Text und Übersetzung von W. Marg. Editio maior. 1972. ISBN 90 04 03505 2
26. GERSH, S.E. Κίνησις ἀκίνητος. A Study of Spiritual Motion in the Philosophy of Proclus. 1973. ISBN 90 04 03784 5
27. O'MEARA, D. *Structures hiérarchiques dans la pensée de Plotin.* Étude historique et interprétative. 1975. ISBN 90 04 04372 1
28. TODD, R.B. *Alexander of Aphrodisias on the Stoic Physics.* A Study of the *De Mixtione* with Preliminary Essays, Text, Translation and Commentary. 1976. ISBN 90 04 04402 7
29. SCHEFFEL, W. *Aspekte der platonischen Kosmologie.* Untersuchungen zum Dialog 'Timaios'. 1976. ISBN 90 04 04509 0
30. BALTES, M. *Die Weltentstehung des platonischen Timaios nach den antiken Interpreten.* Teil 1. 1976. ISBN 90 04 04720 4
31. EDLOW, R.B. *Galen on Language and Ambiguity.* An English Translation of Galen's *De Captionibus* (On Fallacies), With Introduction, Text and Commentary. 1977. ISBN 90 04 04869 3
34. EPIKTET. *Vom Kynismus.* Herausgegeben und übersetzt mit einem Kommentar von M. Billerbeck. 1978. ISBN 90 04 05770 6
35. BALTES, M. *Die Weltentstehung des platonischen Timaios nach den antiken Interpreten.* Teil 2. Proklos. 1979. ISBN 90 04 05799 4

37. O'BRIEN, D. *Theories of Weight in the Ancient World.* Four Essays on Democritus, Plato and Aristotle. A Study in the Development of Ideas 1. Democritus: Weight and Size. An Exercise in the Reconstruction of Early Greek Philosophy. 1981. ISBN 90 04 06134 7
39. TARÁN, L. *Speusippus of Athens.* A Critical Study with a Collection of the Related Texts and Commentary. 1982. ISBN 90 04 06505 9
40. RIST, J.M. *Human Value.* A Study in Ancient Philosophical Ethics. 1982. ISBN 90 04 06757 4
41. O'BRIEN, D. *Theories of Weight in the Ancient World.* Four Essays on Democritus, Plato and Aristotle. A Study in the Development of Ideas 2. Plato: Weight and Sensation. The Two Theories of the 'Timaeus'. 1984. ISBN 90 04 06934 8
44. RUNIA, D.T. *Philo of Alexandria and the Timaeus of Plato.* 1986. ISBN 90 04 07477 5
45. AUJOULAT, N. *Le Néo-Platonisme Alexandrin: Hiéroclès d'Alexandrie.* Filiations intellectuelles et spirituelles d'un néo-platonicien du Ve siècle. 1986. ISBN 90 04 07510 0
46. KAL, V. *On Intuition and Discursive Reason in Aristotle.* 1988. ISBN 90 04 08308 1
48. EVANGELIOU, CH. *Aristotle's Categories and Porphyry.* 1988. ISBN 90 04 08538 6
49. BUSSANICH, J. *The One and Its Relation to Intellect in Plotinus.* A Commentary on Selected Texts. 1988. ISBN 90 04 08996 9
50. SIMPLICIUS. *Commentaire sur les Catégories.* Traduction commentée sous la direction de I. Hadot. I: Introduction, première partie (p. 1-9, 3 Kalbfleisch). Traduction de Ph. Hoffmann (avec la collaboration d'I. et P. Hadot). Commentaire et notes à la traduction par I. Hadot avec des appendices de P. Hadot et J.-P. Mahé. 1990. ISBN 90 04 09015 0
51. SIMPLICIUS. *Commentaire sur les Catégories.* Traduction commentée sous la direction de I. Hadot. III: Préambule aux Catégories. Commentaire au premier chapitre des Catégories (p. 21-40, 13 Kalbfleisch). Traduction de Ph. Hoffmann (avec la collaboration d'I. Hadot, P. Hadot et C. Luna). Commentaire et notes à la traduction par C. Luna. 1990. ISBN 90 04 09016 9
52. MAGEE, J. *Boethius on Signification and Mind.* 1989. ISBN 90 04 09096 7
53. BOS, E.P. and MEIJER, P.A. (eds.) *On Proclus and His Influence in Medieval Philosophy.* 1992. ISBN 90 04 09429 6
54. FORTENBAUGH, W.W., et al. (eds.) *Theophrastes of Eresos.* Sources for His Life, Writings, Thought and Influence. 1992. ISBN 90 04 09440 7 *set*
55. SHANKMAN, A. *Aristotle's* De insomniis. A Commentary. ISBN 90 04 09476 8
56. MANSFELD, J. *Heresiography in Context.* Hippolytos' *Elenchos* as a Source for Greek Philosophy. 1992. ISBN 90 04 09616 7
57. O'BRIEN, D. *Théodicée plotinienne, théodicée gnostique.* 1993. ISBN 90 04 09618 3
58. BAXTER, T.M.S. *The Cratylus.* Plato's Critique of Naming. 1992. ISBN 90 04 09597 7
59. DORANDI, T. (Hrsg.) *Theodor Gomperz. Eine Auswahl herkulanischer kleiner Schriften (1864-1909).* 1993. ISBN 90 04 09819 4
60. FILODEMO. *Storia dei filosofi. La stoà da Zenone a Panezio* (PHerc. 1018). Edizione, traduzione e commento a cura di T. Dorandi. 1994. ISBN 90 04 09963 8
61. MANSFELD, J. *Prolegomena.* Questions to be Settled Before the Study of an Author, or a Text. 1994. ISBN 90 04 10084 9
62. FLANNERY, S.J., K.L. *Ways into the Logic of Alexander of Aphrodisias.* 1995. ISBN 90 04 09998 0
63. LAKMANN, M.-L. *Der Platoniker Tauros in der Darstellung des Aulus Gellius.* 1995. ISBN 90 04 10096 2
64. SHARPLES, R.W. *Theophrastus of Eresus.* Sources for his Life, Writings, Thought and Influence. Commentary Volume 5. Sources on Biology (Human Physiology, Living Creatures, Botany: Texts 328-435). 1995. ISBN 90 04 10174 8
65. ALGRA, K. *Concepts of Space in Greek Thought.* 1995. ISBN 90 04 10172 1

66. SIMPLICIUS. *Commentaire sur le manuel d'Épictète.* Introduction et édition critique de texte grec par Ilsetraut Hadot. 1995. ISBN 90 04 09772 4
67. CLEARY, J.J. *Aristotle and Mathematics.* Aporetic Method in Cosmology and Metaphysics. 1995. ISBN 90 04 10159 4
68. TIELEMAN, T. *Galen and Chrysippus on the Soul.* Argument and Refutation in the *De Placitis* Books II-III. 1996. ISBN 90 04 10520 4
69. HAAS, F.A.J. DE. *John Philoponus' New Definition of Prime Matter.* Aspects of its Background in Neoplatonism and the Ancient Commentary Tradition. 1997. ISBN 90 04 10446 1
70. HABETS, A.C.J. *A History of the Division of Philosophy in Antiquity.* 1997. ISBN 90 04 10578 6
71. ANDIA, Y. DE. *Henosis.* L'Union à Dieu chez Denys l'Aréopagite. 1996. ISBN 90 04 10656 1
72. ALGRA, K.A., HORST, P.W. VAN DER, and RUNIA, D.T. (eds.) *Polyhistor.* Studies in the History and Historiography of Ancient Philosophy. Presented to Jaap Mansfeld on his Sixtieth Birthday. 1996. ISBN 90 04 10417 8
73. MANSFELD, J. and RUNIA, D.T. *Aëtiana.* The Method and Intellectual Context of a Doxographer. Volume 1: The Sources. 1997. ISBN 90 04 10580 8
74. SLOMKOWSKI, P. *Aristotle's* Topics. 1997. ISBN 90 04 10757 6